# Capitalist and Socialist Crises
# in the Late Twentieth Century

# Capitalist and Socialist Crises in the Late Twentieth Century

**JAMES F. PETRAS**

Rita Carroll-Seguin
Miguel E. Correa
Stephen Gundle
Roberto P. Korzeniewicz
Morris H. Morley
Mark Selden

E 70

**ROWMAN & ALLANHELD**
PUBLISHERS

ROWMAN & ALLANHELD

Published in the United States of America in 1984
by Rowman & Allanheld
(A division of Littlefield, Adams & Company)
81 Adams Drive, Totowa, New Jersey 07512

**Library of Congress Cataloging in Publication Data**
Main entry under title:

Capitalist and socialist crises in the late twentieth
  century.

  Includes index.
  1. Economic history—1971–  —Addresses, essays,
lectures.  2. Capitalism—Addresses, essays, lectures.
3. Socialism—Addresses, essays, lectures.  4. Social
conflict—Addresses, essays, lectures.  5. Latin America—
Economic conditions—1945–  —Addresses, essays,
lectures.  I. Petras, James F., 1937–
HC59.C2645  1983          330.9′04          83-16160
ISBN 0-86598-153-1
ISBN 0-86598-156-6 (pbk.)


83  84  85  /  10  9  8  7  6  5  4  3  2  1

*Printed in the United States of America*

330.904
P493

# Contents

# Tables and Figures

# *Introduction*

In recent years the world crisis has deepened, drawing in its wake both capitalist and socialist systems. The essays that follow examine its theoretical and analytical issues, focusing state-class relations in the advanced capitalist countries, scope and depth of industrial growth in the Third World, the relation of the peripheral state to the international division of labor, and the problems of socialist transition in under-developed countries. Historical and empirical analysis of specific country cases further elaborates this theoretical perspective—through close-up case studies, critical textual reading, exposition and analysis of elite ideologies, as well as general reflections on historical experiences.

In some essays analysis is a detailed examination of "facts" and "data"; in others, it is a critical assessment of historical and theoretical concepts. Both analytic-empirical and theoretical discursive styles provide useful points of departure for examining the emerging crisis in the capitalist and socialist systems.

Much has been said about the New Cold War of the Eighties; few, if any, writers, however, have attempted to theorize on the *timing* of its emergence, and the global context in which it occurs. The opening essay, "The New Cold War," looks at the political and economic context that preceded the New Cold War, at the circumstances surrounding the rise and demise of détente, and at the structural forces that compelled Democrats and Republicans, Carter and Reagan, to escalate the arms race, reinvigorate the global policy of confrontation, and militarize U.S. foreign policy. The essay focuses on the centrality of the imperial state in promoting and defending overseas U.S. corporate interests that have become central to the U.S. economy. The very process of "projecting power," however, contains the seeds of conflict and competition, both internal and external, and the essay concludes by examining the dialectical relation between the dynamic forces of military and political expansion and the deepening domestic and international conflicts that accompany it.

The second essay, "Supporting Repression," spells out the meaning of the Cold War for the peasants of the Third World, those directly affected by the new militarism. Washington's alliance with the death squads of Central America signal the end of the era of détente and human rights, and put their distinctive mark on the new period. The essay considers the New Cold War policies as they unfold in a particular setting—El Salvador. The larger policy of intervention, predicated as it is on the "successful" use of military force, required that the Reagan administration come up with a victory to enable it to multiply its application throughout the Third World. Global perspectives are woven into the fabric of regional politics: the repression in Central America provides an intimate view of the consequences of the New Cold War and the militarization of foreign policy.

The issue of Third World industrialization—its nature, scope, and significance—became a point of contention in the *New Left Review,* largely as a result of an exchange between Bill Warren and me during the mid-1970s. The debate was continued by others, but for the most part without any new theoretical insights that would explain why and how "capital" in the metropolitan countries "promoted" or "blocked" industrialization in specific Third World countries.

"Toward a Theory of Industrial Development in the Third World" theorizes on the basis of the changing *composition* of capital in the advanced countries (from industrial to fictitious capital) and the changing *sociopolitical context* in specific Third World countries. The essay establishes a framework that accounts for the particular historical timing of industrialization as it identifies the emerging constraints and con- tradictions. This essay goes beyond the empiricist arguments that theorize from limited conjunctures and isolated cases to provide a comprehensive framework for analyzing the limits and possibilities of Third World industrial growth on the framework of the world economy.

The state, in both the advanced and the Third World, has recently come under scrutiny, with much of the newer writing emphasizing its "relative autonomy." "A Critique of Structuralist State Theorizing" is a critical analysis of the text of a major proponent of structuralism (Nicos Poulantzas). The critique of the "autonomy" concept focuses on its lack of rigor and specificity; accompanying this intellectual laxness is the tendency to dissociate the state from any organic ties to the class structure. The result is that much of what purports to be new critical reflections on the Marxist concept of the state turns out to be little more than restatements of the older Fabian and liberal notions of the "permeable" state. The nexus between intellectual ambiguity regarding the class/state relationship and reformist praxis is underlined in this essay.

The essay on the Peripheral State is concerned with a different set of issues. It establishes the continuities as well as the changes in the role that Third World economies play in the international division of labor. The essay points to the comprehensive role the state plays in almost all Third World societies, regardless of ideology, emphasizing the extreme importance of determining the *class configurations* that define the consequences of state ownership, intervention, and partici- pation in the international economy. The essay challenges the notion that major breakthroughs are imminent in the international division of labor, identifying the limited changes and continual restraints that modify the movement away from dependence on the export of primary products.

While the previous two sections concentrate on the crisis and constraints of capitalist development, the third section, on the Transition to Socialism, focuses on the contradictions and conflicts in socialist countries.

"Social Classes, the State and World System . . ." examines the ideologies of the socialist leadership in two countries, Cuba and China, pondering the shifts in ideology from "political mobilization" to "modernization" and identifying the costs and benefits of each approach. The major contradiction that faces all revolutionary Third World regions that inherit underdeveloped countries is the conflict between socializing production and facing the imperatives of participating in a hostile world capitalist marketplace. The inevitable compromises are described less as the product of "moral betrayals" and more as the result of economic imperatives. "Marxism and World Historical Transformation" discusses a wide range of issues that have been debated among Marxists. Rather than a detailed elaboration, the essay provides an analytical framework for examining specific problems emerging from attempts at long-term, large-scale change within the limited margins of political choice.

"Workers' Self-management and the Transition to Socialism" considers the alternatives to the "statist" versions of socialism discussed above. While sympathetic to the general position, the essay critically examines the political, economic, and social structural factors that diminish or limit the effective operation of "self-managed" enterprises. Four historic experiences illustrate each of the problem areas associated with the blockage of the development of a model of self-management socialism.

The fourth section presents case studies and reflections on recent political, social, and economic developments in the Caribbean, Latin America, the Middle East, and Africa. The essay on Central America identifies the process of social revolution as a direct outcome of the dynamic and destructive impact of capitalist development over the past three decades, rejecting Washington's conspiratorial theories, as well as the orthodox leftist views of revolution, as an outcome of static backward and underdeveloped societies. "Petrodollars and the State . . ." studies the class forces that operate behind the facade of extensive nationalization, controlling and allocating oil wealth to the established elites. Contrary to Soviet Marxism, "state capitalism" is not a vehicle for socialist transformation but rather a mechanism for reproducing the class structure—a point that is further developed in our discussion of the Eritrean revolution. The left-wing's mystification of "state ownership" (as "progressive") is matched by its rather uncritical view of "anti-imperialist forces." The brief reflections on Iran underline the singular importance of understanding that there are right-wing as well as left-wing "anti-imperialists" and that not all forces that oppose contemporary forms of exploitation offer better alternatives. The essay on the Caribbean countries examines the sources of crisis that afflict all "models" of development in the region—market, collectivist, and "mixed" economies; it establishes the basic instability of "mixed" economies, the high social cost of the export model, and the limited capacity for democratic control in centralized economies. The final essay focuses on the long-term, large-scale economic interests that shape U.S. policy in the Middle East and the failure of Arab capitalism or statism to develop any alternative to collaboration. The links and the limited conflict between the United States and Israel are seen in terms of their particular strategic relationship and competing economic interests. The essay identifies the sources of crisis in the Mideast, specifically in the economic transformation wrought through integration into the world economy and in the incapacity of U.S. policymakers to consolidate a set of collaborator rulers in the region.

In summary, these essays reflect my view that contemporary social analysis must come to grips with *class forces* behind the New Cold War, the war against the people of Central America, and the rigidities and constraints of Western capitalism and bureaucratic collectivism.

These essays embrace the hope that understanding the sources of exploitation and repression will enable us to struggle against them to build a more humane and democratic socialist society.

# Part I

## Global and Regional Perspectives

# 1

# The New Cold War: Reagan's Policy Toward Europe and the Third World

JAMES F. PETRAS
MORRIS H. MORLEY

To understand the reemergence of the Cold War, the breakout of détente, and the growing militarization of U.S. foreign policy and its implications for Third World liberation movements, we must first locate these issues in a historical and structural framework. Analysis of recent historical developments will allow us to understand the specific factors that facilitated détente, as well as the reasons for its breakdown: The argument that we will attempt to develop is that détente reflected a particular historical conjuncture, which has since been surpassed. Reagan is less a cause of the end of détente than a consequence of the interaction between structural interests and contextual challenges to imperial interests.

To unravel the source of both Reagan's aggressive foreign policy and the breakdown of détente, we have to turn to examine the global nature of U.S. economic interests and state activity: the long-term, large-scale movement of U.S. industrial and financial capital abroad and the increasing dependence on overseas earnings to sustain these operations.

## Theory of the International Conjuncture

What is striking about the present international conjuncture is the massive, accelerated movement of U.S. military forces into positions of operation throughout the world. The most persistent theme in U.S. behavior today is the "will to power project." Not economic power—even less a capacity to enroll industrialists or financial groups in a massive program to capture markets, raw materials, *through marketplace* activity. Indeed, despite the pervasive rhetoric of free market activity, the central reality of U.S. involvement in the international environment today is through the state: the fastest growing sector of U.S. spending with international implications is the state military budget.

The practical focus of international policy has been to develop new capacities for military planning, military innovations, military bases, intelligence operations, and strategic alliances. The imperial state—in general, and its coercive apparatus in particular—has been made the centerpiece of the new administration's policy for reversing the deteriorating position of U.S. political economy in the world order. In a period of increasing political and economic challenges from the Third World and the Soviet Union bloc, and faced with an incapacity to develop its economic forces to compete and adapt to the new realities of European and Japanese economic competition, the new administration has chosen to revive the global strategy of military confrontation as a way of reestablishing world hegemony. This is not an unlikely choice, as it is in the military and intelligence spheres that the United States has its advantage over its rivals and competitors. To the degree that the U.S. propaganda effort is successful in imposing its military bipolar definitions of world reality on the rest of the West, it hopes to succeed in harnessing or subordinating it to America's economic rulership, undercutting not only the economic and political links with the East, but also the growing diversification of Third World commercial relations and the internal differentiation and polarization that characterize contemporary Third World development.

The current international conjuncture in which the disintegration of détente and the growth of the Cold War are the most striking surface manifestations is thus structurally underpinned by the economic decline of the United States in the world economy and the attempt to recover economic space by projecting politico-military power. The emphasis on the imperial state as the mechanism to shift the balance of power of class forces on a world scale is, of course, one which is wrought with political conflicts and is not guaranteed of success; on the contrary, as we shall discuss later, the entire project of reasserting U.S. global hegemony in the contemporary world conflicts with a vast array of internal and external forces.

## The Imperial Economy and State

Too often discussions of imperialism have focused on the economic dimensions of imperialism—the flow of investments, the terms of commercial exchange, and so on—without explicating the nature of the state that is intimately involved in the organization, and restructuring the international environment to facilitate the growth of overseas economic activities. The boundaries established by the discussion of the "capitalist state" are not adequate—they are time bound, and linked to the world of eighteenth- and early nineteenth-century capitalism in which domination and exploitation were predominantly "national" phenomena. The imperial state, in particular the United States, can be defined as those executive bodies or agencies within the government which are charged with promoting and protecting the expansions of capital across state boundaries by the multinational corporations head-quartered in the imperial centers. In the post–World War II period, the growth of U.S. overseas capital was preceded by a vast network of organizations and activities fostered by the state which established the basis for subsequent massive inflows of private capital. The economic and coercive apparatuses of the imperial state operate to facilitate U.S. capital accumulation and reproduction on a world scale. As more and more of the largest U.S. industrial and financial corporations have expanded abroad, and as a larger proportion of their total earnings are derived from their overseas operations, the activities of the imperial state have become increasingly important for the maintenance of these building blocks of the U.S. economy. The worldwide interests of U.S. multinationals are linked to the growth of a global network of imperial-state activities. What is crucial in this global process is the capacity of the state to sustain the activities and institutions to defend those interests. It is our contention that the revival of the Cold War and the aggressive posture of the Reagan administration is precisely directed at recreating state capacity to sustain worldwide economic activity after a period of disarticulation, largely the product of the Vietnam War.

The interrelationship between the imperial state and capital expansion is evident in the development of post-colonial imperialism since World War II. In the first period, roughly 1945–55, imperial-state investment predominated in rebuilding Europe and constructing capitalist state structures and economies in the Third World. In the second period, roughly 1955–69, massive flows of private investment circulated through-out the globe through the multinational conglomerates. The third period witnessed the enormous growth of finance capital, the massive expansion of banking capital, and the accumulation of massive assets and extension of loans. The logic of imperialism revealed by this historical sequence is largely from imperial-state investment to private industrial and finance capital. Massive imperial-state activity was the necessary precondition for the development of "economic" imperialism. The interrelatedness of overseas state-industrial-finance capital, and the continuous interplay of all three—each with its specific and complementary function—defines the imperial system.

The imperial state can best be conceptualized as a complex web of interrelated but financially specific agencies coordinated at the top levels of the executive branch. The agencies can be divided into three major functional categories: (1) economic, (2) coercive, and (3) ideological. The Pentagon, the CIA, and the other repressive agencies are comple-mented by the State, Commerce, Treasury, and other executive agencies that promote economic expansion. The ideological agencies (the U.S. Information Agency, for example) work on worldwide propaganda activities in association with nongovernmental cultural groups. The important issue, however, is that post-colonial imperialism expands and survives with the growth and incorporation of collaborator groups. In fact, the strength of the imperial system rests in large part on the influence and control exercised by the collaborative classes and strata in the Third World.

## The Imperial System in Crisis

At certain historical moments, the imperial system is made vulnerable by a weakened capacity on the part of the imperial state to sustain a level of cohesion that the system requires. Between 1945 and 1965 the U.S. imperial state could count on a public opinion unified in support of its actions, an organized and mobilized military fighting force, and a high degree of cooperation from its allies in Western Europe, Japan, and the Third World. One outcome of the American involvement in Indochina during the 1960s and early 1970s was a substantial weakening of the interventionary capacities of the imperial state—a consequence of the growing internal divisions among the populace at large, the decline of institutional solidarity and esprit de corps within the armed forces (and their increasing loss of legitimacy domestically), and widespread defections among allies of the imperial-state system.

The gap between the decline of the imperial state and the increase in U.S. economic interests was the first manifestation of the crisis. This problem became explosive when the Iranian revolution took place, expropriating major U.S. oil firms and drastically reducing U.S. military markets and banking operations. The Nicaraguan revolution in Central America merely underlined the issue: without a reconstituted imperial-state apparatus, U.S. collaborators could be defeated and the network that sustained U.S. economic expansion thus undermined.

The crisis of the imperial state and the attempt to resolve it can be understood in three stages: (1) 1969–75—the disintegration of the U.S. military machine in Vietnam, the massive breakdown of the internal consensus in the United States, the international isolation of the United States, and the resulting formulation of détente as a way of "gaining time"; (2) 1976–78—the reconstitution of the armed forces, the promulgation of the "human rights" doctrine as a means of reconstituting internal consensus behind official leadership, the effort to promote linkages with moderate conservative civilian political forces in the Third World, and the pursuit of détente "with reservations"; (3) 1979 to the present—the accelerated buildup of military forces, the promotion of alliances with dictatorial regimes, the attempt to impose definitions of Third World conflicts as reflections of the bipolar world, the end of détente, and the declaration of Cold War Two.

The time frame between 1945 and 1965 was the period of undisputed U.S. global hegemony: Washington was the dominant political, military, and economic force in the world economy. The reconstruction of European and Japanese economies, combined with the enormous waste and cost of the U.S. involvement in Vietnam, eroded the dominant U.S. economic position; the massive internal and external opposition undermined external and internal cohesion. The disarticulation of the imperial-state apparatus created a favorable conjuncture, as Che Guevara had prophetically foreseen, allowing the revolutionary processes in Angola, Ethiopia, Nicaragua, and Iran to proceed successfully, eliminating U.S. client regimes. The growth of the class struggle in the Third World—the consequences of the prolonged transformation in class relations resulting from the expansion of Western capital in the post-war decades—accelerated in the absence of the heavy hand of imperialist intervention.

Faced with a challenge from below and unable in the conjuncture to mobilize and reconstitute the military force to counter, the Nixon, Ford, and Carter administrations sought, through détente, to contain the revolutionary upsurge: they sought to obtain, through Big Power agreements, what could not be obtained through the usual channels of class warfare. Détente then was a transitional policy conditioned by the breakdown of the imperial-state apparatus, attempting to conserve spheres of influence through international horizontal alliances between the superpowers. Détente did not create conditions for the victory of the liberation movements, rather the liberation movements, in particular the Vietnamese revolution, so weakened the imperial network that Washington was forced to attempt to come to terms with its Big Power adversary, at least temporarily. This interpretation is demonstrated by the fact that in the subsequent period in the context of reconstructing the international apparatus, the first casualty was détente: the decline of imperialism was *relative* to a *particular period* and *policy,* and there were no fundamental changes in the structure of U.S. institutions and economic interests that could establish an enduring period of détente. In that sense, détente was an interlude between the political defeat of the late 1960s and early 1970s and the imperial recovery and resurgence at the end of the seventies and in the beginning of the eighties.

The pivotal event that triggered the historical shift from détente to the New Cold War was the defeat of the Iranian Shah, the most favored U.S. client (with Israel) in the oil-rich Middle East. Up to that point, the efforts by the Carter administration to mobilize public opinion in favor of the new militarization had failed: the effort to promote intervention in Nicaragua was unpopular at home and unable to mobilize a majority in the Organization of American States; the effort to heat up the Cold War over Soviet troops in Cuba received limited support at best, even within the Washington political establishment and the mass media. The process of reconstituting the imperial apparatus, in a capitalist democracy, depended on a massive transformation of public opinion. The material losses to U.S. multinationals resulting from the Iranian revolution created the objective conditions (activated capital and mass media support) for the massive rebuilding of the military; the hostage issue gave the President the propaganda weapon to promote the subjective basis (popular consensus) for pursuing policies that (1) mobilized public sentiment for a massive military budget, "unleashing" the CIA and preparing interventionary contingents (Rapid Deployment Force, for example) and (2) pressured European allies to accede to U.S. military programs and to defer to U.S. military definitions of the political challenges in the Middle East, if not in the Third World as a whole.

In February 1979, the shift to a new interventionist policy was signaled with Carter's dispatch of Secretary of Defense Harold Brown as an emissary to Saudi Arabia, Israel, Egypt, and Jordan. As one senior Pentagon official put it, ". . . Harold Brown was sent out to bury [the regional surrogates doctrine]."[1] The notion of a strategic alliance running from Washington, Tel Aviv, Cairo, and Ryahd emerged as a major priority within the Carter White House. In June a number of high-level meetings were convened at the White House, jointly chaired by Secretary of State Vance and Secretary of Defense Brown, out of which "a consensus emerged over the need to bolster what a senior Administration aide called 'our strategic position in the region.' "[2] These discussions produced a general agreement in support of a gradual but significant augmentation of U.S. naval and air force strength, and the parallel development of a network of bases to provide an "infrastructure" for this projected expansion of the American military presence in the Indian Ocean–Persian Gulf area. These goals were viewed as fundamental to the success of the Rapid Deployment Force in the mid-1980s, "when ships crammed with guns, ammunition, food and fuel will be positioned in forward areas, there to be joined by soldiers flown in during an emergency. For that, posts, airfields and staging areas are needed."[3]

In January 1980, Carter unveiled his "new doctrine" of unilateral U.S. military intervention in the event of any attempts to limit U.S. access to the Persian Gulf and its oil fields.[4] Subsequently, Washington began to exert increased pressures on American allies in Western Europe and Japan to upgrade and strengthen their conventional military forces,[5] despite a singular lack of enthusiasm among these governments for the Carter anti-détente policy shift.[6] In any event, the U.S. government was prepared to act alone, if necessary, to keep the oil routes open. "If the United States is unable to get the cooperation [from its allies]," a Pentagon official declared in late 1980, "I would expect we will act unilaterally."[7]

During 1979–80, the Carter administration moved to establish political, economic, and strategic alliances with potential allies in the Middle East region, especially Sadat's Egypt. Cairo emerged as an active support of U.S. regional and global goals, training Afghan rebels, dispatching arms or advisers to Morocco, Zaire, and Oman, and participating in joint training exercises in Egypt with American air force personnel flying U.S. AWACS reconnaissance planes. Sadat also pledged that military "facilities" would be made available to the United States if any situation arose in which an allied Arab state was threatened.[8] At the same time, Washington signed agreements with Oman, Somalia, and Kenya to use their facilities in any "emergency," and obtained the go-ahead to build a military base on the British-owned island of Diego Garcia in the Indian Ocean. Internal U.S. Department of Defense documents outlined a five-year plan to allocate millions of dollars to establish a network of bases within reach of the Persian Gulf in order "to provide launching pads for American military power in the volatile Indian Ocean theater."[9]

The shift toward a more interventionist policy during the late Carter period is reflected in large-scale increase in military expenditures. The total value of conventional arms transfers in 1980 ($15.3 billion) was the second highest in history and only $500,000 less than the 1975 record.[10] In the area of proposed overall defense spending for the 1980–84 fiscal-year period, the shift toward the military buildup is also quite strikingly illustrated. In January 1979 the administration proposed defense outlays for 1980–84 amounting to $738.7 billion. In its March 1980 revision of the 1981 budget, however, it increased this proposed figure to $854.2 billion.[11]

The Iranian crisis allowed Carter to recreate the consensus in the United States between the mass public opinion and the multinationals: A shift in public commitment to military policies took place which the Carter administration would have been unable to achieve two years earlier. Within this larger time frame, it is obvious that the "human rights" policy was a transitional phase, a period in which the U.S. public was strong enough to oppose new military policies but too weak to create an alternative set of institutions capable of insuring enduring peaceful relations. Lacking a firm institutional base, the democratic anti-interventionist mood was ultimately eroded by an effective propaganda campaign which identified Third World revolution with Soviet aggression, and which promoted the idea that the losses of the multinationals were issues of national security and that internal economic crisis was the product of greedy Third World oil countries. The political conclusion that was spelled out by almost all media and official sources was that the assertion of military power could forestall future changes, and that U.S. security interests took precedent over democratic struggles in the Third World.

This political shift by Carter was neither arbitrary nor hypocritical, but reflected the effort to bridge the gap between the far-flung economic empire and the limited capacity of the imperial state. Once having made the decision to reconstruct an imperial state commensurate with the scope of economic interests, the political debate in the U.S. shifted to the issue of which party or candidate could provide the political leadership with the greatest capacity to pursue the new militaristic direction. The conditions for the ascent of Ronald Reagan were thus laid down.

The Reagan administration has pursued a set of policies whose collective impact has the force of a foreign policy doctrine: The ambiguities that were evidenced in the Carter presidency, residual effects from the early years of his administration, have been resolved. The Reagan Doctrine, its assumptions, methods and goals, have become abundantly clear. The Reagan administration is deeply committed to (1) promoting the Cold War and eliminating all vestiges of détente; (2) regaining hegemony within the capitalist world and centering relations between allies and clients in Washington; (3) consolidating a network of clients in the Third World to promote regional-based interventionary forces; (4) challenging Soviet predominance in its own sphere of influence; and (5) developing "strategic alliances" with chosen countries to buttress overseas adventures.

In recent months the initial hostility toward the Carter human rights program has been modified in one particular respect: Reagan policy-makers have come to appreciate the utility of the rhetoric both in neutralizing opposition to the new military posture and in promoting an anti-Soviet, Cold War strategy. A memorandum on human rights prepared by the State Department and approved by Secretary of State Alexander Haig in early November stated in part:

> [on the] positive track [the US should] maintain our reputation as a reliable partner for our friends so as to maximize the influence of our quiet diplomacy. On the negative track, we must reconsider our relations in the light of serious abuses. However, the human rights element in making decisions affecting bilateral relations must be balanced against U.S. economic, security and other interests. We must take into account the pressures a regime faces and the nature of its enemies . . . "Human rights"—meaning, political rights and civil liberties—conveys what is ultimately at issue in our contest with the Soviet bloc.

Influential Congressional figures have wasted little time in giving their benediction to the Reagan "human rights" line. Senate Foreign Relations Committee chairman Charles Percy noted with approval the second White House nominee to be Assistant Secretary of State for Human Rights, Elliot Abrams (after the earlier candidacy of Ernest Lefeber had failed to gain confirmation), commenting that it "signals a real commitment by the administration to seek the high road on human rights."[13] Abrams, in the course of the nomination hearing, had expressed his support for a U.S. policy in the international financial institutions that favored loans to the repressive military dictatorships of Argentina, Chile, Paraguay, Uruguay, and South Korea.[14] This position was in keeping with a previously implemented executive branch decision to vote in favor of loan submissions from allies who had previously been subjected to U.S. abstentions or negative votes in these agencies. In July 1981, for example, U.S. representatives in the World Bank and Inter-American Development Bank voted for a combined total of $484 million in loans to Argentina, Chile, Uruguay, and Paraguay.[15] These regimes, according to Haig, had shown "dramatic, dramatic reductions" in major human rights violations.[16] They had also shown themselves willing to cooperate with U.S. political and economic objectives in the Western hemisphere, which coincided perfectly with the Reagan policy of deciding voting strategy in the international banks, first and foremost, on the basis of "our political/strategic interests."[17] In an address to the Inter-American Development Bank Board of Governors, Deputy Secretary of the Treasury Tim McNamar also linked U.S. votes to the nature of the requesting regime's development strategy, and exhorted the Bank to give priority to the private sector and regimes that "adopt market-oriented economic policies and development strategies."[18] The new policy line in the multilateral development banks is much in evidence in the case of Nicaragua, which is attempting to chart an independent foreign policy and a nationalist-redistributive development strategy. In November 1981, for example, the United States and its client-state supporters in the Inter-American Development Bank forced Managua to withdraw its application for a $30 million fisheries loan as the only alternative to a negative vote by the institution's executive board. "According to U.S. sources, the United States and other countries had an 'overall political problem with the direction' of the Nicaraguan government."[19]

The doctrinaire nature of the Reagan foreign policy, its strident and abrasive character, should not obscure the practical goals that are being pursued: to protect *existing* U.S. corporate interests, to promote U.S. penetration of competitors' markets, to provide access to new sources of raw materials. The new administration's sustained propaganda efforts to reduce a wide variety of Third World liberation movements, political and economic relations and conflicts between states, to being pawns of the East-West struggle, is the principal weapon around which the new foreign policy is being forged.

The Reagan Doctrine is a policy explicitly designed to promote political and military confrontation; the terms under which it is being pursued will pit Washington against all major social and political forces for change, as well as against the Soviet bloc countries, and in more limited contexts, European social democratic regimes. The specific elements that compose the Reagan Doctrine and the strategies that flow from it are increasingly apparent.

## Confrontation on a Global Scale: Components and Strategies

The most salient feature of the revival of the Cold War has been the massive military buildup undertaken by the Reagan administration. The military program is a wide-ranging and comprehensive effort. Multipurposed and multipronged, it is directed at strengthening U.S. military interventionary capacity, bolstering clients and bludgeoning European and Japanese allies into sharing the military costs commensurate with the benefits that they derive from the imperial system. The military buildup is manifested in several interrelated areas: (1) the development of new weapons systems and their location in forward positions; (2) the development of new military bases and the increasing effort to integrate "host" nations in overall U.S. strategy; (3) the strengthening of old military alliances, including demands that allies increase their military spending, including new weapons systems; and (4) developing new military alliances, especially with former pariah regimes (colonial settlers, such as Israel and South Africa) that can serve as "regional police forces" sharing in the destabilization of zones of revolutionary mobilization.

The overarching commitment of the Reagan administration is to out-muscle the Soviet Union as a means of undercutting the growth of Third World political initiatives that choose to break their exclusive dependence on the West and rely on the Soviet Union as a counterweight.

Within days of Reagan's inauguration, the new administration's military goals were articulated in Congressional testimony by Secretary of Defense Casper Weinberger:

> I think it is fair to tell you that the President and I are committed to equipping fully 16 Active Army divisions, building a Navy capable of maintaining a 3-ocean commitment, filling out the 26 tactical wings of the Air Force, and maintaining 3 flexible and rapidly deployable Marine Corps air ground divisions. We are also committed to insuring that the frontline combat forces have adequate lift and support and are backed by fully manned and well trained first line reserves that will complement and increase their capabilities, and also that we can communicate and command these forces at all times under all circumstances.[20]

The Carter administration's shipbuilding allocation for the navy in fiscal year 1981–1982 was immediately increased by 57 percent to $10.5 billion as part of a median range goal to increase U.S. naval strength from 450 to 600 vessels and create a major permanent naval presence in the Indian Ocean.[21] In addition, the Rapid Deployment Force was upgraded "from a subordinate strike force into a full-scale joint command."[22] Reagan's proposed defense spending for fiscal year 1982 is currently $225.7 billion—some $30 billion more than was originally proposed by Carter.[23]

The buildup of the naval and air forces is intended to intimidate Third World regimes in the process of transforming their societies and to inhibit the transfer of material supplies to national liberation movements. Equally important, the military buildup is a form of "armed propaganda," putting recalcitrant democratic allies on notice of the centrality of the United States in the Western scheme of things, as well as providing "moral support" to dictatorial clients in the Third World that the armed might of Washington stands ready to protect regime stability. The new weapons system then is as much a propaganda symbol, signaling a new policy of confrontation, as it is an outcome of the Reagan drive to substitute military solutions for the political, diplomatic, and economic failures of U.S. policy. Unable to construct a meaningful political-economic approach to revolutionary upheavals and North-South conflicts, Washington seeks, through its military power, to reorganize the agenda, establish new political boundaries, impose solutions that basically reflect overwhelming U.S. economic interests.

The quest for military bases has been centered in the Middle East region, where the announced intention of the Reagan administration is to construct, or expand, a network of military bases that will facilitate the movement of U.S. naval, ground, and air forces in the Indian Ocean-Persian Gulf area.[24] This strategic conception has multiple dimensions: "Providing security assistance to regional states; maintaining a military presence in the region; building a reinforcement capability to deploy the necessary additional forces in a contingency; encouraging a role for local states; and gaining support from our European and Asian allies."[25] As the State Department's Director of the Bureau of Politico-Military Affairs declared in March 1981, it is above all the military prism through which the political realities in the region are being viewed and interpreted: "The United States is going to have to become involved militarily in that region. That decision was taken by the last administration and we agree with it. Nobody—the Saudis, the Omanis, the Turks, the Israelis, or the Egyptians—is going to be able to fill the vacuum: that can only be filled by the United States."[26] He further elaborated, "We would like to be able to have the capability to use facilities in that region, and to the extent to which local powers are equipped with American systems, have American fuel, American munitions, this enhances our ability in a time of crisis to move in and take advantage of that equipment."[27] The recent sale of AWACS to Saudi Arabia represents one aspect of this broader-based long-term plan:

> to build surrogate bases in Saudi Arabia, equipped and waiting for American forces to use. The secret strategy, elaborated and pursued by officials in two administrations, would allow the U.S. Rapid Deployment Force to move "over the horizon" to these forward bases and pre-positioned supplies if the Soviet Union or other hostile forces attempted to capture the Persian Gulf oil fields . . . U.S. air and naval forces, as well as the RDF, also could depend upon this military infrastructure if Middle East oil is in jeopardy. In addition, the stage is set, according to an internal Pentagon paper and other sources, for a regionwide air defense network, led by Saudi Arabia and potentially including such moderate states as Kuwait, the United Arab Emirates, Oman, Bahrain and Qatar. According to U.S. diplomatic and military sources, as well as an authoritative foreign official, the Saudi-U.S. arrangement has evolved during highly sensitive discussions over the last two years: a complex plan to help Saudi Arabia construct military facilities with a sophisticated electronic command system that could be the nerve center for U.S. forces fighting in defense of that nation.[28]

The construction of military bases is viewed by the White House as a physical extension of the new military definitions of U.S. foreign policy: the military presence and "exercises" gives literal meaning to the "projection of power" policy currently in vogue at the White House. Most recently, in November 1981, a Rapid Deployment Force exercise involving some 5,000 U.S. troops took place in an area that covered parts of Egypt, Somalia, Oman, and the Sudan.[29] Psychologically, such actions serve to reassure local client regimes that U.S. intervention to save tottering allies, now or in the future, is a credible policy. The bases are not primarily concerned with external Soviet expansion, but are "in place" to provide a point of departure to intervene in critical Third World countries such as Saudi Arabia in situtations where vital U.S. corporate interests are being adversely affected. The argument of "deterrence" against the Soviet Union in practice becomes a means for preemptive action against internal revolutionary forces. In October 1981, for example, the White House invoked the "external threats" argument to justify the use of military force to prevent "another Iran" in Saudi Arabia.[30] One senior official defined the President's statement as "the Reagan codicil to the Carter doctrine" of January 1980.[31] Secretary of State Weinberger spelled out more precisely the "external" and internal dimensions of the new interventionist policy: "We would not stand by, in the event of Saudi requests, as we did before with Iran, and allow a government that has been totally unfriendly to the United States and to the Free World take over. [President Reagan would intervene] if there should be anything that resembled an internal revolution in Saudi Arabia."[32] Nonetheless, the political costs of a U.S. military presence in delegitimizing a regime has precluded ruling groups in Ryahd, Cairo, and elsewhere from openingly embracing U.S. proposals for permanent military outposts;[33] large-scale training missions and bases in adjoining areas, however, effectively serve the same purpose. Not surprisingly, the revised Reagan proposal for financing military bases in the fiscal year 1982 budget exceeds the original Carter request by over $100 million.[34]

Complementing the military buildup is a policy of strengthening old military alliances and developing new ones. The tacit alliances with South Africa and Israel in particular have been swiftly upgraded into strategic ones. The evolution of the new "strategic relationship" with Israel culminated in the December 1981 announcement of an agreement between the two countries on a memorandum of understanding to strengthen military/strategic cooperation against threats to the Middle East "caused by the Soviet Union or Soviet-controlled forces from outside the region."[35] Prime Minister Begin has already announced his willingness to provide air cover for U.S. transport planes and storage space for U.S. armored vehicles on Israeli soil.[36] U.S. military assistance to Israel increased from $1 billion in 1980 to $1.4 billion in 1981,[37] and is projected to remain at that level, or more likely increase during 1982.[38]

In a background briefing in mid-May, the Reagan administration announced that U.S. policy toward South Africa would henceforth be one of "constructive engagement" in contrast to prior policies of "confrontation."[39] The apartheid policies of the Botha government were deemed of secondary importance as compared to its role as an aggressive bulwark against social revolution on the African continent. This strategic alliance, as one of Secretary of State Haig's advisers succinctly put it, "represents an opportunity to counter the Soviet threat in Africa."[40] Assistant Secretary of State for African Affairs, Chester Crocker, outlined in some detail the new U.S. stance that linked a neutral attitude on the issue of apartheid to the protection of Western economic and strategic interests in the southern African region: "In South Africa . . . important Western economic, strategic, moral, and political interests are at stake. . . . South Africa is an integral and important element of the global economic system and it plays a significant economic role in its own region."[41] In keeping with this "new chapter" in U.S.–South African relations,[42] Reagan's United Nations Ambassador cast the sole vote against a U.N. Security Council resolution in condemnation of the large-scale ground and air invasion of southern Angola directed from Pretoria in late August.[43]

These new strategic alliances have been accompanied by the revival of a policy of *de facto* collaboration with right-wing military dictatorships in Latin America and other parts of the Third World. The restoration of close political and military ties with Argentina, for instance, has been a priority goal of the Reagan administration from the beginning. In March the Administration went before Congress to recommend repeal of section 620B of the Foreign Assistance Act, which prohibited all military sales and assistance to Argentina due to major human rights violations.[44] In April General Edward C. Meyer, U.S. Army Chief of Staff, became one of a number of American military officials to visit their opposite numbers in Buenos Aires. According to Argentine officials, Meyer concluded a verbal agreement on increased consultation between the two armed forces that "will facilitate political, military and institutional cooperation—and everything you can imagine—between our two countries."[45] The key executive branch liaison with the Argentine junta has been Secretary of State Haig's special adviser on Latin America, General Vernon Walters, most notable for his active participation in the 1964 Brazilian coup that ousted the nationalist Goulart government.[46]

A similar shift in U.S. policy has been in evidence with regard to the military junta ruling Chile. In Congressional testimony in March 1981, John A. Bushnell, a senior Latin American official in the State Department, stated that the White House had decided to lift existing economic sanctions against Chile and to pursue a less confrontational approach than had characterized policy in recent years.[47] Bushnell pointed to the incongruity between Carter's selective sanctions against the Pinochet regime and the latter's settlement of claims by expropriated U.S. firms "on an equitable basis" and its support of U.S. positions "on many hemispheric and global issues."[48] In June Chilean Foreign Minister René Rojas held confidential discussions with Secretary of

State Haig and other administration officials in Washington on Santiago's role in the new regional military strategy.[49] Soon after, the U.S. cast favorable votes for two international bank loans to Chile totalling more than $160 million. During a visit to Santiago in August, U.N. Ambassador Jean Kirkpatrick said the Reagan administration intended to "normalize completely its relations with Chile."[50]

In the Caribbean-Central American region, the Reagan White House has moved forcefully to bolster the fortunes of allied military dictatorships, especially in El Salvador, Guatemala, and Honduras. El Salvador is the beneficiary of the largest portion of the proposed fiscal year 1982 U.S. military assistance for Latin America, while the Honduras request for $10.7 million is almost double that of the 1981 appropriation ($5.4 million).[51] Furthermore, significant numbers of U.S. military advisory and training officials have been dispatched to both countries.[52] In Guatemala, the administration secretly terminated a four-year Congressional ban on military aid to the ruling junta in mid-1981 with the approval of a sale of 50 military trucks and 100 army trucks, having revised the status of the trucks from "lethal" to "nonlethal" weapons.[53] Reagan also broke a ban on the sale of F16 fighter planes to Latin America instituted by the Nixon administration with its agreement to sell 24 of the sophisticated warplanes to the Herrera government in Venezuela, which had emerged as one of the most active supporters of U.S. policy in El Salvador and other parts of Central and South America.[54] Efforts to promote a South Atlantic Treaty Organization to dominate the region are being pursued by U.S. policymakers as are parallel exertions to promote a Caribbean Basin Organization around a so-called mini-Marshall Plan which would open up the region to U.S. investments and facilitate the creation of a regional military alliance.[55] The Caribbean Basin Organization is also seen by Washington as a vehicle for bringing the Venezuelan Christian Democrats and Columbian Liberals into a confrontation with the revolutionary regimes and movements in the area.

The most sustained and serious Reagan administration efforts, however, have been directed toward pressuring the NATO countries and Japan to increase their weapons procurement policies, to build up their armed forces, and to share the military cost of defending the imperial system. Long-standing tensions have emerged between the United States, Europe, and Japan over the fact that Washington pays the military bill for sustaining Third World regions in which their competitors are extracting high profits. Officials of the Reagan executive branch have aggressively sought to pressure these governments to accept a greater share of the allied defense burden, in the form of increased budgetary allocations for military spending and support for the stationing of U.S.-made medium range nuclear weapons on European soil. "It is essential," Secretary of Defense Weinberger has declared on a number of occasions, "that we develop a more rational "division of labor," under which our NATO allies and Japan will be asked to join in contributing more to the common defense."[56] Japan, in particular, has been singled out for its failure to sufficiently upgrade its military capabilities. "The Japanese will have to do more," observed a senior United States official in a briefing prior to a meeting between Prime Minister Suzuki and President Reagan that Washington hoped would result in a Japanese commitment to increase the proportion of their budget devoted to military spending.[57] In October Secretary Weinberger reiterated the administration's position that America's allies must increase their military contributions to the Persian Gulf area if there is to be "any permanent hope of containing Soviet political intimidation." He continued with an implied threat that the United States could not continue to stand by and watch its allies take advantage of the American military "umbrella" to advance their own commercial and political interests in the region. "Western Europe and Japan dare not settle for merely increasing their trade and diplomatic contacts with nations in Southwest Asia as their contribution toward keeping oil fields out of unfriendly hands."[58]

The U.S. goal is to pressure all its regional allies to accelerate and expand their military programs within a basically United States–centered global alliance. In Europe, where NATO has already agreed to locate 108 Pershing 11 and 464 cruise missiles in West Germany, England, Italy, and the Netherlands, the effort of the Reagan administration is to implicate the alliance membership in U.S. policy through myriad new military deployments. The stationing of new missiles and weapons and weapons systems controlled by the United States underlines the very real loss of sovereignty which this implies in the control over foreign policy—and the terms of negotiation with the Soviet Union. The added leverage obtained by U.S. policymakers enhances their capacity to disregard European initiatives, reverting U.S.–European relations back to the 1950s.

The policies pursued by Reagan toward the Third World are in major agreement with the direction of this approach; arms sales and "strategic" agreements have been, or are in the process of being, hammered out with an array of countries in Africa, Asia, and the Middle East, as well as Latin America. Not long after the administration took office, Under Secretary of State for Security Assistance James L. Buckley outlined the new conventional arms transfer policy: "arms transfers should be viewed as an increasingly important component of our global security posture and a key instrument of our foreign policy."[59] The new policy was subsequently formalized in a White House directive which provided for global transfers of weapons to meet any perceived threat from the Soviet Union, effectively broadening and superseding the selective controls implied in the prior Carter directive of May 1977.[60] In mid-1980, the United States and Pakistan announced agreement on a $3 billion five-year military and economic aid program that will include the sale of F-16 fighter bombers to the Zia regime.[61] More recently, the White House has declared its intention "to significantly increase military aid" to the Mobutu regime in Zaire because of what one State

Department official described as that regime's "central strategic importance" to U.S. policy objectives on the African continent.[62] In the Middle East, combined American military sales to Egypt and Israel for 1981 totals some $2.3 billion.[63] Following the Sadat assassination, the United States announced plans to accelerate arms deliveries to Egypt and Sudan, and to organize a "highly increased U.S. presence in the area."[64] In addition to an already approved $30 million military assistance package, the Reagan administration has requested Congress to provide the Nimeiry government with a further $110 million worth of military equipment.[65] Senior White House officials have also stated the likelihood of U.S. "training teams" being dispatched to Sudan.[66]

The military bases and the joint military activities within these regions serve to bolster the status quo regimes, and directly involves the U.S. armed forces in the role of defending incumbent dictators against popular opposition movements. The military buildup of the United States and its extension abroad has the general political effect of strengthening the coercive apparatus of existing regimes, and marginalizing democratic and reformist forces from any institutional role.

## New Strategies for Direct Intervention

Given the new pattern of emerging arms buildup and military alliances, what policies is Washington likely to pursue in accordance with these developments? The overarching reality that emerges is the growing willingness of U.S. policymakers to sanction and approve, once more, a "regional policeman's" role for its strategic allies. The explicit nature of the relationship with South Africa, the strategic alliance with Israel, the reestablishment of close and friendly ties with Pinochet in Chile and Viola in Argentina, the reconsolidation of relations with the Marcos dictatorship in the Philippines, and the military regime in South Korea are directed at forestalling any new changes in the Third World, as well as reversing processes of change already under way. The U.S. defense of the South African invasion of Angola in August 1981 accorded with the administration's policy of defending South Africa, of destabilizing Angola, and of creating a client regime in Namibia. The invasion reflected the convergence of interests between Pretoria and Washington. The disregard of African bourgeois nationalist and Western European opinion suggests the centrality of the South African connection for U.S. policy. Likewise in the Middle East, the U.S. agreement to deepen its ties with Israel, the doctrine of strategic collaboration including military ties on land, sea and air, involves efforts by Washington policymakers to police the whole Middle East. The growth of radical anti-imperialist forces, the fragility of oil-rich regimes, and the absence of Arab-based forces with a capacity to intervene has led the Washington administration to seek to increase the role of Israel, despite the adverse reactions among pro-United States Arab regimes. The collaboration of Israel would be essential to any direct use of the Rapid Deployment Force, established a large part to protect U.S. corporate access to oil resources throughout the Third World. South Africa's and Israel's military power, and the willingness to use it, thus fits in nicely with the Reagan Third World policy, at a time when other Third World and Western European allies have proven refractory to the current American view of East–West confrontation.[67]

The political rapprochement between Washington and the dictatorships in South America has a similar basis; the common economic interests are rooted in the similar "economic models" that are being pursued—the free market economies and the promotion of growth through large-scale private investment. This convergence in economic policy is reinforced by the belief of both sides that any liberalization of the regimes would immediately destabilize the international balance of power. Moreover, the rather narrow social basis of these regimes and the growth of revolutionary movements elsewhere has served to make them more dependent on U.S. military and political support and accepting of U.S. leadership. The decision of the governments of Chile, Argentina, Bolivia, Paraguay, Honduras, and Guatemala to repudiate the Mexican-French declaration recognizing the Democratic Revolutionary Front in El Salvador as "a representative political force" suggests that the interests of the dictatorships in stabilizing their rule will necessarily involve them in U.S. strategic plans to intervene to prevent or reverse democratic revolutionary processes.[68] This view is reinforced by the substantial involvement of Argentine intelligence and military officials on the side of the existing regimes in Honduras, Guatemala, and El Salvador, and by the apparent willingness of Buenos Aires to act at the behest of the U.S. government "as an instrument of intervention in El Salvador."[69] The political basis or the revival and extension of Washington's military and intelligence programs is built upon the common perception of the vulnerability of internal classes that sustain U.S. hemispheric hegemony. The capacity for U.S. intervention is thus twofold: in the direct support and supply of the established military-dictatorial regimes, and in the effort to construct a regional based police force that can provide for the collective security of any particular regime threatened by upheaval. The impact and consequences for the Third World of U.S. policy are profound in the decline of diplomacy and political negotiations as instruments of policy in the face of the ascendancy of the arms buildup. This does not mean that all negotiations will be eschewed, especially in light of the constant pressures by Western allies. What it does mean, however, is that negotiations and summit meetings with Socialist and revolutionary regimes will be ritualistic affairs in which Washington will hope to "demonstrate" their ineffectiveness; they will become themselves propaganda forums to reinforce the commitment to policies of confrontation. International meetings with adversaries will be arenas to "warn" or "threaten" or "pressure" them to accommodate U.S. interests or face retaliation. Negotiations and meetings thus become an extension of the confrontational relationship—a process that will affect every area of international exchange. The Reagan administration's decision to proceed with confrontational politics was taken unilaterally. The allies are presented accomplished facts and the alternatives of accepting them or being subject to U.S. pressure. The strategy is to "create facts" which polarize East/West, forcing the rest of the capitalist world to follow suit. Those states which refuse to submerse themselves to the Reagan-Haig definition of Western unity are described as susceptible to Soviet blandishments or products of Soviet efforts to "divide the U.S. from its Western allies."

Central to this effort to bifurcate the world is the sustained global propaganda campaign to derive all conflicts and competition in the Third World as emanations of Soviet expansionism. Failing to identify any traces of Soviet involvement, the new concept of "Soviet surrogates" is invented to cover any movement that fails to conform to the traditional right-wing stereotypes of Soviet policy. The main beneficiaries of the new East–West polarization policy propagated in Washington are the extreme rightist regimes—Israel, South Africa, Chile, Argentina, Zaire— who have been ardent upholders of the doctrines as the principal ideological weapon to defend the legitimacy of their rule, lacking any substantial internal justification. The main criteria today in shaping Reaganite policy are a regime's position on the issue of East–West polarization and its willingness to subordinate itself to U.S. leadership in pursuit of the politics of confrontation. The revival of the doctrine of a bipolar world and the attempt to submerge all conflicts into this pattern will be resisted by many allies of the United States: West Germany, with its trade ties with the Eastern bloc; Saudi Arabia, with its fears of Israeli expansionism; Indonesia and Malaysia with their fears of Chinese "hegemonism"; Mexico, with its fears of U.S. domination. The ideology of bipolar global confrontation and the polarizing effects that it evokes will have an adverse effect not only on "nonaligned" forces, but will undercut the position of middle class liberal-democratic and nationalistic movements within Third World countries. The right-wing and repressive political terrain will favor clandestine groups over legalists; the supply and training of military forces will encourage violent, as opposed to electoral, activity; the attacks on the center will force centrists out of politics or over to the left. Global confrontation which polarizes international politics will have a tendency to do likewise internally. The end of policy is to reconstruct the structure of power that existed in the 1950s—and to recuperate the economic position that accompanied uncontested military supremacy.

The commitment of the Reagan administration to the reconstruction of the world in the image of the 1950s requires a number of fundamental changes, most of which are beyond the realm of possibility (including "military supremacy over the USSR," dominating European economic and foreign policy, and so on). Preventing any further changes in power—"containing revolutions" in the Third World—seems to be the first strategic task. This involves a major effort to make El Salvador an example of the "testing of the wills," i.e., the willingness of the United States to maximize the use of force to sustain a repressive regime, even at the cost of massive loss of civilian lives, and even in the absence of allied support. Beyond the revival of preventive interventionism is the serious planning of policies to reverse established revolutionary regimes. The attempt to retrieve the past involves efforts to destroy the present, and the danger is that it can lead to global nuclear war. Washington, under Reagan, is not reconciled with the established revolutionary governments in Nicaragua, Cuba, Grenada, or Angola.

United States policymakers have consistently rationalized their opposition to the direction of socioeconomic change in Nicaragua with tirades over the supposed transshipment of arms to the guerrillas in El Salvador and over the Sandanista efforts to secure militarily the survival of the popular revolution. These two factors have been defined by Washington as the major obstacles to any improvement in bilateral political and economic relations.[70] The Reagan adminstration has pursued a policy of unrelenting hostility toward Nicaragua, culminating in recent statements by senior executive branch officials that the Sandanista government has "very nearly become intolerable."[71] Laying the groundwork for possible intervention, one official declared that it may ultimately be necessary to take direct action: "Something has to be done and done soon."[72] In testimony before the House Foreign Affairs Committee in mid-November, Secretary of State Haig refused to exclude the possibility of U.S. efforts to overthrow the social revolutionary regime in Managua.[73] While there is a general consensus within the U.S. government in opposition to the Sandanistas, and a determination to prevent Nicaragua from becoming "another Cuba,"[74] bureaucratic disagreements have developed over the efficacy of the military option.[75] Secretary Haig emerged as the leading advocate of using military force, in opposition to senior Pentagon officials and the Joint Chiefs of Staff, who fear the possibility of a protracted military involvement in the region lacking domestic social support would endanger the administration's plans to modernize the U.S. armed forces.[76]

The Cuban government's sustained identification with, and support of, social revolution in the Third World—specifically Central America and the Caribbean—has been one of the principal sources of antagonism between Havana and the Reagan administration. Cuba has been singled out as the primary "source" of arms shipments to the Salvadoran guerrillas, leading to Washington's consideration of an array of policy options ranging from a tightening of the existing economic embargo to forms of direct action of a military nature.[77] In the fall of 1981, Secretary of State Haig requested the Pentagon to examine the possibility of blockading Nicaragua and taking various military actions against Cuba, including a show of airpower, a large naval exercise, a quarantine on arms shipments to the island, a naval blockade, and even a possible invasion. More recently, the United States has undertaken an intensive effort to mobilize Latin American allies in support of some form of collective action against Cuba and Nicaragua, or conceivably to provide a multilateral cover for some future unilateral action against the revolutionary regimes. According to U.S. officials, a number of regional governments and their armed forces leadership have been contacted at the highest levels "and asked if they might join in any kind of military action."[78]

Toward the nationalist government of Grenada, the Reagan White House has employed a combination of political ostracism and economic pressures. Despite the maintenance of nominal diplomatic relations, the U.S. government has refused to open lines of communication with the Bishop regime.[79] Meanwhile, political and strategic arguments have been used to pressure Western allies to withhold urgently needed economic aid to the Grenada government. In seeking to limit Grenada's external sources of financing, the United States has attempted, unsuccessfully, to persuade the European Economic Community to withhold a $30 million loan, was temporarily able to block an IMF facility, and engaged in an intense, but unsuccessful lobbying effort to exclude Grenada from the provisions of the Caribbean Development Bank. The United States then sought, again without success, to make Grenada's exclusion the price for a $4 million grant to the regional banking institution.[80]

The United States has not reconciled itself to the permanence of the MPLA government in Angola, and continues to place its support behind the South African-backed forces of UNITA under the leadership of Jonas Savimbi. Determined to reestablish a legal basis for supporting new military and paramilitary operations by UNITA (in collaboration with the CIA) against Luanda, the Reagan administration has asked Congress to repeal the 1976 Clark amendment, which placed a blanket ban on covert or overt U.S. assistance to anti-regime forces in Angola.[81] In a sharp break with the Carter administration, which refused to grant him access to senior executive branch policymakers when he visited Washington in 1979, the Reagan administration held high-level discussions with Savimbi in early December on the grounds that UNITA was "a legitimate political force in Angola."[82]

Reagan policymakers have developed a strategy of confrontation to create the basis for "regionally based" military intervention. The image of revolutionary societies that Haig projected is revealing: according to him, they are crisis-wracked systems devoid of popular support and dependent on outside power to sustain them. The strategy adopted by the Reaganites is to neutralize Soviet assistance (through military buildup) and then, through collaboration between the United States and its regional allies, engage in a military assault for power.

These extremist positions, even by U.S. standards, reflect the new executive branch personnel in Washington whose ideological propensities and styles are divorced from the practical exigencies of day-to-day business operation. The extreme voluntarism manifested in U.S. foreign policy—the will to power—elevates individual desires and powers above the objective circumstances that allow for the realization of policy goals. To the right-wing voluntarist, the assertion of power, the subjective elements, can create the objective conditions; consciousness of the Russian danger properly understood can overcome fear of nuclear holocaust, lucrative trade agreements, and the like. The adventurism in this approach is obvious. The same subjectivity is evidenced in the Reagan approach to the market. The problem is the "psychology" of Wall Street for not investing in industry and stock—not the high interest rates or the availability of other areas which provide higher profit rates.[83] There is an emerging conflict between the militarist-voluntarist policy geared to reversing global trends over the past twenty years and the more sober-minded calculations of pragmatic Western businessmen who recognize the realities of post-revolutionary society and try to maximize opportunities. The divorce between political power and economic power, however, has yet to manifest itself in any clear-cut alternative program. It finds expression only in opposition to particular policy measures.

The first manifestations of the new Reagan offensive strategy appeared early: the deepening ties with Israel found expression in the June 1981 bombing of the Osirak nuclear facility located near Baghdad, Iraq. Despite Washington's disclaimers, the action was followed by a U.S. initiative to formalize a relationship of "strategic collaboration" with Tel Aviv. The rapprochement with South Africa is evidenced in Washington's veto of the U.N. Security Council resolution condemning its invasion of Angola. The invasion established terrain for the operation of the United States–supported UNITA terrorists in Angola and attempts to create a zone between Angola and Namibia to isolate SWAPO from its Namibian supporters. South African troops have continued their attacks on SWAPO inside Angolan territory throughout the latter half of 1981.[84] The agreement of Sadat to the stationing of U.S. troops in Egypt as jumping off locations for Mideastern interventions was followed by Washington's thinly veiled support for Sadat's crackdown on all dissident forces. Massive bombings, full-scale invasions, massive internal political crackdowns, are the first fruits of the new era of the Cold War. While the strategic collaborators thus follow the policy of open warfare, the Reagan administration pursues a policy of unremitting pressure on Europeans and moderate nationalist governments in the Third World. Following the French-Mexican declaration of support for the Salvadoran Democratic Revolutionary Front, twelve Latin American countries were mobilized to denounce the declaration. Vernon Walters, Haig's roving ambassador, the liaison with the most extremist forces in the Latin American military and the key figure in organizing support for the U.S. positions, played a central role in orchestrating this response. The process of integrating and subordinating hemispheric countries within the American orbit has been operating primarily at the military-strategic levels rather than in the economic sphere where a growing pattern of economic diversification (e.g., Argentina's heavy dependence on grain sales to the Soviet bloc) has made a greater U.S. control more difficult to attain. The conference of U.S. military and intelligence officials and their Latin American counterparts in early November is indicative of the Reagan effort to extend and deepen noneconomic linkages with these pivotal sectors of allied states in the region.[85]

The revival and extension of Central Intelligence Agency activity as a factor in destabilizing nationalist regimes in the Third World is evident once again in recent reports of attempts to assassinate the Libyan head of state, Muammar Gaddafi. The activation of terrorist activity against the Angolan government and the ongoing harrassment of the Cuban leadership are also likely indicators of stepped up CIA activity, following patterns established in earlier periods. The authority of the CIA and other U.S. intelligence agencies to collect information from Americans at home and abroad has been considerably broadened by the issuance of an executive order in December 1981 that promises to be another step in the "unleashing" of the Agency and the proliferation of covert operations, especially against nationalist governments and movements in the Third World.[86]

The mounting pressures on Japan and Europe to rearm for confrontation is promoted by a demagogic campaign centering on the efforts of Poland to extricate itself from Soviet and local Stalinist domination. The Soviet–Polish confrontation has been manipulated by the Reagan administration as a means of mobilizing and militarizing Western Europe under U.S. hegemony. By focusing on Soviet–Polish relations, Washington hopes to extend its own brand of interventionism. Brandishing the threat of Soviet intervention in Eastern Europe, it hopes to subordinate Western Europe to its efforts to polarize the world.

The military buildup of Pakistan and the efforts to promote the ASEAN countries as a collective counterweight to revolutionary forces in Asia are the centerpieces of U.S. strategy in the region. The propaganda effort is abetted through efforts to depict the Vietnamese overthrow of the genocidal Pol Pot regime as an example of Vietnamese "expansionism," threatening to engulf Southeast Asia. Likewise, the Soviet intervention on behalf of the Karmal regime in Afghanistan is portrayed as part of a Soviet push toward the oil-rich Middle East. In both cases, the Communist countries acted for very specific sets of objectives rooted in a particular conjuncture—regardless of each one's opinions regarding the ultimate rights and wrongs of the issue.[87] For Washington, however, these actions became the pretext for a wide range of actions destined to head off future changes from within the societies in question. Washington's rationale for Soviet expansionism, declining oil production, was based on studies such as that produced by the CIA in early 1981 stating that Soviet oil production would begin to decline within one to three years. This assertion has since been refuted by more recent studies which show the growth of new sources of production based on increased investments. In its latest analysis of the Soviet economy, for example, the Pentagon's Defense Intelligence Agency describes the Soviet

Union energy prospects as "highly favorable," going on to state that Moscow will be able to increase its oil production and exports for some years to come.[88] The central shift in the region has been the growth of Chinese-American cooperation in promoting instability: in Afghanistan and Cambodia, Peking has provided arms and supplies to U.S.-backed forces. The coordination of efforts with China to promote Western aims is the most significant shift in the revival of the Cold War, placing additional pressures on the Soviet southern and eastern flanks and increasing the isolation of national revolutionary forces in the region.

The current and future goals of the Reagan administration remain: reestablishing U.S. military-economic hegemony over the Third World through the development of a network of stable strategic collaborator states capable of participating jointly in armed occupations of target areas; displacing European and Japanese hegemony in areas that have undercut U.S. positions; deflecting competition and striking a more favorable "balance" between the partners regarding their economic gains and their military expenditures; and rejecting large-scale public funding and proposals for a New International Economic Order in favor of creating new opportunities for U.S. capital expansion and new markets for U.S. goods and services by universalizing the free market economic strategy.

Central to the Reagan strategy of "making the U.S. number one again" is the restructuring of the U.S. society and economy. The federal budget is oriented toward cutting taxes and social services to free capital to accumulate, compete, and increase its share of markets worldwide; the increase in the military budget is to provide the imperial state with the armaments to defend and create the opportunities for expansion. Thus the Reagan approach is a new historical project based on a sharp reconcentration of capital for export which leaves out the labor movement: it represents a shift from "social" or "welfare imperialism," in which domestic reform accompanies outward expansion, to an approach in which internal exploitation becomes a necessary condition for imperialism. The basic difference is the enormous growth of competition between advanced countries and the new challenges from the Third World which have vastly increased in costs of participation in the world economy. The cost of external expansion, however, points to one of many contradictions between the goals of the new historical project of the Reagan administration and the historical realities of the world economy.

### Contradictions of U.S. Policy

There is a strong "voluntarist" streak which runs throughout the policy pronouncements of the Reagan administration—the idea that if policymakers "will" a policy into being, spread the word, create right thinking, they will be able to overcome objective obstacles to the realization of their plans. There is an overvaluation of subjectivity and an undervaluation of the objective circumstances and interests. In many ways, the Reaganites resemble the ultra-left-wing groups of the 1960s New Left who believed that "consciousness," "exemplary action," and acts of will could start the motor of revolutionary mass action going. In this case, the Reaganites believe that pronouncements of confidence in the economy will stir capital to forego high profits in speculative activity in favor of investments in industry; that projections of military power will somehow overcome the interests and linkages that define the relations between Europe and the Soviet bloc. The ultra-voluntaristic policy approach assumes that immediate, day-to-day activities can be overlooked in favor of the grand transformation in the future. But as the ultra-leftist discovered in the 1960s, and as their rightist counterparts are discovering in the present, actions of will that do not take account of the relationship and interests of the present are doomed to failure. The contradictions that have emerged within the Reagan global strategy approach are already evident and are expressed internally and externally.

INTERNAL CONTRADICTIONS

Two important contradictions are maturing within the U.S. political economy. The effort by the Reagan administration to reconstruct the imperial state apparatus through increased military spending and to promote capital accumulation through tax cuts is creating a growing budget deficit. Increases in government borrowing to overcome the deficit have increased interest rates, which in turn slows down investment and deepens the tendencies toward stagnation with inflation. The increased strength of the dollar and the high interest rates, in turn, make U.S. exports less competitive, channel funds into money markets, and weaken the process of global accumulation. Moreover, the incentives to capital have no noticeable effect in stimulating industrial growth, as the costs/benefits are too high relative to alternative areas of activity. The conditions pursued to promote capital growth become the obstacles to growth: a gap emerges between Wall Street and Reagan as the "ideal" world of the ideologues' marketplace fails to square with the practices of bankers and investors. We have the anomaly of free enterprise ideologues in search of a social base.

The second basic contradiction emerging from the Reagan strategy involves the massive cuts in social programs, conditions necessary to stimulate private growth, and the frontal attacks on labor in order to make U.S. capital competitive on a world scale. These measures conflict with the social basis of the political consensus which has underpinned U.S. global expansion since World War II. Empire is now not a source of compensation for both labor and capital, but rather a cost to be borne by labor for capital. The difficulties that this presents to a labor movement whose leadership is deeply wedded to empire, militarism, and the Cold War are immense. The labor bureaucracy's attempt to save its organizational gains without giving up its international commitments prevents them from breaking new political ground. The policy is toward convincing the Democrats to resist social cuts and to embrace the Cold War—a program as bankrupt as Reagan's. Given the international nature of U.S. capitalism, the efforts by the Trade Union bureaucracy to promote internal development to provide employment will find no echo among political influentials: the conditions for external development necessarily require military programs and the consequent cut in wages, both to finance expansion and to protect it. Beyond protesting the Reaganite changes that directly affect it, the labor bureaucracy lacks any global programmatic alternative of its own. The erosion of popular support and the loss of legitimacy that the Reagan administration can experience, however, could seriously weaken its efforts to modernize capital for global expansion.

EXTERNAL CONTRADICTIONS: EUROPE AND JAPAN

The external contradictions that the Reagan administration generates are multiple, and have already manifested themselves. First, to a far greater degree than that of the United States, European and Japanese growth is linked to a policy of détente. Trade relations between Eastern and Western Europe have grown to significance in the past decade, and the new confrontation strategy of the Reagan administration jeopardizes these links without being able to provide any meaningful alternatives. During 1980, the combined value of European Economic Community exports to Eastern Europe (Poland, Bulgaria, Czechoslovakia, Hungary, East Germany, USSR, Romania) totaled almost $26 billion, while imports from Eastern Europe to the EEC reached approximately $30 billion. Total U.S. trade with Eastern Europe (exports and imports) for the same twelve-month period, by contrast, totalled less than $6 billion in value.[89] In addition, West European imports of Soviet Union natural gas have more than tripled since 1975, and in November 1981 the largest East–West business transaction in history was signed between Bonn and Moscow which will nearly double the former's dependence on Soviet natural gas imports.[90] Furthermore, the competition between Europe and the United States over Third World markets cuts across Reagan's efforts to polarize the world in the mold of a rigid East-West confrontation. European opportunities for trade in the Middle East are endangered by the adventurous militarist course adopted by Israel and the United States. One consequence has been an increasing divergence between the United States and Western Europe and Japan over the role of the PLO in the Middle East peace-keeping process. In mid-1980, the European Economic Community put itself on record in support of full self-determination for the Palestinian people and declared that the PLO should be "associated with" negotiations for a peace settlement in the Middle East.[91] Since then, despite persistent U.S. opposition, this position has been steadfastly maintained. The recent willingness of some European countries to participate in the Sinai "peace-keeping" force has been accompanied by reiterations of continued support for Palestine rights and the June 1980 policy statement on PLO participation in the peace process.[92] Japan's identical outlook on the Middle East was underscored in October 1981 when President Suzuki told Yasser Arafat that he considered the Palestinians at the "heart" of the regional problem.[93]

At the same time, the pressure by Washington to increase armaments spending among its European and Japanese allies threatens to disintegrate the social consensus in Europe; social cuts and increased arms spending are likely to provoke sharp class cleavages and resistance—far more profoundly than in the United States. The attempt to deepen European involvement in the New Cold War carries with it the notion of deepening the internal unrest.[93] Simultaneously, the economic policies of the United States—the "monetarist" supply side economics—threatens to deepen the recession: Europeans, fearful of wholesale flights of capital to the United States, have maintained high interest rates, thus blocking any efforts at industrial recovery.[94] The conditions for U.S. recovery then are counterposed to the conditions for European development. Furthermore, the labor-based social democratic parties and governments are under intense pressure to resist supporting U.S.-backed right-wing dictatorships in the Third World. Soon after his election, French President Francois Mitterand expressed "serious reservations" over Reagan's Central America policy of attributing all ills in the area to "communist subversion," to the exclusion of socioeconomic inequalities and repressive regimes.[95] The decision of the socialist government to recognize the Democratic Revolutionary Front faithfully reflects public opinion in France, and is in direct conflict with the "military solution" being promoted by Washington. Greece, Denmark, and the Netherlands have also added their voices in support of political negotiations between the Salvadoran junta and the popular movement prior to the holding of elections.[96] In summary, the terms of the U.S. competitive position and the adoption of a global confrontational approach are in deep conflict with the structural position of the Europeans and the Japanese in the world political economy.

EXTERNAL CONTRADICTIONS: THE THIRD WORLD

European interests and the changing position of Europe in the world economy are only part of the structural constraints that the U.S. government has to confront in the present conjuncture. Significant structural changes have also taken place in the Third World since World War II which constrict Washington's capacity to impose its simplistic formulas of old. The main trend in the Third World has been in the direction of diversification of the economy—increasing industrialization, diversifying trading partners, securing new sources of finance, developing local markets, joining commodity cartels, developing regional ties. This pattern of diversification involves developing a whole series of vital relationships and linkages that cut across the East–West polarity that Washington proposes. Moreover, new classes and trading partners link together state structures which resist fitting into the new U.S. global pattern. Brazil's trade ties with Angola, the Soviet Union, and the Arab countries are a case in point. Moreover, some Third World countries will compete with the U.S. in pursuit of export markets, further constraining an "overidentification" with Washington's pronouncements. Argentine exports of grain to the USSR is a ready example. In addition, while many Third World countries depend on the United States, the latter also depends on the key oil-producing countries in the periphery. The political, ideological and economic ties with some countries (Israel and South Africa) generates conflict with other countries on which the United States is dependent (Nigeria and Saudi Arabia). The image of a "recalcitrant world'" that does not recognize the same dangers as the Reagan administration is a product of the voluntarist fantasies of Cold War ideologues. The deep structural changes and the historical trends of the past decades can no longer be fit into a bipolar straightjacket— and no amount of Cold War rhetoric can undo or reverse them.

EXTERNAL CONTRADICTIONS: THE SOVIET BLOC

The growth of Soviet bloc economic and military power is an indisputable fact of the first order in evaluating the prospects of the new confrontational politics of the Reagan administration. For all of its bluster and bombast, Haig must recognize that any *frontal* attack on the Soviet Union will result in massive retaliation and mutual destruction. Likewise, military intervention against established allied Soviet bloc countries, particularly in Eastern Europe, runs the same risks. These are the outer limits for U.S. action, even in its most adventurous moments. It is only in the Third World, where revolutionary regimes are not yet consolidated and national liberation movements are still in struggle, that Washington will exercise its new military options. Thus, while the Reagan administration's policy envisions a global confrontation, the balance of power forces this confrontation to take place in reduced spheres of the world. Nuclear parity and the formidable array of Soviet arms preclude the kind of political pressure that was evidenced by U.S. policymakers in the early 1950s when Washington maintained a nuclear monopoly or near monopoly. The efforts by the Reagan administration to gain superiority over the USSR in order to recreate the political leverage of the 1950s is unlikely to meet success, in part because of European resistance, in part because of the constraints of the U.S. political economy, and finally because the Soviets are capable of allocating resources to remain competitive.

While Soviet military strength remains an unalterable factor in the current global power alignment, it also serves as a source of possible support for a select number of liberation movements, in particular in Africa and the Middle East. The notion that Washington can simply overwhelm its designated revolutionary adversaries and sustain its dictatorial allies by sheer material might is doomed by the fact that alternative sources of arms exist to buttress the political fortunes of the opposition. While Soviet arms shipments, either in quality or quantity, cannot match those of the United States, still they are sufficient when combined with mass popular support to seriously challenge minority regimes which dominate in the Middle East and South Africa. Recognition of this military equilibrium (objective reality) probably serves to temper the more extreme versions of global confrontation within the Reagan administration. Even as it eschews negotiation and plots the growth curves in arms spending, the Reaganites cannot fail to realize the need to negotiate, to at least attempt to define the terms and locus of conflict—in a word, to establish boundaries within which confrontation will take place. Open-ended conflict, without a sense of place or strategic interests, as surely the Reaganites probably recognize (and with which the Europeans are most concerned) would rapidly end up in nuclear confrontation. The New Cold War then will involve tough talk and extensive U.S intervention in the Third World, but it will be joined with negotiations and an incapacity to reverse relations of global power or to establish domination through exclusive military solutions.

If Soviet military power stands as one constraint on the global aspirations of the Reaganites, Soviet economic growth stands as another factor limiting Washington's efforts to polarize the world between East and West. The links between the Soviet Union and the West have proliferated in recent years. And as the New Cold War heated up and U.S.–Soviet relations declined, the links between the USSR and other capitalist countries grew. The enormous expansion of trade between West Germany and the Soviet Union in the area of technology, energy resources and machine tools is a case in point. The interdependence of Europe and the Eastern bloc—the growing financial ties—inhibits and delimits Western Europe's ability and willingness to follow Washington's conflictual strategy. The scale of activities in certain areas (energy) and the complementary nature of East–West trade (finished goods for raw materials) cannot be matched by the United States, which is more competitive with Western Europe in both what it buys and what it sells. Washington cannot provide a satisfactory substitute for dealing with the East: on the contrary, the nature of Reagan economics is to further depress and constrict overall Western growth in the short run and to increase U.S. competitive advantages in the medium and long run. The arms race, as promoted by Reagan, goes counter to the attempt by Europeans to modernize their industrial plants to maintain a competitive edge and a trading relationship with the newly industrializing countries in the Third World and in Eastern Europe. The growth of Soviet markets and the opportunities for trade thus serve to promote the ascendancy of economic forces in Western Europe over and against the military, especially in times of capitalist stagnation.

The economic ties between the Third World countries and the Soviet Union is another factor which inhibits many countries from joining anticommunist crusades. Moreover, Washington's effort to "confront" revolutionary regimes in the Third World to isolate them economically and to countenance counterrevolutionary activity can be effectively neutralized by these same countries turning more actively toward the Soviet bloc. The confrontation strategy toward Third World revolutionary regimes is less likely to destabilize them and more likely to increase their reliance on the Soviet bloc as an alternative market, source of finance, raw materials, base of military support.

## Conclusion

In summary, the Reagan administration attempt to impose a bi-polar scheme upon a world with increasingly complex links and relations reflects the absence of a realistic understanding of the global changes within the Third World, Europe and the Soviet Union. Romantic reactionary nostalgia for the 1950's is a poor basis to construct a foreign policy in the 1980s. At each critical point, the Reaganites attempt to "force" countries and regions with divergent economic, strategic and political interests to conform to Washington's policy through the trumpeting of new military dangers: failing to grasp the deep structural changes that have narrowed the scope for bi-polar competition, the Reaganites improvise ad hoc explanations; "creeping pacifism" in Europe becomes a means of evading the profound and mutually beneficial economic links with the East; "Third Worldism" becomes a means of reducing the development of regional ties and the growth of commodity producing associations to political rhetoric. These facile simplifications may be fashionable and pass for political analysis in New York or London, but they carry little weight most everywhere else.

## The Role of Latin American Liberation Movements in the Context of the End of Détente

What does all this—the end of détente and the New Cold War—mean for Third World liberation movements? This question can be answered in three parts: first, through a consideration of the likely consequences of Washington's new confrontationist policies on the political economies of the region; secondly, through a discussion of some of the likely political responses by the liberation forces to these emerging configurations; and thirdly, through a discussion of the tactical considerations that emerge within the immediate political conjuncture.

The liberation movements in Latin America face at least four sets of developments, partly but directly attributing to Reaganism, that have important consequences in establishing the terrain for struggle in the coming period:

1. *The decline of centrist political forces.* The push by the Reaganites for greater collaboration in the pursuit of worldwide confrontation has found echo mainly among the most extreme right-wing civilian and military groups. Moreover, the construction of policy on the basis of military security strengthens U.S. ties with the coercive apparatuses of the region. Finally, the new emphasis by Washington on "free market" economics undercuts the basis for local middle class industrialists and their political counterparts in the centrist parties. The withdrawal of Washington's tepid support or encouragement for the centrist groups and the new emphasis on military security has encouraged the repression of the center, forcing it to deepen its opposition to the United States and move to the left, or capitulate to the right. In any case, the center *qua* center is in the process of disintegration and losing its historical identity.

2. *The ascendancy of free market forces.* Both in the United States and in Latin America, the ascent of the political right has been accompanied by the promulgation of policies promoting "free market economics"; this has usually been accompanied by policies promoting export specialization in primary materials. The result has been the undermining of many local industries, the reduction of public services, and the growth of speculative, financial, and commercial capital. The decline of industrial productive and social service state sectors means that a vast array of petty-bourgeois forces, who previously were either conformist to the status quo, nonpolitical, or supporters of centrist or even right-wing political movements, are heretofore available for political mobilization. The mobilization of the petty-bourgeoisie is aided by the disintegration of the centrist parties, the traditional beneficiaries of petty-bourgeois political activism.

3. *Militarization of political life.* The emphasis of the Reagan Administration on military solutions, the new arms programs, and the definition of subversion as the key problem in the hemisphere has set in motion forces toward the resurgence and reconsolidation of militarist regimes. The consequences are likely to adversely affect civic associations (lawyers, doctors), autonomous institutions (church, universities), as well as those political associations which have a limited modicum of freedom of expression.

4. *Greater international coordination and cooperation between the United States and military-rightist rulers.* Efforts are underway once more to promote joint counterinsurgency activities. Reports of Argentine military support for rightists in Guatemala, Honduras, El Salvador, and Bolivia, as well as Venezuelan military advisors in El Salvador, and increasing military cooperation once again in the Southern Core, are precursors to efforts by the United States to form joint interventionary forces to prevent revolutionary transformations. The most likely target areas are Central America, where U.S.-centered counterinsurgency activity could easily mobilize the Guatemalan and Honduran forces to

intervene in El Salvador—possibly as a prelude to a military attack against Nicaragua.

This configuration of forces has established certain parameters for political action by the liberation movements. In the first instance, it means that extraparliamentary activity is the order of the day; emptying all legal institutions of their content imposes few options for meaningful electoral activity. The transitory nature of electoral systems, the incapacity of the regimes to pursue free market economics, and liberal political structures makes it incumbent upon the left to combine legal activity with preparations for clandestine struggle.

The emergence and consolidation of rightist dictatorship and the disintegration of democratic space makes it possible to construct broad democratic antidictatorial forces, capable of attracting the disintegrating forces of the centrist political groupings. The struggle for democratic rights through extraparliamentary coalitions emerges as the central axis for political counterattack to the New Right.

The free market economics have set the stage for the dismantling of national industries. The defense of national industrialization, the public sector, and welfare legislation become essential components in the efforts by the liberation forces to rally the mass of radicalized petty-bourgeois and discontented bourgeois forces marginalized by the new schemes of economic specializations.

The uneven patterns of development, the concentration of growth capital in specific sectors, has deepened the pattern of unequal development, giving rise to regionalist movements, whose demands on the state and methods of struggle approximate those of militant mass movements. These democratic, national, and regionalist movements can find consequential expression only in a coalition whose axis is located in the organized workers and peasants movement; the defense of past democratic gains then becomes the condition for new social revolutionary advances. The complex patterns of imperial exploitation, which adversely affect a variety of social classes, regions, and economic activities, creates the basis for a broad polyclass movement. The capacity of the liberation movements to insert themselves into these diverse struggles within the present conjuncture and retain an essentially class perspective toward a historical transformation will be essential in converting the current right-wing offensive into a defeat, and the basis for a social transformation.

The global conflicts engendered by Washington's attempt to impose its Cold War definition on Europe has engendered new opportunities for the liberation forces. The conflict between the Reagan right in the United States and the European social democrats, most clearly visible in the opposition between Mitterand and Reagan in Central America, opens new possibilities for conjunctural cooperation. Likewise, the alliances fostered by Reagan with the Israelis and the South Africans can open new possibilities for Latin American movements to develop ties in the Middle East, North, and Black Africa. The end of détente and Washington's pressures on the Soviet bloc may increase the latter's willingness to support liberation movements in the U.S. sphere of influence. In the pursuit of external support and alliances, the central and paramount issue is the maintenance of the autonomy and integrity of liberation movements—the decisions to accept or reject support should be rooted in the needs of the national class struggle.

The growth of a worldwide reaction focusing on defeating Reaganism and its political collaborators and their efforts to promote a new Cold War will find echo in a multiplicity of political forces, ranging from European social democrats, nationalist Third World forces, progressive religious forces, the trade union and democratic movements in the United States and Eastern countries. The attempt by the Reaganites to undo the developments of the last decade cut against too many vital interests. The threat to basic social and political rights has the effect of homogenizing a broad array of countries and forces in common opposition to Reaganism, even as their reasons for doing so diverges. The liberation movements have the task of weaving these diverse interests into a mass movement that combines political and military struggle, for democracy and social revolution.

## Notes

1. Quoted in Don Oberdorfer, "The Evolution of a Decision," *Washington Post,* January 24, 1980, p. A14.

2. Richard Burt, "U.S. Buildup Urged in the Persian Gulf," *New York Times,* June 28, 1979, p. 6.

3. Richard Halloran, "U.S. Looking to Leasing of Bases for Easier Access to Crisis Areas," *New York Times,* January 20, 1980, p. 12.

4. See Hedrick Smith, "The Carter Doctrine," *New York Times,* January 24, 1980, p. 1.

5. See John M. Goshko, "U.S. Allies, with Interests to Protect, Offer Vague Support," *Washington Post,* January 26, 1980, p. 15.

6. See Richard Burt, "U.S. Pressing Allies on Arms Rise," *New York Times,* February 22, 1980, p. 10: Richard Burt, "U.S. Asking Allies to Assume More of Military Burden," *New York Times,* April 14, 1980, p. 11.

7. Quoted in Stuart Auerbach, "U.S. Would Act Alone to Keep Mideast Oil Route Open, Aide Says," *Washington Post,* November 16, 1980, p. A27.

8. See Edward Cody, "U.S. Taking Long Gamble on Sadat," *Washington Post,* March 30, 1980, pp. A1, A22.

9. George C. Wilson, "U.S. Steps Up Planning for Mideast Bases," *Washington Post,* August 7, 1980, p. A1.

10. "U.S. Overseas Arms Sales Hit Near-Record in 1980," *Washington Post,* January 1, 1981, p. A2.

11. See Timothy B. Clark, "Defense Report: Everybody Wants More for Defense— But Is There Room in the Budget?" *National Journal* 12, no. 20, May 17, 1980, pp. 801, 803.

12. "Excerpts from State Department Memorandum on Human Rights," *New York Times,* November 5, 1981, p. 10. Also see Barbara Crossette, "Strong U.S. Human Rights Policy Urged in Memo Approved by Haig," *New York Times,* November 5, 1981, pp. 1, 11.

13. Quoted in Don Oberdorfer, "Panel Approves Abrams, Sees 'Commitment' to Human Rights," *Washington Post,* November 18, 1981, p. A3.

14. Ibid.

15. See John M. Goshko, "U.S. Ends Opposition to Loans to Repressive Latin Regimes," *Washington Post,* July 9, 1981, pp. A1, A17. Also see John M. Goshko, "Administration Reiterates Aim of Scuttling Carter Rights Policies," *Washington Post,* July 10, 1981, p. A12.

16. Ibid.

17. *AID MEMO,* Summary of Department of the Treasury, "Assessment of U.S. Participation in the Multilateral Development Banks in the 1980s," September 21, 1981 (Center for International Policy, Washington, D.C., October 20, 1981).

18. Quoted in *Washington Letter on Latin America,* 1, no. 1, October 28, 1981, p. 3. Also see U.S. Congress, Senate, Committee on Foreign Relations. Hearings, *U.S. Contributions to Multilateral Development Banks and International Organizations,* 97th Congress, 1st Session, April 21, 1981 (Washington: U.S. Government Printing Office, 1981).

19. *AID MEMO,* "International Banks Cut Loan to Nicaragua, Increase Loans to Guatemala and El Salvador," Center for International Policy, Washington, D.C., November 15, 1981.

20. U.S. Congress, Senate, Committee on Armed Services, *Department of Defense Authorization for Appropriations For Fiscal Year 1982, Part 1,* 97th Congress, 1st Session, January 28, March 4, 1981 (Washington: U.S. Government Printing Office, 1981), pp. 12–13.

21. See Michael T. Klare, *Beyond the "Vietnam Syndrome": U.S. Interventionism in the 1980s* (Washington, D.C.: Institute for Policy Studies, 1981), p. 61. Also see Michael T. Kaufman, "U.S. Naval Buildup Is Challenging Soviet Advances in Asia and Africa," *New York Times,* April 19, 1981, pp. 1, 12.

22. Klare, op. cit., p. 80.

23. See chart in *New York Times,* August 30, 1981, p. 1E.

24. See Richard Halloran, "Reagan Plan Looks to String of Bases in Mideast and Indian Ocean," *New York Times,* March 12, 1981, p. 8.

25. Statement by Richard Burt, Director, Bureau of Politico-Military Affairs, Department of State, in U.S. Congress, House, Committee on Foreign Affairs, Subcommittee on International Security and Scientific Affairs, *Foreign Assistance Legislation for Fiscal Year 1982, Part 2,* 97th Congress, 1st Session, March 12, 19, 23; and April 9, 1981 (Washington: U.S. Government Printing Office, 1981), p. 170.

26. Ibid., p. 178.

27. Ibid., p. 182.

28. Scott Armstrong, "Saudis' AWACS Just a Beginning of New Strategy," *Washington Post,* November 1, 1981, p. A1.

29. See Richard Halloran, "U.S. Deploying Troops for Maneuvers in Mideast," *New York Times,* November 13, 1981, p. 6. Also see Loren K. Jenkins, "U.S. Paratroopers Land in Egypt for War Games," *Washington Post,* November 15, 1981, p. A27; William E. Farrell, "800 U.S. Paratroopers Open War Games in Egypt," *New York Times,* November 15, 1981, p. 21.

30. See Hedrick, "Reagan and the Saudis," *New York Times,* October 2, 1981, pp. 1, 28.

31. Quoted in ibid.

32. Quoted in George C. Wilson, "U.S. Would Intervene If There Were a Saudi Revolution, Weinberger Says," *Washington Post,* October 5, 1981, p. A5.

33. The Egyptian government has long refused to sign a formal agreement for U.S. access to its Red Sea military base at Ras Banas. See, for example, David B. Ottaway, "Reagan to Face Early Test in Egypt," *Washington Post,* January 19, 1981, p. A21. Although the Saudis were reluctant to permit a permanent U.S. military presence in the country, Pentagon officials argued in support of the proposed AWACS sale on the grounds that ongoing military cooperation would make future access more likely, especially in a crisis situation. See U.S. Congress, House Committee on Foreign Affairs, Subcommittee on Europe and the Middle East, *Saudi Arabia and the United States,* 97th Congress, 1st Session, Report prepared by Congressional Research Service, Library of Congress, August

1981 (Washington: U.S. Government Printing Office, 1981); U.S. Congress, Senate, Committee on Foreign Relations, *The Proposed AWACS/F-15 Enhancement Sale to Saudi Arabia,* 97th Congress, 1st Session, Staff Report, September 1981 (Washington: U.S. Government Printing Office, 1981).

34. See Richard Halloran, "Reagan Plan," p. 8.

35. Quoted in Bernard Gwertzman, "U.S. and Israel Sign Strategic Accord to Counter Soviet," *New York Times,* December 1, 1981, p. 1. For text of memo, see ibid., p. 14. Also see Bernard Gwertzman, "New Gamble in Mideast," *New York Times,* September 12, 1981, pp. 1, 3.

36. See George C. Wilson and John M. Goshko, "Begin Sketches New Relationship in Strategic Plans," *Washington Post,* September 12, 1981, pp. A1, A15.

37. See David K. Shipler, "Begin Wonders, How Reliable in Reagan Anyway?," *New York Times,* July 26, 1981, p. 1E.

38. See U.S. Congress, Senate, Committee on Foreign Relations, *FY 1982 Security Assistance Authorization,* 97th Congress, 1st Session, March 31, 1981 (Washington: U.S. Government Printing Office, 1981), p. 4; U.S. Congress, House, *Foreign Assistance Legislation for Fiscal Year 1982,* Part 2, op. cit., p. 91.

39. Quoted in Joe Ritchie, "U.S. Details Terms for Closer South African Ties," *Washington Post,* May 29, 1981, p. A21.

40. Quoted in ibid.

41. Address by Chester Crocker, Assistant Secretary of State for African Affairs, Honolulu, Hawaii, August 29, 1981, reprinted as *Regional Strategy for Southern Africa,* August 29, 1981. Current Policy No. 308, Bureau of Public Affairs, U.S. Department of State. Also see Bernard Gwertzman, "Official Says U.S. Will be Neutral on South Africa," *New York Times,* August 30, 1981, pp. 1, 19.

42. Quoted in Joe Ritchie, "U.S. Details Terms," p. A21.

43. On the South African invasion, see, for example, Jay Ross, "Angolan Towns Devastated by S. African Raid," *Washington Post,* September 4, 1981, pp. A1, A26, A27.

44. See U.S. Congress, Senate, *FY 1982 Security Assistance Authorization,* op cit., pp. 7–8; U.S. Congress, House, *Foreign Assistance Legislation for Fiscal Year 1982,* Part 2, op. cit., p. 93; Edward Walsh, "Reagan Seeking to Permit Aid to Argentina Forces," *Washington Post,* March 15, 1981, pp. A1, A16; Steven R. Weisman, "President May Repeal Argentina Military Embargo," *New York Times,* March 18, 1981, pp. 1, 14.

45. Quoted in Edward Schumacher, "U.S. Military Courting Argentina Despite Ban on Aid by Congress," *New York Times,* April 8, 1981, pp. 1, 6. See also "End to Argentine Embargo Backed," *Washington Post,* May 2, 1981, p. A7; Edward Schumacher, "The Courtship of Argentina," *New York Times,* June 3, 1981, p. 12.

46. On the Walters visit to Argentina in September 1981 and his extensive discussions with the military leadership, see "Argentina: The Walters Friendship Formula," *Latin America Weekly Report* WR-81-39, October 2, 1981, p. 8.

47. Statement by John A. Bushnell, Acting Assistant Secretary of State for Inter-American Affairs, in U.S. Congress, House, Committee on Foreign Affairs, Subcommittees on International Economic Policy and Trade and on Inter-American Affairs, *U.S. Economic Sanctions Against Chile,* 97th Congress, 1st Session, March 10, 1981 (Washington: U.S. Government Printing Office, 1981), p. 41.

48. Ibid., p. 37. Also see Edward Walsh, "Administration Defends Lifting of Chile Sanctions," *Washington Post,* March 11, 1981, p. A16.

49. See "Chile: Back in the Fold," *Latin America Update,* Washington Office on Latin America (Washington, D.C.), Vol. VI, No. 4, July/August 1981.

50. Quoted in John Dinges, "Kirkpatrick Trip Upsets Opposition in Chile," *Washington Post,* August 13, 1981, p. A25.

51. See "Reagan Seeks Big Rise in Military Aid to Latin America," *Latin America Weekly Report* WR-81-14, April 3, 1981, p. 5.

52. On this and other issues involving U.S. policy toward Central America, see James Petras and Morris Morley, "Economic Expansion, Political Crisis and U.S. Policy in Central America," *Contemporary Marxism* 3, Summer 1981, pp. 69–88; James Petras and Morris Morley, "Supporting Repression: U.S. Policy and the Demise of Human

Rights in El Salvador 1979-1981," in Ralph Miliband & John Saville, eds., *The Socialist Register 1981* (London: The Merlin Press, 1981), pp. 47ff.

53. See "White House Favors Arms to Guatemala," *New York Times,* May 5, 1981, pp. 1, 4; Juan de Onis, "U.S. Sending Envoy to Guatemala with View to Resuming Arms Aid," *New York Times,* May 7, 1981, pp. 1, 12; John M. Goshko, "Military Truck Sale to Guatemala Backed," *Washington Post,* June 19, 1981, pp. A1, A26.

54. See Jackson Diehl, "U.S. to Sell Venezuela F16s in Shift of Regional Arms Policy," *Washington Post,* October 3, 1981, pp. A1, A15.

55. See John M. Goshko, "Reagan Developing 'Caribbean Basin' Policy," *Washington Post,* May 25, 1981, p. A8; U.S. Congress, House, Committee on Foreign Affairs, Subcommittee on Inter-American Affairs, *The Caribbean Basin Policy,* 97th Congress, 1st Session, July 14, 21, and 28, 1981 (Washington: U.S. Government Printing Office, 1981).

56. Quoted in Richard Halloran, "Arms Buildup: Allies Hesitant," *New York Times,* March 27, 1981, p. 7. Also see Bradley Graham, "U.S. Presses Europeans on Defense Outlays," *Washington Post,* February 22, 1981, p. A21; Robert Reinhold, "U.S. Warns Its Allies They Must Increase Military Spending," *New York Times,* February 22, 1981, pp. 1, 8; George C. Wilson and Bradley Graham, "Weinberger Says Allies Must Share Defense Burden," *Washington Post,* April 8, 1981, pp. A1, A17.

57. Quoted in Steven R. Weisman, "Suzuki in Washington for Talks on Arms Spending," *New York Times,* May 7, 1981, p. 16. Also see "Weinberger Presses Japan on Defense," *Washington Post,* April 29, 1981, p. A18.

58. Quoted in George C. Wilson, "U.S. Urges Allies to Aid in Defense of Persian Gulf," *Washington Post,* October 23, 1981, p. A26. Western European governments, however, continued to support the concept of détente and East-West cooperation in the areas of trade, politics, and arms control. See Bradley Graham, "U.S., European Allies Differ on Détente: Schmidt Appeals for Continuity," *Washington Post,* April 10, 1981, pp. S1, A25; Bradley Graham, "West Europeans Cool to U.S. Call for Increase in Military Spending," *Washington Post,* February 26, 1981, p. A21; George C. Wilson, "U.S., European Allies Differ on Détente: Weinberger Assails Soviet Policy," *Washington Post,* April 10, 1981, pp. A1, A26.

59. U.S. Congress, Senate, *FY 1982 Security Assistance Authorization,* op. cit., p. 8.

60. See U.S. Congress, House, Committee on Foreign Affairs, Subcommittee on International Security and Scientific Affairs, *Changing Perspectives on U.S. Arms Transfer Policy,* 97th Congress, 1st Session. Report prepared by Congressional Research Service, Library of Congress, September 25, 1981 (Washington: U.S. Government Printing Office, 1981). Interestingly, U.S. arms transfers agreements with the Third World remained at approximately $10 billion annually between 1974 and 1980. Ibid., p. 13. Also see John M. Goshko, "Carter Restraints on Arms Sales to Friends Are Scrapped by Reagan Administration," *Washington Post,* May 22, 1981, p. A2.

61. See Edward Walsh, "U.S. and Pakistan Agree on $3 Billion Aid Plan," *Washington Post,* June 16, 1981, pp. A1, A12.

62. Quoted in Leon Dash, "Mobutu's Rule in Zaire Seems Shaky," *Washington Post,* November 8, 1981, p. A20. Also see "More U.S. Help Due for Zaire, Mobutu Is Told," *Washington Post,* December 2, 1981, p. A11.

63. U.S. Congress, Senate, *FY 1982 Security Assistance Authorization,* op. cit., p. 4.

64. Quoted in Edward Cody, "U.S. to Speed Arms for Egypt," *Washington Post,* October 12, 1981, p. A1.

65. Pranay B. Gupte, "U.S. to Speed Arms," *New York Times,* October 13, 1981, pp. 1, 14.

66. See Don Oberdorfer, "U.S. Seen Increasing Military Assistance, Other Aid to Sudan," *Washington Post,* October 14, 1981, p. A21.

67. See, for example, Leslie H. Golb, "After Ottawa, Allies Still Far Apart on Third World," *New York Times,* July 26, 1981, p. E3.

68. See Christopher Dickey, "France, Mexico Recognize Left in El Salvador," *Washington Post,* August 29, 1981, pp. A1, A17; "3 Latin Nations Fault Mexico and France on Salvador Issue," *Washington Post,* September 2, 1981, p. 4; Christopher Dickey, "9

Nations Condemn French-Mexican Support of Salvadoran Left," *Washington Post*, September 3, 1981, p. A38.

69. See "Argentines Step Up Their Involvment," *Latin American Regional Reports: Mexico & Central America* RM-81-10, November 27, 1981, pp. 3–4; " 'Che' Galtieri plans his own Vietnam," *Latin America Weekly Report* WR-81-40, October 9, 1981, p. 5.

70. See Alan Riding, "U.S. Official in Nicaragua Ties Aid to Policy Shifts," *New York Times*, August 13, 1981, p. 3.

71. Quoted in James Nelson Goodsell, "Nicaragua Drift to Left Stirs Washington Warning," *Christian Science Monitor*, November 4, 1981, p. 1.

72. Quoted in ibid.

73. See John M. Goshko, "Haig Won't Rule Out Anti-Nicaragua Action," *Washington Post*, November 13, 1981, p. A13.

74. Quoted in Michael Getler and Don Oberdorfer, "U.S. Nearing Decision on Nicaragua: Pressure to 'Do Something' Grows," *Washington Post*, November 22, 1981, p. A1.

75. See ibid., p. A33. Also see Don Oberdorfer, "Haig and Meese Vent Impatience with Nicaragua," *Washington Post*, November 23, 1981, pp. A1, A16; Bernard Gwertzman, "Haig Warns Time Is Growing Short on Nicaragua," *New York Times*, November 23, 1981, p. 15.

76. See Richard Halloran, "Nicaragua Arms Called Peril to Area," *New York Times*, December 3, 1981, p. 12.

77. See Lee Lescaze, "U.S. Action 'Possible' in Cuba Arms Flow, Reagan Aide Says," *Washington Post*, February 23, 1981, pp. A1, A7; Juan de Onis, "Cuba Warned Direct U.S. Action Against It on Salvador Is Possible," *New York Times*, February 23, 1981, pp. 1, 9; Edward Walsh, "Wide Options Against Cuba Noted," *Washington Post*, March 19, 1981, pp. A1, A31; James Nelson Goodsell, "US Considers Tightening Its Quarantine on Cuba," *Christian Science Monitor*, August 3, 1981, pp. 1, 19; Don Oberdorfer, "Haig Says U.S. Is Studying Ways to Put Heat on Cuba," *Washington Post*, October 30, 1981, p. A9; Murrey Marder, "U.S. Sharpening Information Policy Overseas," *Washington Post*, November 10, 1981, pp. A1, A10.

78. Leslie H. Gelb, "Haig Is Said to Press for Military Options for Salvador Action," *New York Times*, November 5, 1981, p. 8. On the U.S. effort to mobilize regional support for action against Cuba and Nicaragua, see Don Oberdorfer, "Haig Asks Joint Action on Cuba," *Washington Post*, December 5, 1981, p. A20; Barbara Crossette, "Haig Presses O.A.S. To Join In Halting A Latin Arms Race," *New York Times*, December 5, 1981, pp. 1, 4. For excerpts from Haig's address, see ibid., p. 4. Amid consideration of the military-quarantine options, Secretary of Defense Weinberger announced a streamlining and consolidation of the U.S. Caribbean Command. See "Pentagon Reorganized Caribbean Command." *Washington Post*, November 24, 1981, p. A10.

79. See, for example, Jackson Diehl, "Grenada Is at Ground Zero in Washington's Great Snubbing War," *Washington Post*, November 21, 1981, p. A23.

80. Karen De Young, "U.S. Presses EEC to Refuse Aid for Leftist Grenada," *Washington Post*, March 20, 1981, pp. A1, A30; "Development Bank Directors Reject US Conditions on Aid for Grenada," *Latin America Weekly Report* WR-81-26, July 3, 1981, p. 7.

81. See "Reagan Urges Hill to End Ban on Aid to Angolan Rebels," *Washington Post*, March 20, 1981, pp. A1, A18. See also U.S. Congress, House, *Foreign Assistance Legislation for Fiscal Year 1982*, Part 2, op. cit., p. 93; U.S. Congress, Senate, *FY 1982 Security Assistance Authorization*, op. cit., pp. 7–8.

82. Quoted in Bernard Gwertzman, "U.S. Plans High-Level Talks With Angolan Rebel," *New York Times*, December 3, 1981, p. 17.

83. See Leonard Silk, "Wall Street, Fearing Deficits, Find Reagan Mixed Blessing," *New York Times*, September 13, 1981, pp. 1, 44.

84. See Joseph Lelyveld, "Raid Kept Secret By South Africans," *New York Times*, December 8, 1981, p. 3.

85. See Jackson Diehl, "U.S., Latin Officers Meet Privately," *Washington Post*, November 6, 1981, p. A11.

86. Judith Miller, "Reagan Widens Intelligence Role; Gives C.I.A. Domestic Spy Power," *New York Times,* December 5, 1981, pp. 1, 19. For the text of the order, see ibid., pp. 18–19.

87. For an excellent analysis of Soviet policy, see Fred Halliday, *Soviet Policy in the Arc of Crisis* (Washington, D.C.: Institute for Policy Studies, 1981).

88. See Bernard Gwertzman, "Soviet Is Able to Raise Production of Oil and Gas, Pentagon Asserts," *New York Times,* September 3, 1981, pp. 1, D14.

89. Figures calculated from U.S. Department of Commerce, International Trade Division, Office of East-West Policy and Planning, *U.S.–Romanian Trade Trends,* January–December 1980 (April 1981), pp. 13, 15; *U.S.–USSR Trade Trends,* January–December 1980 (March 1981), pp. 12, 14; *U.S.–GDR Trade Trends,* January–December 1980 (April 1981), pp. 11, 13; *U.S.–Hungarian Trade Trends, 1980* (March 1981), pp. 11, 13; *U.S.–Czechoslovak Trade Trends,* January–December 1980 (April 1981), pp. 11, 12; *U.S.–Bulgarian Trade Trends,* January–December 1980 (April 1981), pp. 10, 12; *U.S.–Polish Trade Trends,* January–December 1980 (May 1981), pp. 10, 12.

90. See Bradley Graham, "Bonn, Moscow Sign Major Gas Agreement," *Washington Post,* November 21, 1981, pp. A1, A28. Also see "How Europe's Neutralism Harms U.S. Business," *Business Week,* July 28, 1980, pp. 56–59.

91. See Henry Tanner, "Europeans Back Palestine Rights and P.L.O. Link to Mideast Talks," *New York Times,* June 14, 1980, pp. 1, 4. Also see John Vinocur, "Schmidt Sees P.L.O. Role in Europe Talks," *New York Times,* April 30, 1981, p. 3; "France Pursues Mideast Role," *New York Times,* August 31, 1981, p. 3.

92. See Bernard Gwertzman, "U.S. Reports Snags on European Role in the Sinai Force," *New York Times,* November 7, 1981, pp. 1, 4. Also see R. W. Apple Jr., "British Doubt Camp David Terms Can Bring a Mideast Peace," *New York Times,* November 10, 1981, p. 12.

93. Quoted in Tracy Dahlby, "Suzuki, Setting Precedent, Receives Arafat." *Washington Post,* October 15, 1981, p. A18. Also see Henry Scott Stokes, "Japan Sees Arafat Visit as Chance to Seek Wider Accord in Mideast," *New York Times,* October 13, 1981, p. 10.

93a. See, for example, Steven Rattner, "Recession Repercussions Are Making Europe 'Run Scared,' " *New York Times,* December 6, 1981, p. 5E.

94. See, for example, Paul Lewis, "U.S. Aide Defends Rate Policy," *New York Times,* June 17, 1981, pp. D1, D11.

95. Quoted in Jonathan C. Randall, "U.S. Foreign Policy Worries Mitterand," *Washington Post,* July 2, 1981, p. A1. Also see Edward Cody, "Paris' Policy Increasingly at Odds With U.S.," *Washington Post,* September 2, 1981, p. A16.

96. See Bernard D. Nossiter, "Europe Allies Vex U.S. on Salvador," *New York Times,* November 25, 1981, p. 10.

# 2

# Supporting Repression: U.S. Policy and the Demise of Human Rights in El Salvador, 1979-1981

JAMES F. PETRAS
MORRIS H. MORLEY

## Introduction

The U.S. government has been the source of a vast programme of bilateral and multilateral economic aid and various forms of military assistance to the ruling classes of El Salvador since the early 1950s. Between 1953 and 1979, executive branch agencies channelled $218.4 million in economic aid and $16.8 million in military loans and credits to bolster and sustain a state apparatus compatible with American policy goals in the region. During the same period, some $479.2 million flowed from the World Bank, Inter-American Development Bank and other U.S-influenced multilateral financial institutions into the coffers of the dominant Salvadoran political and economic groups.[1] This long-term, large-scale involvement of the U.S. in El Salvador both economically and militarily, has been to a considerable degree responsible for sustaining in power repressive, autocratic regimes that refuse to deal with underlying social and economic problems that persist into the present period. External economic assistance has served to benefit an entrenched oligarchy and its penchant for speculative investments in pursuit of private capital accumulation.

Two general, interrelated crises confronted the U.S. government in El Salvador over the past two years: (1) the disintegration of right-wing

This essay was first published in *The Socialist Register 1981* by The Merlin Press Ltd. © The Merlin Press Ltd. and reprinted by permission.

power traditionally allied with Washington; and (2) the emergence of a revolutionary popular movement challenging for state power. The problem for both Carter and Reagan has been how to reconstruct and reconsolidate right-wing power and how to fashion a set of policies to contain and dissemble the mass opposition to this traditional authority.

These general crises grew out of a sub-set of conjunctural crises which were both cause and consequence of the efforts by U.S. policymakers and their conservative military allies to secure the latter's control over the Salvadoran state structure. These conjunctural crises manifested themselves on three levels: within the governing coalition; within the institutional leadership of society; and within the society at large. Each of these crises was precipitated by the right-wing military's single-minded effort—ultimately supported by Washington—to reassert and consolidate its political rulership. At the level of the governing coalition, the crisis was resolved through the purging of dissident civilian and military personnel. The crisis among the institutional leadership and within the societ as a whole was resolved through mass terror.

### Crisis I: Governing Coalition

In October 1979, U.S. policymakers took advantage of the coup which ousted General Carlos Humberto Romero from office to promote a marriage between rightist security forces, their paramilitary allies, OR-DEN, progressive reformist military officials and representatives of social democratic and Christian Democratic groups. This strategy had several complementary purposes: (1) to preserve the state apparatus and the capitalist mode of production by sacrificing particular individuals (General Romero) and sectors of the land-holding oligarchy; (2) to divide the civilian opposition and subordinate reformist army officers to right-wing military domination; (3) to regain credibility for the repressive apparatus of the state and consolidate the power of a pro-U.S. regime capable of eventually destroying the mass revolutionary movement; and to isolate the anti-junta opposition internationally, especially from its growing government and non-government supporters in Western Europe and Latin America. The outcome of this strategy was to deepen and extend the levels and forms of repression throughout the society which, in turn, alienated reformist social and Christian Democratic elements who began to defect in growing numbers to the revolutionary movement. The internal logic of this struggle under the hegemony of the right, and supported with unfailing consistency by Washington, was to escalate the level of repression while simultaneously drawing U.S. government and quasi-government agencies into providing greater quantities of economic assistance, military aid and the accompanying manpower expertise. And once committed to preserving the right-wing military and paramilitary forces as the ultimate arbiter of the political future of El Salvador, American policymakers, with the ready complicity of the mass media, had no choice but to accept and defend the junta's repressive policies—explaining away the legion of documented examples of massacres and terrorism (by the International Commission of Jurists, the Organisation of American States, the El Salvador Human Rights Commission, Amnesty International and the Legal Aid Commission of the Office of the Archbishop of El Salvador) as the products of anonymous and uncontrollable right-wing violence.

The escalating repression by the right-wing forces in the state apparatus precipitated a major conflict within the post-Romero regime, provoking a rupture between the military and reformist civilians who began to abandon the coalition.[2] With the collapse of the civilian-military junta in January 1980, the U.S. government's immediate response was to try to convince the reformists to stay on—so as to provide a modicum of legitimation for the regime at the international level. When this failed, Washington then sought, successfully, to 'capture' and reinsert a small conservative faction of Christian Democrats into the governing coalition, thus allowing U.S. policymakers to sustain the fiction that the regime was still a civilian-military coalition, that reforms were still being promoted and, on that basis, to continue to avoid the complete international isolation of the junta. Nonetheless, the defection of civilian officials continued and by mid-1980, at least ten senior non-military officials had resigned from the Salvadoran government. Increasingly, then, the U.S. became actively allied with the terror of the military, security forces and the paramilitary organisations—even as it continued to press the ultra right to share power with its compromised, impotent and isolated middle sector client groups.

The rightward shift within the civilian fraction of the coalition was paralleled by a concerted purge by the right-wing military of the reformist elements in the armed forces leadership, principally those centred around Colonel Adolfo Majano, a leading participant in the October 1979 coup. With the steady erosion of influence of the Majano faction during the first half of 1980, conservative officers began to take over more and more of the troop commands—a process which was facilitated by the rigid opposition of Washington to any rapprochement between the reformist military leadership and the Revolutionary Democratic Front. The Carter administration threw its weight behind the policy of 'extermination of subversion' promoted by the military right. The Majano forces, unable to develop ties to the popular movement and unwilling to accept the policies of their fellow officers, saw their influence within the military whittled down.[3] Moreover, because of developed institutional loyalties, they were unwilling to provoke a split within the armed forces until long after they had lost the levers of power which would have enabled them to carry substantial groups of supporters with them. The growing isolation of Majano facilitated his demotion; ultimately, his defection took place with little resonance among the officer corps. Washington's growing economic and military support of the junta (including Pentagon advisers who compensated for the loss of the reformist officers) further served to facilitate the consolidation of the right-wing military within the leadership echelons of the Salvadoran armed forces.

### The Carter Administration: From Human Rights to Military Rights

During the Carter administration, the existence of a so-called human rights policy did not affect the preexisting economic relations between the U.S. and El Salvador that was, in large measure, responsible for creating the social and political unrest. Despite the enormous rise in the number of regime opponents assassinated and tortured by the military, security forces and paramilitary vigilante groups during 1980, for example, direct U.S. economic assistance to the junta totalled a substantial $59 million.[4] In addition to this government-to-government economic largesse, the administration at no point exercised its economic 'muscle' in the multilateral banking institutions to limit the gross human rights violations taking place in El Salvador. On the contrary, between January 1, 1977 and December 31, 1980, the U.S. government supported multilateral development bank loans to the junta totalling $228.4 million and merely abstained on two other loans totalling $38 million.[5] In one of its final acts before leaving office, Carter representatives in the Inter-American Development Bank successfully flexed Washington's 'economic muscle' in support of a $45.5 million agrarian reform loan to El Salvador to be drawn from the Bank's special operations fund in which the U.S. holds 62% of the capital.[6] During 1980, Washington also supported International Monetary Fund loans to the Salvadoran regime amounting to $77 million.[7]

While U.S. economic policy remained consistent under Carter, there were some cutbacks in military aid to the junta—but of the sort essentially resulting from conflicts over discrete isses, of limited duration and which did not denote a clearly defined opposition to repressive military rule in El Salvador. Beyond that, the real impact of these actions was substantially minimised by the emergence of Israel—a strategic Washington ally and 'regional policeman' in the Middle East—as a major exporter of military hardware to El Salvador and other Central American dictatorships during the 1970s. Israel supplied 81% of El Salvador's foreign arms purchases between 1972 and 1977, and over the decade the junta obtained a significant number of tactical transport aircraft particularly suited to counter-insurgency from the state-owned Israel Aircraft Industries.[8]

The limited change in military aid policy under Carter reflected a variety of factors: the relative importance of the human rights lobby within the executive branch; the shifting nature of the bureaucratic debate over tactics and strategy; and the political changes taking place within the Central American countries. The human rights lobby was strongest in the early part of the Carter administration. In the years between 1976 and 1978 it was able to push legislation which successfully limited U.S. military support for specific regimes (Guatemala, El Salvador). By 1979, however, the more conservative forces within the State Department in alliance with the National Security Council had effectively isolated the human rights proponents within the foreign policy bureaucracy. The major change in Washington's policy was the recognition, in the aftermath of Somoza's downfall at the hands of a guerrilla-led nationalist movement in Nicaragua in July 1979, that a major effort had to be made to forge a coalition of civilian business groups and the Army to provide a political, as well as a military, solution in other countries in the area experiencing a resurgence of anti-dictatorial and class struggle. However, the central concern of U.S. policy was first and foremost to undermine the revolutionary popular movements and preserve the existing armed forces.

In late 1979, as the civil war in El Salvador began to assume the proportions of a struggle for state power, the Carter administration decided to reopen the military 'spigots' to the terrorist junta in San Salvador. Between October 1979 and January 1980, Washington shipped $205,541 worth of riot control equipment and reprogrammed (with Congressional consent) some $300,000 in International Military Education and Training funds to El Salvador.[9] In January 1980, the National Security Council tentatively approved a plan to provide additional military assistance to the junta in the form not only of loans and credits but also of combat advisers and training personnel. Residual opposition to this policy change within the State Department was limited to particular individuals and was unable to counter effectively the National Security Council-Department of Defense advocacy of the restoration and deepening of ties with the Salvadoran armed forces. There was also little opposition to the new policy drift at the highest echelons of the State Department. Assistant Secretary of State for Inter-American Affairs William Bowdler reportedly informed a closed session of the Senate Foreign Relations Committee in late January that the new security assistance programme was the only alternative to a 'marxist government' in El Salvador.[10] The desire to prevent 'another Nicaragua' where it was impossible to create alternatives in an open revolutionary situation was a crucial factor shaping the thinking of senior policymaking officials at this time.[11]

In April 1980, the White House 'pressured' a pliant Congress to reprogramme $5.7 million in military aid to the Salvadoran junta. Carter also submitted a request for a $5.5 million military assistance package to help sustain the junta's position during Fiscal Year 1981.[12] In its efforts to maintain the existing state structure intact, the armed forces were allocated the central role in Washington's re-arranged priorities. 'If you eliminate the army in El Salvador', one U.S. official at the time declared, 'then nothing stands between the armed left and a government takeover.'[13] Within the foreign policy bureaucracy, the growing debate over the efficacy, nature and extent of future U.S. relations with the Salvadoran armed forces reflected the extent to which the human rights forces had now been marginalised inside the policy-making process. The National Security Council, Department of Defense, Central Intelligence Agency and the State Department's Latin American Bureau were all forceful advocates of the position that 'military assistance is an essential component of any strategy in El Salvador . . .'[14] Support for the primacy of the diplomatic option, *but not to the exclusion of military assistance,* was largely confined to some State Department officials and the American Ambassador to El Salvador, Robert E. White. Notwithstanding these tactical differences of opinion, however, there was a general convergence on the part of all involved executive branch agencies in opposition to the assumption of state power in El Salvador by the mass-based movement under the organisational direction of the Revolutionary Democratic Front.

While committed to the basic notion that support for the junta must be the focus of U.S. policy, Carter initially opted to limit the open and visible involvement of U.S. military personnel on the side of the junta in the Salvadoran social conflict. Whereas, the 'hardliners' in the administration proposed in early 1980 that some thirty six military training teams be immediately dispatched to El Salvador, Carter preferred to make provision for the acquisition of discipline skills and combat training by the junta officer corps at locations outside of the country. By October, as many as 300 Salvadoran military officers were undergoing training in counterinsurgency warfare at various U.S. military schools in the Panama Canal Zone.[15]

On December 5, the White House announced the suspension of new military and economic assistance to the junta pending clarification of the role of the Salvadoran security forces in the murders of three American nuns and one lay missionary. In mid-January, the suspension was lifted despite Ambassador White's categorical assertion that the regime had refused to undertake a 'serious investigation' into the assassinations.[16] The decision to resume military aid was made with the concurrence of Secretary of State Edmund Muskie and was supported by the executive branch as a whole.[17] The overriding consideration shaping this action was the 'survival of the military' imperative. On this issue, even the 'dissident' American Ambassador lined up with his imperial state colleagues: 'The first priority of our policy is to support a reform-minded government that rejects the extremes of the left and of the right and to preserve the Salvadoran military as an institution. The military is the final barrier against a Marxist-Leninist threat.'[18] On January 17, 1981, Carter authorised an emergency $5 million package of lethal military assistance to the junta (grenade launchers, rifles, ammunition, helicopters), invoking special executive powers in order to circumvent the need for Congressional assent.[19] His term of office ended before futher consideration could be given to operationalising a proposal drawn up by the State Department's Policy Planning Office (with White House approval) to send $50 million in economic aid, up to $7 million in military sales and credits, and thirty eight U.S. army advisers to El Salvador.[20]

The Carter administration continued to proclaim the viability of the regime while the Salvadoran ruling class withdrew $1.5 billion in the midst of the 1979–1980 political crisis.[21] U.S. Agency for International Development officials continued to insist that the junta's agrarian programmes were designed to help the poor while economic resources were channelled to a government controlled by large landholders and financial groups who siphoned off the bulk of the funds for their own use. During 1980, more than 8,000 peasants, workers, students, trade unionists, professionals and churchpeople were assassinated in *non-military* confrontations with the security forces, paramilitary groups and Salvadoran troops commanded by U.S.-trained officers.[22] Hundreds more opponents of the regime 'disappeared' after being arrested.[23] Meanwhile, in the absence of the prosecution of a single military official, the White House perversely continued to label the regime a 'moderate,' 'reformist' and centrist government and to engage in a determined effort to focus the blame for the violence on non-governmental paramilitary organisations. Select cutbacks in U.S. military aid were in no way designed to undermine the internal discipline and cohesion of the armed forces. While on occasion condemning the 'extremists on the right', the 'human rights' administration continued to support the military which practised the violence and provided the recruits for the right-wing terrorist groups.

## Crisis II: Institutional Leadership of Society

The second crisis was located in the institutional leadership of Salvadoran society. Among church organisations, civic associations, peasant unions, trade unions, universities and even among some large landholders, a vast movement emerged, led by a group of men and women increasingly committed to deep-going structural changes in the economic and political institutions of the country. With the coup of October 1979, Washington sought to coopt and promote those sectors of the new institutional leadership viewed both as amenable to external pressures and supportive of efforts to limit the scope and depth of change. Because U.S. policy-makers simultaneously promoted the terroristic right, the social reformers were unable to realise the changes which they sought. The end result was to push the social reformers into an alliance with the revolutionary democratic left and deepen the institutional crisis. With the emergence of the alliance of the centre and the left, the military regime was left with only a small and institutionally weak right-wing Christian Democratic faction. Incapable of incorporating popular support or subordinating the new institutional leadership to the governing coalition, the regime extended and deepened its terror activities; 'extended' it to include the most prominent members of civic society and 'deepened' it to include indiscriminate attacks on peasants and workers. The regime hoped through massive terror to regain the security it was unable to obtain through political means.

One of the major fictions systematically propagated by the U.S. government and the bulk of the American mass media has been the notion that the 'violence' against the Salvadoran people is perpetrated by anonymous right-wing terrorists, who apparently are so clever that they can commit thousands of killings in broad daylight throughout the country and never be apprehended by a junta which claims great military success in ferreting out guerrillas from jungles and rough mountain terrain. The statistics compiled by the Legal Aid Commission of the office of the Archbishop of El Salvador (which has engaged in the most sustained and comprehensive monitoring of human rights in El Salvador), however, tell quite a different story. In the period between May and December 1980, official junta controlled military and police units were responsible for 4,868 (approximately 80%) and the paramilitary organisations for only 1,083 (approximately 20%) of all documented political assassinations.[24] The combined forces of the National Guard, National Police, Treasury Police, Security Forces and the Army killed four times as many civilians as the 'anonymous' right-wing death squads. Moreover, there is clear and precise evidence demonstrating that the death squads and the government forces actively collaborated in carrying through their grisly missions. The Archbishop's Legal Aid Commission provides numerous reports that reveal a pattern of coordinated and complementary operations involving the army, security forces and the paramilitary groups such as ORDEN. Several examples may be cited:

April 17, 1980. Hundreds of members of the paramilitary organisation ORDEN, protected by the National Army and Agents of the National Guard, militarily invaded the Christian peasant communities of 'El Pajal, Tehuiste arriba, El Salto, San Lucas, Ulapa, Santa Lucia, Tepechame', of the jurisdictions of San Vicente and La Paz, departments located in the eastern side of the country, (sixteen assassinations).

April 24, 1980. At least 100 agents of the National Guard, the Army, and the paramilitary organisatin ORDEN, protected by two helicopters with guns and by small tanks invaded the adjacent communities of 'El Campanario, San Benito, Angulo, Llano Grande, El Obrajuelo, Las Lomas, La Joya, La Pita, Santa Amalia', all belonging to the departmental jurisdiction of San Vicente (66 km. west of the capital). Many eyewitnesses declared having seen grenades being thrown at peasant homes, as well as thorough machine gunning, (nineteen assassinations).

July 7, 1980. The town 'Ojo de Agua', jurisdiction of Cojutepeque, department of Cuzcatlan (35 km. east of the capital) was again invaded by agents of the National Guard and members of the paramilitary organisation ORDEN, (eleven assassinations).

Afterwards, the invaders went to the neighbouring towns of San Marin, San Andario, Soledad, El Carmen, San Andres and Candelaris. As they marched they destroyed crops and looted the homes of peasants.

July 10, 1980. At least 1,000 strongly armed and masked men, equipped with bullet-proof vests and identifiable as members of the 'death squad', invaded the 'Mirador' farm with the aid of members of the Army and agents of the National Guard. The majority of the peasants in the farm belonged to the *Union Comunal Salvadorena*. The farm is located in 'Isletas', jurisdiction of Coatepeque, department of Santa Ana, in the west of the country. Eyewitnesses reported that masked men and agents of the National Guard executed sixty peasants, who were selected from among three hundred cooperative peasants. Aid institutions were not allowed to enter the area, which was completely surrounded by members of the army.[25]

The particular savagery that distinguished these 'law and order' operations derived, in part, from the military's adherence to the notion of collective guilt: whole families and villages have been attacked and destroyed because of the activities of particular individuals. The Legal Aid Commission provides a graphic description of this type of 'retribution' carried out by the junta between May and October 1980 which deserves to be quoted in detail:

May 14, 1980. Massacre in the Sumpul River. The army and military bodies (National Guard, *Hacienda* Police), along with members of the paramilitary organisation ORDEN, surrounded villages in a broad rural area. The peasant community remained totally incommunicado for four days. From flame-throwing helicopters, the army burned the homes of peasants. When the villagers ran away they were riddled with bullets by the guards and members of ORDEN. In many operations as it can be seen throughout this report, whole peasant families, including children under five years of age, were executed. The collective deaths of at least 600 peasants, men, women and children, at the shores of the Sumpul River, marks the beginning of the stage of 'Total Cleaning' of the rural areas. The operations were characterised by coordination among the armies of El Salvador and Honduras, which, together with the Guatemalan army, began to extend the 'Sanitary Belt' over Salvadoran territory.

Starting in the month of June, broad rural areas of El Salvador became actual 'stages of military operations of total extermination' against the civilian population ('El Trifinio', 130 km. northwest of San Salvador; extensive areas of the north in the department of Morazan, 170 km. northwest of San Salvador; Aguilares and Guasapa, 35 km. north of San Salvador; and extensive areas of the south, in the department of San Vicente, 60 km. southeast of San Salvador).

Indiscriminate bombings carried out by the airforce and the artillery of the Army have been the principal characteristics of this stage of intentional and systematic extermination. The Association of Humanitarian Aid has calculated that in the area bombed by the Salvadoran army in the Eastern department of Morazan during the month of October and the beginning of November, at least 4,000 people died.[26]

Finally, the depth of the institutional crisis led the regime to violate the sacred and the profane. The Legal Aid Commission reported:

> During 1980, the persecution of the Church which surpassed all previous experiences in relative and absolute terms as well as in cruelty, was extended to sectors which had not been attacked before. And this has all been done with total impunity. Priests, seminary students, gospel teachers and other direct members of the Church have been assassinated. They have machine-gunned and bombed ecclesiastical institutions such as schools, universities, religious residences, and religious facilities. (Twenty eight assassinations, January to October).[27]

These actions, together with the murder of the Archbishop of El Salvador, Oscar Romero, and the four American churchpeople, indicated the degree to which the regime had gone down the road to 'total war' by the end of 1980.

Between January 1 and December 31, 1980, in addition to the six hundred peasants killed in the Sumpul River massacre and the thousands exterminated in the course of bombing missions carried out by the Salvadoran airforce, the Legal Aid Commission documented 8,062 assassinations by the junta and its paramilitary allies. These victims included a wide array of social forces: peasants (3,783); students (692); workers (418); professionals (44); small businessmen (134); and unknown occupations (2,306). Other facets of the regime's activities during this period might also be enumerated. Between January 1 and August 31, some 211 prisoners 'disappeared' following their arrest by members of the regime. Further, between January and July, the army and security forces invaded working class areas on 120 occasions, searched and ransacked trade union, church and civic organisation offices on 90 occasions, and machine-gunned, sabotaged or bombed these same offices on 133 occasions.[28]

Political labels to be meaningful should reflect political realities. Nonetheless, Washington policymakers, determined to sustain the military in power, continued to rationalise their support of its repressive policies on the grounds that it is a centrist government caught between the extremes of right and left. While the most reputable sources of data on the situation in El Salvador speak to the existence of an extreme right-wing terrorist regime, the White House has persisted in its Orwellian deception in which genocide is repeatedly defined as 'pragmatism'.

Each murder that violated a new set of taboos created a crisis, international as well as national, and at each point Washington provided the crucial political support to sustain the regime through the particular crisis—not necessarily because the administration supported each of these murders, but because executive branch officials were more concerned with defeating the revolutionary movement and consolidating the military state apparatus than with preventing political murder. Hence, after expressing ritualistic statements of concern, U.S. policymakers quickly refocused the issue *away* from the regime's crimes to the 'struggle against the Marxist guerrillas' or 'Cuban involvement'. The willingness of Washington ultimately to accept the brutal murders of its own citizens and Archbishop Romero is the best indication of the paramount importance attached to consolidating right-wing rulership. The same pattern was observed in the murder of the seven leaders of the Revolutionary Democratic Front in November 1980—Washington attempted to 'cover-up' the public involvement of the regime and to attribute it to anonymous right-wing terrorists, even though hundreds of government soldiers encircled the building where the initial kidnapping of the opposition leaders took place. The deeper meaning of U.S. complicity is to be found in the profound commitment on the part of both Carter and Reagan to the reconstruction of a network of stable and unconditional allies linked to American global and regional military-corporate and financial interests. In this context, the lives of missionaries and archbishops and social democratic leaders counted for little. Through its arms and military advisory programme, Washington has become an active accomplice in the destruction of the institutional leadership of Salvadoran society.

## Crisis III: Society as a Whole

Parallel to the support for the 'military solution' of the institutional crisis, Washington has sought to build up a social basis of support within Salvadoran society for the remaining faction of the Christian Democrats still supporting the regime. The principal focus of this strategy has been an 'agrarian reform' programme announced by the junta in March 1980. To date, the bulk of the financial, technological and advisory support for the programme has been provided by the State Department's Agency for International Development and the AFL-CIO's American Institute for Free Labour Development.

The most striking characteristic of this so-called agrarian reform programme is an essentially negative one: even its full implementation will in no way benefit an estimated 65% of the rural population in El Salvador who lack any access to land whatsoever.[29] Even the proposed beneficiaries of the programme have experienced minimal gains during its first year in operation. The key 'Land-to-the-Tiller' law (Decree 207) of April 1980, for example, stated that all current tenants on rented plots of less than seven hectares shall become immediate owners of those plots of land. Some twelve months later, less than 1,000 'provisional' titles had been allocated among 150,000 families eligible to become landholders under the law.[30] The exclusionary nature of the programme, its origin in an 'outside and above' development strategy, and the lack of adequate planning and implementing regulations are all discussed in considerable detail in a recent report prepared by two U.S. agricultural experts, based on careful field research and access to unpublished State Department and El Salvadoran government materials.[31] In addition to the flaws in the programme itself, however, the authors also address themselves to the larger political and social context within which the 'agrarian reform' is being promulgated: 'The land reform programme has been implemented in the context of increasing and unrelenting levels of violence against the rural population.'[32] They specifically single out the 'Land-to-the-Tiller' programme:

> The regions most directly affected by Decree 207 coincide almost identically with the areas of greatest repression against peasants by government security forces. It is precisely the Departments of Chalatenanga, Cuscatlan, Morazan and Cabanas that has the highest percentage of renting, as it is also those same Departments which have been the victims of the most brutal repression.[33]

Simultaneous with the implementation of the 'agrarian reform' programme has been the appearance of a combined effort on the part of the armed forces and the paramilitary organisation ORDEN to extend the state's control over rural life, primarily through the occupation of large landholdings and their transformation into collective prisons. This process of the militarisation of the rural productive units has at times conflicted with the efforts by Christian Democratic unions and even the American Institute for Free Labour Development to retain a minimum semblance of civilian influence in the decision-making structure. The resultant intra-bureaucratic struggle has led to periodic assassinations of union members and peasant cooperative leaders. ORDEN, in particular, has been engaged in purging the state controlled 'cooperatives' of any leadership responsive to peasant interests.[34] As a consequence, the efforts by the Agency for International Development and the American Institute for Free Labour Development to harness a peasant-based apparatus to the junta has been stymied by the 'spread effects' of the terror generated from an increasingly homogeneous totalitarian military.

The escalating militarisation of the countryside ('agrarian reform') is eloquently illustrated by the abrupt rise in peasant assassinations in the months immediately following the announcement of the 'agrarian reform' programme. During the first quarter of 1980, assassinations took place at the rate of approximately 150 per month; between April and December, they averaged 370 per month.[35] These figures do not include the hundreds murdered by junta troops in May 1980 as they attempted to flee across the Sumpul River or the thousands killed during the counter insurgency-air bombing campaign carried on during a large part of the year. Furthermore, there has been, and continues to be, a direct constant relation between the flight of refugees from the countryside and the areas designated for 'agrarian reform'. A recent special report by the Legal Aid Commission conclusively demonstrates that the greatest proportion of rural refugees are from those areas targeted by the military junta for the 'agrarian reform'. At the end of 1980, the departments of Cuscatlán, Chalatenango and La Paz, for example, were the areas of origin of over 70% of all the refugees at the *Seminario San Jose de la Montana,* for 64% of those at *El Despertar,* for 100% of those at *Iglesia de Soyapango,* for almost 65% who had taken shelter at the *Noviciado Somascos,* for over 80% in *La Basilica,* and for almost 100% of the peasants who had sought safety at *Parrroquia de San Roque.*[36]

Clearly, the junta's activities have had less to do with transforming land tenure relations and more to do with exterminating any and all forms of independent rural organisation. Yet, American policymakers continue to propagate the pernicious myth that the militarisation of the countryside, including the physical occupation of productive units, is tantamount to agrarian reform and has directly benefited the Salvadoran peasant population.

From supporting terror as a mechanism for securing political rule, as U.S. policymakers sought, the Salvadoran military has turned to terror as the mode of rulership, subordinating all sectors to its domination, violently repressing even those attached to the political apparatus of the regime. The incapacity to distinguish between armed and unarmed opposition, between opposition and and allied peasant associations, is explained by the dynamic tendency of the regime to concentrate all power in its hands, based on the view that a state of war exists and only the military and paramilitary organisations can be trusted to fulfill the mission of 'exterminating communism'. According to this view, those peasants who are not members or collaborators of ORDEN are suspect and potential allies of the enemy. Thus, the efforts by the Christian Democrats and the American Institute for Free Labour Development to create a social base for the regime 'outside' of the state apparatus have failed. The increasing use of terror by the regime is thus a cause and consequence of political isolation: unwilling to allow even a limited autonomy to the Christian Democratic peasant movement, it is condemned to generalising repression to all peasants who manifest the least interest in social organisation. In sum, the rhetoric of agrarian reform, the peasants as beneficiaries, and the transformation of land tenure relations have given way to the reality of escalating repression, the peasants as victims and the militarisation of the countryside.

Having committed itself to the military solution, Washington had no choice but to press on with their support, even as it takes them down the blind alley of totalitarianism. As the number of assassinations in the rural areas increase, and as executive branch policymakers continue to insist that the agrarian reform will become an historical boon to the peasants, we can infer that the U.S. government once again—as in Indo-China—perversely believes that peasants must be saved, even if they have to be killed in the process. This bleak spectacle stands as a monument to those pragmatic and even adaptable liberal policymakers in the Carter administration who chose to stay in Washington and proffer their liberal counsels to the efforts to eliminate revolutionary democratic alternatives in El Salvador. This process of extending the military state's control throughout Salvadoran society, using the vehicle of the 'agrarian reform', has been wholeheartedly supported by the Reagan White House. The ideological utility of 'defending reformers' perfectly serves the new administration's policy goal of exterminating the opposition to the junta: the repressive organisational apparatus, ostensibly implementing agrarian reform, serves to rationalise an all-pervasive police-state apparatus.

### The Reagan Administration: El Salvador and the Militarisation of Civil Society

The transition from Carter to Reagan has been accompanied by a remarkable degree of continuity in terms of overall policy toward El Salvador at the same time as there have been some discernible shifts in strategy and tactics. As part of its overriding goal to revitalise U.S. capitalism both at home and abroad, the incoming administration announced its intention to further marginalise human rights criteria as a factor shaping foreign policy decision-making in pursuit of a related goal which was to seek closer ties with autocratic military regimes in the Third World that supported U.S. political-strategic interests and were willing to open their economies to long-term large-scale flows of foreign capital and commerce.

One of the major recommendations contained in a report prepared by Reagan's State Department Transition Team on Latin America was the following: 'Internal policy-making procedures should be structured to ensure that the Human Rights area is not in a position to paralyse or unduly delay decisions on isuses where human rights concerns conflict with other U.S. interests.'[37] Subsequently, the head of the Transition Team, Ambassador Robert Neumann, put it more bluntly in an address to a group of Foreign Service Officers, declaring that such 'abstractions' as human rights had no central part in a foreign policy that wished to give priority to 'American national interests'.[38] In the lexicon of the new policymakers, allied dictatorial regimes were now described as 'moderately repressive' and even 'pre-democratic.'[39] Referring to the terrorist military junta in El Salvador, United Nations Ambassador-designate Jeanne Kirkpatrick declared: 'I think that the degree of commitment to moderation and democratic institutions within the Salvadoran military is very frequently underestimated in this country. And I think it's a terrible injustice to the Government and the military when you suggest that they were somehow responsible for terrorism and assassination.'[40] In late November 1980, Reagan's senior Latin American policy advisers personally 'assured' leading representatives of El Salvador's business community 'that the new administration will increase military aid, including control equipment, to security forces fighting leftist guerrillas'.[41]

The State Department Transition Team Report designated El Salvador as one of the 'immediate crises' that the Reagan presidency would have to deal with once it assumed political office.[42] Within days of taking over as Secretary of State, Alexander Haig 'actually became the desk officer for El Salvador', according to one executive branch official. 'All reports were going directly to him.'[43] The Report also included a 'hit list' of 'social reformer' envoys to be swiftly removed from their ambassadorial posts.[44] In early February 1981, Robert E. White, the Carter-appointee as American ambassador to El Salvador—and one of the prime 'hit list' candidates—became the first career officer to be removed from his post by the Reagan administration. Both Secretary of State Haig and Under Secretary of State for Political Affairs Walter Stoessel informed White that he had been recalled at the express orders of the White House.[45]

In mid-February, the President inaugurated a two-pronged strategy to mobilise domestic and international support for expanding military relatins with the Salvadoran junta as the most effective strategy for defeating the popular revolutionary movement. The rationale for this new policy was contained in the so-called 'White Paper' on El Salvador which contended that 'the insurgency in El Salvador has been progressively transformed into another case of indirect armed aggression against a small Third World country by Communist powers acting through Cuba'.[46] The most notable feature of the 'White Paper', apart from the chasm that separated its 'evidence' from its assertions, was the complete absence of any account of the numerous political, social and civic movements, representing a wide range of political views and social strata, that had developed over the last decade in opposition to the existing state structure.[47] Nonetheless, the American mass media, liberal and conservative, were virtually unanimous in their acceptance of the 'White Paper's' conclusions which they proceeded to disseminate in the most uncritical fashion.[48] At the level of official Washington, the executive branch, through press conferences, public statements before congressional committees, and confidential briefings of key congressional 'influentials', was able to mobilise legislative support for its position with relative ease. The overwhelming majority of elected officials were basically willing to agree that El Salvador was 'the place to draw the line' against international communist influence in the Western Hemisphere and elsewhere around the globe.[49] Following a closed door briefing by Secretary of State Haig on February 17, the chairman of the Senate Foreign Relations Committee, Charles Percy, spoke for most of his colleagues when he declared: 'I think those outside forces should be put on notice that this nation will do whatever is necessary to prevent a Communist state takeover in El Salvador. . . The Administration is reaching out for Congressional support. They will have that support.'[50] Senate Majority Leader Howard Baker thought it 'entirely appropriate for this country to dispatch noncombat advisers in small numbers—50, 100, 150—to tell these people how to defend themselves against Cuba.'[51] Opposition to increased military assistance to El Salvador was confined to isolated members of the House and Senate who willingly conceded that they lacked the capacity to block any Reagan initiative in this area.[52]

In a concerted and comprehensive attempt to organise worldwide support for the military solution in El Salvador, the State Department sent high-level missions to Western Europe, Southern Europe and Latin America in what one official described as a 'full court press' to line up America's allies behind the Reagan policy.[53] This global 'offensive', however, proved to be a diplomatic disaster in terms of its primary objective. Social democratic and conservative governments in Europe remained hostile to the U.S. position, or neutral at best, generally favouring a negotiated political solution involving all parties in the social conflict.[54] In Latin America, even such staunch supporters as the military governments of Brazil and Argentina, and the Social Christian regime in Venezuela, expressed opposition to *any type* of external intervention in El Salvador. The Mexican response was more pointed. In the aftermath of his meeting with the head of the American 'mission' to the hemisphere, General Vernon Walters, President Lopez Portillo reaffirmed Mexico's fraternal relations with Cuba, warned against the 'unscrupulous arrogance of military power' and decried the fact that Central America had been 'elevated to the undesirable rank of strategic frontier.'[55]

While allied governments preferred to emphasise social and economic reforms over military assistance, the Reagan administration pointedly declared that the survival of the junta was the main order of business and that, henceforth, military and economic aid would not be conditioned, even formally, by regime efforts in these areas. Neither would future assistance be contingent on the outcome of the joint U.S.-Salvadoran investigation into the murders of the American clergy in December 1980. 'I know of no linkage', remarked State Department spokesman William Dyess, beyond the requirement that U.S. aid be used 'efficiently and effectively'.[56] Having 'delinked' the question of aid from the issue of the murder investigation, the administration was sending a clear signal to the junta. As one American official privately admitted, 'the military men know they're off the hook' as far as any pressure for social and economic reforms are concerned.[57]

In devising U.S. policy toward El Salvador, an array of strategy options were considered by the Reagan White House, ranging from the provision of military advisers and equipment on an initial limited scale to reported Pentagon plans that included the training and arming of a helicopter-borne air cavalry unit of 2,000 men.[58] In choosing the most appropriate option at this particular moment, the new administration preferred the strategy of a cumulative indirect military buildup of the junta resources and capabilities instead of a larger-scale, more direct U.S. intervention in the Central American conflict.[59] The benefits accruing from a 'carefully calibrated' strategy were viewed as potentially substantial, while the risks were deemed minimal.[60] 'We're not talking about tanks and missiles', one executive branch official noted. 'There's not even any plan at this stage to send American combat advisers there. What's involved is small arms, ammunition, maybe some helicopters and coastal patrol boats. It's a game we can buy into relatively cheaply, and there's clearly a consensus emerging within the administration that the risks are worth the potential payoff.'[61] Having shaped its policy in terms of a commitment to the survival of the military junta and its Christian Democratic allies, the White House was therefore unwilling to respond to rightist leader Robert D'Aubuisson's call for a right-wing military coup—even though the administration refused to place itself on record as being unalterably opposed to such a development.[62]

In early March, Reagan announced that the U.S. government would provide an expanded package of military assistance to the junta: some $25 million in new military aid and an increase in the number of American military advisers from twenty-five to forty-five. In addition to small arms, radar equipment, military vehicles and helicopters, U.S. naval and military advisers would train their Salvadoran counterparts in the use and maintenance of helicopters and communications equipment and complement Salvadoran naval patrols in the country's coastal waters.[63] The Congress speedily approved the military aid request which included $5 million that the appropriate House and Senate subcommittees voted to 'reprogramme' from already appropriated foreign aid funds.[64] By the end of March, total Fiscal Year 1981 U.S. military authorisations for the Salvadoran junta stood at $35.4 million while the number of Pentagon advisers to be dispatched to El Salvador had been increased to fifty-six, including a number of special forces personnel experienced in counter-insurgency warfare.[65]*

Efforts by Congressional liberals to limit or terminate military aid, but not economic assistance, to the junta continue to be ineffectual. Proposed amendments to end or attach conditions to military funding, and to authorise the withdrawal of U.S. military advisers from El Salvador have elicited minimal support from among the legislative body.[66] At the same time, the small number of Congressional critics of administration policy are basically engaged in a tactical disagreement with the White House—over the most appropriate means to achieve a settlement to the conflict that prevents the transfer of state power to the opposition forces represented in the Revolutionary Democratic Front. In the main, they still cling to the fiction that the formal civilian leadership of the junta headed by Napoleon Duarte is 'responsible' and 'reformist' in contrast to the right-wing terrorist groups acting outside the control of the central government in San Salvador. The major

---

*During March 1981, it was reported that a contingent of Israeli military advisers (perhaps as many as thirty) were providing on-the-spot training in anti-guerrilla tactics for Salvadoran military personnel. See 'Latin Letter', *Latin American Weekly Report* WR-81-13, March 27, 1981, p. 8.

recommendation contained in a report by a 'liberal' member of the House Foreign Affairs Committee following a visit to El Salvador in early 1981 is instructive in this respect:

> The United States should suspend military sales, training, and assistance to the security forces of El Salvador on the grounds that those forces are operating independently of responsible civilian control (i.e. Duarte), and are conducting a systematic campaign of terrorism directed against segments of their own population.[67]

Direct U.S. bilateral economic and military assistance to El Salvador in Fiscal Year 1981 has now reached $143 million. This escalating financial commitment to the junta could, however, skyrocket by a further $380 million during the current fiscal year if various projects currently under consideration by Washington and the multilateral banking community (World Bank, Inter-American Development Bank, International Monetary Fund) come to fruition.[68] In this regard, the Reagan administration has apparently let it be known that it is prepared to apply considerable pressure on allied governments in Western Europe, Canada and Japan to support the 'international bank' programmes for El Salvador presently on the drawing boards.[69] For Fiscal Year 1982, the administration has already requested $26 million in direct military aid for El Salvador and an additional $40 million from the misnamed 'Economic Support Fund' which, in practice, operates as a weapons assistance 'support fund'.[70] These current and projected increases in military assistance to the junta are indicative of Reagan's decision to completely jettison the Carter strategy of attempting to disassociate the regime itself from responsibility for the terror—preferring, instead, to support the militarisation of civil society if that is what is required to defeat a revolutionary movement that has put the issue of state power on the immediate political agenda. At another more important level, however, there was continuity, not rupture. Reagan touched on this shared perspective at the point of overall policy goals:

> I didn't start the Salvador thing (Reagan said). . . I inherited it. (And in any case, he noted, while the previous administration campaigned with warnings that Reagan would be a threat to peace) they were doing what we're doing (in El Salvador), . . . sending aid . . . of the same kind we're sending.[71]

## Conclusion

Like the Carter administration, the Reagan White House is escalating the military build-up of repressive forces in El Salvador to make it a test case for U.S. policy towards the Third World: it demonstrates U.S. willingness and capacity to 'project power', to defend right-wing allies and to put all revolutionary movements on notice regarding Washington's intention to enforce its policy of sustaining docile vassals within its sphere of influence. The new administration continues to propagate the myth of the junta as a 'reformist government' under siege by 'the forces of the extreme right' and 'the forces of the extreme left'.[72] Meanwhile, the military buildup of the junta being carried out with the express authorisation of the White House has served to increase the level and scope of regime repression.

During the first three months of 1981, the Legal Aid Commission reported a total of 5,469 people killed by the regime—2,644 in January, 903 in February, and 1,922 in March—a rate which, if sustained, will at least double the number assassinated by the Junta in 1980.[73] Peasants continue to account for the vast majority of the regime's victims. In a single week (March 7–13), for example, the Commission documented 798 political assassinations by government forces and the paramilitary groups, of which 681 were peasants killed in bombing raids by the 'centrist' regime's airplanes and helicopter gunships.[74] The high proportion of peasants among the victims of junta violence in recent months strongly suggests that the 'agrarian reform' remains a misnomer for government terrorism—the reform rhetoric serving to mask the widespread and destructive use of force to intimidate the rural population. In addition, the rural refugees themselves are constantly attacked in their makeshift camps and on church property which is under seige by the military. Apart from the peasant population, religious, educational and cultural institutions continue to be other focal points of the ongoing regime terror. Military and paramilitary forces killed 170 teachers and 39 Church people between January 1980 and March 1981. Of the three hundred documented acts of violence committed against religious institutions and persons during this period (assassinations, machine gunnings, bombings, beatings, etc.), regime forces were responsible for 224, another 47 were the work of unidentified groups, and only 23 were undertaken by the paramilitary 'death squads'.[75] At the same time, monitoring organisations such as the Legal Aid Commission and Amnesty International continue to find no evidence whatsoever of rightwing terror groups operating independently of the state repressive apparatus. Clearly, the increased political linkages and military aid sponsored by the Reagan administration are *increasing* the level of repression in El Salvador today, not lessening it. The growing professionalisation of the armed forces is not moderating the Salvadoran military but contributing to its extremism.

The build-up of U.S. interventionary capacity in El Salvador is necessarily accompanied by a well-coordinated and orchestrated campaign through the America mass media which portrays this policy as defensive action to counter a mythical Soviet-Cuban intervention in the conflict. Massive U.S. arms flows and the intrusion of Pentagon military advisers are 'legitimated' by the media through the purported discovery of Soviet-bloc arms shipments in the possession of the guerrillas. The fact that most of the weapons used by the insurgents are U.S., Israeli, West German and Belgium-make is explained away by their supposed origin in Vietnam and their transfer via Cuba and Nicaragua to El Salvador.[76]

Intent on creating an interventionist syndrome among the American public and sustaining Congressional support for U.S. intervention in favour of a right-wing dictatorship fighting against the majority of its own people, the mass media focuses on three interrelated themes: (1) the conflict in El Salvador is part of an East-West conflict; (2) the adversaries of the U.S. and the junta are a minority of Marxist guerrillas; and (3) the policy of the guerrillas is to terrorise the majority of 'uninvolved' or hostile peasants into submission, to seize control of the state and pave the way for a new Soviet gateway on 'our doorstep'. What is absent from these accounts is any consideration of the scope and nature of the polyclass opposition to the regime, the downplaying of the large-scale military and economic support that the U.S. government has provided the junta, and the avoidance of any serious consideration of the terroristic nature of the Salvadoran government's policies. This media propaganda effort to legitimise terror by casting the victims as executioners finds further elaboration in the discussions of the growing numbers of peasants fleeing the countryside: these victims of regime repression are presented as objects of guerrilla depredations. In the refugee camps of Costa Rica and among those that we interviewed in Mexico, however, each and every peasant, whether social Christian, leftist or apolitical, spoke clearly and directly to the issue of the junta. Without exception, military repression was the basic reason for abandoning the country.

The attempt to interpret the Salvadoran revolutionary movement as an outgrowth of Soviet-Cuban machinations is so flimsy and fanciful that even close Western allies in Paris and Bonn, Rio de Janiero and Mexico City, remain singularly unconvinced. In the first place, it overlooks at least fifteen years of social history, in which socialist, democratic, and social Christian groups have been actively organising various strata and classes of society to demand improved living standards and representative government. School teachers, peasants, rural wage workers, factory workers, public employees, health workers and others have been organised in public associatins by a variety of political groups. These non-violent, popularly based organisations have been the principal rarget of repression by the combined military and paramilitary forces ofthe junta, accounting for the great majority of the thousands thus far killed. The principal point of cleavage is not East-West, but between peasants, landholders, workers, employers and professionals on the one hand and the military junta on the other. To attempt to superimpose above this historical reality a mythical Big Power conflict is nothing less than a cynical manipulation and rewriting of the past in order to justify present and future intervention.

The growth of the guerrilla and popular resistance paralleled the regime's savaging of the legal, open mass movements: regime repression did not eliminate the popular organisations but forced them underground and into other forms of struggle. The armed resistance grew into a coalition of social Christian, Marxist and social democratic forces linked to a wide array of social groups in society. To portray this plurality of political and social forces as a monolithic military force is an exercise in deliberate deception.

The capacity of the popular organisations to grow and sustain their memberships, despite the severity of the repression, testified to the close relationship between the opposition and the rank-and-file peasants and workers. The widespread disenchantment of all sectors of the peasantry with the military controlled 'agrarian reform' creates ample basis for the growth of the resistance movement. The movement's principal recruits are drawn from the countryside, and much of its support has been drawn from the rural villages. It is precisely for that reason that the junta has engaged in 'search and destroy' missions' throughout wide regions of rural El Salvador and has applied the notion of 'collective guilt' to whole families and villages suspected of harbouring individual resistance members.

The popular resistance movement has passed through several phases in which political conditions have shaped the level and scope of activity. Between the mid-1970s and late 1979, mass public mobilisations were the primary focus of activity: the demands for democratic rights and structural changes were spearheaded and openly expressed by non-violent spokespersons. The armed struggle was largely on the periphery of the movement, essentially a defensive organisation, to counter para-military groups in the countryside. During this phase, repression was 'selective'—several hundred were killed by the regime and its paramilitary forces. Beginning in 1980, and accelerating thereafter, the regime launched a campaign of mass repression throughout the society, directed almost exclusively at the mass of local church, factory, community and coop-erative leaders and activists. The purpose of this extermination campaign was to destroy the organisational support of the mass movement, atomise and terrorise the rank-and-file and drive a wedge between the political leadership and the mass of sympathisers and supporters in the town and country. This task was facilitated by the public activities of the popular organisations, whose members and activists were easily identified by the secret police and other regime officals at large public gatherings.

Strategically, the repressive regime and its backers in Washington hoped that by debilitating the mass organisations, they would eventually isolate the guerrillas and then proceed to a straight military confrontation, in which the heavier fire-power of the U.S.-armed state forces would be decisive. This strategy, when applied, resulted in forcing many members of the mass organisations to join the armed resistance. Those that remain participants in the popular struggle maintain a low profile— the alternative is instant death. The trajectory of mass movement activity which had proceeded upward until 1979, in other words, began to decline in 1980, while the curve of guerrilla activity began a steep ascent. This pattern was evident during the January 1981 revolutionary offensive when widespread guerrilla activity did not coincide with an urban insurrection. The process of reconstructing and sustaining the linkages between the urban mass and rural guerrilla struggle is on the present agenda, but under the most difficult imaginable circumstances.

## Notes

1. U.S. Agency for International Development, Office of Planning and Budgeting, Bureau for Program and Policy Coordination, *U.S. Overseas Loans and Grants and Assistance from International Organizations.* July 1, 1945–September 30, 1979, pp. 49, 219.

2. See William M. LeoGrande and Carla Anne Robbins, 'Oligarchs and Officers: The Crisis in El Salvador', *Foreign Affairs,* Vol. 58, No. 5, Summer 1980, pp. 1094–1095

3. See, for example, 'El Salvador: No-one speaks to the Colonel', *Latin American Regional Reports: Mexico & Central America.* RM-80-09, October 24, 1980, p. 5.

4. See U.S. Agency for International Development, *Congressional Presentation, Fiscal Year 1982, Main Volume* (United States International Development Cooperation Agency), p. 235.

5. Data supplied by Multilateral Development Banks division, U.S. Department of the Treasury.

6. See 'El Salvador: US ready to put pressure on the aid donors', *Latin American Regional Reports: Mexico & Central America* RM-81-03, March 20, 1981, p. 2.

7. Institute for Policy Studies, *Update #2: Background Information on El Salvador and U.S. Military Assistance to Central America,* November 1980, p. 8.

8. 'Problems from the barrels of Israeli guns', *Latin American Weekly Report* WR-80-19, May 16, 1980, p. 9; Institute for Policy Studies, *Background Information on The Security Forces in El Salvador and U.S. Military Assistance,* March 1980, p. 12.

9. Institute for Policy Studies, *Update: Background Information on El Salvador and U.S. Military Assistance to Central America,* June 1980, pp. 6–7.

10. See Karen DeYoung, 'U.S. Weighing a Military Role in El Salvador', *Washington Post,* February 14, 1980, pp. A1, A40.

11. Quoted in Alan Riding, 'U.S. Aid to Salvador Army: Bid to Bar "Another Nicaragua" ', *New York Times,* February 23, 1980, p. 2.

12. Institute for Policy Studies, *Update: Background Information. . .,* op. cit., p. 7.

13. Quoted in Michael Getler, 'New Tack in "America's Balkans",' *Washington Post,* April 17, 1980, p. A28.

14. U.S. official, quoted in Karen DeYoung, 'El Salvador: Where Reagan Draws the Line', *Washington Post,* March 9, 1981, p. A18.

15. Christopher Dickey, 'Salvadorans Training At U.S. Sites in Panama', *Washington Post,* October 9, 1980, pp. A46, A47.

16. Karen DeYoung, 'Carter Decides to Resume Military Aid to El Salvador', *Washington Post,* January 14, 1981, p. A18.

17. Quoted in Juan de Onis, 'Envoy Disputes U.S. on Salvador Deaths', *New York Times,* January 22, 1981, p. 14.

18. 'Interview with Ambassador Robert White: El Salvador's Future—And How U.S. Can Influence it', U.S. New & World Report, January 26, 1981, p. 37.

19. Institute for Policy Studies, *Update #3: Background on U.S. Military Assistance to El Salvador,* January 1981. Also see Christopher Dickey, 'Salvadoran Military Begins Training With U.S. Weapons, Advisers', *Washington Post,* January 25, 1981, p. A15.

20. Karen DeYoung, 'El Salvador: Where Reagan Draws the Line', op. cit., p. A18.

21. 'Common Market: Little to spare in CACM's money box', *Latin American Regional Reports: Mexico & Central America* RM-81-02, February 13, 1981, p. 8.

22. Report prepared by the Legal Aid Commission of the Office of the Archbishop of El Salvador, February 1981, p. 9.

23. Ibid., p. 22.

24. Ibid., p. 99.

25. Ibid., pp. 10, 11, 15, 17.

26. Ibid., pp. 11–12.

27. Ibid., p. 27. For the assassination figures, see Ibid., pp. 29–34.

28. Ibid., pp. 9, 22, 24.

29. See Lawrence R. Simon and James C. Stephens Jr., *El Salvador Land Reform Impact Study, 1980–1981* (Boston, Mass.: Oxfam America, 1981), pp. 36–38. Also see 'El Salvador: Reform imposed from above', *Latin American Weekly Report* WR-81-10, March 6, 1981, p. 10.

30. Al Kamen, 'Beset by Violence and Delays, Land Reform Falters in El Salvador', *Washington Post,* April 5, 1981, p. A21.

31. Lawrence R. Simon and James C. Stephens Jr., op. cit.

32. Ibid., p. 70.

33. Ibid., p. 60.

34. See 'El Salvador: Failure of agrarian reform damages regime's international image', *Latin American Weekly Report* WR-80-32, August 15, 1980, p. 8; 'El Salvador: Counterinsurgency moves into overdrive', *Latin American Regional Reports: Mexico & Central America* RM-80-06, July 11, 1980, p. 5; Philip Wheaton, *Agrarian Reform in El Salvador: A Program of Rural Pacification* (EPICA Task Force, Washington, D.C., November 1980), 22 pp.

35. Report prepared by the Legal Aid Commission. . ., op. cit., p. 9.

36. See Legal Aid Commission of the Office of the Archbishop of El Salvador, *Solidaridad* ('Sobre Los Refugiados'), March 1981.

37. Office of the President-Elect, Washington, D.C., Memorandum to: Ambassador Robert Neumann. From: Pedro A. Sanjuan, State Department Transition Team. *Subject: Interim Report on the Bureau of Inter-American Affairs and Related Bureaus and Policy Areas,* Department of State (Confidential).

38. Quoted in John M. Goshko, 'Reagan State Department Aide Sees "Nationalistic" Policy', *Washington Post,* December 18, 1980, p. A1.

39. Jeanne Kirkpatrick, United Nations Ambassador-designate, quoted in Philip Geyelin, 'Human Rights Turnaround', *Washington Post,* December 12, 1980, p. A23.

40. Quoted in 'Cauldron in Central America: What Keeps the Fire Burning?' *New York Times,* December 7, 1980, p. E3.

41. Juan de Onis, 'Reagan Aides Promise Salvadorans More Military Help to Fight Rebels', *New York Times,* November 29, 1980, p. 1.

42. Office of the President-Elect, Washington, D.C., op. cit.

43. Quoted in Jim Klurfeld, 'How the U.S. Shifted Policy in El Salvador', *San Francisco Chronicle,* March 11, 1981, p. 12.

44. Office of the President-Elect, Washington, D.C., op. cit.

45. Jeremiah O'Leary, 'Lesser Post Is Offered to Fired Envoy', *Washington Post,* February 7, 1981, p. A-3.

46. U.S. Department of State, Bureau of Public Affairs, Washington, D.C., Special Report No. 80, *Communist Interference in El Salvador,* February 23, 1981, p. 1.

47. For a detailed and systematic critique of the 'White Paper', see James Petras, 'White Paper on the White Paper', *The Nation,* March 28, 1981, pp. 352, 267–372.

48. For an excellent analysis, see Jonathan Evan Maslow and Ana Arana, 'Operation El Salvador', *Columbia Journalism Review,* May/June 1981, pp. 52–58.

49. Senator Charles Percy, quoted in Don Oberdorfer, 'Salvador is "the Place to Draw the Line" ', *Washington Post,* February 20, 1981, p. A20.

50. Quoted in Bernard Gwertzman, 'More Salvador Aid Backed in Congress', *New York Times,* February 18, 1981, pp. 1, 3. Also see John M. Goshko, 'Hill Leaders Vow Aid to Salvador to Resist Leftists', *Washington Post,* February 18, 1981, pp. A1, A17.

51. Quoted in Margot Hornblower, 'Ousted Envoy Hits Arms Aid to Salvador', *Washington Post,* February 26, 1981, p. A24. Also see Juan de Onis, 'Baker Supports Added Advisers For El Salvador', *New York Times,* February 26, 1981, pp. 1, 6.

52. See Hedrick Smith, 'House Democrats Seeking to Limit Involvement by U.S. in El Salvador', *New York Times,* March 1, 1981, pp. 1, 15; 'Leader in Senate Predicts Backing For More Salvadoran Military Aid', *New York Times,* March 4, 1981, p. 4.

53. See Juan de Onis, 'U.S. to Seek Support on Salvador Issue', *New York Times,* February 14, 1981, p. 6; John M. Goshko, 'U.S. Prepares to Aid Salvador in First Test of Reagan Policy', *Washington Post,* February 14, 1981, pp. A1, A17; 'Hill Leaders Due Haig Briefing on Salvador Arms', *Washington Post,* February 17, 1981, p. A7.

54. See Richard Eder, 'France Evades U.S. Bid For Support on Salvador', *New York Times,* February 18, 1981, p. 3; 'Europe gives sceptical reception to Haig's "red scare" mission', *Latin American Weekly Report* WR-81-08, February 20, 1981, p. 5; Richard Eder, 'Europe and El Salvador', *New York Times,* February 21, 1981, p. 7; Felix Kessler 'Europeans Appreciate U.S. Envoy's Visit But Shy From a Stand on El Salvador', *Wall Street Journal,* February 23, 1981, p. 27. On the support for a negotiated political settlement, also see 'El Salvador: Bonn and the FDR want talks but Washington stalls', *Latin American Weekly Report* WR-81-18, May 8, 1981, pp. 3–4.

55. Quoted in Richard M. Weintraub, 'U.S. Allies Cool to El Salvador Drive', *Washington Post,* February 27, 1981, pp. A1, A27. Also see 'El Salvador: US launches diplomatic offensive. . .', *Latin American Weekly Report* WR-81-09, February 27, 1981, pp. 9–10.

56. Quoted in Walter Taylor, 'U.S. Eases Standards For Aid to El Salvador', *Washington Post,* February 18, 1981, pp. A-1, A-6. Also see John M. Goshko, 'Hill Leaders Vow Aid to Salvador to Resist Leftists', op. cit., p. A17.

57. Quoted in 'El Salvador: Will It Turn Into Another Vietnam?', *U.S. News & World Report,* March 16, 1981, p. 29.

58. See Juan de Onis, 'U.S. Expands Military Aid', *New York Times,* March 3, 1981, p. 13.

59. See Steven R. Weisman, 'Reagan Vows to Help Salvadorans Buy Says U.S. Won't be Locked In', *New York Times,* February 25, 1981, pp. 1, 4.

60. Quoted in 'U.S. Sends El Salvador 6 Navy Technicians', *New York Times,* March 1, 1981, p. 14.

61. Quoted in John M. Goshko, 'Drawing a Hard Line Against Communist', *Washington Post,* February 22, 1981, p. A8.

62. See John M. Goshko, 'Haig Denies Administration Would Support Coup in El Salvador', *Washington Post,* March 5, 1981, p. A29.

63. John Goshko and Don Oberdorfer, 'U.S. to Send More Aid, Advisers to El Salvador', *Washington Post,* March 3, 1981, pp. A1, A11; Juan de Onis, op. cit., pp. 1, 13.

64. Judith Miller, 'House Panel Approves $5 Million in Extra Military Aid to El Salvador', *New York Times,* March 25, 1981, pp. 1, 3.

65. See Edward Walsh, 'Policy on El Salvador Narrowly Survives First Hill Test, 8 to 7', *Washington Post,* March 24, 1981, p. A14; Edward Walsh, 'El Salvador Protests Called "Orchestrated" Communist Effort', *Washington Post,* March 24, 1981, p. A3; Judith Miller, '15 U.S. Green Berets To Aid Salvadorans', *New York Times,* March 14, 1981, pp. 1, 8.

66. See 'Reagan Backed on Salvador Aid', *Washington Post,* April 9, 1981, p. 7.

67. U.S. Congress, House, Committee on Foreign Affairs, *Central America,* 97th Congress, 1st Session, Committee Print, prepared by Gerry E. Studds, March 1981 (Washington: U.S. Government Printing Office, 1981), p. 29.

68. See Center for International Policy, *Aid Memo: Total Aid Package for El Salvador May Reach $523 Million,* April 1981, Washington, D.C., pp. 1–2.

69. See 'El Salvador: U.S. ready to put pressure on the aid donors', op. cit., p. 2.

70. See Judith Miller, op. cit., pp. 1, 8; 'Reagan seeks big rise in Military aid to Latin America', *Latin American Weekly Report* WR-81-14, April 3, 1981, p. 5.

71. Quoted in Karen DeYoung, 'El Salvador: Where Reagan Draws the Line', op. cit., p. A18.

72. Statement by Walter J. Stoessel, Under Secretary of State for Political Affairs, before the Senate Foreign Relations Committee on March 19, 1981, reprinted in U.S. Department of State, Bureau of Public Affairs, Washington, D.C., *Current Policy No. 265, Statement on El Salvador,* March 19, 1981.

73. Legal Aid Commission of the Office of the Archbishop of El Salvador, *Solidaridad,* April 4, 1981.

74. See 'Central America Watch', *The Nation,* April 18, 1981, p. 455.

75. Legal Aid Commission of the Office of the Archbishop of El Salvador, *Solidaridad* ('Trescientos Actos De Persecucion A La Iglesia En El Salvador'), February 1981.

76. See Francis Pisani, 'Where El Salvador's guerillas get arms', Le Monde Supplement of the *Manchester Guardian Weekly,* March 8, 1981, p. 11.

# Part II

## THEORY

# 3

## Toward a Theory of Industrial Development in The Third World

JAMES PETRAS

The expansion of capitalism on a world scale has wrought a profound transformation in many parts of the Third World. The process of penetration and the impact of Western capitalism has varied according to the stage of capitalist development and the internal structure and composition of Western capital. Moreover, the areas and countries most affected by Western capital at different stages have varied and subsequently the nature of the impact has been different.

More recently, the debate over capitalist development in the Third World has been polarized around two central positions: the "dependentistas" who argued the impossibilities of capitalist industrialization, and their adversaries who argued about the inevitability of capitalist growth.

The first line of thought was most eloquently presented by Paul Baran, who postulated the existence of strong internal barriers—class interests in the periphery—and a Western capitalism strongly linked to primary commodity production and export in the Third World as a serious obstacle to sustained and effective industrial growth. The epigones of Baran failed to appreciate the historical specificity of his argument, understated the importance of internal class relations, and failed to take account of the new capitalist forces and interests in both the West and the Third World. They abstracted the external relations of "dependence" and mechanically tied it to a notion of "surplus extraction" and proceeded to link both to a theory of "capitalist underdevelopment."

The subsequent growth of capitalist industry in a number of countries was either overlooked or simply dismissed through perjorative adjectives, "lumpen development" or "dependent development."

In this context, Bill Warren's writing firmly established the fact that capitalist industrialization was occurring in a number of countries, and that dependency was not an obstacle to growth. His contribution was essentially one of demolishing the notion of the impossibility of capitalist industrialization in the Third World. His essential failure was his inability to theorize about the origins, scope, and process of industrialization. Instead, he inverted the thinking of the dependentistas: where they saw stagnation everywhere, he saw growth; where they saw imperialism generating stagnation, he saw linear progress. Ultimately, Warren's thesis is no more satisfying than those he criticizes: He didn't provide a coherent explanation for the prolonged period of nonindustrialization in the Third World; he fails to explain the persistence of a vast number of scarcely industrialized countries; he fails to discuss the different patterns of industrial growth in advanced capitalist, Third World, and socialist countries; he fails to provide a comprehensive framework to understand the interrelationship between the changing nature of capital in the West and the process of industrialization in the Third World; finally, he fails to discuss the enormous inequalities in industrial development among Third World countries, both in terms of the changes in productive systems and in terms of their stages of industrial growth; moreover, he fails to consider the possibility of the deindustrialization of specific Third World countries.

## Framework of Analysis

The growth of Third World manufacturing industry is a relatively recent phenomenon, occurring primarily in the twentieth century and, for most recently independent countries, since the end of World War II. The timing of industrialization, the initiation and expansion of the industrial process in the Third World, must be seen in relation to the pattern and stages of capital accumulation in the advanced capitalist countries. Essentially, we can distinguish three stages of capitalist accumulation in the West: primitive accumulation, normal accumulation, and the growth of fictitious capital. Each of these stages of capital has a direct effect in shaping the process and forms of capital accumulation in the Third World. To each stage in the process of accumulation, a corresponding process of development occurs in the Third World.

*Primitive accumulation.* In the West, the use of force and violence to establish wage labor relations, to dissociate the direct producers from the means of production, and to create market relations led to the pillage of the Third World: the seizure of wealth and its transfer to the West, feeding into the creation of a monetary economy, commercial networks, and the slow building of manufactures. The primitive accumulation phase in the West coincided with the destruction of the pre-existing forms of production and civilizations in the non-Western world; there was no development of the productive forces—in fact, genocide contributed to the rapid exhaustion of the forces of production, namely labor power.

*Normal accumulation.* Once the capitalist mode of production was firmly established in the West, the relationship with the Third World shifted from a strictly military occupation for seizure of wealth and pillage of precious metals to one of establishing the basis for capitalist production of raw materials for the burgeoning industrial complexes. The growth of this new international division of labor incorporated new plantation and mining enterprises based on investments from the metropolitan country, the growth of "settler capital" in the colony, and the frequently forcible recruitment of subsistence farmers into the labor force. The stimulus to growth and accumulation in the West was the home market and the industrial exports; in the colonies and semi-colonies, the stimulus to growth was the home market of the industrializing West, as the local market was very "underdeveloped": low or non-wage-payments, lack of local industry, the isolation of the interior, the pervasiveness of a large subsistence sector. Where local industry predated colonization, or integration into the world market, it was destroyed either by a deliberate policy of colonial authorities or by market forces unleashed by the free trade doctrines embraced by Western industrial exporters and local primary product producers.

The design of this international division of production originated in the West, but in the process created a class of local producers tied to the system of exchange: mineowners, planters, transport and shipowners, and so on, who began to accumulate capital. The process of local accumulation by comprador groups, and the expansion of the labor force to accommodate the growing demand for raw materials, slowly created a local market, whose basic consumer needs began to be supplied by local manufacturers, despite international competition, colonial state restrictions, and limits on the scale of production. The growth of a home market and light consumer goods industry in the shell of the old colonial division of labor was aided and abetted by the cyclical fluctuations, crises and wars that dislocated the international organization of exchanges: from the interstices of the primary export economy, local manufactures moved out and began the process of the local accumulation, aided by the crisis in the export sector. Crisis-born industrial accumulation in the Third World took hold only in the politically independent Latin American countries; in the colonial states, the absence of state control prevented the local manufacturers from establishing and extending the production of substitutes of industrial imports. Thus in the *advanced stages* of normal industrial capitalist accumulation, substantial internal market began to develop in a select number of politically independent countries, leading to the export of industrial capital; this process expanded rapidly in the post-war period in Latin America and in the post-independence period throughout Africa, but especially Asia. The political changes in the Third World (nationalism, independence), the growing strength of the local manufacturers, and the expansion of the home market contributed to *modifying the internal structures of production within the Third World, without breaking the essential contours of the international division of labor.* Industrial growth and a form of "primitive accumulation" in the Third World was occurring during the period of late industrial growth ("normal accumulation") in the West.

## Fictitious Capital

The 1970s witnessed a transformation of capital, a shift from capital accumulation in industrial production to the growth of fictitious capital— the proliferation of money funds, banking and finance capital, real estate, and the like. The growth of fictitious capital coincides with the relative decline in the profit rate of industry, resulting from the combined pressure of wage increases and the rising power of rentier capital, i.e., the increased costs of energy resulting from the power of the oil producers. The growth of rentier capital—those whose income is derived from land rent, oil being a principal source—reinforced and vastly increased the growth of fictitious capital, as most rentier earnings were channeled into financial institutions of the Western countries, not productive capital. The rising power of financial capital led to the proliferation of speculative investments in urban land, real estate, and money funds and to massive overseas lending. The "de-industrialization" of the West reflects the massive shift toward fictitious capital, and not generally the high information-high technology utopia projected by some pundits. The growth of finance capital has been accompanied by a massive program of selective overseas lending, which has stimulated and deepened the industrialization of a select group of Third World countries: those with a large internal market, with a state and class structure capable of converting loans into productive activity. The stage of fictitious capital in the West then coincides with the development of "normal accumulation" and the deepening of the industrialization process for some Third World countries: the massive growth of capital goods industries, industrial exports, the creation of a substantial home market, a skilled labor force, and so on.

The industrializing Third World countries, the main recipients of overseas financing, provide a higher rate of profit than lending to industrial firms in the West: At comparable rates of productivity, lower wage rates lead to higher profit rates and a greater capacity to pay interest rates above the levels that can be extracted from comparable enterprises in the west. The growth of fictitious capital then means the relative decline of the old division of labor and the emergence of new industrial centers generally but not exclusively centering on the export of light manufactured goods. The continued reproduction of industrial capital has led a few of the industrializing countries to begin to develop capital goods exports, advancing to higher stages of "normal accumulation." The impact of the growth of fictitious capital and overseas expansion has been to heighten the internal differentiation among Third World countries—between those still within the traditional division of labor and little industrial growth, those moving toward the creation of an internal market and light consumer goods industries, to those countries developing capital goods industries, exporting consumer goods and even capital goods.

The interrelatedness of the development of capital in the West and the Third World should not be construed as a linear process in which all Third World countries participate equally; nor are the changes in the composition of capital in the West the ultimate determinant of industrialization in Third World countries. Clearly the growth of capitalist forces and a capitalist state structure with the capacity to harness the massive flow of finance capital toward productive activities is crucial. The growth of finance capital and its internationalization is an *enabling* condition for the *accelerated* growth and transformation of Third World capital. The internal growth of capital, the transformation of peasants into wage labor, the growth of an internal market, and the growth of infrastructure creates the shell, i.e., the framework for capitalist growth. Finance capital expands overseas in search of higher profits, but those profits can be realized only in the context of the more advanced capitalist countries of the Third World—countries with the capacity to create productive activity, increase exports, and hold down labor costs in order to guarantee interest payments.

In summary, the process of capitalist industrialization in the Third World can be understood through an analysis of the interrelation of different stages in the accumulation process in the West and the corresponding impact it has on the accumulation process in the Third World.

## Stages of Accumulation

| Third World | West |
|---|---|
| pillage | primitive accumulation |
| primitive accumulation | normal accumulation |
| normal accumulation | fictitious capital |

Within the process of "normal accumulation," the depth and scope of industrialization varies enormously. Essentially, we can distinguish several phases:

1. Raw material production and export—little or no home market, most rudimentary handicraft industry
2. Raw material production and export and beginning of home market, development of light industry, and service and maintenance shops linked to transport networks
3. Raw material production and export and growth of home market, large-scale import-substitution industries in light industry and beginning of capital goods—beginning of manufacturing exports
4. Light manufactured goods and primary product exports, substantial home market, and expansion of capital goods sector
5. Light and capital goods exports, processed primary products exported, substantial home market

6. Export of technology, diversified capital and consumer goods, fully developed home market

The bulk of Third World countries are spread across, between 2 and 4, with the larger Latin American economies and the more dynamic Asian countries falling into stage 4 and edging toward 5, while the bulk of African and Asian countries are close to stage 2. The vast range of experiences and the enormous variations in levels of industrialization indicate that simplistic formulas suggesting that "as capitalism grows imperialism declines" fails to delve deeply into the specific historical context and relations which have conditioned the very striking patterns of *uneven development within the Third World.* Moreover, the internal differentiation among Third World countries suggests that linear paths of growth for all may not be in order; the more developed industrializing Third World countries may be preempting opportunities, markets and suppliers, as well as establishing their own patterns of regional domination and thus lessening the possibilities of future growth for the less industrialized countries. The following section will outline the overall process of industrialization in the Third World, the emerging patterns, the increasing differentiation among Third World countries, and the impact of industrialization on the class structure.

## Industrialization and the Third World

There is no doubt about the historical turn toward manufacturing in the Third World. The rate of growth of a whole range of manufacturing products was much higher than in the advanced Western countries (see Table 3.1). While manufacturing production increased 26 percent in the developed countries, it grew 60 percent in the developing countries between 1970 and 1977. Likewise, in the area of industrial and manufacturing employment, while the proportion of workers was declining in the developed countries, it was increasing sharply in the Third World (see Table 3.2).

While these growth figures reflect in part the initial low level of manufacturing production in many Third World countries, it also demonstrates the possibilities for capitalist industrialization. How fast and how far this industrialization process can go is problematical. The critical advantage, however, which the developed capitalist countries still wield over the newly industrializing countries is in the high rate of growth of labor productivity. The inability of Third World countries to raise their levels of labor productivity weakens their capacity to enter into international markets and confines the growth process to local markets protected by tariff barriers.

There is strong evidence that the initial industrial push among Third World countries is already tapering off; there is a clear difference between the oil exporting Third World countries and the oil importers. Among the low-income oil importing Third World countries, the annual in-

Table 3.1  Index of Numbers of Manufacturing Production, 1977 (1970 = 100)

| | Total mfg. | Light mfg. | Heavy mfg. | Food | Tex-tiles | Wearing apparel | Wood products | Paper | Chemical products | Non-metallic materials | Basic metal | Metal products | Metal products |
|---|---|---|---|---|---|---|---|---|---|---|---|---|---|
| Developed market economy | 126 | 122 | 128 | 125 | 113 | 114 | 125 | 115 | 143 | 124 | 107 | 129 | 141 |
| Developing market economy | 160 | 147 | 175 | 147 | 133 | 175 | 130 | 149 | 158 | 173 | 160 | 201 | 196 |

Table 3.2 Index of Number of Industrial and Manufacturing Employment, 1977 (1970 = 100)

| | Mining | Mfg. | Light mfg. | Heavy mfg. | Food | Tex-tiles | Wearing apparel | Wood products | Paper | Chemicals | Non-metal | Basic metals | Metal products |
|---|---|---|---|---|---|---|---|---|---|---|---|---|---|
| Developed market economy | 95 | 98 | 97 | 99 | 101 | 84 | 97 | 101 | 97 | 101 | 96 | 92 | 101 |
| Developing market economy | 123 | 140 | 136 | 150 | 137 | 125 | 158 | 141 | 125 | 150 | 142 | 184 | 152 |

*Source: U.N. Statistical Yearbook,* 1978.

Table 3.3   Index of Number of Labor Productivity in Industry, 1976 (1970 = 100)

| | Mining | Mfg. | Light mfg. | Heavy mfg. | Food | Tex-tiles | Wearing apparel | Wood products | Paper | Chemicals | Non-metallic | Basic metals | Metal products |
|---|---|---|---|---|---|---|---|---|---|---|---|---|---|
| Developed countries | 102 | 125 | 123 | 127 | 123 | 131 | 119 | 120 | 117 | 139 | 126 | 117 | 127 |
| Developing countries | 99 | 108 | 104 | 121 | 104 | 106 | 133 | — | 92 | 96 | 118 | 87 | 137 |

Source: U.N. Statistical Yearbook, 1978.

Table 3.4    Third World Manufactures: Structure of Production: Manufacturing Percentage of GDP

|  | 1960 | 1979 |
|---|---|---|
| Low income | 11 | 13 |
| Middle income | 21 | 24 |
| Oil export | 17 | 19 |
| Oil import | 24 | 26 |
| Capital Surplus Oil Exporters |  | 5 |

dustrial growth rate has declined by almost 40 percent, from 6.6 percent during the sixties to 4.2 percent during the seventies. Among middle income oil importing Third World countries, the annual rate of industrial growth has declined almost 20 percent from 7.1 percent to 5.7 percent. Among oil-exporting Third World countries, annual industrial growth rate has increased from 7.6 percent to 7.8 percent; among capital surplus oil exporters, the annual rate of industrial growth during the seventies averaged 11.1 percent. The declining rate of industrial growth among oil importers reflects several factors: the increasing economic surplus extracted for rent payments to the oil export countries; the increasing payment of interest payments to the financial institutions of the west at a time when the economic recession and rising protectionism is closing markets for the industrial products from the Third World. The result is increasing growth of differentials among the rentier-industrializing Third World states, the middle-income, semi-industrialized Third World states, and the mainly agricultural Third World states. As the oil exporters increase their demand for industrial goods, the prime beneficiaries from the point of view of increasing trade will be the most industrialized Third World countries. The uneven growth of manufacturing in the Third World is the most salient aspect, as it suggests a new pattern within the world division of labor. The uneven growth of industry within the Third World is evidenced by the fact that by the end of the 1960s, ten countries accounted for over 90 percent of Third World manufacturing exports to the developed countries (Hong Kong, India, Taiwan, South Korea, Mexico, Pakistan, Philippines, Iran, Argentina, and Brazil). Moreover, the same ten countries account for the bulk of all Third World manufacturing output. While significant changes in industrial development are taking place among a select number of Third World countries, the aggregate growth in Third World share of world manufacturing output and trade is still small and it is growing at a snail's pace. The attempts to devise a theory based on the notion of a *global* realignment of forces clearly lacks substance. The selective changes within the Third World, the dynamic transformation in the productive structure—the growth of manufacturing on a large-scale—

in a few countries suggests that the critical issue is the particular configuration of internal factors: class and state features, market and resource bases, geographical and geopolitical locations. The scope of industrialization in most Third World countries is still quite limited— only most of the middle-income countries have a quarter or more of their productive activity located in the industrial sector (see Table 3.4). The predominance of agriculture, even as industrial change is taking place, reflects the strong class linkages between primary producing classes and the state, the enduring power of the "traditional division of labor" and the weakness within the state sector of any public industrial entrepreneurial groups capable of taking up the slack by the private sector.

All the constraints, however, are not political and social: the limited resource base of some Third World countries constrains their capacity to finance industrial imports; their geographical location (landlocked countries, long distances from markets) increases the cost of transport, the absence of "basic development"—infrastructure, fully developed market and productive systems (subsistence agriculture)—inhibits finance capital from lending, as the interest-earning possibilities are found primarily in the larger, more developed Third World countries. These same factors affect the recycling of rent income from the oil exporting countries, with the bulk of financial resources concentrated in the more industrial Third World countries. Finally, Third World countries not at the cutting edge of the superpower confrontation are not likely to receive large grants and loans that serve to create "propaganda showcases." These large financial outlays were *initially* important, especially for poor countries like Taiwan and South Korea, and are hardly to be found in the rest of the Third World; in fact, in the present context of economic recession and military confrontation there is little likelihood that economic showcases are on the agenda—we are more likely to find the use of rapid deployment military forces to contain revolutionary upsurges. For all these reasons, the "scope" of industrialization in the Third World (the proportion of gross national product accounted for by industrial production) can be expected to increase among the semi-industrialized countries, while the poorest, least developed agricultural areas will tend toward stagnation.

### Depth of Industrialization

If we examine the depth of industrialization, the growth of capital goods, transport, and chemical goods industries among Third World countries, we find a similar pattern. Only in seven countries is 30 percent or more of the value added in manufacturing derived from manufacturing other than light consumer goods industries: India, Kenya, South Korea, Mexico, Brazil, Argentina, and Singapore (see Table 3.5). (We are including only capitalist countries.) Of 48 countries analyzed, only 12.5 percent have manufacturing sectors in which 30 percent or

**Table 3.5   Distribution of Manufacturing Value Added: 1978 Percentages**

| | Light industries | Capital goods/ Chemical/ Transport |
|---|---|---|
| Low Income Countries | | |
| Burma | 51 | 6 |
| India | 29 | 30 |
| Malawi | 63 | 0 |
| Sri Lanka | 53 | 4 |
| Mozambique | 62 | 6 |
| Haiti | 50 | 1 |
| Pakistan | 58 | 14 |
| Tanzania | 57 | 13 |
| Zaire | 63 | 9 |
| Central Africa Rep. | 81 | 3 |
| Madagascar | 28 | 0 |
| Indonesia | 36 | 0 |
| Sudan | 78 | 3 |
| Middle Income Countries | | |
| Kenya | 35 | 30 |
| Ghana | 34 | 0 |
| Senegal | 62 | 9 |
| Zimbabwe | 39 | 20 |
| Egypt | 49 | 20 |
| Zambia | 33 | 24 |
| Honduras | 57 | 7 |
| Cameroon | 52 | 10 |
| Philippines | 49 | 18 |
| Congo Peoples Rep. | 22 | 9 |
| Nicaragua | 62 | 11 |
| Peru | 42 | 22 |
| Morocco | 48 | 18 |
| Dominican Republic | 76 | 6 |
| Colombia | 48 | 23 |
| Syria | 64 | 7 |
| Ecuador | 45 | 16 |
| Paraguay | 53 | 11 |
| Tunisia | 42 | 24 |
| Jamaica | 60 | 14 |
| Turkey | 37 | 0 |
| Malaysia | 30 | 22 |
| Panama | 63 | 8 |
| South Korea | 39 | 30 |
| Algeria | 49 | 12 |
| Mexico | 33 | 31 |
| Chile | 26 | 22 |
| South Africa | 26 | 27 |
| Brazil | 24 | 39 |
| Uruguay | 52 | 16 |
| Iran | 27 | 17 |
| Argentina | 24 | 39 |
| Venezuela | 27 | 14 |
| Trinidad & Tobago | 17 | 17 |
| Singapore | 11 | 48 |
| Greece | 46 | 17 |

Table 3.6   Middle Income and Low Income: Value Added in Capital Goods and Chemicals
(number and transport)

|       | Middle income | Low income |          |
|-------|:---:|:---:|----------|
|       | 6 | 1 | over 35% |
|       | 9 | 0 | 20%–29% |
|       | 12 | 2 | 10%–19% |
|       | 8 | 10 | under 10% |
| Total | 35 | 13 |          |

more of their value added is generated by the capital goods sector. On the other extreme, 37.5 percent have manufacturing sectors in which less than 10 percent of the value added comes from capital goods industries (see Table 3.6). Clearly, whatever industrialization has taken place is overwhelmingly located in light consumer goods areas. Only one of the low income countries (India) and only one of the African countries (Kenya) are found in this group. The diversification and deepening of industrialization occurs in the first because of its enormous size and longstanding manufacturing presence, and in the second because it has become the prime location for multinational capital in East Africa. What is striking is that six out of the seven countries are "middle income," suggesting that the deepening of industrialization is at least in part a product of the growing internal market and associated with an increasingly differentiated class structure in which industrial entrepreneurship, public more likely than private, has emerged to take hold and direct the industrial process.

This latter point is evidenced by the fact that three of the seven are Latin American countries with the longest and largest involvement in industrial production in the region. All three have a very substantial public sector involved in basic industry and resources; all three possess a large internal market; all possess large and developed ties to the financial centers of the West. The deepening of industrialization beyond the production of consumer goods is thus associated with two types of development strategies. The older, larger countries have, over time, been able to develop a capital goods industry in relation to the growth of the internal market, even as they increasingly promote the export of light consumer goods. More recently, small industrial countries developing a capital goods sector and, in particular, South Korea and Singapore, have capitalized on large surplus labor pools and external markets. The divergent paths to deepening industrialization and the internal and external factors that historically condition each route suggest that attempts to impose a single strategy as some international agencies propose (export oriented industrialization) may have disastrous consequences. The combination of factors of labor, capital, and entrepreneurship that facilitate the deepening of industrialization in one cir-

Table 3.7   Debt Service as Percentage of Exports of Goods and Services

|             | 1970 | 1979 |
|-------------|------|------|
| Brazil      | 12.4 | 34.6 |
| Mexico      | 24.1 | 64.1 |
| Argentina   | 21.5 | 15.5 |
| Singapore   | .6   | 1.3  |
| South Korea | 19.4 | 13.5 |
| Kenay       | 7.9  | 7.5  |
| India       | 10.9 | 9.5  |

cumstance may be obstacles in another. The imposition of the policies of Singapore on Argentina have led to massive industrial bankruptcy.

The dominant pattern for industrializing countries is the growth of a home market—even South Korea exports only 20 percent of its industrial production. The world market plays an important supplemental role among these countries, despite the free market rhetoric espoused by their political leaders and unfortunately indiscriminately disseminated by some social scientists. Moreover, with the exception of Singapore and Kenya, all of these countries have a powerful and obtrusive state sector which combines heavy public investments and financing with central allocations of resources. The growth of direct state involvement accompanies the expansion of export industries and the deepening of industrialization.

Finally, the sources of financing for the industrializing Third World countries vary. In the case of Brazil and Mexico, external financing is playing an increasingly important role. While in the cases of South Korea, Argentina, Singapore, India and Kenya internal financing seems to be much more significant, as shown in Table 3.7.

The "deepening" and "widening" of industrialization through the growth of a home market and internal accumulation are thus demonstrated to be possible, though the reduced number of cases suggests that the likelihood is improbable. The same is true for the externally oriented growth pattern. The bulk of the Third World is heavily loaded at the light consumer stage of industrialization—with only the most rudimentary elements of advanced industry. Only with heavy state intervention in direct productive activities can the process of industrial growth begin to take hold. Linkages to the world market become the basis for growth only where there is in place a state-class configuration anchored in a productive apparatus that can absorb and direct capital flows and exchanges.

The growth of capital goods industry has not been accompanied by the homogenization or even diffusion of technology throughout the society. On the contrary, the growth of capital goods in most of the countries has been accompanied by a deepening of the pattern of uneven development. The countries with the high preponderance of capital

Table 3.8  Percentage of Labor Force in Agriculture, 1979

| | |
|---|---|
| India | 71 |
| Kenya | 78 |
| Brazil | 40 |
| Mexico | 37 |

goods industries includes a majority with a large poor, agricultural population.

The growth of capital goods industry is not necessarily a *general* index of the level of development of the productive forces in society at large. Rather, it suggests enclave developments with slow and limited effects in stimulating the transformation of other sectors of the society.

## Industrialization and the Transformation of the Labor Force

The growth of both the industrial and the "service" sector continues roughly at the same proportion for all capitalist Third World countries. Within the "service sector" there are essentially two groups, the new bureaucratic and commercial classes that form a distinct minority, and the huge army of unemployed and underemployed ("self-employed") street vendors, day laborers, domestic workers, and other low-paid workers in low-productivity activity. Thus the service sector is made up in large part of the reserve army of unemployed (or what some writers refer to as the "marginal population"). As capitalism grows, so does the service sector. The only countries manifesting a declining ratio of industrial workers to service workers is the low-income countries; overall figures, however, are distorted by the presence of China, a socialist country. Accompanying the growth of wage labor among the industrializing Third World countries is the proportionate marginali-

Table 3.9  Growth of Industrial to Service Labor in Collectivist Countries

| | Services | | Industry | | Service industry ratio | Service industry ratio |
|---|---|---|---|---|---|---|
| | 1960 | 1979 | 1960 | 1979 | 1960 | 1979 |
| China | — | 12 | — | 17 | — | .71 |
| Democratic Rep. of | | | | | | |
| Korea | 25 | 34 | 9 | 30 | 2.77 | 1.13 |
| Cuba | 39 | 45 | 22 | 31 | 1.77 | 1.45 |
| Mozambique | 11 | 16 | 8 | 17 | 1.37 | .94 |
| Albania | 11 | 14 | 18 | 25 | .61 | .56 |
| Mongolia | 17 | 22 | 13 | 22 | 1.23 | 1.00 |
| Vietnam | 14 | 19 | 5 | 10 | 2.80 | 1.90 |

Table 3.10    Ratio of Service to Manufacturing Labor among Middle and Low Income
Countries

|  | 1960 | 1979 |
|---|---|---|
| Middle income socialist countries | 1.59 | 1.03 |
| All middle income countries | 1.60 | 1.50 |
| Low income socialist countries | 2.09 | 1.18 |
| Low income without China and India | 1.60 | 1.70 |
| India | 1.36 | 1.63 |

zation of large sectors of the population (see Table 3.9). While almost one quarter of the labor force in the middle-income countries is incorporated in industrial activity, over one third is involved in "services." Among low-income countries, the proportion is almost even. This suggests that the rate of marginalization increases more rapidly than proletarianization as the industrial process deepens; put another way, the growth of a reserve army of surplus labor reflects the incapacity of the capitalist accumulation process to employ the displaced peasantry. Capitalist development in the Third World does not lead to a society polarized between capital and labor, but one that is polarized between capital, labor, and an underemployed mass superior in size to both. The pattern of class formation and industrialization in the collectivist countries demonstrates a very distinct pattern to that occurring in the capitalist countries (see Table 3.9).

In the collectivist countries, industrialization leads to increasing proletarianization, accompaned by a decline in the "marginal" surplus labor force. In every country, the ratio of service to industrial workers has declined. Socialist industrialization is clearly leading to the transformation of the marginal masses into industrial workers, in sharp contrast to the middle-income countries where growing proletarianization is accompanied by a proportionate growth in the service sector.

In the collectivist countries, industrialization reduces the reserve army of unemployed, and accelerates the proletarianization process. This pattern holds for both low-income early industrializers, as well as among the more industrialized Third World countries (Table 3.10). The impact of collectivist ownership is further strengthened by the fact that low-income collectivist countries start with a much higher ratio of service to industrial workers (2.09) than the others (1.6), but after almost 20 years of development they have significantly lower ratios. In contrast to the capitalist industrializing countries, there is an inverse relation between proletarianization and marginalization.

## Industrial Exports and the Third World

The growth of industrial production within the Third World has been accompanied by the growth of exports of manufactured goods. The

Table 3.11   Structure of Merchandise Exports (in percentages)

|  | Primary commodities | | Manufactures | |
| --- | --- | --- | --- | --- |
|  | 1960 | 1978 | 1960 | 1978 |
| Low income | 82 | 70 | 18 | 30 |
| Middle income | 87 | 64 | 13 | 36 |

most striking change is found in the "middle-income" Third World countries which have witnessed almost a threefold increase in their percentage of industrial exports (see Table 3.11). While middle-income Third World countries show the greatest gain, low-income Third World countries have also moved away from sole reliance on primary product exports. There seems to be a basis for discussion of a historic trend away from the traditional division of labor. The assumption, however, that a new pattern involving exchanges between the high technology Western countries and the capital intensive low-income countries is emerging is too simplistic. Rather, what is emerging is a pattern in which the low-income countries increasingly exchange manufactured goods *within* the Third World, while the more developed and industrialized countries are increasing their exchanges with the advanced capitalist countries. In 1978 almost half of the manufacturing trade of the low-income countries was with other developing countries, while only a little over a third of the trade of the middle-income countries trade is with the developing countries (see Table 3.12).

Clearly there is a growing international market based within the Third World for the early industrializing countries; on the other hand, as industrialization takes hold, there is an increasing need by the middle-income Third World countries to import more advanced industrial goods and hence it must increase its exports to these countries.

The lowest wage areas are not the prime regions exporting goods back to the advanced capitalist countries. The wage factor is important, but not a sufficient factor in shaping the growth of industrial exports. The notion of the growth of export industrialization as a result of industrial redeployment from the advanced countries to the low-wage

Table 3.12   Trade in Manufactured Goods

|  | Industrial market economies | | Developing countries | |
| --- | --- | --- | --- | --- |
|  | 1962 | 1978 | 1962 | 1978 |
| Low income | 56 | 45 | 38 | 48 |
| Middle income | 51 | 58 | 44 | 33 |

Table 3.13 Destination of Merchandise Exports

| | Industrial market economy | | Developing countries | | Non-market industrial economy | | Capital surplus oil exports | |
|---|---|---|---|---|---|---|---|---|
| | 1960 | 1979 | 1960 | 1979 | 1960 | 1979 | 1960 | 1979 |
| Low income Countries | 51 | 61 | 29 | 29 | 19 | 5 | 1 | 5 |
| Middle income countries | 68 | 67 | 24 | 26 | 8 | 4 | — | 3 |
| Oil exporters | 68 | 73 | 27 | 26 | 5 | 1 | — | — |
| Oil importers | 68 | 64 | 23 | 27 | 9 | 6 | — | — |
| Capital surplus oil exporters | 83 | 70 | 16 | 29 | 1 | — | 0 | 1 |

Table 3.14    Declining or Stagnant Industrial Labor Force among Middle Income Countries:
Percentage of Labor Force in Industry

|              | 1960 | 1979 |
|--------------|------|------|
| Yemen PDR    | 15   | 15   |
| Nicaragua    | 16   | 14   |
| Ecuador      | 19   | 18   |
| Paraguay     | 19   | 19   |
| Jordan       | 26   | 19   |
| Jamaica      | 25   | 25   |
| Chile        | 20   | 20   |
| South Africa | 30   | 29   |
| Argentina    | 36   | 28   |

areas fails to account for the fact that there is a *range* of low-wage areas, and those that are most involved in industrial exports to the Western countries are *not* the *lowest* wage areas.

While Third World countries demonstrate some diversification of trading partners in manufacturing exports, there is little in the way of diversification in the export of primary products: the major exports are still directed toward the developed economies.

The growth of industrialization is financed by primary goods exports to the advanced countries. In a period of recession and declining demands within the developed countries, there is declining possibilities of continuing industrial growth within this framework. Greater emphasis and importance on local or regional markets and exchanges are likely to emerge. The deepening downturn in the advanced capitalist countries is leading to increasing pressure for protectionism, less demand for primary materials, less finance capital available for overseas financing. The crisis of export industrialization could lead to even greater and more decisive pressure for structural changes to widen the home market: the convergence of development imperatives and redistributive pressure could lead to significant political and social conflicts in precisely those middle income countries which have advanced the furthest on the industrial front. The industrialization process in some countries has also been adversely affected by a multiplicity of factors with the result that the proportion of industrial workers employed over a two decade period has declined (see Table 3.14).

The causes for stagnation are numerous: the migration of skilled and unskilled labor from Yemen to the oil-rich Gulf States; the civil war and the destruction of industry during the late 1970s in Nicaragua; the pursuit of free-market economic policies in Chile and Argentina, which has contributed to the decline of local industries under the impact of cheap foreign imports. The process of industrial growth is not a linear one spreading throughout the Third World; it reflects the uneven growth of capital on a world scale, the alignment of class forces, and elaboration of internal development policies. The absence of a cohesive industrializing class linked to a coherent policy, promoting an internal market and selective insertion in the international market has hindered the growth of a growing number of previously industrializing countries.

## Finance Capital and Industrialization

The growth of industrial enterprises has not been primarily a result of the redeployment of industries from the west. Though foreign capital financed 10 to 20 percent of total investments in the Third World in the 1960s and 1970s, most of the flow of capital, especially in the 1970s, was increasingly in the form of commercial loans (see Table 3.15).

The shift from direct investments to commercial loans reflects the transfer of capital from industrial productive activity to finance and banking in the developed countries. The decline of industry in the West is not so much due to its deployment abroad as it is because of shifts toward nonproductive activity and its increasing flow abroad as loan capital. The greater attractiveness of indirect investment is due to the higher rates of profit, the low risk, and the relative immunity from class struggle and nationalist expropriation. Any defaults would jeopardize a county's standing with all lender countries, since loans are increasingly lent by consortiums.

The growth of industry in the Third World has been mainly through state-promoted and -financed local investment, not foreign direct investment; external financing of state and local investment has been increasing in importance, especially the financing of trade and the import of capital inputs and technology. The growth of Third World industrialization is directly related to the internal transformation of capital in the advanced capitalist countries, in particular the United States and England: The greater the growth of finance capital, the greater the growth of industrial capital in the Third World.

The second point important to note is that almost all commercial bank lending was concentrated in the more developed Third World countries (see Table 3.15). Eight countries (Mexico, Venezuela, Algeria, Brazil, Argentina, and South Korea) accounted for over 50 percent of total bank debt outstanding in 1979. Finance capital does not go to the lowest wage and income areas where the productive forces are least developed and therefore costliest to start up and where there are less tangible assets to attach. Finance capital flows to those countries where the productive forces are already in place and where there is a regime heavily oriented toward export growth (which can provide the foreign exchange for interest payment remittances) and possesses a capacity to extract surplus value from labor to meet payments. Capital is recycled to semi-industrialized Third World countries, thus absorbing a disportionate amount of capital to develop their productive forces; yet insofar as variable interest rates lead to increased interest payments to finance capital, the long-term effect may be to put a squeeze on new investment.

Table 3.15 Oil-importing Developing Countries' Current Account Deficit and Finance Sources, 1970–1980 (in billions of 1978 dollars)

| | Oil Importers | | | | | | | | | |
| | Low income | | | | | Middle income | | | | |
| Item | 1970 | 1973 | 1975 | 1978 | 1980 | 1970 | 1973 | 1975 | 1978 | 1980 |
|---|---|---|---|---|---|---|---|---|---|---|
| Current Account Deficit[a] | 3.6 | 4.9 | 7.0 | 5.1 | 9.1 | 14.9 | 6.7 | 42.8 | 20.4 | 48.9 |
| Financed by | | | | | | | | | | |
| Net capital flows | | | | | | | | | | |
| ODA | 3.4 | 4.1 | 6.6 | 5.1 | 5.7 | 3.3 | 5.3 | 5.3 | 6.5 | 7.9 |
| Private direct investment | 0.3 | 0.2 | 0.4 | 0.2 | 0.2 | 3.4 | 5.1 | 3.8 | 4.6 | 4.5 |
| Commercial loans | 0.5 | 0.6 | 0.8 | 0.9 | 0.7 | 8.9 | 13.7 | 21.0 | 29.4 | 27.1 |
| Changes in reserves and short-term borrowing[b] | −0.5 | −1.1 | −0.7 | −1.1 | 2.4 | −0.8 | −11.7 | 12.7 | −20.1 | 9.5 |
| Memorandum Item: Current account deficit as percentage of GNP | 1.9 | 2.4 | 3.9 | 2.6 | 4.5 | 2.6 | 1.0 | 5.5 | 2.3 | 5.0 |

[a] Excludes net official transfers (grants), which are included in capital flows.
[b] A minus sign (−) indicates an increase in reserves.

The outcome of the tension between the inflows of capital and outflows of interest depends upon whether the capital inflows locate in productive sectors which can capture external markets and thus generate earnings to pay back loans; if not, the cumulative interest payments can become a serious obstacle to sustained development of the productive forces and can lead to stagnation.

The scope and growing importance of finance capital involvement in the third world is indicated by a recent World Bank Study:

> Banks' gross claims on oil importers rose from 49.6 percent of total bank capital in 1975 to 61.5 percent in 1978, while claims on developing countries as a percentage of total assets rose from 2.6 percent to 2.9 percent. For U.S. banks, the ratio of developing country loans to capital rose from 49.4 percent (1975) to 57.5 percent (1978) and the ratio of loans to total assets rose from 3.6 percent to 4 percent. [*World Development Report 1981* (World Bank), p. 61]

Investment capital was rapidly displaced by finance capital. The multinational corporations rapidly adapted to the new context, becoming increasingly integrated with the finance capital. These changes were duly noted in the World Bank study:

> After 1975, foreign equity investment did not even keep up with inflation. However, with the expansion of commercial bank lending, the form of foreign investment in developing countries itself changed. Intra-company loans supplemented equity participation. The financing needs of transnational companies were covered increasingly from sources other than the parent company, such as borrowing from local banks or the Euro-currency market.

Private commercial bank lending was the component of external finance that grew most rapidly, from about $4 billion in 1970 to $36.1 billion in 1980. By the end of 1980, the outstanding debt of the developing countries to private sources of market capital had reached $284 billion, up from $32 billion in 1970.

The growth of finance capital has also had a significant effect in reducing official (state) bilateral and multilateral lending, obvious competitors in the loan business. As a recently published study noted:

> Over the past decade, there has been a sharp fall in the share of net borrowing from bilateral official sources; a marginal increase in the share coming from multilateral institutions; and a large increase in the proportion of loans from private creditors—especially from financial institutions. As a result, debt to private creditors increased at 28 percent a year, debt to financial institutions at 41 percent a year. Private financial institutions held 12 percent of outstanding private and publically guaranteed debt in 1970 and some 43 percent in 1980. . . . The share of official creditors in the debt of the middle income oil importers fell from 43 percent in

1970 to 27 percent in 1980, while private creditors accounted for almost three-quarters of the total by 1980. [*World Bank Report 1981*, p. 57]

While the role of the state lending was important in the initial stages of economic expansion, in particular for the "middle income industrializing countries," over the past decade private banks have come to dominate the financial markets of the more dynamic Third World countries. Low-income Third World countries in the early stages of accumulation still depend on official state financing. State loans finance the large-scale, long-term investments that create market conditions, productive forces, and a wage labor force which subsequently encourages capital investment. It is in this context that private commercial finance capital moves in to capture interest earnings.

STAGE I (initial accumulation)
multi-lateral and state financing                    local, state and private investment

STAGE II
finance capital (commercial banks)              local, state and private capital and multinational firms

The industrializing Third World economies have become much more integrated into the financial networks of international capital and less tied to the overseas development agencies and the multinational corporations. On the other hand, the least industrialized economies have witnessed a decline in net capital flows in real terms after 1975. This decline in loans and aid to the so-called poor countries reflects the lack of interest by the private sector in long-term investments (and initial low earnings), the unattractiveness of the internal market (small consumer demand). The political concerns over possible social upheavals that motivated official state loans to finance economic and social development has been replaced by increasing arms sales and programs. The West—the U.S. government in particular—is more willing to contain political threats resulting from economic stagnation through repression than economic development.

Faced with an incapacity to develop their productive forces, the less industrialized Third World countries have taken to exporting labor. The Third World oil exporters are in the process of converting rent income into industrial capital and in the process are draining labor from the labor reserves of the poorest countries. The latter category of countries became, in turn, a kind of rentier labor contractor state. As one study notes:

Most of [the poorest of the developing countries] benefited from the oil exporters' increased economic prosperity through the export of labor and the corresponding inflow of remittances. Total remittances to the developing countries mainly from Europe and from the Gulf countries rose from about 3.5 billion in 1970 to 24 billion in 1980—two billion more than the developing countries total ODA receipts and equivalent to about 13 percent of the major recipient economies merchandise exports.

Labor surplus from primary commodity producer states moves to the new sites of accumulation in the rentier states as the industrial cycle begins to take hold. The global convergence that provides rent income and surplus labor produces accelerated growth—one which, however, accentuates the unevenness between "rentier" and "primary producing" Third World states. The capital-intensive nature of the industrial growth and the lack of national anchorage for much of the working class means that the stability of employment is quite limited. Once industry is in place, labor exports will decline, and labor will be repatriated. Meanwhile, the bulk of remittances has not been invested in productive activity, but rather in consumer items or commercial activity, thus lessening the prospects for long-term industrial transformation in the labor-export countries.

The increasing industrialization of the Third World has, however, not been aided significantly by the accumulation of rent income in the oil exporter states. The trade, financial, and investment nexus has led to greater integration between the industrialized countries and the oil-exporters. The latter spent 44 percent of their export earnings on imports from the advanced capitalist countries and only 8 percent on imports from the Third World. The conversion of rent income, appropriated from Third World and advanced capitalist countries, draws in its wake labor from the Third World, finance capital, high technology, and consumer goods and arms from the industrial countries. Only the deepening and diversification of industry among the advanced Third World countries allows them to increase their share of the market among the rentier states.

The shift in the composition of capital within the advanced capitalist countries and the growing importance of private finance capital is leading to a profit squeeze on the industrializing Third World countries. For private loans, the average maturities for loans fell from 20 years in 1970 to 12.7 years in 1980. Grants as a percentage of debt dropped from 32 percent in 1970 to 6 percent in 1979. Shorter maturities and higher interest rates mean that the net transfers are less. In 1970, after amortization and interest payments 43 percent of borrowed funds were available for development; in 1980 the figure was only 22 percent. Clearly debt payments and bank accumulation are putting a tremendous squeeze on the productive forces: fictitious capital is increasingly subordinating productive capital to its needs, extending and deepening the crisis from the already stagnant industrialized countries to the newly industrializing countries.

# 4

# A Critique of Structuralist State Theorizing

JAMES PETRAS
STEPHEN GUNDLE

In recent years there has been a remarkable upsurge of interest in the state as an object of social inquiry and analysis. It would certainly be no exaggeration to assert that in the past decade and a half the state has been elevated from a position of secondary importance to one at the forefront of political and sociological discussion. On the whole, this upsurge of interest is to be welcomed. Current discussions reflect a reaction against both the tendency to reduce the state to the status of a political afterthought, a mere receptacle of economic pressures, and the tendency to bypass the state in favor of analysis of "public policy", "public administration", "government", and the like. To a large degree, the new wave of interest represents a positive move away from simplistic and misleading modes of studying the distribution of power and should be seen as a part of the general revival of interest in the "superstructure" of society which followed the tumultuous events in Western societies in the late 1960s and has sharpened as a result of recent developments in certain of Western Europe's Communist parties.

The centrality of the struggle for power, which has been characteristic of twentieth-century revolutionary movements, has also perhaps been instrumental in increasing the attention paid to the state. In recent decades popular forces in several parts of the "third world", including Cuba, Vietnam and Nicaragua, have succeeded in displacing existing ruling classes and seizing state power, while in other parts this struggle is still continuing. The problem of the nature of the state and the manner in which it can be taken over and either transformed or dismantled is therefore a vital topic for analysis. Further impetus to

This essay was first published in *Contemporary Crises* 6 (1982), pp. 161–82. © Elsevier Scientific Publishing Company, Amsterdam; reprinted by permission.

the study of the state is found in the incorporation of Socialist and Communist parties within the state in the advanced capitalist societies. Social Democratic parties in Austria, West Germany, and Sweden have almost become "natural" parties of government in their respective capitalist countries, while Communists in France, Italy, Spain, and Japan participate in the administration of the state at the local level and have become ensnared within national parliamentary politics. In these cases, discussion of the state has served an ulterior purpose in providing a political rationale for reformism and an ideological rationale for new rising strata within the party-organizational machinery.

The discussion of the state has also highlighted the complexity of interaction between state and society and, in the best of cases, the connecting linkages or collective mediations between them. No longer is there any discussion of a simple and mechanical transmission between the economic "base" and the societal "superstructure". The debates over the nature of the state and the fashion of conceptualizing the state-society relationship have embraced different strands of opinion and given rise to several markedly contrasting schools of thought. The intellectual products which have emerged are of varying degrees of usefulness in understanding the historical meaning and empirical content of state-class relations. In particular, Althusser and his followers have been responsible for the propagation of a variety of inadequate and misleading conceptions which in some quarters have assumed the same mystifying role and hallowed status of old and discredited formulae. The work of Poulantzas has been especially influential in two crucial areas which have been the sites of the greatest controversies: the mode of conceptualizing the state-ruling class relationship and the implications for the struggle for socialism which arise from the conceptualization of this relationship. The appropriate formulation of these problems is among the concerns of this paper.

The effort to carve out space to discuss the state as an area of study has, in some instances, led toward a tendency to break away from concrete analysis of the interrelationship of state and class structure: the state is constituted as a theoretical "thing-in-itself", and social classes, particularly the ruling class, become devoid of any historical referent. Abstract "fractions" of the ruling class are discussed with reference to the equally abstract and ill-defined "hegemony" of "monopoly capital".

The lack of class specificity is matched by the problem of the obscurity over the meaning of the terms of discussion. A dense fog of impenetrable jargon has enveloped many strands of the debate, depriving them of political relevance. The lack of conceptual specification has had the effect of vitiating the usefulness of much of the analysis. Terms defining the state's behavior in advanced capitalist countries are often assumed to have a universal validity, and the particular representative form of the state presently to be found in these societies is viewed as the normal, or usual, form. Concepts also shift according to context, taking on ad hoc meanings according to the particular problem to which they are directed. In Poulantzas these problems of analysis are compounded by an inability to grasp either the historical character of the state as a changing entity or its concrete empirical form within a social formation.

One of the key notions that tantalizes many writers and which has led to confusion is the "relative autonomy of the state", a formula sufficiently slippery to allow for a variety of loose constructions and improvised analysis which leaves little room for rigorous and systematic study. Lacking any fixed locus in historical time and space, the notion is often carried to the point where the activities of the state become unified in a conceptually disembodied entity acting on the class structure without any notion of the conjunctural limitations and social boundaries which determine state action and differentiate between different kinds of state. In these cases, the state subsumes the class and social structure and, in the true spirit of the Hegelian ideal of the state, fashions the whole ensemble of activities. All class struggles and political movements are understood through the development of the state. However, since the state bears the burden of all significant social action, there is nothing left to explain the origins and concrete development of the state, unless a notion equivalent to social or political parthenogenesis is introduced.

The responsibility for theorizing and propagating the notion "relative autonomy" lies to a large degree with Poulantzas, whose work on political power and the state must be subjected to a vigorous critique if future discussion is to proceed along a path which is both analytically fruitful and free of theoretical aridity.

## Poulantzas and the State

The focus of the majority of Poulantzas' work is on the state in advanced capitalist society. It represents an attempt to constitute a theory of the state from the allusions and fragmentary discussions to be found in the classical texts of Marxism. In two books, *Political Power and Social Classes* and *State, Power, Socialism*, a comprehensive theoretical scheme is mapped out, embracing formulations on the form and functioning of the state, the composition and reproduction of class power, and the state-society relationship, each of which has had a profound influence on discussions of the state.[1] The reasons underlying the extent of this influence cannot be reduced to any single consideration, although two factors are clearly of importance. Firstly, the original French publication of *Political Power and Social Classes* coincided with the events of May 1968, which gave a practical demonstration of the inadequacy of traditional Maxist interpretations of politics and society and of the need for new analyses.[2] Secondly, Poulantzas benefited from the fashion for structuralist Marxism in the 1960s and early 1970s which followed publication of Althusser's two books of essays on Marx.[3] The superficial rigor and apparent originality of his ideas provides a third reason for the success enjoyed by this body of work. On closer examination, these attributes are found wanting, for in reality Poulantzas' conceptualization of the state is marked by incoherence and inconsistency. Insofar as political prescriptions for socialist strategy are elaborated, these merely serve to provide a new and theoretically sophisticated legitimacy for reformism.

Poulantzas presents the definitive account of what is often called the "stuctural-relational" concept of the state. The state is conceptualized not as a simple instrument of the ruling class which is set apart from society but as a relationship within the structure of capitalism: the political relationship of dominance of the bourgeoisie over the working class and the other subordinate classes. The state crystallizes the domination of capital over labor[4] and is the material condensation of the relationship of class forces in society. The class relations of capitalism are seen as being inscribed in the bureaucratic and hierarchical relations which constitute the state. Political power therefore is not an attribute of particular institutions but is a reflection of the ability of a class to promote its political position in the class struggle. It is based on class relations and exercised through the apparatus of the state. The conception of the state as located in the class relationships of a social formation is crucial to the manner in which the relation between class struggle and the state apparatus is analyzed by Poulantzas.

The "power bloc" is the central concept used in analyzing the relationship between class struggle and the state. It includes all the segments or fractions of the bourgeoisie, a class which is internally divided by the competition of different capitals and by the contradictory position of various forms of capital in the circuit of the extended reproduction of capital, as well as the dominant classes of other modes of production which are present in society although subordinate to the capitalist mode of production. Each class fraction inside the power bloc occupies a place within the state apparatus, although the state as a whole is seen as relatively autonomous of any individual class fraction. Under the hegemony of the leading bourgeois fraction, the power bloc is unified and organized politically through the state apparatus. The power of different fractions within the power bloc is represented and exercised through their occupation of particular branches and agencies of the state apparatus. A unified and coherent policy for the power bloc is formulated through the process of "structural selectivity" between the branches and agencies of the state apparatus. The filtering of both decisions and non-decisions is permitted by the hierarchy of the various branches and agencies in which the relations between various fractions of the power bloc are manifested. In this way the disagreements and contradictions within the bourgeoisie are resolved inside the institutional framework of the state, allowing capital to achieve a certain degree of unity in its struggle with the working class and other subordinate classes in society.

The organizational stucture of the state is seen as sufficiently flexible to allow the centers of the exercise of political power to be shifted inside the state from one branch or agency to another, with changes in the relationship of forces within the power bloc. Such permutations between the different class fractions within the power bloc are provoked by shifts in the balance of forces between the power bloc and the dominated classes. But the state has a double political function: it not only organizes the class struggle of capital, it also disorganizes the class struggles of those who are oppressed and exploited by capital. The process of disorganization is accomplished primarily through the integration of certain dominated classes and strata into subordinate positions within the hierarchical framework which constitutes the state apparatus. Thus, although the working class and other subordinate classes may be present in the state, the state as the material condensation of the power of the dominant class functions to reproduce their position as dominated classes. The struggles of dominated classes inside and outside the state do have some effect on state policy but should be seen principally as points of resistance to the struggle of capital which is unified by the state itself.

To summarize briefly, Poulantzas views the state as the product of a certain relationship of class forces characterized by the ability of capital successfully to maintain and reproduce capitalist relations of exploitation. This relationship of class forces, which is the basis of capitalist political power, is evidenced in the state apparatus. Thus, while remaining relatively autonomous of any particular capitalist fraction, including the hegemonic fraction, the state organizes and unifies the class struggle of capital while disorganizing the struggles of dominated classes.

Within Poulantzas' discussion of the state, several specific theoretical and methodological problems may be isolated. Grounded in what is termed "the Marxist scientific problematic", the approach to the analysis of the state is uncompromisingly theoretical. Concepts are developed not as a result of empirical work but on the basis of a reading of the classical texts of Marx, Engels, Lenin, and, to a lesser extent, Gramsci. These texts themselves constitute the object of the analysis, not the actuality of politics and the state. The approach is therefore not only theoretical but also abstract in that the concepts which are developed are purported to be universal and scientific while actually being completely devoid of concrete referent. Difficulties become apparent when efforts are made to utilize such concepts for historical or empirical analysis: their static and abstract character does not lend itself to the analysis of ongoing processes. The problem of operational notions to cut into reality becomes extremely difficult. The method employed usually results in an analysis which takes the following form: an elaborate framework is outlined in the introduction; this is followed by a detailed, if often schematic and anecdotal, account of the events or processes under discussion which is accompanied by the insertion, on an ad hoc basis, of particular notions as descriptive labels in an attempt to link the theoretical framework to historical or contemporary analysis. In any study in which this approach is adopted, Poulantzas' assertion that there is always "a structural distance between theory and practice, between theory and the real" is embodied with a vengeance.

The problem of theoreticism in Poulantzas is related to the location of his work within the theoretical world of structuralist Marxism, whose practitioners, through an emphasis on a highly technical and inaccessible theoretical practice, have succeeded in radically separating theory from both political practice and from reflection within the working class movement. In this way the social division of labor between intellectuals and workers is reinforced and intellectual elitism relaunched as a point of scholarly principle.[5]

The precise relationship between Poulantzas and his intellectual master Althusser is not always clear nor is their relation to structuralism as developed by Saussure, Lévi-Strauss, and others. Poulantzas has admitted in an interview that "there are some remnants of structuralism in Althusser and the rest of us, in the theoretical conjuncture in which we were working". It is clear that his analysis of the state-society relationship relies heavily on Althusser's theory of structuralist causality and on the determination of economic, political, and ideological "levels" or "instances" in society.[6] The deployment of this framework gives rise to a basic theoretical, practical question which Poulantzas cannot adequately answer: if capitalism is conceived as a structure and social classes as over-determined and complex effects of the unity of the instances within the structure, what concrete role is played by the class struggle? As class struggle cannot be presented as a subsidiary effect of the mechanical movement of the instances of the structure, the category of "practice" is used in an attempt to resolve the problem. An element of dualism enters the analysis here, since practice cannot be fully integrated into the framework of structuralist causality but only posited as a complement to it. Each element within a social formation is therefore presented twice in the analysis, as the "effect of the structure" and as the "effect of a practice". This problem occurs first in *Political Power and Social Classes* and is not resolved in later works.

Dualism, no matter how skillfully disguised, cannot conceal the analytical and intellectual gap left by the absence of the subject from any model of structuralism. In the exposition of the articulation of the instances of the structure and the various class practices, there is no place for any human element, whether in the form of a class or an individual. The displacement of the subject from the center of analysis has a distorting effect on the study of politics since it removes any possibility of grasping the historical or empirical content of particular institutions and actors. Objective interests and structural determinations also override any consideration of spontaneity and consciousness. By banishing such factors, Poulantzas arguably succeeds in transcending psychological and personalized interpretations of the class struggle, but in the process he foregoes any possibility of accounting for the paradoxes and contradictions which arise in the intensity of heightened class struggle. Realizing the poverty of analysis which is produced by this deficiency, Poulantzas resorts to ad hoc devices which are completely incompatible with a structuralist model in order to capture the spirit of otherwise unexplainable subjective class interests and action: namely, anthropomorphic terminology. For example, in the case of the bourgeois revolution in Germany, it is said that one of the errors of judgment of the bougeoisie was that it "could not make up its mind" to break with the nobility and that it found itself confronted with an organized workers' movement when it "finally woke up".[7]

The relationship between the state and the ruling class and its correct conceptualization forms a central problem in Poulantzas. The categories of "power bloc", "hegemony", and "class fraction" represent key elements in an analysis which seeks to go beyond the idea, which was predominant in Marxist orthodoxy for several decades, that the state in class societies is the simple instrument of whichever class is dominant. However, the mode in which each of these categories is conceptualized prevents the formulation of a coherent alternative theorization of the state-ruling class relationship. Each category is developed and integrated into an abstract theoretical whole separated from the empirical world, with the result that none is operationalizable as a tool of analysis. The entire framework used to conceptualize political power and the state does not even enjoy a reflective relation to reality; it is situated uncompromisingly above and apart from it. Furthermore, each individual category is conceptually deficient, either through vagueness or internal inconsistency.

Two elementary difficulties may be located in the conceptualization of social classes. Firstly, Poulantzas fails to elaborate a concept of class which is independent of his definition of class interest. Class is defined in terms of ownership of a factor of production, such as capital, land, or labor, which in turn gives rise to the economic, political, and ideological interests of the class. As a result, the definition of class is nothing more or less than a tautology. The second problem concerns the notion of class fraction. Despite the centrality of this term in Poulantzas' analysis of the ruling class and the exercise of political power, its definition is left curiously imprecise. It may be more or less deduced that a class fraction is a sector of the ruling class based on the political organization of a particular capital or combination of capitals. Such a definition, however, creates further difficulties. How, for example, does a class fraction differ from the old-fashioned interest group which figures so prominently in political science textbooks? Only in terms of its economic roots. Even this serves to obscure the problem, for, if fractions arise as a result of political contradictions within the capitalist mode of production, for example, between monopoly and non-monopoly capital, then the number of possible or potential fractions would seem to be limitless. Every time a conflict occurs within capital, a new fraction should make its appearance on the political scene. Yet how would such a fraction be identified? Since not all groups in the political scene are related to classes, the methodological problem of identifying with precision which groups are class fractions and which are not is considerable.

The confusion surrounding the notion of class fraction derives in part from the awkward fact that, although Poulantzas attempts to locate it within Marxist class theory, no such notion is present in Marx's own works. A similar term employed by Marx is that of "faction", which is to be found in *The Eighteenth Brumaire of Louis Bonaparte* and other works. But the term "faction" simply refers to a transitory alignment of interests on a single issue, not to a constitutive division of the bourgeoisie. To support the argument that the idea of fractions can be legitimately read into Marx, Poulantzas is compelled to rely on two quotations from Engels and the assertion that fractions are implicit in Marx's conceptualization of class.[8] The latter claim merits a brief examination. Poulantzas suggests that by using terms such as "coalition", "union", and "fusion", Marx implied that several fractions of the bourgeoisie co-exist in political domination. However, these terms clearly entail the idea of the fundamental unity of capital, whereas "fraction" suggests division and separation. For Marx, commercial, industrial, and financial capital are not separate capitals, as Poulantzas sees them, but rather separate forms of the same capital. Poulantzas views capital as intrinsically divided, only united through the state and in relation to labor; the notion of capital-in-general is completely absent. This view diverges from that of Marx, who explicitly located the unity of capital in the fundamental relations of production.

A concept such as that of "power bloc" is the necessary corollary of the idea of fractions. Having divided the dominant class into competing and contradictory fractions, Poulantzas must explain the political unity of this class or, at the very least, the limits of its political disunity. The power bloc is the concept employed to perform this function. It "indicates the particular contradictory unity of the politically dominant classes or fractions of classes as related to a particular form of the capitalist state."[9] In other words, it represents the political coalescence of the dominant class in capitalist society under the direction of its most powerful segment. But the notion of the power bloc is not free of conceptual flaws. As used by Poulantzas and his various disciples, it is a purely descriptive category which adds little to analysis except to label a particular configuration of power without tracing the origins and internal development of the social forces involved. It functions simply as a device to indicate the political unity of capital after its conceptual division into fractions.

It is by no means clear that the idea of a power bloc is of use even as a descriptive category. By referring to only a "relative homogeneity" in the relations between the components of the power bloc, Poulantzas unwittingly undermines the power bloc itself.[10] If one begins with the idea of class fractions whose number and relative power is subject to continued change, it must be assumed that the composition of the power bloc is also subject to change. Thus, the ability of the power bloc to function as a bloc at all must fluctuate. This instability limits the extent to which the power bloc can be usefully employed as a means of describing the organization of political power in capitalist society.

Further difficulties arise in attempting to identify empirically the "hegemonic fraction" within the power bloc, i.e., the particular fraction which plays a dominant role in relation to the other fractions in the power bloc. In the face of the increasing internationalization of capital and shifting fractional alliances, identification poses a major method-ological problem. Yet Poulantzas gives no precise criteria for identifying which fraction is hegemonic, with the result that the problem of identification is rendered largely subjective in practice. Difficulties such as this occur partly because the notion of hegemonic fraction, like those of class fraction and power bloc, is not truly a practical concept designed to be utilized in empirical analysis. Its origins, function, and role are entirely contained in the great theoretical artifice which Poulantzas has constructed to explain the state. The problems which have been located in the concepts used to analyze the relationship between the state and the ruling class are compounded by confusion on the question of power and a muddled notion of hegemony.

Hegemony plays a double function. Gramsci's idea is taken in order to describe, but not to specify or analyze, the means by which one fraction of the ruling class politically dominates the other fractions. By extension, it is also used to denote the class leadership which the ruling class as a whole exercises over the rest of the social totality. Yet Gramsci is constantly derided for failing to give a true theoretical grounding to the concept to hegemony, which remains a "practical concept" in all his writings.[11] Poulantzas attempts to correct this deficiency by incor-porating the concept into his own theoretical universe, but in so doing he mutilates Gramsci's original idea by reducing its practical function to description and restricting its field of application to the political practices of the dominant class. It is of course true that hegemony is not fully developed in Gramsci, but it is precisely the quality of practicality dismissed by Poulantzas that allows it to be fruitfully employed in analysis.

Poulantzas' confusion over the problem of power arises from the dichotomy between structure and practice. In structuralist analyses of the state, power is not a property of particular institutions but rather a relationship: the capacity of a social class to realize specific objectives in the class struggle. Power relations would therefore appear to be equivalent to class relations. But power only properly exists insofar as it is organized in actual institutions ("power centers") which, since they possess an autonomy and "structural specificity" of their own, are not simply instruments of the power of social classes.[12] The question therefore arises of how power relations can be equivalent to class relations when power centers are not centers of class power. This contradiction can be resolved on a superficial level but only with a further reinforcement of dualism. Poulantzas does this by consigning power and class relations to the realm of class practices while relating power centers to "the structure", as the organizing matrix of institutions. Nevertheless, a real problem remains unresolved here. Poulantzas fails to grasp concretely the meaning of power; he operates a narrow and exclusive conception of political power which orders and links together the political concepts of power bloc, politically dominant class, and hegemony without any basis in an analysis of capital accumulation and class struggle. The political level is therefore split off from the global system of power relations in society, aloof from and structurally autonomous of the economic. It is in this context that the idea of the relative autonomy of the state must be examined.

## Relative Autonomy of the State

"Relative autonomy" is a notion that has become common currency in the analysis of the state, yet it is a category which not only fails to explain the social and political relationships within a social formation but actually serves to obscure them. This nebulous and often imprecise notion is used variously to describe the relationships between certain spheres of society and also relations within these spheres: politics are "relatively autonomous" of the economy; the state is "relatively autonomous" of the ruling class; the various branches of the state and fractions of the ruling class are all "relatively autonomous" of one another, and so on. A whole series of complex and often contradictory relationships within society is analyzed in terms of the same vague category. The multiple dimensions in which the term is used point to its elasticity and the role it plays as a catch-all bag for a variety of theoretical perspectives that allow the drawing of a wide range of conclusions. Use of the term is by no means confined to Poulantzas, although "relative autonomy" is central to his conceptualization of the state. "Relative atuonomy of the state" as seen by Poulantzas will therefore be examined in some detail before problems of a more general nature are discussed and possible alternative conceptualizations considered.

Originally, relative autonomy was used to overcome the idea that the superstructure of a society is a simple reflection of its economic base and the related idea that the state in capitalist societies is simply the political instrument of the dominant class. It is used by Poulantzas to establish the political as an "autonomous and specific object of science" and to review the interrelationship of political power, the state and social classes.[13] It permits distinct conceptualizations of separate instances and practices within the "complex whole" of a social formation and the transcending of the base-superstructure model: "the economic, the political and the ideological are not already constituted essences, which then enter into external relations with each other, according to a schema of base and superstructure . . . ".[14] But, although relative autonomy performs this role, it does not actually clarify the nature of the relationship between the economic and other levels; it merely posits a static conceptual separation which gives no real indication of their complex functional interrelationship. The concrete problems of how the economic, the political, and the ideological are integrated within a social formation, of how each conditions the others and their collective interaction, is scarcely discussed. It is merely stated that the nature of the relations between the different levels is governed by the structure, which embraces them all, assigns them their places, and distributes functions to them within a social totality.[15] This tautological proposition is of no use whatsoever in empirical analysis.

In a famous letter written to J. Bloch in 1890, Engels talks of a reciprocity between base and superstructure: "According to the materialist conception of history, the ultimately determining element in history is the production and reproduction of real life".[16] The theory of the economic being "the ultimately determining element", or determinant in the last instance, although raised to the level of dogma in certain varieties of Marxism, was never more than an extraordinarily vague and inadequate theory of social causation. It clearly fails to give any indication of how the nature of the determination may be measured or linked analytically to the empirical world. As long ago as 1935, Karl Korsch suggested that this theory was of no use as a workable hypothesis:

> Without an exact quantitative determination of 'how much' action and reaction takes place, without an exact indication of the conditions under which one or the other occurs, the whole Marxian theory of the historical development of society . . . becomes useless . . . And the logic of the matter is not affected by such verbal evasions as 'primary' and 'secondary' factors or by the classification of causes into 'proximate', 'mediate' and 'ultimate', i.e. those which prove decisive 'in the last analysis'.[17]

The attempt by Poulantzas and others to replace Engels' principle with a theory of structural causation may be subjected to much the same criticism. Despite its pretensions to be scientific, the structuralist model contains no quantitative determination of the interaction and interpenetration of the economic, political, and ideological spheres or any indication of the conditions under which such movements occur. It is also true that the structuralist model of a social formation shaped by a multiplicity of determinations is not free of reductionism, the very problem it seeks to overcome.

The idea of relative autonomy has paradoxically produced a hybrid form of social analysis in which the link between politics and economics has been both weakened and obscured, while vestiges of reductionism still remain. This inconsistency is a prominent feature of Poulantzas' work. Two aspects of the conceptual separation of the political and the economic are problematic. Firstly, the state is set apart from the valorization process with the result that the needs of capitalist accumulation and state policy are not directly linked. Production of surplus value is seen as taking place in the economy, while only its distribution is mediated by the state. This problem arises from the second problematic aspect: the clear distinction that is drawn between the economic interests of the dominant class and its political interests. The role of the state in this model is to organize the political struggle of the dominant class. The state is seen as being completely absent from the sphere of economic struggle. For this reason, the mode in which the political is separated from the economic is both artificial and dangerous; it produces a situation in which politics cannot be analyzed in terms of contradictions in the relations of exploitations which are the major force of social change.

This conceptual separation relies in part on an asocial conception of the economic. Poulantzas strips the economic of any social aspects by restricting its field to specific individual material interests, thereby ascribing all social characteristics to the political level of a social formation. In practice this means that a class must be based on a specific material interest, but it can only become fully fledged and assume a social form when it exhibits pertinent effects at the political and ideological levels through class struggle. This much at least is clear in the statement that a class "can only be considered as a distinct and atuonomous class, as a social force, inside a social formation, only when its connection with the relations of production, its economic existence, is reflected on the other levels by a specific presence".[18] In other words, it is claimed that classes are demarcated in terms of material interests but only properly exist through political representation. It is at this point that the problem of reductionism arises, for, if this idea is to have any practical meaning or application, the political must be directly reducible to the economic: parties and political groups must be simple reflections of economic interests. The only other alternative would be to sever completely the links between politics and economics and adopt a pluralist model. This option, however, cannot be seriously entertained within a Marxist conception of the state.[19]

Relative autonomy lies at the center of Poulantzas' discussion of the state. The relative autonomy of the contemporary state vis-à-vis the dominant class is held to be a reflection of "a new articulation of the political and the economic in the relations between the structures and the field of the class struggle", which is constitutive of the capitalist type of state.[20] By means of a reading of *The Eighteenth Brumaire of Louis Bonaparte*, Poulantzas seeks to enlist Marx and Engels in support of his claim that relative autonomy is a defining feature of the state in capitalist society:

> Marx and Engels' texts concerning Bonapartism contain in the first place the analysis of a concrete political phenomenon in a determinate formation. However parallel to this, Marx and Engels *systematically conceive* Bon-

apartism not simply as a concrete form of the capitalist state, *but as a constitutive theoretical characteristic of the very type of capitalist state.*[21]

Here Poulantzas establishes a rudimentary theoretical justification for his generalization of concepts to be found in Marx and Engels' analysis of the French state under Louis Napoleon into generic features of the capitalist state. This operation is carried out despite the fact that no such generalization may be found in the texts themselves where the degree of autonomy of the state from the ruling class is explicitly presented as a feature of the specific historical conditions under which Bonapartism prevailed.[22] Autonomy only emerged in the short term as a result of a temporary dislocation within a social formation. It arose, like Bonapartism itself, as a result of transitory contradictions in the ruling class.

The idea of relative autonomy requires specification in terms of historical time period. If the notion of relativity is only employed as a means of establishing linkages between arbitrary theoretical boundaries, it cannot indicate whether autonomy is a function of immediate circumstances (conjuncture), medium term tendencies (historical stage), or long-term trends (historical epoch). Theorizing on the basis of conjunctural circumstances, in the manner of Poulantzas' treatment of Bonapartism, has the effect of transforming moving configurations of social forces into systemic categories. This form of generalization, which is also to be found in the impressionistic and anecdotal accounts presented in Poulantzas' discussion of modern dictatorship,[23] is a form of sub-theorizing that provides no insights into the long-term, large-scale processes of change. Whatever is present in the form of immediate interests in a conjuncture can become the historic interests of a class, not least as a result of the long-term historic forces discretely operative in the epiphenomenon of a momentary constellation of forces.

Underlying relative autonomy are two distinct notions, relativity and autonomy, which require scrunity. To begin with, the notion of relativity is inherently somewhat imprecise; without specifying precisely and rigorously the spatial entities within or around the social formation under discussion, the term is vacuous. To have any meaning, the problem of relativity must be posed in relation to the class structure and, more specifically, in relation to the process of class formation, the internal composition of class and class relations. This issue cannot be resolved merely by looking at class structure; rather several other key dimensions of the problem must be considered: the impact and determinant role of other states (dominated by their own ruling classes), of state institutions such as the church, and the military and the class interests they embody, and of the class struggle. All these dimensions influence, shape, and ultimately determine the degree of autonomy. In many cases, the notion of relative autonomy indicates a one-sided approach which has the analytical effect of prematurely exhausting the operative class factors determining state power. In such cases, relative autonomy displaces comprehensive class analysis and disguises an incapacity to conceptualize the various mechanisms and channels through which class power determines the state. Finally, the notion of relativity requires a global as well as historical context: what appears as an absence of determinant forces within a particular social formation can be concretely located in the historical expansion of global capitalism. The dissolution of all the boundaries of autonomous state action has been one of the characteristics of the ascension of world imperialism, and, conversely, the wave of revolutionary regimes has created areas of limited maneuverability with new sets of social determinations. In either case, it is not a question of autonomy, relative or otherwise, but of locating the social fulcrum for state action. Abstract political categories devoid of class content are of no use in identifying the position of the state within the world capitalist system, or the particular class forces that are dominant.

If the notion of relativity is an intellectual and political evasion of the problems of class power and class struggle, the notion of autonomy is even more ambiguous. Assuming that there is some spectrum of degrees of autonomy, some specific criteria for assessing these degrees are necessary to even initiate discussion. This operation in turn cannot be meaningfully conducted unless one proceeds to specify the contexts in which autonomy functions. The lack of clarity in these issues has led to the most elusive and ultimately useless forms of theorizing. The meaning of terms is stretched to fit a variety of historical experiences, with little regard for the temporal, spatial, and systemic context.

These tendencies are especially regrettable in state studies, for the original impetus away from economism and dogma toward a grasping of the political, ideological, social, and economic spheres as crucial elements of the same totality was necessary and potentially very promising. The distorted and mechanistic views of the state which depend on ahistorical theoretical efforts and abstract sociologizing for their proofs have not advanced Marxism but rather undermined the development of Marxism as a tool of analysis and a mode of praxis.

There are several problem areas that require attention. The whole idea of state autonomy needs clarification, and the terms of discussion must be specified in such a way as to make the notion operable for rigorous historical and empirical analysis. Such a clarification can only proceed by organizing the discussion within a framework encompassing the class structure located within the larger universe of the world capitalist system.

Outside of a particular historical conjuncture, the state is neither an autonomous force nor a merely derivative phenomenon, but rather an "actualizing" structure linked to the organizations of class power. The specification of state activities is intimately related to the economic and political demands of the ruling class in each historical moment; it is embedded in patterns of capital accumulation and class confrontation.

## A Basis for Relative Autonomy of the State

If any sense is to be made of the notion of the relative autonomy of the state, it must be anchored in an empirical or historical reality. Only by precisely isolating the form of autonomy, the nature of its relativity, and the time sequence within which it occurs, can the elements of vacuity and imprecision, which have characterized its usage hitherto, be overcome. An essential prerequisite for this approach is identification of those features of a social formation which allow for relative autonomy. These can include at least the following:

1. state personnel in influential policy-making positions are not drawn from or related to a single sector of capital, but the entire spectrum of capitalist forces;
2. the scope of state activity is dependent upon the volume of capital accumulation in general; funding of state activity is therefore based on material resources derived from a great diversity of capitalist activity and not from a single sector;
3. the state's extensive network of administration and specialized agencies permits and reproduces an internal motivation and a mode of functioning which are not entirely reducible to capital. Acting through its own channels, with its own personnel and perspective, the state circumscribes and promotes patterns of capital accumulation.

The greater centralization and concentration of capital lessens the autonomy of the state by tying its interests more directly to the state, which in turn functions as the nerve-center of corporate life. On the other hand, the growth of the state apparatus itself, in the present phase of imperialist development, gives the state a scope and a capacity to act which far exceed that of any particular monopolistic corporation. Hence, the state finds itself with less of a role as the arbiter of competitive capitals and yet with more direct involvement in fashioning the framework within which great concentrations of capital operate. The state is at once more autonomous and more instrumental.

As against this conception, there are a number of ahistorical, asocial notions of the relative autonomy of the state that require a brief discussion. The formulations of Althusser, Poulantzas, and others have given rise to the idea that the autonomy of the state is a function of its independence from the class structure. The state is not seen as being subject to specific class determinations and interests but rather as obedient to some abstract "logic of the system". This quasi-functional approach fails to explain, except in an ex post facto fashion, why certain capitalists benefit and why others lose in any particular historical conjuncture. The differential returns to various capitalists simply cannot be explained by the general notion of the state responding to the imperatives of capital. Nor does a category such as "power bloc" add much of significance to analysis beyond abstract designation of the organization of power. Tied to a set of deductive functional conceptions abstracted from history, the notion of relative autonomy is little more than a short-hand device for appropriating a particular moment of empirical reality as the basis for political discussion. The obtuse vocabulary of Poulantzas and many of those influenced by his work provides an illusion of profundity which ultimately cannot disguise the redundancy of this type of "abstracted empiricism" in analyzing long-term, large-scale social changes.

A second erroneous notion is associated with the "Bonapartist state", or "state of exception". Here the state is described as "mediating" between classes and creating its own policies based on its own interests and conceptions of capitalist imperatives. But the idea of the state of exception mistakenly assumes that the capacity of capitalism to renew and reproduce itself within the framework of democracy is a norm and the best system for its development. Such an assumption cannot be historically justified, least of all in the Third World. The conditions for capitalist reproduction are not rooted in any abstract set of social relations, productive forces, or even state-society relations but rather derive from two sets of contradictions: one expressed in the class struggle and the other located in the insertion of the whole ensemble of social relations and productive forces into the world economy. The articular set of mediations which come about within a "Bonapartist" regime reflects a series of capital movements, that in turn reflect struggles between capitals and within productive units between capital and labor. The resolution of these struggles within capitalism, in the assertion of the economic project of a particular sector of capital as that of the ruling class as a whole in relation to labor, leads to the dissolution of any transient state of exception.

Underlying these erroneous notions is a set of indeterminations regarding the interrelationship of the class structure and the state. Static and abstract categories which cannot be fruitfully operationalized can neither clarify nor explain this interrelationship. Clearly, what is required is a set of propositions and a forceful reminder that state-society relations are complex, in flux, and subject to reciprocal influence. There are several interrelated issues that can be identified and that could serve as a point of departure for historical or empirical analysis:

1. the state's representation of capitalist interests is not the identity of these interests;
2. the timing and modes of realization of capitalist interest by the state vary with the forms of legitimation and the capacity of a given state to act coherently within a particular ensemble of political and social forces;
3. for the state to act as a force of repression, ideological and organizational discipline must subsist within the state apparatus;

the class struggle must be absent from the state, and state personnel must be seen to be isolated from the interface of class conflict;
4. the state must be seen dialectically as both interpenetrating with society and standing above it. The state, through public expenditure and provision of services, enters into the reproduction of classes and strata in a way that is both intertwined with and independent of the needs of capital. In relation to the class structure, the institutional structure of the state and its hierarchical organizing principles function to shape the orientations of state personnel and related categories in favor of the existing order. In periods of class polarization and mobilization, the organization of vertical allegiances is subject to cross pressures from the class struggle: the working class and its allies seek to shatter the myth of the ideological neutrality of the state and disarticulate the administrative and repressive apparatuses.

## The State in the Age of Imperialism

In both Europe and the United States, abstracted formulations on the nature of the state have had certain practical political consequences. The absence of comprehensive class analysis has served to heighten the illusory belief in permeationism: the notion that the accession of leading members of workers' parties to the higher reaches of the executive and the legislative of piecemeal changes can act as bridges to socialism. Within this conception, the universe of social and political action shrinks; class struggle is replaced by collaboration with bourgeois forces and the demands of the working class are manipulated and suppressed to permit the historical compromises that enable state permeation. Reality is reconstructed to eliminate the historical experiences and class basis of revolutionary action. The process of class struggle is reduced to a set of political formulae fitted into abritrary stages by bureaucratic tacticians with the aid of intellectual apologists. A static empiricism in interpreting class action fuels a rhetoric of political "realism" which provides an ideological gloss over the whole proceeding.

Poulantzas' discussions of the state must be viewed in the context of these tendencies. Theoretical incoherence and conceptual inconsistency in his work are compounded by elements of reformism which find a more or less explicit expression in *State, Power, Socialism*. In the final chapter of this book, Poulantzas proposes a "democratic road to socialism", which in practice legitimates the aspirations and political orientation of Western Europe's Communist leaderships in the phase of "Eurocommunism".

*State, Power, Socialism*, Poulantzas' final book, reassesses the nature of politics and the state in capitalist societies in the light of the major developments which occurred in the years after *Political Power and Social Classes:* the upheavals of 1968, the new movements of social minorities, the Chilean experience, the advent of Eurocommunism, and the tendency towards authoritarianism in European states. Although some earlier positions are criticized and reformulated, no basic changes are made to the theoretical system elaborated in the earlier work. There is a change of style—notably absent is the air of dogmatism and rigid orthodoxy which pervades *Political Power and Social Classes*—but in the essential approach only changes of emphasis are made. Althusser's concentration on apparatuses is replaced by the idea of the "institutional materiality" of the state as a complex of apparatuses;[24] the notion of the state as the "condensation of the relations of class forces" in its relation to political struggles is explicitly developed;[25] in relation to economic functions, the state is seen as not only producing the general external conditions of production but as actually entering into the constitution of the relations of production.[26] These changes of emphasis are made in order to tailor the model of the state to the changed political conjuncture in Europe. In this enterprise, considerable use is made of the work of Foucault. Here it transpires that the absence of theoretical fixity does not signal serious discussion and engagement of new analyses but rather expropriation of their central ideas. Foucault's notions of "disciplines", "bourgeois discourses", and "techniques of knowledge" are employed in a descriptive fashion as a device for disguising the lacunae and analytical poverty of Poulantzas' own analysis. Poulantzas seeks to assimilate Foucault into his own theoretical universe without confronting the implications of such an assimilation and without recognizing that the latter is developing a distinct problematic. The superficiality of the treatment of Foucault is underlined in the elaboration of the "democratic road to socialism". This strategy is neither novel nor innovative; it consists of a tired reformism in which the class struggle is seen as largely contained within the institutions of representative democracy, and revolution as a protracted process proceeding in stages.

Although the political posture in *Political Power and Social Classes*, in which it is stated that "Lenin said that it was necessary to win state power by smashing the state machine; and I need say no more" would appear to be a straightforward Leninism, there are elements of reformism present in the analysis of the state which are not explicitly linked.[27] Therefore, the reformist positions put forward in *State, Power, Socialism* cannot accurately be viewed as a radical break in Poulantzas' thought; rather they must be seen as the logical political extension of a strand of reformism present in the corpus of Poulantzas' theorization of the state. Four aspects of the discussion of political power and the state in the earlier work lead to this conclusion.

Firstly, although the emphasis placed on the balance of dominant and dominated class forces has led some commentators to conclude that the class struggle lies at the center of the structural-relational conception of the state, in fact both the class struggle and the working class itself are largely absent from the analysis. This is an inevitable consequence of Poulantzas' methodology. The status of the class struggle is diminished in an analysis which focusses principally on the ruling class and its heterogeneity. Although the state is seen as the site of the representation and resolution of disputes amongst capitalist fractions, the working class is not seen as playing any significant role in class struggle at the level of the state. Emphasis on the plurality of the components of the dominant class also produces an underestimation of the fundamental antagonism between capital and labor. In Poulantzas, the class struggle is not seen as an effect of the struggle for the conquest or retention of state power but rather as an effect of the struggle between fractions of the dominant class for hegemony within the power bloc. As a result, the opposition between the ruling class and the subordinate classes is conceptualized in a formal and static fashion, and the problem of the working class struggle for power is not properly addressed.

Secondly, although great pains are taken to reject Gramsci's view of the relations between the dominant ideology and the dominated classes, in which the proletariat may become ideologically dominant before it is politically dominant as a result of an historical dislocation between hegemony and domination, the possibility that the hegemonic functions of the dominant class may be dislocated or displaced is not definitively discounted.[28] Of course, discussion of the possibility of the proletariat winning hegemony before taking state power does not necessarily signal a capitulation to reformism, but a working class party which strives for hegemony must also actively seek the conquest of state power if it is not to lose its sense of purpose.[29] The real issue concerns the nature of the struggle for hegemony. For both Gramsci and Lenin, it consisted of a battle waged against existing institutions for the construction of alternative centers of power. This, however, is not what Poulantzas has in mind. A very different version of the struggle for hegemony is proposed, one which focusses not on the expropriation of state power but on winning influence within the existing democratic branches of the state. The centerpiece of the later "democratic road to socialism", this strategy is classically reformist.

The third aspect is directly related to the second in that it concerns the role of universal suffrage and parliamentary institutions. These are seen as defining and integral features of a state "which has gained autonomy from the economic and which presents itself as the incarnation of the general interest of the people".[30] This is a dangerous and misleading view. Although such institutions undoubtedly are important in the functioning of certain states, many other capitalist states have functioned and presented themselves as the incarnation of the popular interest without them. There are numerous historical examples of dominant classes discarding democratic institutions when working class parties have achieved an unacceptable presence within them. The weight Poulantzas gives to parliaments and elections in conceptualizing the state leads to a mistaken political strategy which places similar weight on them.

The fourth aspect of Poulantzas' theoretical accommodation of reformism may be seen in his view of the "Welfare State". Although it is recognized that this term "merely disguises the form of the 'social policy' of a capitalist state at the stage of state monopoly capitalism",[31] the welfare state is mistakenly seen as a reduction of the economic power of the ruling class which is "imposed on the dominant class *by the struggle of the dominated classes*".[32] In fact, the welfare state emerged historically as the response of capital to working class struggle against the state itself. It was a solution imposed in an unfavorable conjuncture of the class struggle by the dominant, not the dominated, class. The welfare state does not represent a working class victory but rather a means of guaranteeing the maintenance of a healthy and technically skilled labor force which also plays an ideological role in the stabilization of capitalist power. Poulantzas recognizes that it "cannot under any circumstances call into question the capitalist type of state," but completely fails to grasp the nature of its role in the disarticulation and disorganization of working class struggle.[33]

These problematic aspects of Poulantzas' conceptualization of the state are symptomatic of a more general failure to grasp correctly the dynamic of capital. In the present period, neither the state nor modes of production can be adequately conceptualized at the national level. What is striking in the contemporary period is not the continued elaboration of internal functions but the extended jurisdiction of the state far beyond territorial borders. The state cannot be usefully conceived within a national unit, nor the "national state" be taken as the point of departure for most discussion of classes and class struggle, in an era when the internal and external interface is increasingly determinant of the character of the state. The organization of production and labor, essential to the functioning of a given mode of production, and the state's capacity for coordination of interests and repression are not activities that can accurately be deduced from the internal configuration of forces.

Many bourgeois writers now downplay the operational distinction between domestic and foreign policy, stressing instead the growing interdependence of the international order as a whole. It is time that Marxists began to understand the global nature of the state and the centrality of international domination in defining its contemporary character. The United States, for example, cannot be adequately conceptualized as a "capitalist state" or "state in capitalist society", but only as an "imperial state". Imperialism must be correctly theorized in all its dimensions, with the imperial state at its center: the activities of multinational corporations cannot be considered without the institution which created the universe in which they function, nor can any discussion of capital accumulation on a world scale become meaningful unless the central role of the imperial state in creating the conditions for it is properly understood. The efforts to analyze the post-colonial and the peripheral state must also be put in the context of the multiple activities of the imperial state.

No international movement of capital can take place without the sustained involvement of the imperial state, whether in the form of initial entry, expansion, or the survival of capital. The centrality of imperial capital within the U.S. social formation defines the domestic and external structures and functions of the state, as well as its policy. The roots of the imperial state are anchored in the United States, while its branches span the globe; its origins lie in th national unit, while its functions and operations extend into a multiplicity of societies and transnational organizations. The crucial task for state theorists today is to develop a theoretical framework anchored in the new realities: the system of international domination and exploitation needs a new theoretical conception of the state.

## Notes

1. Nicos Poulantzas (1975), *Political Power and Social Classes*, London: New Left Books; (1978), *State, Power, Socialism*, London: New Left Books.
2. Nicos Poulantzas (1968), *Pouvoir Politique et Classes Sociales*, Paris: Francios Maspero.
3. Louis Althusser (1970), *Reading Capital*, London: New Left Books, 1970; (1969), *For Marx*, London: New Left Books.
4. This notion is only implicit in the first work cited above and is fully developed in the second.
5. These aspects of structuralist Marxism have been subjected to a scathing critique in E. P. Thompson's highly commendable essay "The Poverty of Theory," in (1978), *The Poverty of Theory and Other Essays*, London: Merlin Press, pp. 193–397.
6. Stuart Hall and Alan Hunt (1979), "Interview with Nicos Poulantzas," *Marxism Today*, 23 (7): 198.
7. Poulantzas (1975), op. cit., p. 181.
8. Ibid., pp. 234–6.
9. Ibid., p. 234.
10. Ibid., p. 241.
11. Ibid., p. 137.
12. Ibid., pp. 104–117.
13. Ibid., p. 29.
14. Ibid., p. 17.
15. Ibid., p. 14.
16. F. Engels (1970), Letter to J. Bloch, in K. Marx and F. Engels, *Selected Works*, Vol. 3, Moscow: Progress Publishers, p. 487.
17. Karl Korsch (1935), "Why I am a Marxist," *The Modern Monthly*, 9 (2): 88–95.
18. Poulantzas (1975), op. cit., p. 78.
19. Poulantzas did at least recognize this problem. See Hall and Hunt, op. cit., p. 198.
20. Poulantzas (1975), op. cit., p. 274.
21. Ibid., p. 258.
22. "Only under the second Bonaparte does the state seem to have made itself completely independent," Marx and Engels, Vol. 1, op. cit., p. 30. They also qualified their remarks on autonomy by noting that "the state is not suspended in mid-air", p. 302, and that the historical function of Bonapartism was "to safeguard the bourgeois order", p. 308.
23. Poulantzas (1976), *The Crisis of the Dictatorships*, London: New Left Books.
24. See Poulantzas (1978), op. cit., pp. 49–120.

25. Ibid., pp. 123–160.
26. Ibid., pp. 163–199.
27. Poulantzas (1975), op. cit., p. 96.
28. See Ibid., pp. 204–205, 240.
29. Particularly cautionary in this respect is the case of the Italian Communist party. This party's idea of hegemony, neither dynamic nor revolutionary, is conceived solely in terms of existing institutions and in static and manipulative forms of mass mobilization.
30. Poulantzas (1975), op. cit., p. 230.
31. Ibid., p. 193.
32. Ibid., p. 194.
33. Ibid., p. 194

# 5

# The "Peripheral State": Continuity and Change in the International Division of Labour

JAMES PETRAS

Discussions focusing on the "overdeveloped" or "underdeveloped" state, the "strong" and "weak" states miss the essential point: the class relationships and class struggles that provide the social context that shapes and gives meaning to these terms. The assumption behind these writings is that the 'state' stands above society and has its own logic and momentum. Nothing could be further from the truth. The growth of the state apparatus is directly proportional to the weakness of the local ruling classes in exercising hegemony: the absence of intermediary groups in civil society, their dissolution by colonial authorities, by capitalist and commercial expansion, urbanisation, secularism, etc., has forced the dominant property groups to strengthen the repressive apparatus of the state. The cost at times is high because their representatives in the police and army frequently extort a high price for protecting their interests. At times, the level of extortion and the modus operandi adversely impinge upon the dominant groups creating a breach between the governing class and the practical interests affecting the local dominant classes. The strength of the 'state' is an ambiguous term that can only be understood in context: (1) its measurement can be gauged in terms of its capacity to sustain the existing social relations of production, specifically its power to control the labour force in the interests of dominant property groups and (2) the collective power of the state in extracting surplus in the international market and converting it into productive activity. The capacity of the state to act within the internal and international division of labour is fundamentally dependent on the level of class conflict: high levels of conflict erode the basis for state

Reprinted from and with the permission of the *Journal of Contemporary Asia.*

action; hence the weak state lacks social cohesion, the strong state possesses it. The discussion of 'strong' and 'weak' states is thus a *derivative* phenomenon. One must begin with the nature and process of class formation and class struggle to understand the sources of strength and weakness of the peripheral state: social relations of production create the need for coercion, even as the use of force by the state is absolutely essential for sustaining and reproducing the productive system.

The development of the productive forces, class relations and the growth of a differentiated class structure shapes the specific importance of the state. The growth of the state apparatus, in the first instance, parallels the growth of productive forces—and the vulnerability of local ruling classes. The over-staffed bureaucracies, soaring military budget are "overdeveloped" only by the standards of ahistorical, asocial rationality—abstract notions that fail to relate the state to the specific class conjuncture or historical situation. The periphery has for a number of historical reasons—which are well known—experienced the development of the class struggle far in advance of the development of the productive forces. And it is in response to this phenomena, the fear of revolutionary upheaval ("instability"), that the state has expanded beyond what appears as "economically rational". Moreover, the expansion of the state apparatus beyond other institutions of civil society reflects the deep insertion of the metropolitan powers in the social structure: the transfer of military resources from the advanced capitalist countries (and, why not, the socialist countries) to sustain peripheral states had led to the 'disequilibrium' between state and civil society. The peripheral state apparatus grows out of the *logic of the imperial state* (adopting modern military technology to repress petty commodity producers) *in relationship to the development of the class struggle*. The uneven growth of technology, between military and economy, characteristic of many Third World countries, can only be understood not in terms of the logic of the state or by some mystical bureaucratic imperatives within the state, but by the crises in class relations: the loss of hegemony by the dominant classes over the labour force.

The principal distinctions are not found in the degree of autonomy of the state (relative or absolute) or by the capacity of states to repress or by their technical proficiency but in the particular classes they represent.

## Common and Differentiating Features of the Peripheral State

It has become commonplace to speak of peripheral states responding to "imperatives" of development through the elaboration of similar policies and institutions. Thus it is important to distinguish between common and differentiating features found among peripheral states. For while most peripheral states have adopted common policies and practices because of common circumstances, they have also pursued vastly different goals and methods.

There are at least five features of the peripheral state that have appeared almost universally: (1) extensive and prolonged intervention in the economy; (2) growing public sector activity; (3) expanding and deepening of external ties; (4) the creation and, in varying degrees, elaboration of planning institutes and mechanisms; and (5) the promotion of industrialisation. Independently of ideology, all peripheral states— from the most self-denominated "free enterprise" regime to the most unabashed socialist—has taken on a multitude of economic functions and roles, even as it retains its special status as the ultimate repository of coercion. While extensive state activity is expected from radical regimes, what is striking is the size and scope of state activity in regimes commonly associated with "free-enterprise"—they are statist almost against their ideological will. The state not only collects taxes and protects property but has been actively involved in the growth of productive units in a variety of sectors over a period of time. The organisation of co-operatives, the investment in infrastructure, basic industries, munitions factories, strategic industries—all have involved the state. The reasons vary: in some areas the initial investments are beyond the capability of private capital (capital goods industry); in others the returns are long-term and problematical, thus discouraging foreign capital investment (steel industry). Beyond that there are areas like infrastructure development in which state policy is to keep the costs cheap in order to subsidise and promote private investment (electricity and power). Finally, there are specific power groups within the state apparatus which have special interests in maintaining control over particular productive activities (i.e., military in regard to weapons production). Hence *state* interventionism has become necessary for the growth and security of peripheral capitalism, even when the ideology of the state eulogises its opposite. Having pointed to the *complementary* nature of state interventionism to private enterprise, there is a further development that is a direct outgrowth and which goes beyond these policies. The establishment of a public sector involves the growth of a class of bureaucratic capitalists whose status, wealth and power expands or contracts with the fortunes of their sector. The initial impetus for state activity, rooted in the needs and weaknesses of local capital, are, in some cases, supplanted by the driving force of the bureaucratic bourgeoisie which, while lacking formal ownership, exercises decisive control. The enormous growth of autonomous public corporations, parastatals and state investment and trading houses are part of a new empire in which millionaire bureaucrats exercise the same prerogatives and manifest the same conservative social views as their private coun- terparts—often forming joint business ventures and joining the same social clubs. The growth of international finance capital, especially as Western banks recycled petrol-dollars to the periphery, created a vast source of direct financing for new state activity. The growing state debt and the expanding financial ties of all peripheral states to the private money markets is another common feature found independently of ideology. The soaring energy, food and industrial commodity costs have had a tendency to homogenise the external conditions of all peripheral states, even as the manner in which they deal with the problems varies enormously. The common effort to control external fluctuations through cartels and the efforts by the peripheral states to renegotiate the terms of dependency, bringing together Cuba and Brazil on sugar for example, illustrates the common circumstances.

Finally, the disintegrating and chaotic effects generated by the market has finally forced even the most laissez-faire regimes to resort to planning and to efforts to create state organisations to mediate the fluctuations— even if only to save the local capitalists from destruction. The planning process itself is, in many cases, haphazard, data is frequently unreliable and the coincidence between the plan and the behaviour of business is only an occasional occurrence. Nevertheless, most business would hardly survive if it were not for the financing and allocations of the state legitimated by the Plan. The ritual of planners proposing targets and allocating resources thus is not altogether useless, though the effort to amalgamate socialist planning, with its counterpart elsewhere, is more than slightly far fetched.

The push for industrialisation results, in the case of radical regimes, from a programmatic position—the desire to overcome underdevelopment and dependency on an imperial centre. On the other hand, the dependent peripheral countries have also pursued industrialisation programmes, in part because of the conversion of merchant groups to industrial activity, in part because of programmes of import-substitution and shortages of foreign exchange (a problem that persists however) and partly because of the pressures from the metropolitan countries interested in capturing local markets and/or exploiting cheap labour in order to create industrial export platforms. The irony here has been that it is precisely among some of the most 'dependent' outwardly oriented peripheral states that the most extensive industrialisation has occurred—a process, however, which has its own specific features that will be discussed further on.

While one should recognise that the state in the periphery possesses certain common attributes, it is even more important to note the specific features that differentiate revolutionary from capitalist states.

Before one can effectively discuss the issues of intervention, planning, etc., there is a prior question that must be addressed: what is the class nature of the state? That is, apart from its acknowledged general activity, the state also plays a definite role with regard to the class interests of specific classes, and it is that order of activity that allows us to distinguish the *class state* from the state-in-general. The issue is which classes are represented by the party in power, organisations in the bureaucracy that decide who bears the cost and who benefits from state intervention and ownership? More fundamental than the notion of nationalisation is the question for whom? How is the surplus distributed? Who contracts the foreign loans and who pays them back? The capitalist regimes and their defenders of all hues and colours mystify the relationship by referring to the "state" or the "nation". While both revolutionary and dependent capitalist states have incurred debts, in the former, the loans have usually gone to finance consumption and productive activities benefiting the producers while in the latter they have overwhelmingly benefited the property owners. Moreover, the payments and subsequent austerity programmes have not been equitably borne by all classes in the peripheral capitalist countries—selective restrictions and austerity have primarily affected the working class. In the revolutionary societies, the burdens have been more uniformly borne, though where incipient bureaucracies have emerged they tend to escape most of the costs. While a substantial public sector has grown in many dependent capitalist societies, the private sector continues to draw substantial personnel, resources and subsidies from the public. Moreover, there is a tendency, especially at the top, for employees and executives who gain power and wealth in the public sector to convert these resources into private investment. The interchange of roles (between private and public) and the linkages between the two contributes to the subordination of the public to the private sector. As public enterprises become profitable, and as a wealthy private sector emerges with links to top executives in the public, there is a tendency to sell off the profitable public firms and for the state to remain with the less lucrative operations, thus serving a polemical material for the advocates of the virtues of the free enterprise system. In effect, the growth of public enterprise becomes a trampoline for the upwardly mobile propertyless political leaders who eventually transform themselves into prominent enterpreneurs: the familar career pattern begins with a mass nationalist leader, who proceeds to organise and promote public enterprise (perhaps dubbed "socialist") and then participate in joint ventures and become the possessor of private wealth and capital. In Western eyes, this transition is described as the shift from 'ideological' to 'pragmatist'.

In the initial phase, the scarcity of capital, popular expectation and the negative image of capitalism, force the political leaders of peripheral capitalism to develop state enterprise. Through linkages with the multi-nationals, the peripheral state forges an alliance to promote industrial exports. However, the introduction of large-scale public enterprises, the recruitment of local personnel and the increasing demands for upward mobility and greater rewards among the public employees, creates pressure for bureaucratic-nationalism. Within dependent capitalism, as the capacity for local administration increases there is a tendency for the bureaucratic bourgeoisie linked to local capital to expand through foreign financing at the expense of multinational capital. In these exceptional circumstances, the combined forces of state and local capital seek to modify their role in the world division of labour, entering into competition with the imperial countries for industrial markets. In some instances, the collaborator classes, spawned by the multinationals within dependent capitalism, become the agents of competitive capitalism in the world economy.

The revolutionary regimes in developing their capacity for production continue to depend on external financing and technology. The priorities, however, are shaped by the mass organisations and relatively egalitarian norms. Nevertheless, as the revolutionary society must produce, in part, for the world market (none able in any rational sense to produce all that it needs) its competitive conditions shape the terms of production. The products of the revolutionary society must be produced efficiently and at competitive costs with countries based on capitalist social relations. The exploitative conditions of production embedded in world exchanges get inevitably transferred in part to the revolutionary society. Within the latter, however, constraints on market influence are vested in the revolutionary political organisations of the masses, who can significantly improve the quality of life within production and without, through institutions of popular power. Nevertheless, while socialist revolutions occur in peripheral states with low levels of development in the productive forces they will be in a contradictory position: socialised production will continue to form part of the international division of labour.

The growth of public sector enterprise in peripheral capitalist states should not lead us to amalgamate these with revolutionary societies in transition to socialism since, in many cases, in the former the public sector is socialising the costs of capitalist production, while in the latter elements of capitalism (including relations to the world market) are harnessed to socialism. For example, under peripheral capitalism the state sector is growing in the high cost-low profit upstream and in-frastructural sectors while the low cost-high profit downstream man-ufacturing and processing sectors are in private lands. The process of comprehensive socialisation undertaken by social revolutionary regimes ensures that these occurrences are few and far between.

In summary, while common circumstances and imperatives do cause similar features to appear among all peripheral states, fundamental qualitative differences in the nature and consequences of state activity clearly separate capitalist and revolutionary states. The notion that the world capitalist market is "homogenising" the state, that the very term "peripheral state" is an appropriate denotation involves a false amal-gamation of very different structures. This approach is similar to the earlier "convergence" theory in which some commentators claimed the industrial imperatives eliminated the differences between socialist and capitalist societies. From the point of view of social-revolutionary activity, the revolutionary states are the *epicenter* of a worldwide transition to a new social order even as they stand at the periphery of technico-economic development. The "economistic" bias inherent in the classification of states by the latter criteria is compatible with the Euro-centric views of its proponents. The more complex position of

Table 5.1 Country Groupings by Percentage of Total Exports Accounted for by Primary Exports (N = 47)

| Percentage of exports, primary commodities | Percentage of countries | |
| --- | --- | --- |
| 100 to 90 | 40.4 | |
| 89 to 80 | 21.3 | 80.8 |
| 79 to 70 | 19.1 | |
| 69 to 60 | 2.1 | |
| 59 to 50 | 2.1 | |
| below 50 | 14.9 | |

the states—being sociopolitical centres and technico-economic periphery—requires a different conception of the world order and the process by which it is being transformed.

The rate of economic change in the present capitalist world order is much slower than is acknowledged by many observers. Despite the growth of politically and juridically independent states and a spate of international forums and projects, the international division of labour has been little changed over the past two decades. The capacity of capitalism to redefine the traditional division of labour has been greatly exaggerated, a point we will proceed to examine in some detail.

## A New International Division of Labour

There have emerged a number of theorists who have called into being a "new international division of labour" in which the old colonial division of labour involving Third World exports of raw materials and importation of finished goods has been transcended.[1] According to this new division, Third World countries have been industrialised to produce cheap labour-intensive manufacturing goods to be exported to the core capitalist countries for more advanced capital-intensive goods. The proponents of the new division of labour argue that the accompanying industrialisation of the Third World reflects the new world capitalist rationality and logic. In order to assess these assertions, we will examine a select number of countries (47) drawn from a World Bank study* which has data for both 1960 and 1976.

In 1976, in the 80 per cent of selected Third World countries, primary commodities accounted for 70 per cent or more of exports. What is more, in half of these countries primary commodities accounted for upward of 90 per cent of their exports (see Table 5.1).

---

*World Bank Development Report 1979 (Washington: World Bank, 1979).

What is striking about these results is the *continuity* in the pattern of the world division of labour, 20 years after most countries have achieved formal independence. Despite the growth of industrial production in many areas of the Third World, the main role of the Third World countries in the capitalist world economy is still as suppliers of primary commodities. It is clear that trade diversification and the growth of industrial exports were not greatly influenced by the political changes accompanying independence. It appears that the continuing socio-economic links with the markets and classes within the core capitalist countries are stronger than changes in political leadership.

The evidence thus far does not substantiate the claim by the advocates of a new international division of labour (NIDL)—the overwhelming majority of Third World countries are still predominantly exporters of primary products.

The NIDL argument might take the form of arguing that as Third World countries become more "developed" they will begin to modify their position in the world division of labour. If we consider level of income among Third World countries (again using World Bank measures) and divide them into low income/middle income countries, we find that over four-fifths of the middle income countries are predominantly primary goods exporters (70 per cent or more), compared to less than three-quarters of the low income countries (see Tables 5.2 and 5.3). Clearly, level of development in the national economy is not a good indicator of any propensity among Third World countries to shift their role within the international division of labour. In low income countries, like Pakistan and India, the great unevenness of development manifests itself in a growing industrial export sector, side by side with typical Asiatic poverty. In the "middle income" countries, the huge labour pools, massive infusions of outside funding initially, at least, products of politico-military strategic interests, have led to industrial exports in the three leading countries (South Korea, Hong Kong, and Taiwan).

It is clear that the simple growth of income within Third World countries is not incompatible with a continuing dependence on primary commodity exports. In fact, the industrialisation for export patterns seems to be more attracted toward the lowest income countries, rather than the higher income Third World countries.

While it is clear that the old division of labour still defines the global relationship between Third World and core capitalist countries, there is a *trend* away from this pattern. Almost two-thirds of the selected countries show a shift in exports toward non-primary goods between 1960 and 1976 (Table 5.4).

While the claims of the NIDL are grossly exaggerated, there is some basis for examining *modifications* of exchange within the global marketplace. It should be kept in mind, however, that the general trend of diversification still has a long way to go and that almost one-quarter of the countries show no changes or are *increasingly* dependent on primary product exports.

Table 5.2  Percentage Share of Primary Commodities by Level of Income

|  | Low income countries | | |
| --- | --- | --- | --- |
|  | 1960 | 1976 | Percentage difference 1960–76 |
| Ethiopia | 100 | 98 | + 2 |
| Mali | 96 | 99 | − 3 |
| Burma | 99 | 99 | 0 |
| Malawi |  | 96 |  |
| India | 55 | 47 | + 8 |
| Pakistan | 73 | 43 | +30 |
| Tanzania | 87 | 91 | − 4 |
| Sri Lanka | 99 | 86 | +13 |
| Haiti | 100 | 49 | +51 |
| Central African Repub. | 98 | 82 | +16 |
| Kenya | 88 | 88 | 0 |
| Uganda | 100 | 100 | 0 |
| Indonesia | 100 | 98 | + 2 |
|  | Middle income countries | | |
| Egypt | 88 | 73 | +15 |
| Cameroon | 96 | 90 | + 6 |
| Ghana | 90 | 99 | − 9 |
| Honduras | 98 | 90 | + 8 |
| Nigeria | 97 | 99 | − 2 |
| Thailand | 98 | 81 | +17 |
| Yeman Arab Republic |  | 87 |  |
| Philippines | 96 | 76 | +20 |
| Congo Peoples Republic | 91 | 87 | + 4 |
| Papua New Guinea | 92 | 99 | − 7 |
| Morocco | 92 | 84 | + 8 |
| Ivory Coast | 99 | 92 | + 7 |
| Jordan | 96 | 79 | +17 |
| Columbia | 98 | 78 | +20 |
| Ecuador | 99 | 98 | + 1 |
| Republic of Korea | 96 | 12 | +74 |
| Nicaragua | 98 | 84 | +14 |
| Tunisia | 90 | 74 | +16 |
| Syrian Arab Republic | 81 | 90 | − 9 |
| Malaysia | 94 | 84 | +10 |
| Algeria | 93 | 99 | − 6 |
| Turkey | 97 | 76 | +19 |
| Mexico | 88 | 69 | +19 |
| Jamaica | 95 | 44 | +51 |
| Chile | 96 | 95 | + 1 |
| Rep. of China (Taiwan) |  | 15 |  |
| Costa Rica | 95 | 71 | +24 |
| Brazil | 97 | 75 | +22 |
| Iraq | 100 | 100 | 0 |
| Argentina | 96 | 75 | +21 |
| Iran | 97 | 99 | − 2 |
| Trinidad and Tobago | 96 | 94 | + 2 |
| Hong Kong | 20 | 3 | +17 |
| Singapore | 74 | 54 | +20 |

Table 5.3   Comparison of Low Income and Middle Income Countires of Third World
and the Percentage of Exports Accounted for by Primary Products in 1976
(N = 47)

| Level of income (countries) | Percentage of countries with 70% exports (primary or over) | Percentage of countries with less than 70% primary exports |
|---|---|---|
| Low | 72% | 23% |
| Middle | 82 | 18 |

Moreover, in analysing this trend, it is important to examine the
rate of change. We examined 32 countries from the World Bank sample
for which we have data for a 16 year period.

The actual growth of industrial exports indicates a very diverse
pattern in which over three-quarters of the selected countries evidenced
low to moderate growth and only slightly more than one-fifth demonstrated substantial growth. In evaluating these growth figures, one
should also take account of the fact that most Third World countries
started with very low base figures and the subsequent striking gains
leave many heavily dependent on primary commodities. Of the 20
countries showing substantial increases of non-primary exports, 13, or
65 per cent, still were heavily dependent (70% or more) on primary
product exports. In fact, in only seven Third World countries do non-
primary products account for more than 50 per cent of the total (Hong
Kong, India, Pakistan, South Korea, Taiwan, Haiti and Jamaica).

By focusing on these exceptional seven cases, NIDL advocates have
attempted to theorise about the Third World—overlooking the particular
strategic military *political* positions that some of these countries occupied
in the global confrontation between capitalist and socialist countries
(namely, Hong Kong, South Korea, and Taiwan) and the historical
roots of *national* industrial development (India).

Moreover, in part, industrial growth and diversification of exports
has been stimulated by exports to non-metropolitan countries, quite
the opposite of what NIDL theorists propose. For many of the more

Table 5.4   Comparison of Percentage Exports of Primary Commodities among Select
Third World Countries between 1960–1976

| | |
|---|---|
| Third World Countries Decreasing Percentage of Primary Commodities in Exports | 63.8 |
| Third World Countries Increasing Percentage of Primary Commodities in Exports | 17.0 |
| Third World Countries Maintaining Percentage of Primary Commodities in Exports | 8.5 |
| No Data | 6.4 |

Table 5.5    Percentage Increase of Non-primary Exports among Industrialising Countries
between 1960–1976 (N = 32)

| Percentage increase | | Percentage of countries | |
|---|---|---|---|
| Less than 5 | 18.8 | | |
| 5–10 | 18.8 | low | 37.6% |
| 11–20 | 40.6 | medium | 40.6% |
| over 20 | 21.9 | high | 21.9% |

dynamic industrialising Third World countries, regional expansion is becoming much more central to their growth patterns.

The trade patterns of the past are only partly evidenced in the destination of their exports. Among the low income, Third World countries exports to the non-metropolitan areas account for 37 per cent and 34 per cent in 1960 and 1976. Among the "middle income" Third World countries, there has been a shift upward from 29 per cent to 33 per cent in the proportion of industrial exports to non-metropolitan areas.

It is within this context of continuing dependence on primary commodities, of very selected industrial diversification, that a limited trend toward "a new international division of labour" should be discussed. By 1976, about 52 per cent of the low income manufacturing exports and 64 per cent of the middle income exports were going to the core capitalist countries. Among the more industrialised Third World countries, textiles and clothing accounted for 20 per cent of Indian, 32 per cent of Pakistani, 36 per cent of South Korean, 30 per cent of Taiwanese and 44 per cent of Hong Kong's industrial exports. The predominance of textiles and clothing suggests the quite fragile and limited nature of the industrial push, even in these, the most dynamic Third World countries. Essentially, the availability of cheap labour for labour intensive manufacturing is a major consideration in the advance of industry— but hardly a basis for sweeping assertions concerning a new international division of labour.

The NIDL theorists have obscured many of the fundamental issues that confront the Third World. Rather than seeing the growth of a new division of labour growing from the logic of industrial capital in the metropolitan countries, the real issue is the very limited opening of industrial markets in the metropole, the constraints on industrial financing, the construction of barriers to the transfer of technology, etc. The intellectual bankruptcy of the NIDL school reflects their incapacity to analyse the class forces that shape state policy in the metropole and the real behaviour of the multinational corporations. Operating from an abstract deductive model of capitalism, haphazardly selecting illustrative 'cases' to buttress their arguments, they have failed to deal with the fact that over 90 per cent of multinational industrial production in the major countries of Latin America are geared toward capturing the internal market.[2] Fixated by the Hong Kong, South Korea, Taiwan experience, they fail to come to grips with the major conflicts between North and South over precisely the *incapacity* of the Third World countries to break into new markets and the intransigence of the metropolitan countries in resisting the creation of a new international division of labour. What industrial exports have taken place is largely a result of the combined pressures of bourgeois Third World countries and limited sectors of metropolitan competitive capitalism (electonic, clothing, capitalists). The NIDL theorists have been largely taken in by the rhetoric of Trilateral Commission position papers, which are *not* the operating basis on which the economic policies of the member nations are formulated.

The very terms with which the NIDL arguments are framed are suspect. The notion of 'industrialisation' means very different things in different settings.[3] In the metropolitan countries, it refers to the routinisation of innovation, large-scale research and development, elaboration of machinery, processing, assembly, sales and shipping. In the periphery, 'industrialisation' refers to only elements—all of the technology is imported, as is much of the machinery and sales. Moreover, in many countries the location of industries is contingent on a specific set of social factors—low wages, no taxes, no strikes—which, on the one hand, limit the "spread effects" of industrial development and, secondly, could lead industry to pack up and abandon a country if their conditions changed.[4] Both the historical and contemporary experiences should cause us to reject the simplistic notions that Western "industrialisation" is the 'mirror' of the East.

If one looks closer at the nature of Third World industrialisation, one discovers that much of it is assembly plants, involving little industrial training and investment. Moreover, the growth in Southeast Asia, Mexico, Central America and the Caribbean of free trade zones in which the corporations, for all intents and purposes, exercise sovereignty in the areas of production means that the production is "national" only in the most vacuous, juridical sense: the territory is "national", the operations, laws and production are in fact run by foreign nationals. Moreover, the fragmented nature of industrial production in most Third World countries suggests that we are not dealing with integrated processes of production but with partial and limited production controlled and dependent on metropolitan forces.

Clearly, capitalism is transforming more and more of Third World societies. Primary products are being subject to mechanisation, transportation and commercial expansion is being promoted by the capitalist state and industrial processing of agro-mineral products is clearly on the ascent. With the national political-economy, industry is growing and primary goods production is declining. Proletarianisation is accomplished and exceeded by the growth of a mass of semi-proletarian rural and urban labour pools with temporary and seasonal employment. Yet this industrial growth is overwhelmingly dependent on the continued growth of traditional exports, to finance and to sustain it. Moreover, the most dynamic growth sectors of industry are not only internal, but largely directed to the purchasers of durable goods, namely the 20 per cent of the population found in the affluent middle and upper classes. The *lack* of a new international division of labour and the very dismal prospects of Third World countries achieving even 15 per cent of world industrial exports by 1990 heightens the internal contradictions between a growing industrial capacity and ever-increasing surplus labour force uprooted from primary production. Rather than looking for a new division of labour, we can expect a new round of Third World labour-based social revolutions.

## Peripheral States and the Old and New Division of Labour

From the previous discussion we can conclude that there is a division among different types of peripheral states, some of which participate in the traditional and some in the new division of labour. What is more interesting perhaps is the fact that participation in one or the other cuts across ideological cleavages that define regimes within the periphery. We can identify at least four different types of regimes which are still part of the traditional division of labour—overwhelmingly primary commodity exporters. (1) *Neo-colonial* regimes which still depend heavily upon metropolitan political and military support to sustain their ruling class. These include countries like Zaire, Gabon, Thailand, and the Cameroons, among others. (2) The dependent *developmental* regime possesses and depends on its own political and military forces, but its economic expansion is greatly fueled by metropolitan financial and investment resources. This includes countries like Kenya, Egypt, Colombia, which depend on traditional exports even while they industrialise. (3) The third variant of peripheral states that persists within the traditional division of labour are the *state capitalist* countries like Algeria, Libya, Iraq. In this case, strong state ownership and the development of heavy industry has led to heavy dependence on oil exports to finance new projects, which as yet are not competitive in international markets or have not yet been completed. (4) Revolutionary regimes such as Cuba, while opening new areas of production and transforming the class structure have been unable to shift out of the primary commodity role. In part because of the scarcity and high cost of strategic resources, lack of skilled personnel, favourable arrangements with the Soviet bloc—Cuba remains firmly embedded as an exporter of primary commodities.

In summary, we find that while political and social changes of major significance have taken place among a number of peripheral countries and a wide range of regimes has emerged, they have been unable to redefine their position in the international division of labour. Yet, the similarities in type of export—primary commodities—should not obscure the differences in the type of imports and how they are disposed: while in the neo-colonial states luxury imports and consumer items benefit the upper classes and limit the growth of new productive forces, in the revolutionary regimes the consumer imports benefit the great majority of the population. Likewise, the capital goods imported by the 'national developmental' regimes become the patrimony of the national bourgeoisie while in the state capitalist they are under the juridical control of the public, managed by a bureaucratic strata. While the external relations remain the same, the type of internal regime makes a major difference in the way that the economic surplus obtained through the exchanges is distributed. The historic possibilities of redefining a state's relation to the international division of labour are in part related to the peripheral state's capacity to channel the surplus toward classes and institutions capable of creating new products and innovations. While all but the neo-colonial state seem in varying degrees involved in generating the capacity—only the revolutionary state seems capable of ensuring that the fruits of innovation will rebound to the benefit of the majority of the producers.

Just as we found that a variety of peripheral state regimes are found in the old division of labour, a similar range of regimes is found in the new division of labour (1) *colonial* regimes such as Hong Kong, *colonial settler regimes* such as South Africa are found among the industrial exporters; (2) *dependent development* regimes include South Korea, Brazil, Taiwan, Singapore; and (3) *state capitalist* regimes probably would include India; and (4) *revolutionary* regimes might include China.

The role of these states in the New International Division of Labour is, in part, based on the existence of cheap labour supplies and the willingness of the regime to increase foreign exploitation of this labour force through industrial export platforms (especially in the cases of the Southeast Asian countries). In the large countries of Brazil, India and South Africa, a formidable state industrial sector oriented toward exports is promoted through a combination of export subsidies and low costs of local inputs. The existence of a long-standing national entrepreneurial group with external linkages is an added factor. While in Asia multinational capital seems to have played a major role in redefining the country's participation in the international division of labour in Latin America, it has been "national" capital, local big business and public corporations. South Korea appears to combine both patterns: state and multinational firms, with the former increasingly important. There is a more fundamental distinction that needs to be drawn among these peripheral states that are redefining their participation in the international division of labour regarding the *durability* of their new position. Among the Asian and, in some of the Caribbean countries, export industries lack any and all *backward linkages*: only *territory* and *labour* has been appropriated by the multinationals in the setting up of assembly plants. Hence there are sharp constraints on their long-term stability. Growing protectionism in the metropolitan countries, an eruption of class conflict or nationalist movements could increase labour costs and cause the corporations to pack up their screwdrivers and hop to another island. The industrial transformation is in these cases superficial and *subject to reversal.*

The apparent displacement of the political bureaucrats by the managerial elite in China appears to be a historic change—leading to China's reinsertion into a traditional role in the world market: sending contract labour abroad, offering concessionary industrial zones to foreign capital, accumulating foreign debts, etc. The political context appears to be somewhat different: the strong bureaucratic centralist state prevents any effort to fragment the nation between rival imperial states. Nevertheless, the push by the bureaucratic collectivist leadership is to maximise its industrial exports through the exploitation of cheap labour, even undercutting the labour intensive export products emanating from South Korea and Taiwan.

In summary, we can conclude that the relation of peripheral states to the world economy vary with the *class nature* of the state and their *position in the old or new division of labour.* Looking only at one or the other does not allow us to understand the constraints and boundaries on political and social action.

### Peripheral State Strategies and the Transition to Socialism

If we look specifically at the interface between social revolutions and world economy, we can distinguish at least four distinct strategies:

(1) *Rupture and autarky.* The Cambodian experience under Pol Pot, certain tendencies during Mao's China and Stalin's Russia indicate an approach which attempted to withdraw from world exchange and to develop the productive forces on the basis exclusively of internal resources: self-reliance, according to this school accommodated personal virtues and economic commonsense. This approach led to force-draft efforts to telescope centuries of development in a few decades, requiring large-scale and sustained repression and control. The attempt sought to produce internally many of the goods obtained through the international division of labour—leaving out all those areas considered superfluous by the regime. Austerity caused the society to approximate a form of primitive communism rather than modern socialism.

(2) *Capitalist rupture and integration in the Soviet bloc.* Cuba and Vietnam entered into a traditional division of labour with the Soviet Union—even as the terms were more generous than previously with the West. A product of international conflict with the US, this policy is, in part, the product of circumstances imposed on these countries, more than the result of an ideological choice.

(3) *Rupture with Soviet bloc and reinsertion in the world market.* China is the clearest expression of an attempt to maximise the growth of productive forces through association with Western and Japanese

capital and its share of international markets through export of labour intensive products. The emergence of dependent bureaucratic collectivism is evidenced by the new world which the Chinese leadership is pursuing in the world market place. The linkages between the "modernising" bureaucratic leadership and Western capital are accompanied by the heightening of contradictions between socialised production and the increasingly 'managerial' appropriation and allocation of the social surplus (and its siphoning off through world exchanges). The capacity of the bureaucratic leadership to redefine "socialist consciousness" in terms of *managerial-technocratic* criteria is crucial in sustaining their legitimacy, if not with the producers certainly with the party-military apparatus.

(4) *Capturing the commanding heights and negotiating with both blocs.* Nicaragua is attempting to maximise the advantages of world trade and the transfer of technology from the Western countries with its *mixed economy,* while attracting political and economic support from the socialist countries through its political and ideological changes in the state. In this approach a revolutionary state possesses the crucial financial and external trade sectors and part of the productive areas, and through mass organisation controls the rest of the private sector. This approach attempts to gradually evolve a process of socialisation without the dislocation of the rapid rupture approach (Cuba), avoid the austerity and repression of the self-reliant approach, while maintaining the revolutionary integrity so clearly absent in the Chinese case. The possibility of this transition enduring, however, is questionable given the pressures of international capital and the increasing political opposition of local capital.

## Conclusion

The most striking fact about the peripheral states is the growth of *industry* combined with the continued dependence on export of primary production. The major 'transformation' has been in response to 'national capital' (public and private) oriented toward internal production. External financial association with the state has led to the promotion of traditional exports and growth of import substitution industries. The changes from colonial to independent states in most countries have not led to qualitative changes in the international division of labour but in the internal division of labour: urban industries and services at the expense of agriculture. The exceptions are largely countries that have been strategic military centres benefiting from imperial wars (South Korea, Taiwan and Hong Kong) which have been net recipients of huge capital inflows that led the merchant capital class to convert to industrial production.

The growth of industry and new classes—bureaucratic, entrepreneurial, petty commodity—and the transformation of labour into wage and salaried finds expression in state regimes based on coalitions of forces.

Increasingly, the problems of 'general development' have been replaced by class demands—how the development product is distributed, the social relations of production, denunciation of new ruling classes. The production ethos and the struggle against underdevelopment through which the state and the dominant periphery ruling classes organised the cohesion of society is giving way to specific class demands and denunciation: production for whom? The 'new ruling class' of the periphery which legitimates itself through expropriation of multinational property (including Saudi Arabia's ARAMCO) itself is now seen as the source of exploitation. The peripheral state involved in deepening the inequalities and uneven development within society cannot any longer sustain power by pointing to "North-South" dichotomies—the specific sources of appropriation of surplus are mediated by the local apparatus of power, even as the transfers to the 'outside' persist. Growing economic diversification, economic concentration in the local public and private clans and ruling classes has provoked a fundamental contradiction between the claims of 'national development' and private (elite) enrichment and appropriation. The bureaucratic commandism of the high growth capitalist states and the new market openings of the bureaucratic collectivist states both decrease the political and social space for the emerging wage and salaried workers and petty commodity producers. The increasing similarity in structure between bureaucratic collectivist and authoritarian capitalist state is manifest in the common opposition of the civilian-military bureaucratic strata to popular control. Authoritarian capitalism adopts the hierarchical political organisation (of their collectivist enemies) and harnesses it to capitalist development. The collectivists adopt the market and managerial structures (of their capitalist enemies) and harness it to bureaucratically planned economies. The fundamental programmatic convergence is not found in the assimilation of one or the other of different property forms (there is neither "capitalist restoration" nor "creeping socialism") but in the all-embracing role of the state as the principal buttress for sustaining exploitative social relations facilitating the alienation from the working class of the social surplus and its transfer to their respective dominant groups. The simultaneous growth of markets and bureaucracy parallels the expansion of the working class and the growing contradiction embedded in the spread of social production and alien appropriation. To conflicts generated by the historic appropriation at the international level (the anti-imperialist struggle) is now added the appropriation by the public (and socialist) and private dominant interests at the national level. The political alternatives posed by the bourgeois societies of 'bureaucracy' or 'market' are two totally false anti-working class choices. The state in both instances alienates the surplus: in both cases the working class does not exercise hegemony over the process of production or the disposition of the surplus. Both bureaucratic collectivist and market oriented states must repress the working class to force it to submit to the 'laws' governing the operation in favour of the dominant interests.

The demise of bureaucratic "socialist" states in the periphery and the use of extreme force against the organised working class (Argentina, Chile, etc.) to 'free markets' indicates that the peripheral working class has formed a clear conception of its exploitation even if, as is the case, it has not formulated an alternative.

The peripheral state inserted in both the international and national division of labour hence becomes increasingly the target of any mass political movement—especially those initiated at the point of production. The absence of class conscious, working class organisation and the proliferation of civilian/military bureaucratic strata creates conditions for old ruling classes rooted in old property relations to be displaced and new propertyless groups to seize power—always in the name of the masses but consistently to rule over the masses. The mass overthrow of the authoritarian capitalist state has not led directly to socialism but to 'transitional' states in which property forms are collectivised but social relations remain hierarchical. The crisis of bureaucratic regimes in the periphery has never been resolved through demoncratisation— extending effective power to those below—but through liberalisation— the extension of power horizontally from the political apparatus to the techocratic managerial groups. Liberalisation retains the hierarchical order: the market opens new privileged sectors; the transition from bureaucratic collectivism to "market socialism" is structurally more feasible, politically more acceptable. This "historical compromise" within the apparatus is based on a consensus in maintaining labour discipline. The real change in peripheral state domination, hence, is for the working class to define itself in relation to both the bureaucracy and the market. The movement today is underway. In Bolivia, Peru, Nicaragua, it occurs in demands for self-management and among the more advanced sectors for a class based democracy.

In more general terms, this movement is manifest more widely in a rejection of existing state integration rather than in the affirmation of a new democratic alternative: the most elementary demand is for autonomous class organisation against both the corporatism of the capitalist state and the party dominated mass organisation of the collectivist state.

### Notes

1. See Folker Frobel, Jurgen Heinrichs, Otto Kreye, "The New International Division of Labour: Origins, Manifestations and Consequences" (mimeo). Bill Warren, "Imperialism and Capitalist Industrialisation", *New Left Review* (Sept./Oct. 1973). See also Martin Landsberg, "Export-Led Industrialisation in the Third World: Manufacturing Imperialism", *The Review of Radical Political Economics*, Vol. II, No. 4, pp.50-63.

2. See James Petras, "Comment l'Amerique latine alimente la prosperite des Etats-Unis", *Le Monde Diplomatique*, Aug. 1979, p.3.

3. Philip McMichael, James Petras, and Robert Rhodes, "Industrialisation in the Third World", in James Petras, *Critical Perspectives on Imperialism and Social Class in the Third World* (New York: Monthly Review, 1979), pp.103-136.

4. James Petras and Juan Manuel Carrion, "Contradictions of Colonial Industrialisation and the Crises in Commonwealth Status: The Case of Puerto Rico", in Petras, *Critical Perspectives on Imperialism and Social Class in the Third World*, pp.253-270.

# Part III

## Perspectives on the Transition to Socialism

# 6

# Social Classes, the State, and the World System in the Transition to Socialism

JAMES F. PETRAS
MARK SELDEN

During the 1960s, renewed interest and attention was directed to the "social relations of production" and the "superstructure" as the center piece of the discussion on the "transition to socialism." Previous emphasis on the "forces of production" revolved around the idea that development of the technical-material base determined the form and context of social relations and political institutions. Once state ownership and planning mechanisms were in place and the party's political primacy firmly established, the measure of socialism was taken to be the level of development of the productive forces: the greater the quantitative output of goods, and particularly the greater the strength of the heavy industrial sector, the closer to socialism. Some were content to measure "socialism" in terms of its ability to "catch up with and surpass" the level of production of the advanced capitalist countries. The dynamic agency of change was located in the realm of production and technology, from which all else followed. In 1950, Stalin summing up Soviet practice of two decades of forced draft industrialization, provided the authoritative formulation of the primacy of the productive forces and of the base over the superstructure:

> Every base has its own superstructure corresponding to it. The base of the feudal system has its superstructure—its political, legal, and other views and the corresponding institutions; the capitalist base has its own superstructure and so has the socialist base. If the base changes or is eliminated, then following this its superstructure changes or is eliminated; if a new base arises, then following this a superstructure arises corresponding to it.[1]

Such mechanistic formulations left their imprint on subsequent discussion, both inside and outside the Soviet Union. In this perspective, absolute obedience to party and state fiat, hierarchical organization in factories, one-man management, piecework, no strikes, were all justified as conducive to "building socialism," that is, to developing the productive forces efficiently. The notions of worker self-management, egalitarianism, and the restriction of class privilege which had inspired earlier socialist revolutionaries in Russia and elsewhere were attacked as petty-bourgeois or relegated to a misty, distant future state of "full communism." No serious effort was made to bridge the gap between contemporary policies and institutions, which seemed to be leading in the opposite direction, and the final goal of communism. The promise was that with abundance, socioeconomic and organizational divisions would simply wither away.

## The Challenge to Productive Forces Theory and the Limits of Mobilization Politics

In the late fifties and sixties this orthodox perspective which Stalin enshrined and his Soviet successors perpetuated came under direct attack from two major sources: Fidel Castro in Cuba and Mao Zedong in China. Both argued that changes in social relations and ideas were the essence of the socialist transition.[2] To be sure, the abundance of communism required extensive economic development, and both leaders attempted to formulate bold strategies for accelerated growth. But neither Castro nor Mao focused his energies on strategies for development of the productive forces per se. Operating on the political terrain which they knew best, they sought to foster changes in the realms of ideas and institutions which they proclaimed would propel the economy forward while insuring that the larger society was advancing not toward capitalism but to higher stages of socialism. In practice, both insisted not only that the effort to expand the productive forces had to be compatible with the eventual transition to communism but on the primacy of politics—hence, Mao's ideas of "politics in command" and uninterrupted revolution, and Castro's notion of "creating wealth with political awareness, not creating political awareness with wealth and money."

This approach struck a responsive chord among leftward-moving forces throughout the world, notably among radical intellectuals in the advanced capitalist countries where the productive forces were already highly developed, but also in the ranks of many Third World revolutionary nationalists who believed it offered a strategy for simultaneously unleashing the productive forces in their own stagnant or subjugated economies and regaining control of the reins of the national economy. In both China and Cuba the overriding preoccupation with politics in some quarters led to the relegation of issues pertaining to the productive forces to a secondary plane, part of the general environment which "conditions" the development of social relations.

This voluntarist reached its zenith in Mao's leadership during the Great Leap Forward and cultural revolution and in Castro's mobilization for the ten million ton Zafra of 1969–70 and criticism of the mechanical determinism of the Soviets.* In the late sixties, from China and Cuba to France of May '68 and the United States and Japanese new left, the attack on Soviet-style preoccupation with production indexes led to a renewed emphasis on "culture" (cultural revolution), "consciousness" (moral over material incentives), "class struggle" (including "red" over "expert"), and popular participation (mass mobilization). Inspired by the heroic Vietnamese resistance to the U.S. war machine, many drew the conclusion that "human will" could transcend the constraints imposed by underdeveloped capitalism or underdeveloped state socialism, or, in the core nations, could overwhelm the entrenched power of mature capitalism. The creation of a new "Socialist Individual," it was held, would lead directly to national liberation and the values and structures of a communist society. Both Mao and Castro asserted that their efforts to provide leadership for these changes would accelerate development of the productive forces. And both insisted on the necessity to take large economic risks to assure the desired changes in the realm of ideas and institutions.

In China and to a lesser extent in Cuba, the initial phases of the revolutionary transformation opened the way to development of the productive forces.[3] China's land revolution not only reduced inequality and improved living standards for poor peasants but made available new resources for investment by individual cultivators and the state. The early stages of cooperative formation, based on voluntary participation and gradual development by stages and resting on the explicit promise of mutual prosperity, sustained the process of expanded accumulation and rapid growth. By the mid-fifties China had embarked on a path of planned economic development leading toward nationalized industry and collectivized agriculture. China appeared, moreover, to have learned many of the lessons of forced collectivization which paved the way for long-term stagnation of Soviet agriculture and the antagonistic relationship between state and peasantry.

As the United States tightened the economic screws on Cuba beginning in 1959, Castro and his associates responded with successive edicts for nationalization of United States enterprises and the expropriation and collectivization of large-scale sugar plantations, ranches and mines, culminating in central planning and investment. The result was a mixed economy with leading industries in the hands of the state and collective

---

*Criticism of the Soviet Union, however, took very different forms in the two countries. While China coupled its critique of Soviet domestic policy with wholesale condemnation of Soviet foreign policy, Cuba, despite notable tensions in the sixties, eventually aligned itself closely with Soviet policy, notably but not exclusively, in Africa. Moreover, Cuban leaders never publicly aired a comprehensive critique of Soviet domestic policies.

agriculture, preserving, however, a significant private sector in the countryside. These measures increased the capacity of the state to capture and reinvest the surplus and to shape social and economic priorities. Large-scale aid and trade from the communist countries enabled Cuba (as China earlier) to survive and cushion the shock on living standards of the U.S. economic blockade and the necessity to redirect trade and technology from the U.S. and other capitalist nations.

Yet landlords can be expropriated only once, and the fruits of struggle channeled toward accumulation. By the summer of 1955, China's leadership, committed to ambitious industrialization goals, confronted the painful choice of cutting back the targets of its first Five-Year Plan (1953–57) or devising a new strategy to spur development. In the summer of 1955, Mao decisively intervened in the internal party debate and launched China on a new course dubbed "the socialist upsurge." In less than one year, China completed the projected 15-year program of full-scale collectivization of agriculture (Stalin's forced collectivization by comparison seems like "creeping socialism") and nationalization of industry. Noting that China accomplished this extraordinary organizational feat with a virtual absence of violence, and without apparent disastrous consequences for production, we may have missed the more important point about the upsurge and the Great Leap Forward which extended it two years later: These movements drove a deepening wedge between the party state and large elements of the peasantry as the Chinese leadership abandoned principles of voluntary participation and development by stages. Close to half the rural population moved directly and essentially by official fiat from private cultivation of land to large-scale collective agriculture. A substantial percentage of the peasantry, perhaps as high as one third, probably experienced collectivization not merely as imposed, but as a form of expropriation and loss of security (loss of title to and income from land they regarded as their own). For those who suffered a loss of income, including much of the middle peasantry, collectivization was emphatically not the fulfillment of the party's promise of mutual prosperity. Three years later, in the wake of the Great Leap, when the Chinese economy collapsed and the nation once again hovered at the brink of mass starvation as a result of policies associated with the Great Leap—reinforced to be sure by the 1960 withdrawal of Soviet aid and successive years of natural disaster—the most utopian elements of the commune system (e.g., premature establishment of accounting at the commune level, costly and wasteful village steel production, communal dining halls) were abandoned along with unsustainable rates of accumulation. Nevertheless, the entire structure of collective agriculture as well as the credibility of party leadership were seriously undermined, producing the subsequent "retreat" from the communes.

The Great Leap Forward was initially presented at the first stage in a technological revolution. Facing an acute capital shortage, however, Mao and his closest supporters in the leadership sought to press ahead rapidly with accumulation by tapping the remaining reserves of social labor (predominantly women), pressing the labor force to the limit (and often beyond), in short, turning labor into capital. To do so, they promised the peasantry that three years' hard labor would produce a thousand years of happiness: Communism, it appeared, was just around the corner.

When the politics and economics of the Leap were discredited in the eyes of many by the economic collapse of the early sixties, labor utilization rates declined below pre-Leap levels. Voting, so to speak, with their feet, many peasants partially withdrew from the collective economy by devoting more of their energies to their private plots and individual economic activities.

In the Great Leap and the cultural revolution, Mao Zedong led the party and people in political movements designed in part to curb the undoubted excesses of bureaucracy and reduce inequalities (the three great differences) in the name of workers and peasants. If the preceding analysis contains any grain of truth, however, the framework popularized during the cultural revolution—Mao's "socialist" road pitted against the "capitalist road" associated with Liu Shaoqi and much of the party leaderships—distorts far more than it explains. Problems associated with Mao's mobilization path, unending hastily conceived and ill-conceived economic innovation, unsustainable economic pressures on all classes, the increasing divorce of leadership from economic reality, and the abandonment of collective leadership principles require closer analysis.

In Cuba, beginning in 1968 with the Revolutionary Offensive which led to further expropriation of private property (though leaving an important private sector for agriculture) and culminating in 1970 with the Gran Zafra, the leadership attempted, through radical challenges to economic privilege, private property, and the division of labor, to lay the basis for the development of the productive forces. The offensive and the Zafra did curb one form of incipient bureaucratism and parasitic economic activity, but the state proved incapable of creating alternative forms of rulership or of managing many of the services that were replaced. The results included not only the decline of certain basic services and consumer items, but a thriving black market and tendencies to bureaucratic rigidity.

There was a further set of constraints on social transformation imposed by the backwardness of the productive forces and by the fact that these fragile economies (and Cuba's was both much richer than China's and more vulnerable to international pressures) remained dependent on the world market. No amount of exhortation and mobilization could substitute for the development of the technology, raw materials, petroleum, machinery, and food that were absolutely necessary to generate sustained growth. "Self-reliance," in both cases, initially imposed by the U.S. embargo and blockade, and then elevated to the level of a virtue, contributed to short-run national survival in the face of powerful external pressures. Yet turned into a principle rather than a survival strategy and carried to extremes, it could result in long and costly delays in development and transformation of resources and technological isolation. Frequently, where the resources were not available internally or could not be extracted with indigenous technology, the population, because of the priorities of leaders who still lived comfortably, if not opulently, had to go without. The virtues that resulted from the practice of "self-reliance"—discipline, national pride, class solidarity—were accompanied for ordinary citizens by austerity, rigidity, and sacrifice.

Reading Mao Zedong's writings of the forties and early fifties, one is struck by the socialist promise of mutual prosperity. Like Lenin earlier, Mao insisted that cooperation in the countryside must take place voluntarily through the demonstrated ability of co-ops to improve their members' livelihood (and not just the livelihood of the poor peasants).[4] Particularly by the time of the Cultural Revolution, that is, nearly two decades after liberation with its promise of abundance, the tone had become predominantly one of demanding self-sacrifice and belt tightening. Land revolution and the early cooperative movement had eliminated the most egregious forms of exploitation and inequality of the old society in each village of the Chinese countryside. This left, however, the residual problems of overwhelming poverty, as well as a range of inequalities. Among the contributions of the Chinese revolution was its clear recognition of the persistence of inequality and the threat it posed to socialist development. Some of these inequalities could be addressed, but none quickly eradicated, by the mass movement, between city and countryside, between educated and uneducated, between plains and mountain areas, between fertile and infertile regions, between coastal and inland regions, and among neighboring cooperative units, to name a few. The language of egalitarianism and even intense participation in social movements which continued after the completion of collectivization in 1956, notably during the Great Leap Forward and the Cultural Revolution, raised expectations but did not eliminate many remaining hierarchial divisions and pockets of privilege, though the pockets could sometimes be found in different parts. Socialism in both Cuba and China increasingly became identified in the minds of many citizens of those countries with moral virtue at the expense of material rewards. For those socialist workers who saw socialism as bringing a better material life in an egalitarian society, the experience surely presented a dilemma.

In the case of Cuba, economic dislocations and shortages that accompanied the supposed revolutionary offensive of 1968 (the expropriation of all private retailers, atrisans, petty commodity producers and manufacturers) and the failure of the targeted ten million ton sugar harvest resulted in a shift in emphasis from mass mobilization to economic planning and programming, from a stress on moral exhortation to greater emphasis on material incentives, from a focus on revolutionary ascetism to expanded consumer rewards.[5]

Political changes soon followed. Decisions affecting education and administration were delegated to local assemblies, which were elected by popular vote with a choice of multicandidate listing. Decentralization and self-financing has strengthened enterprise managers at the expense of central political authorities, but without greatly increasing workers' control over basic planning.

The shift in Cuban internal developments toward a more decentralized rational-bureaucratic model has probably increased the availability of consumer goods and inequalities. The shift from mass mobilization to "party building" may have facilitated more efficient planning, but not necessarily greater political accessibility for the majority of working people. Moreover, the differences between mental and manual, skilled and unskilled, rural and urban labor which were contained through the mass mobilization campaigns are reappearing as the division of labour reasserts its centrality in the new scheme of things.

Internationally, Cuba continued to support revolutionary movements throughout most of Latin America—Nicaragua, El Salvador, Chile, Brazil and Uruguay. In some of these countries, it supports the revolutionary left; in others the orthodox communist parties; and in still others, both. At the same time, in some Caribbean, Central American, and South American countries Cuba has extended political support to social democrats, like Manley in Jamaica or nationalist opportunists like Burnham in Guyana, and has refrained from criticizing its biggest trading partner in the Americas, the Videla dictatorship in Argentina. Cuba's international policy thus reflects the contradictions between its revolutionary origins and social base on the one hand and, on the other, both its "state needs" to break the U.S. economic blockade and extend trade ties in order to develop the productive forces, and popular pressures to improve living standards. The revolutionary transformation of Cuban society, the overarching changes in socioeconomic structure, particularly the redistribution of wealth and nationalization of foreign and Cuban enterprise, come into conflict with the need to engage in exchange in the capitalist world market. The result is that the Cuban position can be adequately explained neither by exclusive reference to its position in the world system nor by simply extrapolating from the internal changes in class relationships. The contradictory international position of revolutionary states is observable in the imperatives derived from the commitment to internal transformation of social relations and the imperatives resulting from the necessity of participating in capitalist exchange and production operating through the world market.

## The World Economy, Social Classes, and Contradictions of the Transition Period

World system analysts, operating almost exclusively at the level of the world market and the relationship of countries to it, have highlighted one important element of constraint on revolutionary societies. They often fail, however, to comprehend the significance of the changes that have taken place within revolutionary socialist societies and which sharply differentiate them from neocolonial "peripheral societies" whose national independence has left intact the sinews of the colonial economic and social order. Changes in social relations of production, the egalitarian and redistributive measures, tend to be ignored as a result of the all-determining preoccupation with the role of the world capitalist market. Since "the relations of production that define a system are the relations of production of the whole system, and the system at this time is the European (i.e., capitalist) world economy," ergo any nation which participates in that system must be capitalist.[6] Class struggle, social revolutions, and changes in state power are reduced to efforts to change positions in the world market. What then was the significance for Russia of the Bolshevik revolution? As Immanual Wallerstein observes in an influential article, following the World War II "Russia was reinstated as a very strong member of the semi-periphery and could begin to seek full core status." In short, the revolution strengthened Russian ability to compete within the world capitalist system.[7] No less, no more.

World systems analysis fails to comprehend the role that "peripheral" revolutionary socialist societies play in extending revolutionary struggles throughout the capitalist system. At the same time, pressures generated within the world economy intensify contradictions among socialist states. The accomodation of some reflects the push and pull between internal revolutionary dynamics and the pull of the capitalist market.

This critique applies equally to those "mode-of-production" analysts who in the same mechanical fashion reduce the whole problem of socialist revolution to changes in social relations and ideas, ignoring both domestic economic constraints and the operations of the world market. Thus, changes in policy, especially in external relations, are described as results of irreversible changes in the class nature of the regime, as if the internal classes lived independently of the constraints and demands of the world market and apart from the need for market participation to develop the productive forces.

Beginning in the early to mid-1970s, following the economic dislocations of the "ten million ton" sugar harvest and the Cultural Revolution, a shift occurred with respect both to the urgency of the development of productive forces and the role of foreign technology and capital in Cuba and China. Having officially downplayed economic and technological factors in the development of productive forces, their impact did not disappear; on the contrary, the underdevelopment of technology and the continuing need to penetrate competitive markets and to earn foreign exchange began to seriously impair the capacity of each society to grow. Throughout the 1970s, and well before Mao's death, pressures intensified for rapid economic growth, acquisition of foreign exchange, and technological development, leading to the renewal of political and economic ties with the United States, Japan, and Europe to achieve these goals. In the event, technological specialists and administrators who had been the object of repeated attack during the Cultural Revolution became still more indispensable as political priorities retarded the broadening and deepening of the technological base. Tendencies toward stagnation led to a crisis of the whole regime. At the very moment when Mao was pressing for an opening to the United States and Japan, specialists and administrators who saw foreign technology as crucial to China's development were making a comeback from their defeat in the Cultural Revolution. Changes in domestic policy went hand in hand with China's new international alignments.

By the early 1970s the continuing blockade of Cuba, the defeat of the revolutionary upsurge in Latin America, China's hostility, and the continuing dependence on the USSR all led Cuban policy in the direction of increasing emphasis on developing the productive forces and developing ties with nonrevolutionary societies. If anything, these pressures were stronger in a China which from the 1960s experienced its major international threat as coming from its one-time ally and protector, the Soviet Union.

From these multiple crises, pressures built internally to give greater scope to market forces and technical specialists and to view with increasing distrust the demands of an internally divided party. The phenomenon was not of course limited to China and Cuba. We can trace the response to these pressures for reform to the Liberman proposals in the Soviet Union and Yugoslav experimentation with self-management in the mid-fifties. In differing ways each sought to overcome bureaucratic rigidity and excessive centralization in order to insure higher productivity and increased personal incomes. At the same time, there was growing recognition of the need to relate to the world market,* including imports of technology from more advanced industrial countries, to expand the scope of foreign trade and earnings, and in general to accept a larger role for foreign capital. The dangers of market ties—increasing Western leverage—tended to be neglected.

In both Cuba and China, the initial impetus for industrial development and diversification rested in part on substantial technological and financial support from the Soviet Union. By the early sixties, however, the tie between China and the USSR had broken and the period of bitter recrimination had begun. While Soviet—Cuba relations were firm, both China and Cuba looked increasingly to participation in the world capitalist market. In the Chinese case, this took on added importance as a means to build ties which might blunt the danger of Soviet encirclement. And U.S. imperialism, which had spurned Chinese communist overtures in the 1940s and 1950s, now sought to play the China

---

*The evidence is clear that the Mao group in China consistently understood this necessity and sought to prevent its isolation and dependence on the Soviet Union from at least 1944. U.S. policies of confrontation and blockade thwarted such possibilities for more than two decades.

card to increase its leverage against the USSR, Vietnam, and the Third World. The United States recognized the economic and military advantages in a diplomatic opening to China. In the mid 1970s, the United States attempted to harness Castro to its imperial interests, but the effort floundered in part because of Cuba's support of the Angolian revolution and its ties with the USSR, especially Ethiopia.

The revolutionary socialist regimes, whether China, Cuba, Vietnam, Mozambique, Yugoslavia or Angola, without exception, have had to come to terms with their basic material conditions.

Over the medium run, the underdevelopment of the productive forces within revolutionary Third World countries has forced increasingly compromising relations with imperial countries. The objective constraints imposed by the uneven distribution of productive forces on a world scale has been and will continue to be a much more important factor shaping regime behavior than the "betrayal" of this or that revolutionary group or leadership. This is not to negate the importance of revolutionary leadership, political program, and relationship between party and class. Political choices with differential impacts on and in response to the demands of particular social classes condition the impact of international economic relations including technological constraints which reinforce bureaucratic, hierarchical, and technologically derived perspectives in the socialist transitions, frequently at the expense of egalitarian and participatory socialist goals. No nation, whatever its revolutionary credentials, can escape these constraints so long as all must participate in the world economy, accumulate capital, and apply advanced technology. International market relations, moreover, find resonance within the political structure, converging with the interests of managerial and technological personnel and petty commodity producers. These tendencies affect not only domestic class relations, but resonate in state-to-state and broader international situations.

## Mobilization Politics, the State and the Problems of Socialist Democracy

To understand post-capitalist socioeconomic and political development and particularly the social nature of the political regime, it is important to recognize two basic facts: (1) the social forces participating in the revolution, and heavily represented in the party and state structure include a wide array of nonworking class, nonpeasant social forces, namely intellectuals, administrators, small businessmen, and diverse professionals, and (2) a substantial part of the officials from the previous government, police, managerial, and educational systems are incorporated along with revolutionary cadres and newly educated technicians and administrators into the new state. The nationalist coalitions which bring about anticolonial revolutions aspiring toward socialism share in varying degees common anticapitalist and socialist convictions and widely divergent understandings of the content of those categories and the methods to achieve them. Once the initial period of revolutionary euphoria passes, sharp differences inevitably emerge over the nature and program of the revolutionary state as it confronts such monumental problems as poverty, underdevelopment, and external threats. New and old officials, in the state, party, and army, as well as intellectuals and technocrats, all experience expanded power with the enlarged economic and political role of the state as a direct function of revolutionary changes in ownership and planning.

Once the initial phases of revolutionary transformation have passed and the initial gains of land revolution, cooperative formation, and central planning have been consolidated, what Mao Zedong described as contradictions between state, collective, and individual emerge with increasing clarity. The issues cut far deeper than the corruption of "betrayal" of individual cadres ("capitalist roaders" in Chinese parlance of the Cultural Revolution). State goals such as accelerated accumulation, rapid industrialization, and military modernization clash, for example, with the efforts of peasants and workers to translate the gains of the revolution into improved living standards; the "correct plans" of the state conflict with the desire for greater local control over resources for both investment and consumption; and where the center prevails the results may include bureaucratic rigidity and passivity at the grass roots. Moreover, the desire for autonomy of individual cooperatives (self-reliance) tends to produce greater inequality among units and regions as the strong prosper; by contrast, the state could use its expanded powers to narrow differences.

The main tendency in early periods of the transition nevertheless is clear: The party-state tends to create centralized hierarchical production-oriented regimes in which "masses" are "mobilized" to fulfill production quotas—the realization of which is defined as "achieving socialism." The principal struggle is not between capitalist roaders and revolutionaries but involves post-capitalist forces struggling to shape the social relations of production and the class character of the state which will facilitate economic-technical development and preside over the collectivist society.

The most striking development of national liberation and revolutionary socialist politics is the capacity of workers and peasants to initiate and particularly to participate in shaping revolutionary processes—notably the overthrow of the old regime and transformation of ownership and political institutions—but their capacity to gain and retain control over the emerging state. Even where the commitment to popular welfare is genuine as it clearly is in China and Cuba, the growth of the party-state emerges as the distinct social solution which intellectual functionaries impose to mobilize and discipline the producers while maximizing their control and disposal of the economic surplus. While the mechanisms of wealth, power, and privilege differ in capitalist and state socialist societies, political power in the bureaucratic party-state apparatus translates into economic power. Moreover, the evidence suggests that in many cases privileges and prerogatives can be transferred to offspring. The decisions and power of this bureaucratic stratum are, however, conditioned by the values and other constraints of the originally mass revolutionary movement. Ironically, the party whose leadership is so vital in helping to eliminate old modes of exploitation and to bring working people to the center of the historical stage in the national liberation and early phases of socialist transition tends to become the principal obstacle to the full realization of a democratic socialism attentive to the goals of progressive worker mastery over society. The interface of the two processes of market integration and bureaucratism define the essential political problem confronting working classes in the transition to socialism.

Against this background we may consider the dramatic shifts in emphasis that have taken place between the 1960s and 1970s in both China and Cuba. The startling rapidity of the pendulum swing, from the preoccupation with social relations and revolutionary politics to a focus on developing productive forces and to meeting popular needs and wants, represents in part a powerful popular reaction across class lines (though hardly evenly or universally) to the intense and sustained politicization of the proceeding decades and the repeated calls for personal sacrifice.* This swing was facilitated in both countries by the high level of political and economic centralization characteristic of the expanded state power of the socialist period. Despite development of a range of approaches to popular participation at the rank-and-file level in these and other socialist countries, they share powerful party-led bureaucracies capable of dominating the major national and particularly international decisions. The speed with which shifts initiated at the center take place, and the wide swings of policy characteristic of both Chinese and Cuban politics, attest to the lack of built-in institutional safeguards which might challenge such shifts. In both China and Cuba the lack of firm institutional anchorage for "mobilized masses," linking the point of production to the national level, and the lack of organizational autonomy (independent of state and party hierarchies), place limits on sustained collective activities which are not initiated or supported by the centre. Moreover, where mobilization failed to give rise to sustained institutional expression of the people, as in the case of chaotic labour mobilization for the Cuban harvest, or as in the inability to create effective new popular institutions during China's cultural revolution, mobilization frequently produced dislocations, declining production, and falling living standards for a large segment of the labor force. When

---

*In the case of China, the reaction was strengthened by the fact that one aspect of the campaign to permanently discredit the Gang of Four focused on their opulent personal lifestyles while they had called on others for spartan self-sacrifice in the name of revolution. This was, of course, a politial weapon used by their opponents (as they had used it previously). However, at least in the case of Jiang Qing, Mao's widow, we have independent evidence to corroborate some of the charges.

revolutionary changes in social production became associated with day-to-day dislocation, and arbitrary uses of power, or with the goals of young worker or student activists at the expense of experienced workers, the result was to reinforce those political forces pushing for "modernization" rooted in technical rationality and discipline, i.e., development of productivity within a stable hierarchical pattern. In short, the very power and persistence of the political movements of both countries created preconditions for a sharp swing to the opposite pole.

The challenge to orthodoxy provided often brilliant but sometimes murderous and self-serving opposition to prevailing practice. Intensified frustration with erratic economic performance reinforced the backlash against arbitrary and cruel uses of power. This left the door wide open to resurgence of those who recognized the limits of political mobilization for transformation of production relationships and ideas in an economy of scarcity, who focused instead on new approaches to stimulating the economy and improving people's livelihood. We observe important shifts within the top echelons, from mobilization from above and below, to modernization and stabilization from above combined with wider play to market forces from below. The consequences of the changes throughout the social system promise to be profound and far-reaching, though the pattern of recent decades should alert us to the prospect that the current phase may provoke anew these counter forces which are presently quiescent.

Socialist regimes have tended to oscillate among three poles, emphasizing at given periods political mobilization, stabilization of centralized bureaucratic power, or reliance on market forces. Historically, the mobilization approach has tended to recede in importance with the elimination of old exploitive classes (particularly landlords and capitalists), the completion of the transition of ownership to state and collective forms, and the growth and consolidation of bureaucratic power. Both China and Cuba, in part because of the vigor and longevity of the revolutionary generation which initiated the socialist transition, and in part as a result of the deep imprint of the earlier guerrilla struggle, have exhibited unusual tenacity in the persistence of mobilization politics.

But if a central goal of socialism remains the formation of an institutional order which makes the regime fully responsible to and subject to control by the direct producers, not China, Cuba, nor any other socialist state has yet approached solution to the problem. Here we touch on the institutionalized power of the party state and the weakness of democratic tradition.

"Mass mobilizations" continue to play a political role, planning and direction tend to be monopolized from above, as is evidenced by the fact that when the pendulum swings the other way there is virtually no public outcry or counteraction. The press heralds the new line and officially organized mass meetings legitimate it. Rather than a full assessment of former policies, what passes for public discussion typically illuminates only their failures while continuing to claim the omniscience of the party. All too often, the transcendent goals, the ten million tons, the Great Leap Forward, are imposed by the party-state on society. While resistance to particular policies is evident, what is lacking is genuine public debate and discussions; still less, legitimate channels for organized opposition. The sometimes erratic shifts from market to bureaucracy and from centralist to decentralist managerialism are reflections of the absence of institutional power of the direct producers. Workers' democracy, beginning in the workplace and radiating throughout society, is not something that is extraneous or a luxury if the goals are genuinely socialism and not state capitalism. It is integral to the effective operation of a socialist economy and politics. The initial stages of mobilization politics during national liberation movements and the struggle for the land provide organizational and experiential foundations for subsequent efforts to create socialist democracy. The more difficult task is to sustain and build on these foundations in subsequent phases of the revolution.

## International Solidarity: Prospects and Constraints

The constraints imposed by the uneven development of the productive forces on diverse revolutionary societies are widely visible. Mozambique, Yugoslavia, Cuba, Vietnam, North Korea and China have all experienced liberation struggles involving the mobilization of significant numbers of workers and peasants, as well as sections of the bourgeoisie. These revolutionary movements have proceeded to expel imperialist and neocolonial forces, to eliminate the power of landed wealthy classes, and to collectivize and nationalize principal means of production. Each has proclaimed its fundamental adherence to the principles of revolutionary socialism. In none of these cases was socialism "imposed" from outside by invading armies as in parts of Eastern Europe. Rather it grew upon the basis of unique institutions, largely the products of the interaction between indigenous mass forces and leadership responding to exploitation imposed by imperialism and by domestic ruling classes. In each of these cases, the main social base of the revolutionary regimes unquestionably derived from worker-peasant forces.

Yet each of these regimes, the product of mass-based revolutions deriving their legitimacy and strength primarily from oppressed classes, has developed international policies and relations with capitalist and imperialist countries which seem to substantially contravene elements of the logic and process that brought them to power. Having broken the power of local ruling classes and banished foreign capital and military power from within the boundaries of the nation-state, and having once overcome the efforts of core capitalist countries to crush the revolution by armed intervention or blockade, every revolutionary regime has moved to reestablish linkages with the nations and capital of the core and, in some cases, to pursue active collaboration with imperial power. Having reached the summit of political power internally, the revolutionary regimes, typically emerging from colonial or semi-colonial bondage, confront the international power of the capitalist marketplace from a markedly disadvantageous position.

A few illustrations highlight the issues and the painful choices facing these revolutionary nations. Mozambique, under the leadership of Frelimo, went through a profound national and social revolution, destroying the Portuguese colonial regime and its local collaborators, and establishing mass-based political committees as the new basis of power. Yet the main source of the revolutionary regime's foreign exchange, $80–100 million per year in 1976 and 1977, remains the cash produced by contract laborers working in the mines of the racist South African regime. Both South Africa and Rhodesia, moreover, brought immense pressure to bear on Mozambique in an effort to crush the guerrilla opposition to the Smith-Muzorewa regime in Zimbabwe, including armed attack and sabotage.

The contrast is striking with the policies adopted by Mozambique immediately after its own liberation. In an act of revolutionary solidarity, the new Frelimo-led government of Mozambique closed its border with Rhodesia, suffering a loss of revenue estimated at $50 million annually. This position could not, however, be sustained. Indeed, within a week Mozambique and Rhodesia reestablished political and economic ties in contrast, for example, to the long-term post-liberation experience of Castro's Cuba and Mao's China under U.S. blockade. In this case the pressures included the need for external markets and finished goods provided by Mozambique's more developed neighbor, and foreign exchange provided by migrant workers. These factors contributed to Mozambique's decision together with other front line states, to exert pressures on ZANU to make the transition from armed struggle to an electoral strategy which eventually led to the formation of the Mugabe government in coalition with settlers, ZAPU forces on a pro-capitalist program.[9]

Like Mozambique, Cuba has maintained strong ties to revolutionary movements and provided material support including its own troops in Africa. In the course of two decades, however, the Cuban economy has been integrated into economic domain of the Soviet bloc in ways which have in fact reinforced its economic position as a primary commodity producer heavily dependent on sugar.[10] In the foreign policy area we observe the (conflicting) consequences both of Cuba's alliance with the Soviet Union and the need to preserve working relationships with major (capitalist) trade partners. Cuba has moderated its support for armed revolutionary struggle in much of Latin America in ways often consistent, though not identical, with Soviet policy and it has also developed numerous relationships of convenience with repressive regimes. In the cases of Guyana, Argentina, Brazil, Ethiopia, and the Soviet invasion of Afganistan, for example, Cuba has either avoided public criticism because of important economic ties (Argentina, Brazil, and the Soviet

Union's Afganistan adventure), provided propagandistic support because of political ties (Guyana), or furnished material support (to Ethiopia, yet apparently stopping short of armed intervention in Eritrea).

China's policy in recent years furnishes us striking examples of accommodation and cooperation with the leading capitalist nations. In the course of the past decade, the Chinese economy has increasingly tied itself to the world market in ways which have reinforced its political ties with Western and pro-Western regimes. The displacement of the "mobilization" faction by a leadership group preoccupied with technological and economic growth has facilitated the transition to greater market linkages and political accommodation with pro-Western forces. Continuing scarcities and underdevelopment as well as a popular reaction to the clique politics and extremism associated with the cultural revolution have provided the new leadership group with a rationale for governance—"modernization." The border conflict with the USSR has reinforced the socioeconomic factors predisposing the current Chinese government toward increasingly close economic and political ties with the West. The decision by the Chinese leadership to seek Western sources of capital and technology, the emergence within the leadership of a dominant group intent on economic modernization and rapid improvement of living standards even at the cost of growing inequality, and hostility to the class struggle perspective of the cultural revolution period converge to reinforce new elements in Chinese foreign policy. What is ironic about China's conflict with the USSR is that it intensifies as the difference over domestic policies recede. Deng Xiaoping charges that "the Soviet Union pushes hegemonism and commits aggression abroad, it bullies, enslaves and exploits other countries." Hence it is a "social-imperialist country."[11] Such charges are no longer accompanied by an attack on Soviet domestic policies. The current Chinese leadership has quietly abandoned significant elements of its critique of Soviet policy, including the charge of revisionism.

As in other societies, socialist or capitalist, China's policies are primarily influenced by the development of internal class forces and the constraints of the world capitalist market. Notions that attribute changes in international policy to decisionmakers' "perceptions" of military conflict with a political adversary are not capable of explaining the all pervasive shifts in world alignments, the massive and sustained internal shifts in socioeconomic relations and long-term goals and the transvaluation of values.

Given the internal changes and the external pressures of the market, it is not surprising that China has lent moral or material support to a number of repressive and counterrevolutionary Third World regimes, e.g., Pinochet's Chile, Savimbi in Angola, the former Shah in Iran, Zia in Pakistan, Marcos in the Philippines. Edward Friedman has analyzed the economic component of certain policies which have brought China, Cuba, and others into economic relations with certain Third World dictatorships:

Peking, a copper importer (still trying to develop copper mines) cooperates with copper producers Zaire, Zambia, and China as Cuba, a sugar exporter, cooperates with Brazil's murderous rulers, who are also sugar exporters. The alternative to such cooperation is deep injury to one's own citizens from ruthless world-market forces.[12]

At the same time, opposition to the Soviet Union has drawn China close to a number of the most retrograde forces in the West, including Franz Joseph Strauss in West Germany, Senator Henry Jackson and Zbigniew Brzezinski in the United States, and Prime Minister Margaret Thatcher in England. And China's condemnation and punitive invasion against Vietnam as "the Cuba of Asia" reveals just how far the demise of the socialist bloc has proceeded.

In looking to the United States and Japan, the present Chinese leadership hopes to alleviate its major military problem (the Soviet threat) and to obtain sources of capital and technology. In noting the fact that China is actively seeking foreign capital, including direct investment and public and private loans, is planning the formation of free export zones, and has joined the IMF, it is worth observing the continuing emphasis on the primacy of internal factors. Thirty years of revolution and industrialization have transformed the environment into which foreign capital and technology is now being infused.

Unlike China and Cuba, Vietnam completed national liberation at a time when Sino–Soviet conflict had peaked and the clarity of division between a socialist and capitalist bloc had blurred. Vietnam's long struggle to preserve an independent position between the Soviet Union and China quickly came to grief following the defeat of the United States in 1975. While defeated militarily, U.S. policies of isolating Vietnam at a time of increasing Sino–Vietnamese tensions reduced Vienamese options. When relations with China ruptured entirely as a result of Vietnam's invasion of Kampuchea, the expulsion of Chinese residents and the Chinese military invasion of Vietnamese territory, Vietnam entered the Soviet camp.

Two elements of Vietnamese policy vividly reflect the pressures to overcome its isolation and reintegrate itself within the world capitalist economy. First, Vietnam's overtures to the ASEAN states included the public promise to end its support for fraternal liberation movements in neighboring Thailand and the Philippines. Secondly, Vietnam quickly entered into agreements with Western oil companies to develop her offshore resources and with Japanese firms permitting foreign investment in Vietnamese industry. Both policies reflect the material constraints on the Vietnamese revolutionary leadership, more than subjective leadership failings.

The revolutionary regimes without exception confront a formidable array of problems, many of them the legacy of earlier protracted colonial or semi-colonial domination, including acute shortage of capital, technology, and industrial base, distorted monoculture and export-oriented economies, and the destruction by ruling classes in defeat of important productive forces. Each of the revolutions considered here has achieved impressive gains, particularly viewed against the record of the prere-volutionary condition. Yet each remains vulnerable in economic, tech-nological, and financial terms. This phenomenon has generated pressures to reenter the world market in order to develop the nationalized and collectivized productive forces. Underdevelopment of the productive forces which once contributed to the anti-imperialist upsurge and the search for socialist institutions can now be seen to place constraints on revolutionary practices both domestically and internationally. These constraints are manifest in both their internal development policies and their external relations with capitalist countries. Inevitably, they limit the degree and scope of international solidarity between post-revolu-tionary regimes and emerging revolutionary movements both in the stage of national liberation (as in Zimbabwe, South Africa, East Timor, Thailand, and the Philippines) and in those seeking to forge a socialist strategy (for example, Angola, Kampuchea and Guinea-Bissau).

Nevertheless, as a result of the pressures outlined above, but also because of changes in world alignments, notably the disintegration of the socialist bloc and the Sino–Soviet dispute, contradictory elements in the foreign policies of each of these nations are clearly evident. These include Mozambiquan pressures on ZANU to accomodate in Zimbabwe; Cuban support for Ethiopian efforts to crush the Eritrean national liberation movement; Vietnamese public renunciation of support for the liberation movements in Thailand and the Philippines; and China's opposition to liberation movements in many parts of Africa and Latin America.

World market forces may have distorted internal processes, encour-aging technocratic and market tendencies; they have not, however, been effective in undermining public ownership, economic planning, or the education, health, and welfare programs initiated by socialist programs. Market pressures to produce more efficiently, the inequalities in pro-ductive forces on a world scale, and technological backwardness in the underdeveloped socialist societies all converge to strengthen the status and position of mangerial-technocratic strata. The demands of the world market mediated through these strata, however, are constrained by power relations established by the revolution, and the mass expectations enshrined in the organizations and programs that legitimate the state. Distortions in post-revolutionary societies generated by the world market are repeatedly challenged by egalitarian impulses reflected in continuing class struggles. World systems anaylsis, through a classificatory approach that considers only the position of societies in the international economy, fails to capture essential changes of the contemporary epoch—the contradictory process of capitalist expansion and socialist revolution. Moreover, the assumption of some world systems theorists that basically nothing has changed in revolutionary societies (since they still participate in the world capitalist system) fails to account for the dual nature of participation and rejection. The class-based regimes resulting from the national and class struggles cannot simply be reduced to components of the capitalist system. The great (if incomplete) transformation of the Chinese countryside and Cuba's historic defeat of South African forces in Angola can best be understood as aspects of the anticapitalist class struggle and not as marginal shifts within the world capitalist system.

Revolutionary socialist states are in a contradictory position; they have eliminated gross patterns of exploitation and privilege centered on the ownership and control of major means of production; collectivized agriculture and nationalized industry; initiated far-reaching changes in health, education, welfare, and employment; reduced many forms of privilege and inequality; ended external control over their natural and human resources; and many have made a significant start on creating the foundations for a democratic politics. Yet they must compete from positions of weakness within a capitalist world market which imposes its own rules of conduct: competition, profit-making, unequal exchange, and so on.

The contradictory position of revolutionary states has evoked a variety of responses, including: (1) policies to extend revolutionary movements throughout other areas (international solidarity); (2) selective support of some revolutionary struggles while developing ties with nonrevolutionary regimes in other areas; (3) alignment with counter-revolutionary forces seeking to maximize advantages through the market at the expense of class struggle; (4) unification of Third World and other states to oppose the hegemony of the core nations in general and the superpowers in particular.

Three conflicting factors—the world market and the related market exchanges, the party state and its administrators and cadres, and the struggles of working people to widen their sphere of political activity while improving their livelihood—shape the contours of the socialist transition within and among nations.

## Notes

1. Joseph Stalin, *Marxism and Linguistics* (New York: International Publishers, 1961), p. 9.

2. For Mao, the classic texts are "Reading Notes on the Soviet Text Political Economy" in *A Critique of Soviet Economics* (New York: Monthly Review Press, 1977), and "On Kruschchev's Phoney Communism and Its Historical Lessons for the World," *Peking Review*, July 17, 1964. Substantial extracts of both texts are available in Mark Selden, *The People's Republic of China. A Documentary History of Revolutionary Change* (New York: Monthly Review Press, 1979). The emphasis on production relations and the primacy of politics were not new themes for Mao. However, they took on new dimensions from the late 1950s. For Castro, see "We Will Never Build a Communist Conscience with a Dollar Sign in the Minds and Hearts of Men"; 'The Revolutionary Offensive: We did not make a revolution to establish the right to trade'; "Creating Wealth with Political Awareness, not creating Political awareness with money and wealth" in *Fidel Castro Speaks*, ed. James Petras and William Kenner (New York: Grove Press, 1969).

3. Victor Lippit, *Land Reform and Economic Development in China: The Contribution of Institutional Change to Financing Economic Development* (New York: International

Arts and Sciences Press, 1974). Selden, *The People's Republic of China*, introduction: James O'Connor, *The Origins of Socialism in Cuba* (Ithaca: Cornell University Press, 1970); Edward Boorstein, *the Economic Transformation of Cuba* (New York: Monthly Review Press, 1968).

4. See in particular Mao's "Jingji wenti yu caizheng wenti" (Economic and Financial Problems) in *Mao Zedon Ji*, ed. Takeuchi Minoru (Collected Works of Mao Zedong), vol. 8, pp. 183–324, and Mao's first major statement on agricultural cooperation, "Zuzhichilai" (Get Organized!) in ibid., vol. 9, pp. 85–94. Selden has explored this issue at length in a paper prepared for the Conference on the Socialist Transition in China's Countryside.

5. Carmelo Mesa Lago, *Cuba in the 1970s* (Albuquerque: University of New Mexico, 1974); Frank Fitzgerald, "Critique of the Sovietization of Cuba Thesis," *Science and Society*, vol. 42, Spring 1978, pp. 1–32; Arch Ritter, "Growth Strategy and Cuba: Past, Present, and Perspective," *Social and Economic Studies*, vol. 21, no. 3, September 1972, pp. 313–37; David Lehmann, "The Cuban Economy in 1978," *Cambridge Journal of Economics*, vol. 3, 1979, pp. 319–26.

6. Immanuel Wallerstein, *The Modern World System* (New York: Academic Press, 1974), p. 127. Parallel criticisms apply to the treatment of capitalism in Latin America by André Gunder Frank and a number of other dependence theorists whose preoccupation with world market relations has tended to obliterate or distort internal class and other factors. See, for example, his *Capitalism and Underdevelopment in Latin America* (New York: Monthly Review, 1967).

7. "The Rise and Future Demise of the World Capitalist System: Concepts for Comparative Analysis," in *The Capitalist World-Economy. Essays by Immanuel Wallerstein* (Cambridge: Cambridge University Press, 1979), pp. 30–31. Recently Wallerstein has begun to address a number of issues pertinent to the relationship among classes, states, and the world system—always, however, from the perspective of the primacy of the latter. See, "The Withering Away of the States," *International Journal for the Sociology of the Law*, forthcoming.

8. Samir Amin, "Self-reliance and the New International Economic Order," *Monthly Review*, vol. 29, no. 3, July-August 1977, pp. 1–21. Harry Magdoff, "The Limits of International Reform," *Monthly Review*, vol. 30, no. 1, May 1978, pp. 1–11.

9. John Saul, "Mozambique—The New Phase," *Monthly Review*, vol. 30, no. 10, March 1979, pp. 1–19 alludes to the problem of migrant labourers. See also Allen Isaacman, *A Luta Continua. Creating a New Society in Mozambique*. Southern Africa Pamphlet (Binghamton: Fernand Braudel Center, 1978), pp. 49, 63. A special editorial in *Review of African Political Economy*, no. 14, January/April 1979, just prior to Robert Mugabe's victory at the polls observed of the situation in Mozambique:

The front line African states led by Tanzania's Nyerere, but particularly Zambia and Mozambique which had hosted the guerila forces, withdrew their commitment to prolonged struggle and told the PF (Patriotic Front) parties that they had to accept some deal; they must get the best they could out of Lancaster House. . .

More recently, internal changes have also taken place; the Mozambique state accepted an expanded role for the marketplace. As Machel has recently pronounced, the new economica policy is one in which "the state will create the conditions to support private traders, farmers, and industrialists. Private activity has an important role to play in straightening out our country" (*Washington Post*, March 21, 1979).

10. A recent assessment of the issue of pre- and post-revolutionary Cuba's economic "dependency" concludes that while it remains high, it has in fact been significantly reduced by comparison with the period of U.S. domination of the island's political economy. William M. LeoGrande, "Cuban Dependency: A Comparison of Pre-Revolutionary and Post-Revolutionary International Economic Relations," *Cuban Studies*, vol. 9, no. 2, July 1979, pp. 1–28.

11. Statement to Sekou Toure, May 5, 1980, *Beijing Review*, May 19, 1980, p. 5.

12. Edward Friedman, "Maoist Conceptualization of the World Capitalist World-System," in *Processes of the World System*, ed. Terance Hopkins and Immanuel Wallerstein (Los Angeles: Sage, 1980), p. 220. Cf. John Gittings, *The World and China, 1922–1972* (London: Eyre Lethuen, 1974). Both Friedman and Gittings point to important continuities as well as basic changes in one of orientation of Chinese policy.

# 7

# *Marxism and World-Historical Transformations*

JAMES PETRAS

## *Introduction*

In the Third World, several issues related to the Marxist discussion of the transition to socialism have recently come to the fore. For purposes of our discussion, let us focus on four issues: (1) the possibility of incorporating capitalist cooperation over a prolonged period of time in order to avoid internal and external dislocations; (2) the concept of capitalist development as the economic basis for socialist transformation; (3) the idea that capitalist production simplifies the tasks for production, thus obviating the need for specialists; and (4) the notion that mass organizations involved in the struggle to overthrow capitalist regimes become the basis for worker and peasant self-rulership.

## *Marxism and the Transition to Socialism*

Recent experience in Latin America provides us with a set of cases that throw considerable light on the effort to incorporate capitalist cooperation in the transition to socialism. In the not too distant past in Chile (1970–73) and in Jamaica (1972–80), efforts were made to induce private capital to cooperate in the economic development of the country. In both cases, capital responded by fleeing the country, running down plant and equipment, and working in tandem with international capital and the imperial state in destabilizing the regime and eroding the popular base of the democratic-socialist regime. Subsequent to the downfall of the socialist regime, the capitalist forces have effectively established themselves as the sole interests shaping governmental policy.

More recently, we can observe the efforts by the Nicaraguan government to fashion a coalition of public and private capital aimed at reactivating the economy. While in the initial months the capitalist spoke of a commitment to national development, as the revolutionary process unfolded through the rapid growth of mass organizations the bourgeoisie began to disinvest and to run down production. The inevitable result of the failure of private investment has been the growth of the state sector—the capitalists have engaged in a self-fulfilling prophecy: creating the very conditions they claimed to have sought to avoid. Rather than cooperate with the revolution in developing production and profits, the private sector chooses to join with imperial state induced counterrevolution to overthrow the regime, even at the loss of the enterprise.

It is clear from the above that the attempt to develop a socialist strategy that incorporates private capital results in a very unstable equilibrium. The efforts to provide guarantees of economic profits, state loans, and export incentives to capital do not satisfy their demands. Rather, the fundamental issue that is posed by capital is not economic (profits and loans), but political, control over the state and development of the social conflicts that alter the political balance of power in the state. In this context, capital is more likely to prefer to lose money in order to gain political power. In this context, if the left pursues a policy of sharing political power in order to obtain economic cooperation, it runs the risk of losing political control without securing any substantial increase in economic production.

The behavior of the private sector, its overt political concern, cannot be separated from an analysis of the international political-economic context in which it operates. The presence of the U.S. imperial state provides political subsidies to cushion economic losses and alternative sites for investors to relocate their operations. Thus the willingness of the private sector to take "risks" internally as an adversary of the regime are balanced by its knowledge of guarantees externally.

Given this international setting and the domestic behavior of the local capitalist class, socialist transitional strategies cannot count on capitalist cooperation without seriously jeopardizing the very process itself. Dislocation occurs from both ends of the policy spectrum, when capital is expropriated and when capital is "incorporated." The notion that somehow "incorporation" of capital into a prolonged transition will avoid ruptures in the productive process fails to accord with recent historical experiences. Successful socialist transition involves the creation of the political organization (of the worker and peasants) to confront inevitable dislocations—and to sustain the regime during the restructuring of the economy.

Marx envisioned socialism growing out of contradiction between forces and relations of production, transforming social relations and building from the productive forces generalized by capital. Recent experiences of capitalist development in Vietnam and Nicaragua suggest a different historical outcome. Productive forces were developed and class antagonisms did emerge; however, as the class struggle approached the stage of a revolutionary upheaval, the capitalist class began to transfer its capital and to destroy the productive forces. The problem of socialist transition in the Third World is not only the "underdevelopment" but, more importantly, the destruction and pillage of the productive forces. Moreover, the growth of an international division of labor, alternative trade networks and multiple overlapping production centers means that after Third World revolutions, international capitalists can disrupt the circulation as well as production of goods as part of the continuing class struggle. Thus if mines are expropriated by a revolutionary regime, the multinational corporations increase production elsewhere and close off marketing outlets. The same strategy can affect export industries. The tourist industry is similarly vulnerable: The hotels and other local facilities are dependent on a network of tourist agents, transportation networks and exporters of specialized goods to bring in the tourists. The expropriated local facilities can become the hostage of the large networks.

In the recent period in Vietnam and Nicaragua, we have an example of capital, faced with political defeat, massively destroying the productive forces (lives and property) and pillaging the economy (e.g., Somoza transferring hundreds of millions, leaving behind substantial debts). Rather than see socialism growing out of the economic development of capitalism and building on the productive forces already created, recent history teaches us that capitalist development leads to an intensified class struggle in which capital destroys the productive forces, leaving the revolutionary regime with the task of rebuilding the productive forces. Without the advantages of socializing the existing productive forces and building upward toward newer and higher standards for living, the needs to rebuild means that for a given historical period the standard of living of segments of the labor force may actually be lower than that reached at the highest point under the previous regime. We can reformulate Marx's law of capitalist development to include the effects of the class struggle. Under conditions of increasing conflict, capital's historic role is to destroy the productive forces. The general regression of the level of the productive forces imposes a new set of conditions on the revolutionary regime in its effort to promote the transition to socialism. It must reactivate the productive forces (incorporte unemployed labor and reconstruct physical plants and factories, farm equipment, and so on) and sustain the loyalty of those segments of the labor force with a standard of living reflecting the conditions of production prior to capital's destruction of the productive forces. The problem is, in the first instance, political and ideological; those skilled workers engaged in operating productive facilities, whose social existence and social consciousness was shaped by the previous level of productive forces must become aware of the uneven [destructive] impact of the revolutionary struggle on the productive forces; the burned out factories and the need to rebuild them are integral parts of the social reality that defines revolutionary consciousness. The latter includes the totality of social reality—the historic role of capital in destroying productive forces, the uneven impact of the class struggle on the emergence of productive forces in post-revolutionary society and the paramount needs to reconstruct the working class through the reconstruction of productive forces.

In many ways, Marx exaggerated the simplicity of the production process, underestimated the ideological hold of capital over skilled/ technical workers and failed to take account of the degree to which knowledge over the whole productive process was separated from individual workers. These factors have serious political consequences in the transition period. Displacing nonrevolutionary technicians causes losses in production which, in turn, has repercussions in sociopolitical organizations: Scarcity breeds authoritarianism. Despite the flight of some trained personnel in Nicaragua, the Sandanistas' effort to maintain production and retain nonrevolutionary personnel while gradually increasing the political consciousness of the country has been generally successful, even as it is fraught with tensions between revolutionaries and technicians.

The revolutionary leadership in Nicaragua is acutely aware of the importance of maintaining the skilled labor force in the country to sustain production. The managers and technicians, however, were reared and trained under capitalism, accepting its production methods, conception of the class structure, and its ideology. The revolutionary forces arc vulnerable because they lack "red-experts" and thus must modify programs to accommodate necessities. Thus while social equality is a consequential concern among the leaders, they are afraid that extreme measures would cause a wholesale flight of trained personnel. Hence, the reduction of salary/wage differentials in the public sector has been very gradual.

In Vietnam and Nicaragua, organs of popular power were first and foremost manifest in the military struggle to destroy the dictatorial regime. During the political military stage, all mass organizations were subordinated to the immediate task of carrying through the combined guerrilla and mass struggle to its victorious conclusion. The mass organization's primary function was to support and sustain the armed struggle; the fight against the dictatorial regime was at the same time the affirmation of the right to political representation. The central feature of the popular organizations in the immediate post-revolutionary period continues to be the preoccupation with military-police tasks—to defend the revolution from counterrevolution forces. Equally important, the destruction of the forces of production, and the massive unemployment which resulted, have focussed mass organizations on the task of economic reconstruction, and the tasks of production. Within the boundaries set by these overriding conditions (production for reconstruction and defense against counter-revolution), the issue of popular representation and democracy becomes central. The locus of representation is found in the defense and productive units—the militias, neighborhood committees, state farms, factories. Mass participation and initiative play an important role in mobilizing resources, implementing plans, and sustaining the regime. The crucial correlation here is the relationship between the state and the mass organization, the degree of autonomy that exists between the two, the flow of influence—essentially, the degree of political freedom that exists within the mass organizations for discussion and debate. The egalitarian-collectivist policies pursued by the revolutionary regime based on the mass organs reflect the representative character of the political system.

A representative system, however, need not be a democratic one. The degree to which the political institutions are built on procedures and safeguards that guarantee to the working class and peasantry legislative and executive power over the productive system defines a working class democracy. The crucial distinction between a popular representative government and a workers' and peasants' democracy is found in the issue of workers' and peasants' control—the capacity of workers and peasants to criticize and elect their leaders through their own organizations; the ability of workers to form their own parties and through legislative and executive organs to decide on the development path.

In the early phases of the revolution, in which all efforts have been concentrated on the most immediate tasks of survival, legislative and executive power has tended to be concentrated at the top. The mass organizations which have incorporated hundreds of thousands into political, social, and economic activity here, of necessity, developed close relations with the state. The problem is to continue the necessary collaboration between mass organization and the state and at the same time maintaining a viable and autonomous political life within the organizations that allow the producers to play an independent role in governing society.

## Class Struggle and Economic Crisis

Orthodox Marxists analyze the class struggle as a consequence of economic crisis. Class action is usually described as a derivative phenomena dependent on the demise of the capitalist system. Recent comparative historical experience demonstrates that the reverse relationship may be more to the point; that economic crisis can be the result of sustained high levels of class conflict. The collapse of expanding economies can be the result of the social and poltical contradictions that have accompanied dynamic growth, namely socioeconomic displacement, proletarianization, and social polarization.

Recent experiences of intense class struggle in Chile (1972–73), Nicaragua (1977–79), El Salvador (1979–82), Guatemala (1980–82), Jamaica (1976–80), Argentina (1969–73), Brazil (1962–64) coincide with significant decline in economic growth, suggesting that there exists an *inverse relationship between class struggle and capital accumulation*: The higher the level of class struggle, the more it is national and challenging to the system, the more likely it is to set off a decline in investment and an economic crisis.* Where local struggles occur which are not sustained or consequential in national terms, there appears to be little, if any, relationship to economic development. In order to understand the relation of class struggle to economic crisis, we need to adequately conceptualize: (1) the different levels of struggle (local, national); (2) the kinds of demands; (3) the durability of the struggle; (4) the organizational strength of the class forces; (5) the location of the forces of struggle in the economy; (6) the level of capitalist development. These factors, in turn, are in part shaped by the degree of historical centrality of class struggle in the social formation, i.e., whether the action is embedded in a "tradition", and by the centrality of the organized labor-owner relationship.

This conceptualization of the notion of class struggle allows us to classify the different levels of class struggle so that we can derive models of *effective* and *ineffective* class struggles—those that have consequences in terms of determining economic crisis as opposed to those that have little or no impact. For our discussion, the *nature* and *scope* of class struggle is more important than the mere existence of class struggle. The question of the relationship between class struggle and economic crisis revolves around the issue of identifying the level of class struggle that impacts on capital accumulation.

Broadly conceived, we can identify four levels of class struggle:

1. *revolutionary situation*: continued mass mobilization and increasing radicalization, including direct challenges to the incumbents of state power leading to massive armed confrontation.
2. *mass mobilization*: the growth of mass organizations and the increasing incorporation of new layers of the population into electoral and mass opposition activity, leading to the redefinition of the conditions of domination by the regime.
3. *incremental opposition*: sporadic activities, occasional strikes and protests confined to limited sectors of the population.
4. *stagnation and repression*: little or no active opposition with occasional protests by isolated groups or individuals.

In this framework, it is clear that strikes may or may not have political and economic significance. Only in the context in which class struggle reaches the level of mass mobilization and a revolutionary situation will it have a direct role in precipitating economic crisis. In countries, such as in Peru in the late 1970s, where there were a number of *unsustained* (24 hours) and *ineffective* general strikes (leading to rejection of worker demands, mass firings), the class struggle did not precipitate or deepen the economic crisis. In the cases mentioned earlier,

---

*Of course, other factors besides class struggle might lead to a decline in accumulation and the drying up of investment, e.g., declining exports, lack of markets, primary commodity price declines, worldwide economic depression, corrupt governments.

the high levels of class struggle led to massive capital flight, decline of production, growing government deficits, unemployment and inflation—in a word, a major economic crisis. The decline of capital, however, was not uniform. Our hypothesis is that in periods of mounting class conflict, capital declines in the following order: private direct investment, private bank capital, state capital. Private direct investment is especially prone to flight because it is likely to be substantially and directly affected by class struggle at the point of production. Unlike the state, private investors have few resources to cushion substantial losses over time. Private banking loan capital is not always directly linked to production; as long as the state can continue to pay interest, bank capital is less concerned with class struggle at the point of production. Bank capital begins to dry up when the government is perceived as beginning to lose control over the overall situation—when class struggle threatens to change the state. Finally, state loans may be the least affected by class struggle, since they are not motivated by profit or interest but serve strategic political interests. The role of state loans is to take the "risks" rejected by the private sector. Whereas private banks would probably discontinue lines of credit as the class struggle deepens, thus provoking an economic crisis, imperial governments may continue to prop up regimes with financial resources to consolidate political and military structures. "Political capital" (state to state) may actually increase with the class struggle to compensate for the outflow of private capital.

Foreign and domestic capital may respond differently to rising class struggle, depending on the political character of the leadership of the movement. Under social-revolutionary leadership both types of capital will hasten their departure. However, where the class struggle is directed by nationalist leadership, there is likely to be a greater flight of foreign capital.

The outflow of capital capable of precipitating an economic crisis depends on the high levels of class struggle. Lower levels of class struggle may not reach the "social tension" threshold capable of triggering "risk anxiety" among the holders of capital. On the other hand, we do not hold the opposite notion that high levels of repression *per se* are conducive to growing investment. The absence of class struggle may be a necessary but not sufficient condition for capital flows and capital growth.

While this theory of economic crisis is premised on the centrality of class struggle, it assumes a certain dynamic development of productive forces, economic expansion that produces antagonistic class forces. What it suggests, however, is that the logic of class struggle intervenes and directly and adversely affects the "laws of motion of capitalist development" and sets in motion a process of disaccumulation, leading to economic crisis. The very process of dynamic economic expansion creates the social polarities and class conflicts that act on the economic accumulation process, provoking economic crisis which, in turn, further deepens the class conflict, in a continuing reciprocal, dialectical fashion, until either capital or labor reasserts its absolute authority.

## Marxism and the Transformation of the Third World

Marx's effort to equate the development of capitalism with the development of "free wage labor" is fraught with many difficulties, foremost of which is the fact that wage payments were the least likely form in the initial period of growth of Western capitalism. Furthermore, the expansion of capital into the Third World found societies which lacked labor "freed" from the means of production and which possessed alternative sources of economic activity. The coercion of labor was a necessary condition to alienate labor from precapitalist economic activity and to sustain labor's exclusive activity within the capitalist mode of production.

Capitalist social relations of production thus were defined by the coercion necessary to produce the requisite labor surplus for the organization of capitalist production. Surplus value was produced by coerced labor, not unlike wage labor; the notion that "coercive labor" was less "efficient" is belied by the enormous surplus generated, accumulated, and transferred to other sectors for reinvestment.

The notion that "capitalism" progressed by eliminating the "precapitalist" barriers to production and thus, despite its terrible exploitative role, played an important civilizing role, e.g., liberating the "forces of production," is open to serious question on a number of counts.

First, capitalist expansion may have eliminated some precapitalist institutions and laws, for example, inhibiting its growth. Yet it maintained others (precapitalist forms of control) pertaining to control over labor, harboring many systems of payments, housing, and obligations from the "previous period." Second, the freedom to buy and sell, to hire and fire, to produce and consume, without impinging on state prerogatives did not necessitate a breakdown of social obligations in relations between labor and capital. Third, the transfer of capital on a world scale and the reorganization of precapitalist societies in the Third World did not usually create new productive forces, but the reorganization of labor to serve the process of external accumulation, a process that served to alienate labor from its means of production and to alienate the surplus from the nation. This dual phenomenon of alienation defined a process of exploitation without the development of the productive forces, since accumulation was externally anchored and required, in the absence of "revolutionizing" the mode of production, the permanent implantation of a coercive relation of production. Furthermore, the selective entrée of capital in the forms of extractive enterprises led to the existence of a heterogeneous social formation. However, the existence of more than one mode of production belied the fact that capitalism quickly assumed a "hegemonic" position and instrumentalized the early forms and converted them into additional sources of surplus extraction.

The (inter-) penetration of capitalist and precapitalist social formation hence placed a variety of social relations of production within the same sphere of production, albeit as tributaries rather than as direct producers. The "immediate" context of economic activity, the patterns of ownership and control, continued in some cases to resemble "precapitalist forms" but the dynamic which accelerated the rhythm of production and appropriated the surplus was none other than the original source of capitalist accumulation, which operated from the periphery to the capitalist center.

Marx focused on the social relations of production in defining capitalism rather than on the total organization of production because he assumed the laws of motion of capitalism were compatible only with free wage labor; the optimal conditions of capitalist expansion were essentially the "ideal types" of labor/capital relations extrapolated from the English experience. Marx was historically wrong: Capital accumulation, reproduction, and expansion occurred under a variety of experiences which included slavery, peonage, and forced labor. Indeed, these social forms were more common and contributed a very great proportion of the surplus to the initial and even advanced stages of accumulation. It turns out that wage labor was the *exceptional* form of capitalist social relations and only belatedly became the dominant form of payment. Meanwhile as the wage payment became dominant, the area of "freedom" associated with the selling of labor has become increasingly circumscribed as the state has increasingly intervened to dictate the levels and kinds of payments labor will receive. Indeed the growth of nonwage payments (fringe benefits) and the quasi-coercive dictation of wage/labor payments in the modern capitalist world (income policies), in the capitalist democracies of Europe, as well as the capitalist dictatorships in the Third World, suggest that "free wage relations" have led to a rather brief and aborted existence within the capitalist mode of production. The very limited sway that this particular form of social relation has had within the capitalist mode of production and the rather limited areas in which it has operated suggests that the arguments about the existence or nonexistence of capitalism based on this rather superfluous (and rather superficial) set of criteria have blinded analysts from understanding the process of social transformation in the twentieth century. The rapidity with which twentieth-century revolutions have seemed to move from "national" or "bourgeois democratic" to socialist is not a function merely of considerations of political power but is rooted in the objective economic systems; since the productive systems in revolution are already capitalist, the transformation of those systems cannot pass other than toward a new system of production. The revolutionary process which mistakenly defines the social system through the notion of "free wage labor" proceeds to shift toward a set of political and social categories ("national," "democratic") independent of the mode of production, resulting in a set of anomalous situations in which the class that controls the means of production is excluded from a definition of the state. The problem is further compounded when a social revolutionary movement overthrows a capitalist ruling class, proceeds with a set of formulas defining an "antifeudal" or precapitalist social formation and sets up political and economic tasks with no accompanying appropriate class to fulfill the functions described.

If, as Lenin claims, Russia was a "semi-feudal" society which required the "democratic dictatorship of the workers and peasants," where did the workers and peasants emerge who overthrew "feudalism" and established socialism? On the contrary, if one conceives of Russia as a backward and unevely developed capitalist country that combined a dominant capitalist sector with its class conscious proletariat and a backward agrarian capitalist sector based on an export oriented bourgeoisie exploiting peasants through "pre-capitalist social relations," one can understand why socialism was immediately on the agenda: no stages were skipped between *feudalism* and *socialism* because the Russian revolution emerged essentially as a combined revolt of workers in the advanced sectors of capitalism, uniting with the peasants from the backward sectors of capitalism. Both revolted against the common practice of their exploitation. The process of accumulation and reproduction was equally damaging to their interests, though the transfer of surplus from the countryside to the cities inflicted a particularly heavy burden on the peasantry as petty commodity producers. The accumulation pole outside of the rural areas exacted a particularly heavy toll on the petty commodity producers and hence required more severe "repressive" social relations. These *exactions*—transfer of capital—and the *coercive relations* which accompanied, both necessary ingredients to the overall process of capital accumulation in the countryside, are what many commentators confused with *feudalism*, in Russia and in the rest of the Third World. The process of accumulation and reproduction was as present in Russia as in the West; the capacity of the local bourgeoisie and foreign capital to expand was not hindered by these coercive relations but facilitated by them. The goal of the bourgeoisie was to attempt to capture as much of state power to *further the process already under way*, to accelerate it with the Czarist state if possible—without it if necessary—not introduce a "new mode of production" or carry out another "bourgeois-democratic" revolution.

Likewise, the growth and emergence of a substantial communist movement in China coincides with the expansion of capitalism and its penetration of Chinese society. The large-scale growth of industry, the accumulation of capital through tributary measures and other exactions over the peasantry set the stage for the rapid conversion of China from dictatorial capitalist exploitation to socialism (with lip service to a transient or "national democracy" phase). The only coherent explanation for the rather vapid existence of the "national democratic" state is that it never had a distinct existence, either as a state formation or with its own ruling class. It did not define a turning over of power from a feudal landowning class to a "national bourgeoisie." But rather the overthrow of capitalism provided the setting for a relatively rapid and continuous transformation of China toward socialism within the same state with the same hegemonic group. Whatever the forms of social relations, the substance of the productive system, capitalism, left no other option. The fiction of a "national democratic" stage to "end" feudalism was maintained more as an ideological ploy for international consumption than as a definition of the social process within China.

No "national democratic" classes exist either as organizers of a distinct mode of production or as durable social forces sustaining a regime distinct from the ensuing socialist regime. The same actors define and carry out a succession of measures all tending to one predetermined goal: the socialization of the means of production. They do so because they all emerge from a common cohesive group sharing a common experience shaped by the only system that produced its subverters: the capitalist mode of production.

The tendency to identify the particular "mix" of "coercion" and "payments in kind" with precapitalist formations and to prescribe political formulas that substitute so-called new and modern forms of domination to "raise" or "liberate" the productive forces is nothing more than an exercise in classical reform politics—substituting an amelioration of the form of exploitation for an anlaysis and transformation of the whole. Furthermore, the shift from "coercive" to "free wage" determination in itself will not liberate productive forces. Insofar as the expansion of capital has become socially and historically attuned to a given set of coercive social relations, sudden and abrupt changes could lead to a sharp decline in total output and a process of disinvestment. The long-term tendency toward capital accumulation envisioned by capital in the Third World depended on a stable, docile labor force from which the surplus could be extracted and reinvested with maximum freedom. The "freedom of capital" was thus strengthened by coerced labor; capital accumulation was heightened; the transfer and opening of new ares of exploitation were widened. The loss of labor control or shifts from coercive to free wage forms was not a function of capitalist imperatives but of the struggle of the enslaved proletariat in *political conflict with the economic needs of the bourgeoisie.*

The growth of wage/labor social relations did not signal the development of capitalism in struggle with precapitalist social formations but the political struggle of the proletariat against the coercive shackles of the bourgeoisie. The efforts by self-styled Marxist theorists to define this as a bourgeois democratic revolution was an attempt to transform the workers' struggle into an instrument for "modernizing" capitalism or of appropriating the political power of the proletariat toward the fashioning of an alternative form of bourgeois domination, hegemonized by the local petty bourgeoisie.

*Alternative Conceptions of the Capitalist World Economy*

The conception of the world economy as divided into core, semi-periphery, and periphery does not adequately capture the dynamic growth, specialization and multiple points of accumulation, which increasingly characterize capitalist world development. The old tripartite conception fails to focus on the highly significant internal differentiation within these categories. An alternative conceptual framework designed to account for the increasingly important and highly specific functional relations within and between regions is required. Concretely, any approach must recognize the process of capital accumulation in newly developed regional centers and the internal class transformations that have allowed previously "colonized," "peripheral" raw material exporters to diversify their relations, develop the productive forces, and appropriate surplus from both imperial centers (finance capital) and less developed regions (raw materials). The active role in regional accumulation adopted by these countries requires that we look beyond the notion that these areas are mere mediators between the core/periphery and examine their role as competitors in surplus appropriation, developing multiple exchange relations: exporting finished durable goods, providing loans and credits and selling low-level technology to less developed countries while importing high technology, securing major loans and investment, and selling a mix of raw materials and manufactures to advanced capital countries. The grouping together of a new complex of capital exporting, commerical, financial, and industrial centers from the formerly undifferentiated periphery requires the mapping out of the new networks and relationships.

World capitalism can best be understood as a system of hierarchically organized competitive networks in which regimes and countries "specialize" in one or more activities. Our analysis focuses on the changing pattern of networks linking nations and defining their positions and functions in the international division of labor.

Historically, those countries which achieved the highest development of productive forces and the most powerful military-political state apparatus have shaped the international division of labor to their needs, organizing "specializations" within subordinate regions and countries and incorporating the emerging ensemble in the service of their economic and strategic needs. The classical pattern involved the production and export of finished industrial goods from the metropolitan centers and the import of agro-mineral products from the colonized or semi-colonized countries. Two points require emphasis here: first, while colonies were typically reduced to mineral or agrarian monoculture economies in the service of the metropolis, the economic supremacy of the latter rested on the diversification of its economic base and the global sweep of its multiple economic activities, including manufacture, finance, shipping, agriculture and mining, as well as on its ability to control and profit from dynamic sectors of the colonial economy. In short, in a world in which capital accumulation was frequently equated with specialization, hegemonic power lay in fact with optimum diversification. Second, even in the colonies, diverse patterns of specialization began to develop. For example, personnel within India were recruited and served as regional police within southern and eastern Asia; a similar pattern was evidenced in the French use of Sengalese forces in the occupation of Africa. Hundreds of thousands of Korean laborers were impressed to work overseas in Japanese coal mines, as were Mozambiquan workers in South African mines. These patterns not only defined the fabric of imperialist relations to the detriment of the colonies but set in motion important processes of class differentiation.

More important, certain arcas and regions, even in the colonial period, served as banking, administrative, and commercial centers, accumulating capital and creating the basis for dynamic growth in the post-colonial period. Lebanon, Singapore, Hong Kong, became banking and commercial centers, retaining some of the surplus appropriated by the imperial countries. The appropriation of surplus, even in the colonial systems, did not reflect the direct transfer from so-called periphery to "core." In the post-independence period and especially by the 1970s, industrial and commercial centers in the Third World created a complex grid of relations between and among Third World countries, radically altering the composition of trade between some more dynamic regions. Increasingly industrializing Third World countries were capturing regional markets, supplying credits and low-level technology to less developed areas, while increasingly importing high technology and borrowing financial resources from the imperial centers. The changing networks and the multiple and multi-tiered relations defining the world economy are severely strained by efforts to force them into a trichotomous system of stratification.

The triumph of national independence movements in the decades following the Second World War made possible a margin of discretionary power for former colonial nations in selecting lines of economic activity within the world economy. The degree of autonomy of choice was governed by such diverse internal factors as class composition, the nature of the state, geographical locus, natural resource endowment, technological level, and capital accumulation, as well as by the structure of relationships with regional and international configurations of power. The result was that while many countries experienced little change in the post-colonial division of labor, some have dramatically transformed their position, becoming the centers of complex regional networks.

Both imperialist and former colonial countries "specialize" in particular forms of economic activity. In the case of the metropolis, these principally take the form of advanced technological centers (United States), heavy industrial (Germany, Japan, Italy), financial (Switzerland, England), and agricultural or resource surplus (United States, Canada,

Australia, France) centers. However, there is obviously considerable overlap here as the metropolitan centers vie to establish multiple specializations, indeed, multiplicity of activities on a far-flung scale becomes the *sine qua non* of being a "metropolis."

In the contemporary world economy, we find a rapidly growing diversification of specializations among many former peripheral countries redefining their position in world networks. If many of these nations or regions not long ago fit the mold of monoculture economies, we can now observe a panoply of activities whose range is suggested by the following: trading centers (Singapore, Hong Kong), industrial export bases (South Korea, Taiwan, Brazil, Hong Kong), financial centers (Lebanon, Singapore, Panama), agricultural export centers (Argentina), military base areas (Philippines, Puerto Rico, Panama), mineral export centers (Venezuela, Saudi Arabia, Iran, Chile, Libya, Indonesia), labor export platforms (North Africa, Mozambique, Mexico, Caribbean), and tourist centers (Caribbean). These specializations are in constant flux. The image of stagnation, central to much of the dependency literature, fails to encompass the dynamic changes occurring in important sections of the former colonial world as they are progressively encompassed in a capitalist economic nexus. Surplus appropriated from the metropole and the less developed countries has created new dynamic areas and sets of relations in which regional linkages of domination and subordination begin to preempt the global patterns established earlier by the metropolitan countries.

The world capitalist system operates through networks organized within and between each of its regions. These reciprocally derive from and affect state policy, class structure, and class formation throughout the network. The competitive activities between similarly specialized imperial countries and their firms is extended to and shapes larger networks embracing the former colonial nations. When capital in industrial countries competes, for example, over the sale of technology, its activities are complemented by the existence of financial and trading centers which compete among themselves to facilitate investment and circulation of goods. Increasingly, exchanges between industrial and agro-mineral areas are taken over by financial and commercial centers within each region. The functional specialization of the parts—economic, political and military—and the interconnectedness of the whole are essential elements for the reproduction of capital on a world scale. "Strategic interests" of hegemonic powers must be comprehended in terms not of gains and losses of a single specialization but of changes in *networks* and the possibility of local powers substituting or replacing specialized functions of former imperial countries within the network. The breakdown of networks or their reorientation away from their complementary role within a given imperial system can have a significant adverse affect on the hegemonic position of an imperial power.

International economic specializations are overlaid by politicomilitary structures organized by the hegemonic powers to maximize their access to markets, labor and resources. The proliferation of independent nation-states and the declining capacity of the United States to intervene unilaterally and militarily led to an effort to create what some refer to as "subimperialist" or "regional" powers. Initially, these countries were designated by the imperial centers to fulfill a role of gendarme within a given region. The attribution of this role was preceded by a close relationship between the imperial state and the regional power—one in which the specialized agencies of repression and the greater part of the state apparatus had been trained and penetrated by the imperial state.

Recent history suggests that these changes have occurred *only* in the case of a small number of nations. Moreover, it is by no means certain that underdeveloped states that succeed in achieving regional power status are capable of sustaining their new roles, above all because of the contradictions generated within their own polities by the profound internal changes required. Subimperial nation-states of recent vintage have not had the ability to fulfill their roles. The Iranian regime collapsed before the combined opposition of Islamic and Marxist nationalists, undermining the very underpinnings of U.S. strategy in the Middle East. South Africa was incapable of preventing the victory of the MPLA in Angola, in part because without U.S. military intervention it was unable to sustain its drive against Cuban MPLA forces. The collapse of white minority domination in neighboring Rhodesia, further isolated the regime and inevitably stimulated black revolutionary forces in South Africa.

Brazil, increasingly caught between internal opposition forces, the decline of external markets, and increasing debt payments, has begun to experience a deepening economic crisis, combining stagnation and inflation. The assassination of Pak Chung Hee in South Korea, the explosiveness of student led mobilization, followed by the declining economy, casts a shadow on the brightest of economic performers. This is not to suggest the imminent collapse of regional powers. However, the declining effectiveness of regional powers in shaping the political universe sustaining the current international division of labor has increasingly forced the United States to reconsider the case for unilateral intervention.

The critical issue, however, that requires emphasis is the growing autonomy of the regional powers and their increasing contradictions with the advanced capitalist centers. Increasingly, they compete over trade in the Third World, for loans in the financial market places, for access to cheap raw materials. Given the heightened economic competition, it is not surprising that these regional forces increasingly refuse to be tied into U.S.-directed alliances that constrain economic opportunities. Brazil's break with the United States over Angola, the Middle East, and Central America responds to its growing competitiveness for economic markets and resources. The establishment of new industries among the Southeast Asian countries could lead to greater competition and conflict between them and Japan. The autonomous regional powers increasingly preempt previous dominant capitalist centers and create the basis for polycentric market-financial centers, increasing the level of competition, destabilizing the structure of control, creating multiple sources of conflict and cross-ideological coalitions that define the early classifications.

## Conclusion

The world historical transformations that have taken place in precapitalist and capitalist societies and the process of transition to socialism have raised several important issues for Marxist theory.

1. The revolutionary transformation of a number of Third World countries has served to refocus discussion on the nature of the historically specific conditions under which capitalist penetration took place. The experience of class formation and the growth of revolutionary movements in conditions in which capitalist development was not accompanied simultaneously by the growth of wage/labor relations calls into question *aspects* of the *global-historical universality* of Marx's original conception. Marx's notion that capital separates the direct producers from production and subordinates them to wage labor in Third World conditions needs to be revised to take into account not only the logic of capital to rationalize production, but the need to defend its class interest by incorporating and subordinating precapitalist relations as mechanisms of labor control. Equally important, the absence of historical conditions that limited labor alternatives to wage labor necessitated that capital rely on coercion rather than the market to recruit labor.

2. Historical practice over the past several decades has served to highlight some of the strengths and weaknesses of efforts to apply "revionist" and "orthodox" conceptions of Marxism to the problems of the transition to socialism. In the first instance, efforts by "revisionist Marxists" to incorporate capitalist cooperation to socialist transformation in the present world economy has been demonstrated to create conditions of unstable equilibrium, leading to the very socioeconomic dislocations that they sought to avoid. Historical practice suggests that the Marxist notion of transition to socialism must incorporate the problematics of "dislocation" as a necessary (though certainly not welcomed) accompaniment of the early stages of a restructured society. The consolidation of political power and the establishment of the foundations of the new sociopolitical order can then become the new basis for the selective rearticulation of the collectivist society in the capitalist world economy.

3. Marxist theory of the Second and Third International had developed a very mechanical and economistic conception of socialist revolution based on a notion of optimal technical-productive development and catastrophic collapse. These notions conceived of class struggle and class consciousness as passive derivatives. Yet historical experience in a number of Third World countries demonstrates that the logic of class

consciousness and struggle becomes a determinative factor in certain historical conjunctures "interfering" with the strictly economic processes and setting in motion a process of social transformation that (temporarily) reverses the accumulation process.

In this regard, the post-revolution conditions for development themselves become problematic as the disaccumulation process creates a double set of problematics for the revolutionary leadership: the simultaneous rebuilding of the conditions for the socialization of production and the expansion and creation of socialist consciousness. Marxist science, premised on the notion that socialism grew out of the conditions of socialized production engendered by the reproduction of capital, becomes modified: Marxism becomes both a creative ideology—a means of recreating what was destroyed by capital—and a means of selectively socializing that which grows out of the capitalist world.

The so-called crisis of Marxism emerges from the effort to create a political system of representative workers' democracy in the context of sustained military, political and economic warfare. The tendency toward bureaucratization and nondemocratic forms of representation are in fact the consequences of the "over-development of the mass organs of defense" at the expense of democratic organs at the point of production.

4. The growth of neo-Marxist attempts to refocus attention on the world economy as the basic unit of analysis is a positive break with the previous Marxist orthodoxy that was firmly embedded in examining political economy from the perspective of "building socialism in one country." The preliminary efforts led to a conceptualization that dichotomized or trichotomized the global system. This paradigm was most appropriate for the colonial and immediate post-colonial period. Over the past decade, however, new theoretical conceptions of the growth possibilities among third world capitalist countries and the emergence of new regional powers leads to the need for a more complex and elaborate schema. A system of hierarchal networks representing both the emergence of new more autonomous power constellations and the continuation of the older sets of imperial-peripheral relations defines the contemporary world economy. The reconceptualization of the emerging world-economy requires that we build upon and go beyond the neo-Marxist and orthodox Marxist schemes to mapping out the new forms of world capitalist development recognizing the new polarities and divisions between former "peripheral" states as well as the deepening internal class contradictions that accompany the external shifts in the world economy.

# 8

## Workers' Self-Managment and the Transition to Socialism

JAMES F. PETRAS
RITA CARROLL-SEGUIN

### Introduction

The past decade has witnessed a growing interest in workers' self-management within the international labor movement. The debate over self-management has spread from the advanced industrial countries to a number of newly indusrializing Third World countries. Several factors account for this growing consciousness within the working class: (1) dissatisfaction with the consequences of nationalization of the means of production and growing stratification of society; (2) the increasing discontent among workers with the alienating conditions of work and the authoritarian relations of production; (3) the rising levels of political education and the decreasing preoccupation with issues of wages and salaries; (4) the increasing understanding by labor that rapid technological changes and their introduction by hierarchical managerial authorities can lead to permanent displacement, hence the need for greater labor conrtrol; (5) in the context of ascending class conflict, workers observe the tendency for capital to disinvest, to run down plant and capital, and to flee to "safe havens" making workers' control a necessity to prevent the dismantlement of enterprises; and finally (6) the increasing transnationalization of production and the increased tendency for corporate capital to relocate plants or reallocate investments has demonstrated the inadequacy of orthodox trade unionism and increased worker pressure for control over investments and decisions affecting plant location.

This forward momentum toward worker self-management has received severe jolts and backward pushes in various countries and historical periods. The violent seizure of power by terrorist rightist regimes in a number of Third World countries has led to the dismantling of workers' councils and repression of their discussion. In these circumstances, the focus of the struggle has shifted toward more immediate issues directed toward economic and political survival and elementary democratic demands. In the advanced capitalist countries, the combination of deepening economic crisis and, in some cases, rightist regimes has forced the workers' movement onto the track of defensive struggles, organizing against restrictions on trade union rights. While the initial responses to dictatorial regimes and economic crisis may appear to put the issue on the back burner, struggles that emerge as defensive responses may combine with efforts to enlarge the direct role of the workers over the production process. In fact, since the current crisis is profoundly structural and systemic, the labor movement's struggle against deteriorating conditions logically leads to reopening the issue of control over the production process. In this context, the issue of workers' self-management can re-emerge in a more dynamic context linked to a more volatile struggle against a declining social system unable to meet the elementary needs of labor.

The current context for workers' self-management is not uniformly bleak. In Greece, France, and Sweden, governing parties are programatically committed to some form of self-management. In Spain and Italy there continues to be constant syndicalist pressure to increase the role of labor within the sphere of control over production. In Third World countries, in countries as diverse as Nicaragua, Iran, Angola and China, discussion of forms of worker participation have been broached in the recent period. In the Eastern bloc, apart from the continuing discussion and practices in Yugoslavia, sections of the Polish workers' movement have raised the issue of self-management in a programatic fashion. The discussion of workers' self-management in an increasingly global context suggests that the political conditions for its practical application have arrived. Dynamic capitalist penetration and the ensuing contradictions that have emerged in recent decades have transformed most areas of the world economy sufficiently to allow for the development of new forms of social organization of production.

Yet workers' self-mangement does not evolve out of the heads of idealistic thinkers. Nor is it the mere derivitave of large-scale economic processes. Many efforts have been made to establish workers' self-management in isolated enterprises, largely through the initiative of individuals who were concerned with the plight of workers made redundant through plant closings or who assure that successful small-scale experiments can become pilot projects or models to successfully convince others of the rationality and practicality of workers' control (Matejko 1971; 25–26) (Cole 1953). A classic example occurred in the General Foods plant in Topeka, Illinois. The program was an economic success—workers handled the responsibilities given to them, production increased, and labor discipline improved. But when labor made overtures toward expanding its area of responsibility, threatening several layers of managment, the program was abandoned (*Business Week* March 8, 1974). A general pattern exists in these small-scale experiments: Where they are successful they threaten management and are quickly dimantled; where management retains control, little effective participation takes place and workers lose interest. Kelley (1968) discusses this phenomenon in the Glacier Metal Comapny experiment in England. Despite half-hearted attempts to solicit worker input and to change job titles, flattening the bureaucratic hierarchy, traditional manager/subordinate relations remained. (See also Hyatt 1975 and Argyris 1973). Sufficient time has elapsed to note that isolated examples of individual experiments have few sustained effects.

In the following discussion of self-mangement, we will focus on a number of aspects of the issue: (1) the contextual determinants of self-mangement and its long-term prospects, (2) self-management and the transition to socialism, and (3) general problems of self-management, focusing in particular on the controversies accompanying it in the context of a market economy.

## Algeria

### INTRODUCTION OF SELF-MANAGEMENT FROM BELOW

Self-management in Algeria developed out of the disorganization and lack of central authority that were part of the immediate aftermath of the Algerian independence struggle.[1] The French had withdrawn after an eight-year battle (1954–62), leaving behind empty houses, unmanned shops, factories, and farms. They also left empty many of the administrative posts in government and most of the technical positions in industry and commerce. The exodus brought the economy to a standstill and caused massive unemployment.[2]

At the same time, because the struggle had no clear class base, no coherent Algerian nationalist group had emerged to man the state apparttus. The revolutionary army, the FLN, consisted of a broad-based coalition of elements, all vying for state control. Within this context, and without any direction from the state, workers throughout the country spontaneously took control of farms, factories, and shops.

The government was slow to recognize what was essentially a grass-roots movement. Many factories and apartments had been vacant since April of 1962; takeovers began toward the end of June. It wasn't until August 24 that the FLN government, the Executif Provisiore, published a decree, ". . . allowing prefects to requisition abandoned industrial and agricultural enterprises and to nominate managers to administer them until the return of the owners" (Clegg 1971, 47). The Decrets de Mars was issued by Ben Bella (who had emerged at the center of power by September 1962) the following March. In essence, it gave the government unlimited power of nationalization. At first the government responded only to UCTA (Union General des Travailleurs) organized labor protests or legitimated preexisting worker management firms. Later it began a more systematic attempt to bring the dynamic sectors of the economy under state control without introducing workers' control.

ORGANIZATION OF WORKERS' COUNCILS

The UGTA was responsible for organizing the social sector. It decided that the "comite de gestation," or "workers' council," was the organizational form best suited to its goal of socialized production. A "Commision de Gestation" was established to advise workers on how to set up councils. Each firm was to be organized in the Yugoslav pattern. There was to be an assembly of all qualified workers which, if it were large enough, would elect a council which, in turn, would elect a committee or board of directors. In practice these groups were nothing more than rubber stamp organizations. Apart from electing the council, the assembly's only function was to vote upon plans and proposals generated elsewhere, in the beginning by the board of directors, later by government agencies.

The crucial factor was the knowledgeability and organizational capacity of the workers, and this varied greatly from the masses of illiterate agricultural day workers to the small urban proletariat. Membership and election rules were never uniformly enforced. In many cases the "annual" elections were held only once and in some cases not at all. The board of directors was dominated by the state-appointed director, who was the legally acknowledged representative of the state's interests. The director was the chairman and secretary of every committee, controlling what issues were discussed and how the discussion was entered into the minutes. The director decided how membership laws were to be interpreted; in agricultural firms for example, where seasonal workers were excluded from the assembly by law, the director could, by altering the interpretation, either pack the assembly with supporters or eliminate enemies.

SPREAD OF SELF-MANAGEMENT

By September the UGTA was ready to move into the countryside where it ran into conflict with the military.

The army, the FLN, and the UGTA all attempted to harness the spontaneous seizures and organize them into a national movement, each for its own reasons. Only the UGTA had a clearly socialist position. The army controlled much of the western part of the country and, while it shared the UTGA's desire not to let the country fall back into the hands of a foreign bourgeoisie, it was in no way wedded to the concept of socialized agricultural production. Army leaders wanted to distribute individual plots of land to excombatants in order to secure their political base. In addition, some two-million land hungry peasants were returning from French "regroupment camps"[3], and army leaders were in favor of distributing land to them individually. Where self-management committees had formed, often on the largest, most modern farms best suited to collective operation, the committees were dissolved and the workers forcibly removed (Clegg 1971, 50–51). Thus the UGTA's efforts were limited to a tiny portion of the countryside.

The spread of workers' self-management was also limited in the industrial sector. Most of the abandoned factories and shops were in the competitive sector: Small firms operating on a labor intensive basis with very low profit margins. The growth poles of Algerian industry, natural gas and the petrochemical industry, were owned by the French government and by the multinationals. They remained unscathed by both the war and its aftermath.

From the beginning the state worked to restrict self-management to the least profitable, least productive sectors. When pressured in the latter part of his rule, Ben Bella increased the self-managed sector with a wave of nationalizations intended to increase popular support. However, most of these were tiny shops, small restaurants, and hotels. There was no pattern to these nationalizations and, in the end, they formed an insignificant part of the total economy.

The economy was clearly divided into four sectors, two private and two social. The private sector was controlled in part by the Algerian petty bourgeoisie who had purchased many of the small shops and restaurants from the colons on the eve of independence. Second, multinational corporations controlled all of the larger privately owned firms including the textiles, metal and petrochemical industries. In the social sectors there were those firms that were operated by the workers and those administrated by representatives of the state, called societes nationales. During the first two years, all societes nationales were created by the conversion of worker-managed firms. Later, the government nationalized many profitable industries and immediately set them up as state managed firms. Compensation often accompanied this second wave of nationalization with foreign loans supplying the funds. The pattern that evolved included the following sequence: As nationalization progressed from the shops of the petty bourgeoisie to the firms controlled by foreign capital, efficient, capital-intensive, industries were managed directly by the state while the least modern, labor intensive firms were abandoned by state bureaucrats and left for the workers to control.

WEAKNESSES OF ALGERIAN SELF-MANAGEMENT

To maintain a system of self-management, labor must control the state. In Algeria, labor struggled against a bureaucratic elite bent on turning the social sector into a state capitalist one. The working class and the revolutionary cadres lost the struggle because they never controlled the state. At the top administrative level where policies were created, 43 percent of the employees had been part of the previous colonial administration. At the intermediate level among those persons in charge of policy execution and routine decision making, 77 percent were former colonial adminstrators. Only at the lowest levels of government, were there large numbers of FLN members and many of these positions merely paid for the political support of individual leaders (Clegg 1971, 116).

Almost immediately the UGTA and the committees entered into a losing battle against the growing tendencies toward autocratic leadership by Ben Bella and the FLN. The government began to preempt workers' control. Committees established after October were state appointed, not elected by workers. The Decretes de Mars seemed to outline a socialist ideology to underpin the takeovers. In point of fact however, only legal structures were provided; monetary and organizational support were never forthcoming. Self-management atrophied, leaving room for Boumedienne to introduce what was obviously state capitalism after he ousted Ben Bella on June 19, 1965.

The state further weakened self-management by controlling access to capital.

> . . . the reasons for creating some form of integrated financial and marketing organization lay, initally, with a quite rational desire to integrate the socialist sector . . . But the mechanisms created on this basis soon came to determine the total operation of the comites, making a farce of their nominal autonomy.   [Clegg 1971, 70]

On RA (Office National de la Reforme Alagire) and its subsidiaries CCRA (Coopratifis de la Reforme Algaire) in agriculture and the BCA (Banque Centrae d'Algerie) controlled revenue and credits for the socialist sector. In practice this meant that firms, already heavily in debt because of massive capital flight and destruction of capital goods that had taken place in the months before independence, were starved for capital, unable to get out of debt, unable to reach full production, and unable to increase wages. The councils were thus left open for criticism by the supporters of state capitalism on the grounds that they were inefficient. In reality it is clear that the rate of absolute exploitation actually increased under self mangement.[4]

The nature of the original struggle, guerrilla warfare as opposed to industrial class conflict, meant that the most committed, organized members of any would-be workers' movement toward a socialist transformation had just completed an eight-year stay in the countryside as the left-wing element of the FLN. On the other hand, those who instituted workers' control were the least class-conscious workers who had stayed in the employ of the French colonizers. Workers lost interest in self-management when they were unable to obtain their primary goal: increased salaries. Large numbers of unemployed were never incorporated into the working class and were never organized, giving the self-managed sector almost no power base of popular support.

## REVERSAL OF THE REFORMS

In 1962 Ben Bella outlawed both the communist and the socialist parties. He also attempted to bring the UGTA and radical elements of the FLN under control. When he was unable to do so, he merely eliminated UGTA leaders from the legislature and replaced them with his own supporters. This left the UGTA paralyzed until 1965. Local unions would strike for higher wages which government-appointed national leaders would not support. Through 1963, Ben Bella continued to eliminate elements within the government which supported self-management.

When Ben Bella was ousted, Boumedienne made room for the further collapse of the self-managed sector by abandoning it to market forces.

The workers of autogestion must pay their enterprise taxes; they will get no more loans. . . . in a word they must run their sector rationally. [Boumedienne quoted in Clegg 1971, 134]

Shrinkage in the self-managed sector was nevertheless accompanied by expansion of the state sector.

First, Boumedienne returned a number of small worker-managed shops to their previous owners, his petty bourgeoisie supporters. Next, the regime nationalized transportation, insurance, banking and petro-chemical distribution. It gained control of most of the foreign trade sector and many of the oil and natural gas related industries. These firms were brought under the direct control of state managers, their organization and operation excluding labors' participation in management.

In agriculture, the cumbersome and inefficient central bureaucracy was dismantled. However, the same set of bureaucrats took charge of the newly decentralized structures. Successful self-managed firms in construction and transport which had been in existence since the first days of independence were reorganized. The committees became powerless advisory organs. The same thing happened to every other firm in the self-managed sector large enough to pique some bureaucrat's interest.

During much of 1967, union leaders and socialist members of government were imprisoned or went into exile. By the middle of 1967, UGTA leaders met in secret only, forming the nucleus of a clandestine workers' party. By 1968 state capitalism was firmly entrenched and any progress toward socialism was reversed.

Self-management in Algeria was instituted from below by workers and farmers in the period immediately following liberation. Using the Yugoslav experience as a guide, progressive elements within the government attempted, after the fact, to organize what was essentially a grass roots movement. However, the scope of self-management was limited in several ways. The state never fully supported a transition to socialism. Sectoral conflict among members of the government precluded the widespread organization of the agricultural sector. Legislation regarding the implementation of self-management was never uniformly enforced. Firms were not introduced into the self-managed sector in any systematic fashion. Only the least profitable, labor-intensive firms were represented. Credit and supplies were virtually unobtainable. Though production increased, the rate was slow enough to allow the new national bourgeoisie to blame the sector for the country's economic problems supplying the ideological justification for the devolution of self-management into state capitalism.

## Chile

The Chilean example presents a high degree of labor participation at all levels of firm management. When workers in Chile seized the first factories they were acting from a long tradition of labor organization, electoral democracy and state intervention in the economy. Firms in the social sector were managed jointly by state and labor representatives. Unlike the firms managed by Algerian workers, Chile's social sector contained the most dynamic sectors of industry and thus presented possibilities for real improvement in workers' living conditions. Of course, there are both external and internal constraints upon the development of industrial democracy. The history of trade unionism so necessary in that it provided a base of organized support, carried with it an ideology which limited the participation of some members to the level of economic concerns. Externally, contradictions in Chilean society—Chile's democratic tradition which the left had utilized for decades, culminating in the election of a socialist government—precluded the forced ejection of bourgeois elements from the political arena. These elements were thus able to topple the regime. Once supporters of workers' councils lost control of the state, it was not long before they were completely dismantled.

### PRECONDITIONS FOR SUCCESSFUL IMPLEMENTATION OF COMANAGEMENT

Chile's labor organizations first developed in the late nineteenth century among miners. By the early twentieth century, several trade unions existed, and a number of wider-based, more radical organizations were developing, eg., FOCH (Federacion Obrero de Chile), established in 1909. The first labor code was enacted in 1924, legalizing unions and strikes. Other aspects of the code were crucial to the later development of participatory democracy. Separate blue- and white-collar unions were created, preventing white-collar workers from becoming elite union representatives. Paid union staffs were prohibited and officials, elected for a maximum of one year, had to remain at their jobs. Collective bargaining was allowed at the plant level only. Federations and strike funds were illegal. These last two measures were created in a futile attempt to keep unions weak. This attempt was only partially successful. While, perhaps the measures retarded the development of a nationwide organization, they also hindered bureaucratization and stratification, promoting instead the involvement of the rank and file. The code also instituted profit sharing. Unions were legally entitled to 10 percent of the firm's profits. Five percent served as a wage supplement; the other five as a union fund, giving the unions a monetary base independent of the government. Until the late sixties most union demands were economistic, i.e., they demanded higher wages. Still, the period 1958–65 is one of increasing labor militancy. Union membership doubled. The annual number of legal strikes rose steadily from 120 in 1958 to 723 in 1965. (Espinosa and Zimbalist 1978, 29).

The government's role in the economy began in a massive effort to promote import substitution industrialization and slowly increased until, by 1970, the public sector accounted for 46 percent of all value added in the economy (Ramos 1972, 78). State control of industry and the nationalization of private sectors was not introduced by Allende. The initial attempts at self-management also predate him. The Unidad Popular government reacted somewhat ambivalently toward the growing movement to change social relations from below as it caused tension between Socialist Executive and Christian Democrat (petty bourgeois) elements within the Parliament (Raptis 1971, 11–16).

INTRODUCTION OF WORKERS' SELF-MANAGEMENT

The first worker-owned and state-owned/worker managed firms were actually created while Frei was in office. However, they do not represent a commitment to socialized production on the part of the government. Rather, the government allowed the social sector to expand only in response to worker protests. Only twenty-two small worker owned firms were established but they were enough to encourage increased militancy among workers in the state sector. The first spontaneous factory seizures occured in the last two years of the Frei regime, ". . . all had less than 80 members . . . and each was a firm where the owner had abandoned the factory or the firm had gone bankrupt . . . " (Espinosa and Zimbalist 1978, 42). By the end of Frei's term in 1969, thirty such enterprises had been reorganized as state-owned/worker-managed firms, bringing the total number of firms in the state sector up to 110.

The change from the Frei to the Allende government greatly enhanced the promotion of workers' control. By September 1972 the number of state-owned/worker-managed firms had risen to 100 and by September 1973 it stood at 120. At the same time a national organization had formed, the National Federation of Producer Cooperatives, to which seventy-five percent of the employees in the cooperative sector belonged. But at that point there was still a long way to go before socialist productive relations would be established. Though it was expanding, the social sector still represented only a small segment of the working class.

The social sector expanded using five legal mechanisms. The first two, intervention and requisition, were in existence prior to Allende's victory but rarely enacted. In both cases the state stepped in and operated firms because of actual or threatened declines in production. Intervention gave the state-appointed manager more power than requisition, especially over the firm's finances. The state usually intervened in response to actions taken by owners: lockouts, destruction or sale of capital goods, or outright capital flight. In many cases labor acted with the intention of forcing intervention, knowing they could, through increased agitation, pressure the state into appointing a director of their choosing. Third, the state sector expanded through the outright expropriation of the country's natural resources from multi-national corporations, one of the acts which prompted international capital to organize efforts to cripple the economy and hastened the regime's demise (Petras and Morley 1975). Fourth, new firms were created and run solely by the workers. Although only eight such enterprises were ever officially created, many more were in operation awaiting final approval by the fall of the Allende government. Finally, the state, in conjunction with workers, purchased firms from owners anxious to leave a climate they perceived as less than hospitable to private property.

THE NORMAS BASICAS

To understand the forms industrial democracy took in Chile, it is necessary to know what organizational patterns and structures emerged. To measure real participation it is also necessary to be concerned with the variety of contexts into which these structures were inserted. The manner in which the state and the workers managed firms in the social sector became the subject of a joint CUT (Central Unica de Trabajadores)[5]—government commission which issued a set of guidelines (without force of law) during June of 1971. Called the Normas Basicas, these guidelines suggested that the decision making bodies within a firm in the state sector should be comprised of both state and worker representatives. The administrative council, the principle decision-making body, was to consist of eleven members. Six were to be from the government and five were to be elected from among workers' ranks by a general assembly of all workers. Three of the five labor representatives had to be blue-collar workers. Labor representatives received no compensation for their services, served a short term, and could be recalled at any time by a majority vote of the general assembly. In reality, the 6–5 split actually favored the workers. Government representatives were often absent from the biweekly meetings and in many instances the representatives were selected from among the ranks of the workers.

Although better than 80 percent of the firms in the social sector had elected a functioning administrative council by the time of Allende's overthrow, a wide variation existed in application of the Normas Basicas. Some sectors had a richer tradition of organized labor activity than others. Their workers were more readily engaged in self-management tasks. Unfortunately, attempts at sectoral organization met with difficulties resulting in wide variations among different firms in the same industry. But the most significant factor affecting the implementation of the Normas Basicas in any particular plant was the response of its union leaders. Many perceived the new organizations as rivals and wished to maintain their positions as the exclusive representatives of labor's interests. Still others could not transcend traditional trade union ideology and so remained interested only in wage and benefit issues. They were thus unable to encourage active decision making on the part of the workers (Espinosa and Zimbalist 1978, 53–56).

The Chilean experience with workers' self-management provides insights into the determinants of workers' attitudes toward participation. Informal interviews with a wide range of workers, from copper miners to migrant workers in squatter settlements, revealed that the workers who were more influenced by the extraparliamentary left and whose immediate struggles were infused with a global vision of change were much more disposed to the program of self-management than those workers organized in unions led by electorally oriented trade unionists. In a related finding, Zimbalist and Espinosa found a greater recepitvity to the ideas of worker self-management where the class struggle was strongest. Their findings, based upon a survey conducted in the social area in mid-1973, representing 30 percent of the industrial labor force shows that executive decision making by workers is dependent upon rank and file interest. Conversely, if the rank and file have no real power, they will quickly lose interest in any self-management scheme. Besides association with class-oriented political views, high levels of participation were also associated with better "labor discipline" and smaller differences between highest and lowest-paid members of a firm. Productivity increased with participation despite an increase in the number of persons employed. Their study refuted the notion that effective worker participation led to a decline in productivity. Finally, the Chilean study demonstrated that the higher the degree of participation, the greater the rate of capital reinvestment by workers. Increase in capital stock in participatory firms was only 3.9 percent from 1959 to 1964. From 1965 to 1970 it was 4.6 percent among all firms in the self-managed sector. Among firms in the survey with more than twenty employees reinvestment averaged 15.5 percent.

WEAKNESSES OF SELF-MANAGEMENT IN CHILE AND
THE REVERSAL OF REFORMS

Intervention and requisition were at the disposal of the working class, but the opposition also had legal devices to delay, limit, or reverse takeovers. During 1971 and 1972 the government intervened and requisitioned a total of 318 firms. Sixty-five of these acts were reversed. Many more were delayed. Often a delay of only a few weeks provided sufficient opportunities for massive capital transfers. Originally Allende and his staff had planned to incorporate the largest, most dynamic industries into the state sector so that the government would control the leaders in each industry. A list of 74 of the most important privately owned firms was submitted to the legislature by Allende for nationalization. During October of 1971, a long series of parliamentary debates and juridical delaying tactics was used to prevent these acts, culminating in a constitutional impasse. By 1973 only 50 of the 74 firms had made it into the social sector.

The Chilean experience demonstrates the importance of two critical elements in the develpment of council socialism. On the one hand it points out the central importance of class struggle in creating the conditions for worker self management. The necessary ingredient for effective self-management is the large-scale autonomous participation of workers. In no other country looked at in this study was there as high a degree of real participation. Workers were involved in every aspect of management. They chose product lines, made decisions about the introduction of new technology, make organizational changes, and controlled accounts. Unfortunately, the Chilean experience shows also that a class society on the verge of civil war is a lethal environment for newly created workers' institutions. Existing in a pluralist framework, the Allende government never acquired sufficient control of the state or of financial mechanisims external to it to insure the longevity of the reforms. The more conservative elements of the Christian Democratic Party and right-wing extremist groups, their private property threatened, had nothing to lose in the violent curtailment of "representative democracy," and everything to gain. Through the military coup led by Pinochet in 1973, these groups were able to dismantle the social area and, through the use of terrorism and violence, erase the workers' organizations associated with self management.

Three aspects of Chilean history made the Chilean experience with workers' control unique: (1) the existence of a system of participatory democracy; (2) a history of direct government intervention in the economy; and (3) a strong tradition of class-based collective action and trade unionism. These factors were both strengths and weaknesses. Chile had a participatory system of industrial democracy with a very strong class base. However, those factors which promoted organization and participation also meant that the classes which supported industrial democracy were never in complete control of the state, and therefore once the state mechanism fell into the hands of class members who were opposed to participatory democracy, the organizations quickly fell apart.

Durable workers' self-management emerges from an organized struggle-tempered working class which strives to develop a workers' state while organizing its self-management councils. If either or both of these conditions is not met, as has been seen in the cases of Algeria and Chile, the impulse toward a self-managed economy is short lived. But self-management schemes do not always arise out of the experiences of the working class, however ill-formed. In many cases plans are drawn up by state functionaries with interests very different from those of workers.

Bolivian codetermination and then Peruvian industrial communities will be discussed in this section. Similarities between the two cases, which also distinguish them from the Algerian and Chilean cases are: (1) the "top-down" organization which resulted in decreased workers' involvement in management and more labor unrest; (2) the fact that both cases represent attempts on the part of corporatist, nationalist, governments to industrilize while minimizing class conflict; (3) both codetermination and the industrial communities created the unforseen consequence of increased labor mobilization, highlighting the limited power of a corporatist regime in a developing capitalist country; (4) in both cases, lack of unity among fractions of the bourgeoisie made it possible for these organizations to survive and (5) in both cases when a single fraction, which did not support self-managment, established political dominance the programs were quickly dismantled.

The Bolivian experiment was limited to the tin mines. This discussion highlights the unions' dependence upon the state bureaucracy, which made it an ineffective representative of the miners' interests. Contradictions develop when workers' organizations play the dual role of guarding labor's position and serving in a capitalist managerial capacity. Finally, the nature of a movement whose existence depends upon the political space afforded it by divisions within the capitalist class is short lived.

Moving to the Peruvian case, many of the aspects of "top-down" management noted in the Bolivian case will be seen again. In addition, the mechanisms through which labor attempts to extend the function of the appartuses for participation supplied by the state will be discussed. The Peruvian case also demonstrates the role coercion plays in maintaining corporatist unity and in dismantling participatory organizations, in this case the industrial communities.

## Bolivia

Workers' control in Bolivia was instituted "from above" to encourage increased production without escalating class conflict. Six months after the MNR government took control it nationalized the tin mines. The delay allowed time for capital flight. In addition, the mines were old and not as productive as they had been. Thus the stage was set for an escalation in class conflict as the state struggled to maintain production without incurring additonal costs for labor or machinery. In response to steadily worsening living and working conditions workers' protest movements developed. The new government therefore sought to "involve" the workers in management enough to increase the amount of labor supplied without increasing wages or causing more conflict.[6]

At first the miners cooperated with the government but the honeymoon between miners and government ended when the miners realized that COMIBOL (National Tin Mine of Bolivia) officials were enriching themselves instead of financing exploration. Productivity fell and miners stopped reporting evidence of new veins. Miners' wages had not risen. An increasing segment of the payroll at each mine and in the government went to the growing white-collar mine staffs and the COMIBOL bureaucracy, the ranks of which were inflated with the names of managers' and bureaucrats' nonworking relatives. It was during this period that the unions and FSTMB (Federation of Bolivian Mine Workers' Unions) lost their autonomy. Union leadership, dependent upon its role in the government's codetermination program for funds, was unresponsive to worker demands, as is evidenced by the fact that miners' wages had not risen. This added to the disillusionment of the workers.

The radical miners at Siglo XX struggled to push the comanagement scheme beyond what the military government intended. By design, workers originally had no power to combat managerial abuses. Miners at Siglo XX refused to participate in the original program in which workers' assemblies served only in an advisory capacity. They demanded that workers council be given the right to veto *any* managerial action. All expenditures had to be approved by the union. Unfortunately, the effectiveness of the veto was limited. Unions rarely had enough money to hire auditors to check mine accounts. Second, the veto also placed labor in an adversarial position in regards to management. Because of their position as watchdogs, instead of participating in management, they remained concerned with monetary issues.

Government was forced to attempt to dismantle comanagement almost as soon as it began. The price of tin collapsed after the Korean War and international capital was called in to bail out the economy. Predictably, BID (Bank for Interamercian Development), and U.S. and West Germany private banks, lent the government $37,750,000 on the condition that the operations of the market be unrestricted and social programs be cut. For the miners this new "liberal" policy translated into attempts to "rationalize" the operation of the labor market and production. A scheme to reorganize the comanagement program was put forward by the government which would have eliminated the veto power won by Siglo XX miners and many other benefits including a reduction in the number of less strenuous above-ground mining jobs which served as the only available old age, disability and welfare services.

Through strikes, slow-downs, and protests, the workers were able to defend their position and prevent the enactment of the reforms for four years. During that time, political and economic tensions mounted, culminating in a coup by General Barrientos who ended the first phase of so called comanagement by sending troops into the mines in May 1965.

An analysis of this phase shows that worker militancy and organizational capacity grew in self-defense against the government's attempts to worsen conditions under the ideological guise of comanagement. The councils did not, therefore, succeed in their intended role of co-opting labor. On the other hand, labor remained weak, demanding only higher wages and improved living conditions. Being but weakly organized and internally divided, labor could not serve as a mass base of support for socialized production and participatory democracy.

A wave of criticism of mine operations took place after Barrientos came to power. Everyone agreed that the mining operations had been a disaster, losing $106,000,000 since the revolution. Labor costs had risen, no new veins had been discovered, and the price of tin had not recovered on the world market. The vested interests of the class of state functionaries who gleaned their livings from COMIBOL saw to it that the principle of nationalization was never discussed. For them the issue was not a question of returning the mines to the private sector but of extracting more value from labor and cleaning up alleged managerial inefficiency. They therefore launched a bogus campaign in an effort to renew labor's enthusiasm for self-management, promoting the idea that it was the Bolivian middle class which had somehow falsely nationalized the mine and which, ". . . maintained control of the decision-making apparatuses and continued as servants of international private capitalists" (Nash 1972, 116).

Between the fall of Barrientos in 1969 and the rise of Colonel Banzer in 1971, two nationalist military figures, Ovando and Torres, ruled, providing political space for the workers' movement. In this interim the miners gained room to maneuver as their support became important to the nationalist military leaders. By this time workers' organizations had acquired enough organizational experience to particpate in a substantive manner in the management of the mines. An entirely new workers' control program was introduced. "Union leaders pointed to the error of letting COMIBOL fall into the hands of the politicians . . . bourgeois bureaucrats and the military" (Nash 1977, 166). Wages were increased and the veto reinstated. The new proposal, issued May 1, 1971, described an organization which would elicit more participation from below. In the old system, top union officials automatically sat on boards. Now a general assembly was to elect all labor representatives to the boards of directors. The president of COMIBOL was to be selected from a list drawn up by a directory which was elected by and composed of miners. Managerial responsibilities of workers were to be enlarged and all members would have a vote at board meetings. In retrospect it is impossible to gauge the exact nature of the new plan which also eminated "from above." Nevertheless, workers had already demonstrated their capacity for extending the limited powers granted them. On the other hand, radical unions rejected these proposals on the grounds that they failed to deal with the basic contradiction between watching management and being co-equal with it.

The question is moot. The Banzer coup in August 1971 insured that the plan would never be implemented. A faction of the capitalist class had clearly emerged as dominant and any room to manuever quickly disappeared. Banzer announced the removal of all veto powers and a return to "rational" labor policies. All pretense of participation was thus eliminated. As Nash concludes:

> Bolivia's experience with workers' participation reveals the contradictions implicit in any compromise form of entry into management short of a socialist reorganization of the aims and structures of the industrial enterprise. [1972, 169]

## Peru

Successful coparticipation of labor and capital, introduced from above, occurs only in the context of a rapidly expanding economy. Bolivia and other underdeveloped capitalist countries do not possess the resources to provide both welfare concerns to labor and incentives to capital to allow for class collaboration. Second, coparticipation operates for an extended period of time when the state enters into a relationship with a highly organized unionized labor force with its own power base, in a position to influence state policies and mangerial decisions, as was the case in Western Europe during the 1950s and 1960s. In France (Ross and Hartmen 1960), in Germany (Deppe et. al. 1969), and in England (Kendel 1973), workers' control programs were instituted during periods of economic growth and increased demands for labor, as an answer to organized labor's challenge to the capitalist's "right" to the lion's share of profits and their "right" to control production. Workers in these countries made demands which exceeded the typical wage-benefit packages. The programs established in response to those demands were often attempts to co-opt labor and quell unrest. They therefore offered little in the way of substantive changes. More often than not, the rank and file preceived them correctly and were less than enthusiastic participants.[7]

In contrast to the Euopean situation, coparticipation in Peru was a specific response to the burgeoning class conflict engendered by industrialization and growing peasant discontent in an underdeveloped country. Instituted "from above," it was an attempt to integrate autonomous working-class forces within the political and economic projects of the capitalist class. The Peruvian experience thus offers an example of the limitations and contradictions inherent in reforms instituted from above in a capitalist environment.[8]

In 1968 Velasco and his military supporters seized control of the state from his predecessor, Belaunde, using a nationalist platform similar to the MNR's platform in Bolivia during the 1950s. The Belaunde regime's support for international capital had aliented many nationalist forces. Urban growth poles and foreign capital had drained the agricultural sector leaving unrest, peasant uprisings, and land seizures. Velasco took control in order to preempt revolutionary mobilization among the popular classes during a period of disintegrating relations among fractions of the capitalist class.[9]

At first the government underestimated the role coercion plays in maintaining corporatist unity. Peruvian leaders' control of the labor movement could often be achieved through a series of tactics designed to prevent the formation of new class-based organizations, to dissolve existing ones and to co-opt those portions of the labor movement it could not disperse. At the same time they planned to increase productivity. The cornerstone of this ultimately unsuccessful plan was the Industrial Community, or IC. The ideology which underpinned the IC stated that labor was to share in the responsibilities and the risks of capitalist development. Supposedly, this would diffuse class conflict and decrease labor's tendency to organize. From this point of view, the program was a failure. It caused a great increase in unionization. However, the struggle that ensued was not between labor and private capital but rather between workers and the state itself, which was forced into an adversarial position vis-à-vis both labor and capital.

THE INDUSTRIAL COMMUNITY

Velasco presented a compromise program of coparticipation that alienated private capital while giving little to labor besides a small profit-sharing program. Called decree law number 18350, it was enacted in July of 1970. Part Two, Titles Seven and Eight, required that 25 percent of a firm's net profits be turned over to the IC for distribution. Five percent was to be divided equally among all workers. Five percent was to be differentially distributed to *all* employees in proportion to their regular salaries, and the remaining 15 percent was to be annually reinvested until the IC owned half of the enterprise.

Several critical points need to be raised here before describing the other elements of the IC. First, equality and the possibility of wage redistribution was never addressed. The 5 percent proportionately distributed included managers with large salaries, so that in effect, this act perpetuated imbalances.[10] Second, law 18350 made no mention of "self-management." There was no way for workers to ever own more than 50 percent of an IC firm. Workers could, therefore, never control a majority on the board of directors. Third, no time limit for reaching the 50 percent level was ever established. By investing in and enlarging the company, management could make sure that the IC never even controlled the 50 percent allowed by law and, thus, never achieved parity on the board of directors.[11] Fourth, the IC's were supposed to promote labor discipline as an aid to industrialization. They were not supposed to reduce unemployment, which averaged 35 percent of the economically active population; all industrial workers accounted for only 7 percent of the active population. Only medium and large industrial firms were included in the IC legislation. Very few workers were, therefore, included in the IC program. Further, no controls were ever created over investments in technology, exacerbating the unemployment problem by allowing IC enterprises to eliminate jobs through the introduction of capital intensive production processes.

Other aspects of the plan were designed to minimize worker participation. IC legislation was binding upon all industrial firms with more than five employees. At the top of the organization was the board of directors. The board consisted of representatives of labor and private capital in proportion to the amount of stock held by each. Below the board was the workers' council consisting of six to twelve members elected by a general assembly of all workers. Participation was minimal. The general assembly only had the power to elect the council and rubber stamp council activities. The elite within the IC were elected to the council and quickly became part of the bureaucracy. All disputes between labor and capital were mediated by the state. Council members were the only representatives of workers' interests recognized by the state. In their capacity as company board members they often left their jobs in the plant and came to have more contact with other board members than with fellow workers. The council had complete control over IC discretionary funds giving council members defacto control over all daily IC operations. It also administered the distribution of monies to workers leaving the firm in compensation for their portion of IC owned company stock. Finally, as Espinosa and Zimbalist's model would have predicted, the rank and file, cut off from their leaders and unable to participate in decision making, quickly lost interest in the IC and returned to their unions (Stephens 1980).

ORGANIZATION OF PERUVIAN WORKING CLASS

The Peruvian working class was organized prior to the initation of the industrial communities and thus had developed sufficient class consciousness to resist efforts at cooptation. Peasant unions had been increasing in number since 1963 and they continued to grow throughout the decade. By 1968, 85 percent of all sugar cultivation was done by unionized workers (Stephens 1980). At that time strikes in the agricultural sector accounted for 18.9 percent of all strikes (Petras et al. 1981, 225). Several haciendas were seized by workers, indicating the beginnings of spontaneous change from below (Matos Mar. 1970), (Bourque 1975). When Velasco came to power, more than 50 percent of all value added in production came from unionized firms. There was a high correlation between the number of workers in a firm and the likelihood that there was a union present. In 1963, 1461 shops had more than twenty workers. These shops emploeyd 69 percent of the labor force in manufacturing. Among them there were 503 unions and 34 percent of the shops were unionized. The Peruvian industrial labor force was also capable of organized collective action. From 1965 to 1968 there were 392 strikes per year on the average in all sectors and 192 per year in industry (Stephens 1980, 129).

The effect of the IC on this base of organization was a pronounced increase in union activity. There were a number of reasons why the military's program promoted unionization. The industrial communities provided a legitimate platform for union organizations during the process of soliciting enough names to transform an enterprise into a union shop. The presence of the IC with its, albeit few, benefits to workers coupled with management's obvious resistance to complying with the regulations, made it clear that an independent organization was needed capable of defending the workers' interests (Stephens 1980, 108). After 1971, unions formed outside of the industrial sector when mining, fishing and telecommunications were added to the areas covered by IC legislation.

In addition to the industrial communities a number of rural and industrial cooperatives were formed during the Velasco regime (Petras et al. 1981, 222–37), (McClintock 1977). The experience of the industrial cooperative is informative. Though the sector was too small to be an economic or political force, it was characterized by higher degrees of participation than the rest of the social sector. These co-ops shed light on the question of workers control over wage rates. Initially bankrupt enterprises were turned into cooperatives. By May 1976 there were thirty in Lima and they were largely successful in increasing productivity, something that usually occurs only when there is real participation. Horvat (1982), among others, argues that workers tend to raise their own wages faster than productivity increases. It can look like a no-win situation. External control may guarantee "correct" wage–investment ratios but lowers participation which, in turn, lowers productivity. Absence of state control, so the argument goes, may bring about an initial rise in productivity, as workers begin to act like capitalists, but will mean falling returns in the long run because of too much profit taking. Although very limited in scope, the Peruvian industrial cooperatives show this to be a false dichotomy. Constraints may be placed upon wages without limiting other aspects of self-management. In this case, the workers were, by law, limited to paying themselves no more than twice the official minimum wage. Second, these co-ops started out heavily in debt and the state would only lend them money on the condition that the borrowed amount be invested in capital stock (Vanek 1977). This prevented them from doing what their capitalist counterparts had—borrow money from the government and invest it in real estate rather than in industrial development.

**Table 8.1  Growth of the State Sector During the Allende Regime (November 4, 1970 to September 11, 1973).**

| Year | # of state enterprises | # of state enterprises in the industrial sector | industrial production in state sector as % of total industrial production. | industrial employment in state sector as % of total industrial employment. |
|------|------|------|------|------|
| 1970 | 43  | 30  | 11.8 | 6.5  |
| 1973 | 420 | 270 | 40.0 | 30.0 |

*Source:* Espinosa & Zimbalist: 1978:42, 49, 50.

## LABOR AND THE IC

The IC was not able to effectively monitor the activities of management. At first the IC did not have the authority to audit the firm's accounts. Even after that right was won in January 1972, most IC officials lacked the accounting expertise to enable them to audit. And, if the company had not shown a profit, the IC was left without funds and could not hire independent auditors.

Organized labor's reaction to the IC was mixed. The communist-party-controlled CGTP provisionally supported the IC as a transitional phase in a process ending in social ownership. Other unions, fully aware of the co-optive nature of the IC, were cautious. At first, they supported profitsharing but not worker representation on the board of directors. Later, union officials softened that position. They argued that the IC helped them to organize and therefore was not a threat. Also, the IC gave unions access to company information they would not otherwise be entitled to. A few union officials were co-opted but many left their positions as union officials to become IC representatives while retaining contacts with other union officials—a strategic gain for the unions not for those groups that would have used the IC's to dissolve them.

Like Chile, the overall success in implementation of IC reforms depended upon the prior organizational experience of workers. First, unionized firms were more likely to have an IC. By the end of Velasco's term, 91 percent of the unionized manufacturing firms had an IC while only 58 percent of the nonunionized firms did. Second, Peruvian labor leaders were experienced in dealing with a state bureaucracy, an important skill as all collective negotiations, grievances and contracts had to be presented by worker representatives to the Ministry of Labor for approval (Stephens 1980, 107). Workers in unionized plants had less difficulty adjusting to working within the IC guidelines than did those workers for whom the IC represented the first experience with collective action and bureaucratic relations.

Unlike Chile, where participation by unionized workers resulted in substantive changes in work organization, the number of strikes, the rate of pay, the amount of theft, and so on (Espinosa and Zimablist 1981, 127–75), in Peru few real changes were made (Stephens 1980, 101–144). The IC's largest affects were to aid organizing and indirectly to increase strike activity.

Often workers could not utilize IC legislation to its fullest because of ignorance. In Chile, autonomous union organizations were responsible for informing workers of their position. In this case a series of government agencies, each more conservative and less effective than its predecessor, were given the task of education. Five years after the enactment of IC legislation, ". . . 56 percent of blue collar workers simply didn't know anything about the rights granted them as members of the IC and among the 44 percent who knew something there were many with very rudimentary or even incorrect ideas" (Stephens 1980, 112).

But as in Chile, legal provisions that were meant to fragment labor, ". . . ended up politicizing and strengthening the defensive power of the labor movement" (Espinosa and Zimbalist 1981, 36). In Peru, unionization was increased because the limited role afforded labor by government in the IC forced labor to rely upon independent trade unions in self-defense. Labor's demands were never won in IC council meetings, or in meetings with state functionaries. Most of the issues labor was interested in were not permissable topics for discussion at board meetings. And when the worker representatives brought non-compliance problems to the OCLA (Office of Labor Communities), the agency was reduced to writing letters to the offending owner. OCLA had no legal sanctioning power. Workers' only recourse was the strike. Increases in strike activity during this period can easily be seen.

From 1965 to 1972, strike activity was fairly constant. The IC's were first announced in 1970 and were instituted by the end of that year. From 1972 to 1975, when IC's were operating in most large firms, the number of strikes and the number of lost manhours increased.[12] Finally, wages and working conditions remained the primary reasons for collective action. Workers did not alter their demands to include what is normally associated with workers' control.

CAPITAL'S REACTION TO THE INDUSTRIAL COMMUNITIES

IC legislation was not designed to limit capital's prerogatives in any way, yet there was massive resistance to the IC program. No significant changes were made in the daily operations of most firms. Supervisors and managers maintained their positions. The profitsharing scheme was an immediate nuisance to capital; however, the danger of workers ever acquiring half ownership was minimal. Capital's immediate reaction included layoffs and disinvestment. Next, there were many irregularities in the sale of shares to IC's as they tried to capitalize the 15 percent of annual profits earmarked for reinvestment. Medium size firms would be broken into smaller firms, each with less than six employees. Firms were divided into two companies, one in manufacturing and one in the service or commercial sector, both of which were not subject to IC legislation. Profits would then be declared only in those companies which did not have an IC and where the distribution of 25 percent of the firms earnings to labor was not required. Reminiscent of Bolivian mine managers, Peruvian factory owners would hire their relatives at very high salaries in order to capture most of the differentially distributed profits. Padded expense accounts and phantom employees were the norm.

GOVERNMENT RESPONSE AND THE DESTRUCTION OF
THE INDUSTRIAL COMMUNITY

Peru differed from Chile, where obvious attempts were made to diminish the power of the bourgeoisie and from Algeria, where the Bourgeoisie

**Table 8.2 Unionization before and after 1970 by Size of Enterprise**

| Number of workers in enterprise | Percentage of enterprises where a union was established | | | Percentage of enterprises in size category | N | Percentage of workers employed by enterprises in size category |
|---|---|---|---|---|---|---|
| | Before 1970 | After 1970 | By 1976 | | | |
| Under 20 | 0 | 0 | 0 | 28.9 | (577) | 4 |
| 20–49 | 4 | 22 | 25 | 32.5 | (648) | 11 |
| 50–99 | 23 | 51 | 74 | 17.0 | (339) | 13 |
| 100–499 | 51 | 58 | 78 | 19.3 | (385) | 42 |
| 500+ | 93 | 41 | 98 | 2.2 | (44) | 30 |
| All | 17 | 28 | 38 | 100.0 | | 100 |
| N | (338) | (551) | (758) | (1938) | | (190,762) |

*Source:* Stephens: 1977:108.

fled. Here, attempts were made to encourage capital investment, but to no avail.[13] Faced with capital's refusal to invest, the Velasco government buckled under and began dismantling the IC. The original plan called for labor to gradually control 50 percent of a firm, then to purchase half of the remaining 50 percent so that the workers owned 75 percent. This process was to be repeated until virtually all stock was controlled by the IC. Alarm in the private sector forced Velasco to renounce this idea and to state that 50 percent was the maximum amount the IC could ever control. Despite this and other concessions, private capital refused to cooperate with Velasco's development strategy. The state was, therefore, forced to take on the task of industrialization on its own and in joint ventures with multinationals. As the state reluctantly took over more control of investment and development, public debt increased (Hunt 1976, 302–49). Still the state stopped short of a direct attack on the national bourgeois.

Increased unionization external to the IC and an increase in the number of strikes, as well as continued noncooperation by private national capital indicate the failure of the corporatist scheme to absorb and suppress class conflict. Each side made increasing efforts to exert hegemony independently of the state mechanism. At the same time, several other factors, including collapsing mineral prices, the disappearance of the anchovy, one of Peru's major exports, and debt repayment problems, forced Velasco to seek aid from the IMF which he received only after agreeing to "liberalize" trade policies and drastically reduce public spending (Stallings 1978, 29), (*Latin America Economic Report* 1976).

Spending cuts further polarized capital and labor. The redistributed profits had amounted to over one month's additional wages per year for 67 percent of all workers in IC firms. Now, inflation and unemployment eroded the previously made gains. Strikes increased and the government retaliated. It was made easier to fire striking workers, and when employers illegally fired workers the government turned a deaf ear to labor's complaints. After Bermudez took control in 1976, signaling the defeat of all prolabor forces inside and outside of the government, a state of emergency was declared and strikes were made illegal. Many union leaders were arrested and many members of government, suspected of labor connections were exiled. At this point, right wing extremist groups were no longer restrictred in the use of coercion. Organizations of thugs, within the state fishing company (PESCAPERU), were used to "discipline" other unions.

Several decrees gave the government increased power over unions. The structure of the IC was altered. Representation on the board of directors had to be divided proportionally between blue- and white-collar workers. Fifteen percent of the firm's profits were still handed over to the IC but now they were placed into a special fund. When the fund reached the equivalent of 50 percent of the company's net worth, contributions ceased. The bulk of the fund was distributed to individual workers in the form of labor shares which carried a fixed rate of interest, were redeemable after five years and, most important, were transferable.

. . . given a high enough price, a sufficient number of workers or white-collar employees can certainly be found who would be willing to sell their shares back to the enterprise or to whatever intermediary . . . [Stephens 1980, 234]

This would gradually reduce worker representation on the board of directors back to zero.

The failure of the Peruvian experiment with industrial democracy illustrates the weakness of "top-down" efforts and suggests again that any scheme of participation that lacks effective moblization of its constitutents is likely to generate opposition. Deep-seated hostilities, and histories of sharp conflicts involving managerial intransigence and labor militancy, are not propitious climates in which to attempt to implement coparticipation schemes. The Peruvian experience demonstrates the transitory nature of coparticipation. By the mid 1970s both labor and capital attempted to assert their hegemony independently of the bureaucratic state formulas for joint association. In the end, the schemes disolved as the previous forms of class organization reemerged.

### Yugoslavia

The Yugoslav experience is sufficiently long and well documented to allow a detailed look at the relationships between labor, the enterprise and the state over time. Its experience with self-management can be divided into three periods. The first from 1950 to 1965, the second from 1965 to 1974, and the third from 1974 to the present. In terms of the relationship between the enterprise and the market, the first period was characterized by central planning and a state controlled economy. In contrast, the second period was the most "liberal." Planning was abandoned in favor of reliance upon market forces. In the last period, reliance upon market forces has been greatly reduced. However, regional governments have replaced the central government as the sources of control. Important aspects of the first period include: (1) the historic genesis of workers' councils out of Yugoslavia's role in World War II and its relationship with the Soviet Union; (2) the limited scope of self-management confined, for the most part, to skilled workers and the limited purpose of self-management at this time, to encourage increased productivity; (3) the development of regional and sectoral inequalities caused by certain aspects of the relationships among the firm, the municipality and the central government; and (4) the specific conflicts which developed into the impetus toward the introduction of the market.

In the second period: (1) the party-state retreated from economic planning; (2) the market exacerbated regional and sectoral inequalities and increased inequality of wage rates within individual enterprises; (3) the power of the municipality dwindled and was replaced by regional governments; (4) international capital came to play a greater part in firm operations; (5) individual workers began to question firm management by technicians; and (6) self-management, under the imperatives of the market, makes workers responsible for production quotas, capital investment, and labor discipline. During this period, workers chose to maximize individual gains at the expense of capital accumulation. A crisis ensued in which managers, workers and state officials called for the reimplementation of economic planning.

The 1974 constitution marks the beginning of the third period during which firms were reorganized and market forces were curbed. However, the problems which first developed during the 1950s and 1960s have yet to be dealt with.

ORIGIN AND PURPOSE OF THE ORIGINAL SELF-MANAGEMENT SCHEME

Three experiences separate Yugoslavia from other East European countries: (1) the antifascist movement which served as the base of Tito's regime; (2) Tito's break with Stalin and Yugoslavia's explulsion from the Cominform in 1948; and (3) the existence of an antifacist, anti-Stalinist base of popular support upon which a system of participatory democracy could be founded. Expanded participatory schemes were a method of rallying grass roots political support to Tito's isolated regime. Separation from the Soviet Union allowed for criticism of the highly centralized bureaucratic model of state planning, prior to which the original workers' councils had been completely organized from above, their only function the execution of the initial five year plan (Comisso 1979, 42).

After 1948 self-management organizations in Yugoslavia were still subject to forms of external control. The councils were designed primarily to neutralize sources of conflict while increasing productivity. Local governments controlled the firm through taxation. Managers were left with little money to redistribute in the form of production bonuses so workers' control did not immediately result in improved living conditions. The power of the municipality over the firm was augmented by the fact that representation at the national level was based not upon plants or individual workers but rather regions.

> . . . (Which) meant that, to the degree formal organs of representation were responsive to pressure from below, they were by and large responding to territorial based interests . . . which . . . meant ethnically rooted ones."
> [Comisso 1979, 47]

Subsequently, territorial inequalities that had developed because of this system of regional representation would feed interethnic conflicts.

STRATIFICATION WITHIN FIRMS AND BETWEEN SECTORS

An examination of the workers' roles as both capitalists and exploited labor reveals three issues. First, Yugoslav firms were stratified from the beginning. Skilled workers were always overrepresented on workers' councils. But this does not necessarily imply a class division between skilled and unskilled workers at this time. Most thought that the skilled workers and technicians were managing the enterprise to the benefit of the entire group. Evidence would seem to support this impression. From 1952 to 1966 the average annual rate of growth in industrial production was 8.2 percent. Employment in industry increased at a rate of 5.3 percent per year while labor productivity also rose an average of 4 percent. Illiteracy declined. Health facilities were improved and the infant mortality rate decreased (Comisso 1979, 55–57). Second, while intersectoral inequality increased, intrafirm inequality was rather low. The ratio between the highest and the lowest paid worker within a firm was restricted by law to no higher than 3:1 in fixed salaries and 5:1 in production bonuses. In a longitudinal study of industrial, mining, agricultural, and service industries from 1956 to 1961, Macesich (1964, 24) found the difference to be somewhat less. Salaried employees made an average for the period of only 39.3 percent more than hourly wage earners in regular salaries and bonuses. Note however that the trend which was to become problematic once legal restraints were removed was already apparent: This indicator had already risen from a low of 30.6 percent in 1956 to 47.7 percent in 1961. Third, the firm was run much like any capitalist enterprise. Productivity was the key word. Piece rates were often used and workers' salaries were closely linked to production.

The reactions of workers to these conditions were mixed. According to Adizes (1978, 214), prior to 1965 workers identified with and often approved of what otherwise might be called "rate busters." Fantastic stories were told of "worker heroes" who could double and triple their production quotas. Later, workers reported missing the days when bells rang announcing that plant production quotas had been surpasssed. Strike data from this period also seems to indicate that workers were either unconcerned with self-management or actually satisfied with its stratified operation. Of the 1,750 strikes that were reported between 1958 and 1969, almost all concerned *personal* incomes rather than aspects of self-management. Still, there were high rates of absenteeism and worker turnover during this period, seemingly indicating dissatisfaction with work and only a superficial involvement with plant management (Jovanov 1972).

The evidence seems to bear out Espinosa and Zimbalist's contention that high absenteeism and worker turnover are associated with minimal participation. The large majority of workers did little more than elect skilled workers to positions on workers' councils because they had little prior organizational experience. In addition, many were incompletely proletarianized:

> According to the 1953 census, 21 percent of manufacturing laborers, 38 percent of miners, and 17 percent of all transport workers retained ties to the peasant community. Thirty-eight percent of all unskilled laborers lived in villages but were employed in industry. [Commisso 1979, 61]

Absenteeism was highest during planting and harvest seasons.

Workers also reported that they felt their councils fairly represented their interests and they thought reinvestment and firm expansion would benefit them (Meisler 1964, 99), (Barrat-Brown 1960, 39–45), (Kolaja 1961, 27–31). Workers' impressions are borne out by the workers' councils' management of discretionary funds. According to Comisso (1979, 59) enterprise use of autonomous funds can be summarized as follows:

| | |
|---|---|
| Economic investment | 41% |
| Consumption | 27% |
| Charitable donations | 10% |
| Commune funds, legal and advertising | 22% |

In addition, the proporation of internal financing to all other sources doubled from 1953 to 1960, from 10.9 percent to 20.8 percent (Pejovich 1966, 70).

MUNICIPALITY-ENTERPRISE RELATIONS

Having discussed the internal composition and character of the Yugoslav enterprise in the 1950s and 1960s, we now turn to the relationship between the firm and the municipality–the governmental unit, which interacted with the firm most frequently. This relationship is unique to the Yugoslav case. In addition to such common municipal services as roads, utilities, and the provision of zoning regulations, the municipality was responsible for economic growth, employment and social services within its jurisdiction. The municipality and the firm were mutually dependent. The municipality was dependent upon the firm for all its income, which it garnered in the form of taxes. At the same time, the power to tax gave the municipality influence over the operations of the firm. "Recommendations" would be made to the firm's director that no inflationary wage/price increases be made which would increase the amount of tax revenue needed by the municipality. The two often worked together, especially when dealing with the federal government, or when creating wage/benefit packages to attract labor from other regions.

The regionalism that grew out of the municipality-enterprise relationship negatively affected production. Grants-in-aid and loans from development banks were all given to regional governments which in turn distributed the funds to local enterprises. In an effort to protect the local standard of living the municipality used these funds as leverage to prevent industrial specialization through the application of capital over a wide variety of industries. Often a single plant made many diverse items, making little use of economics of scale. Local-level bureaucracy expanded, as did the number of "political factories." Each enterprise became less and less productive, able to rely less and less upon market mechanisms, requiring more and more preferential treatment from the municipality. The municipality was, of course, forced to comply with enterprise demands for cheap loans to insure both its tax base and the jobs of its residents. These conditions were worse in lesser-developed regions which contained fewer dynamic industries (Comisso 1979, 49). Poorer regions thus remained underdeveloped, trapped in a cycle of inefficient production, protected markets, and low interest debt financing of the same inefficient production processes.

Uneven development during the planned phase of Yugoslav economic history aroused the discontent of the wealthier regions which saw a disproportionate portion of the national budget pouring into impoverished areas without any increase in productivity. The most developed sectors, of course, seemed to have the more successful, dynamic, competitive industries. Thus, planned allocation was villainized because it didn't lead to the highest possible national growth rate. Pressure on the party/state mechanism to allow for more reliance upon market forces came from regional/ethnic groups as well as from workers and technocrats in growing industries. The growing number of highly skilled laborers also pushed for greater autonomy and more reliance upon market mechanism for wage and price determinations, placing their own interests above the interests of the entire class.[14] First, they argued, only increased reliance upon the market would make planning at the firm level possible and that would make improved investment decisions possible which would increase overall productivity. Second, the specific elimination of wage and price controls would be to the direct advantage of skilled workers, because they were in demand by both industry and the state and because they were concentrated in high growth sectors of the economy where prices and profitability would skyrocket once released from state control.


STATE, MARKET, AND SELF-MANAGEMENT

The central government began its retreat from economic planning prior to the 1965 reforms. The communist party formally separated itself from various state organs. Communist party members declined as a proportion of total industrial labor force in the late fifties and early sixties, though they were still overrepresented in industry compared to their proportion of the total labor force (Kolaja 965, 21). There was a decrease in the number of party members who were firm directors and an increase in passivity among the rank and file, resulting in a less-organized labor force. Nevertheless, the party managed to maintain some degree of economic control because distribution of funds at both the local and the national level was still a highly politicized affair (Meisler 1964, 32), (Johnson 1972, 210).

State bureaucrats were not in favor of either more local autonomy or greater reliance upon the market. They were unwilling to relinquish the privileges their position afforded them, and there was much debate over whether the market would allow for the achievement of social goals. The bureaucrats also argued that the "modern, rational" production processes, while allowing for increased wages for some workers, did so by reducing the total number of workers employed, leaving the state, at some level, to provide for the increased number of unemployed.

Thus three areas of conflict emerged in the early sixties: sectoral conflict between growth industries and less productive sectors; state–industry conflict between some level of government and either individual firms or entire sectors; and intrastate conflicts among various organizational layers of government. In the struggle between the supporters of autonomous, worker-controlled firms and the supporters of central planning, firms and local governments in high-growth sectors along with those regions which contained natural resources prevailed against the supporters of the state: the bureaucrats, the least developed regions and the communist party.[15] The final blow came when severe economic problems—inflation, declining growth rates, unfavorable trade balances—forced the Yugoslavs into the hands of the IMF which required "liberalization" in exchange for credit (Paver 1974, 132).

THE 1965 REFORMS AND THE INTRODUCTION OF THE MARKET

The 1965 reforms thus represent a major shift toward greater reliance upon the market, a more decentralized government, and more control over wage rates and production decisions at the firm level. The reforms also caused deepened regional and sectoral conflicts, and increased reliance upon external financing. The central government still issued periodic plans but, unlike the original Five Year Plan, these were simply projections of what the economy would be like in the future given industry's current nondirected activities. The municipality's role was limited to functions usually associated with a local government in a capitalist state: welfare, police, and infrastructure. The growth of private banks released the enterprise from the government's influence to some degree. The power of the municipal government was further reduced when the region was made the new locus of distribution of government funds.

The reforms increased inequality between regions and sectors. Not only did workers in the agricultural or peasant sectors make less money than workers in industry, the health care and social services they had access to were inferior because most of these programs had been carried

Table 8.3   Total Number of Strikes, 1965–1975; All Sectors, and Manufacturing Only

| | All sectors Strikes | | Manufacturing only Strikes | |
|---|---|---|---|---|
| Year | Number | Index | Number | Index |
| 1965 | 397 | 100.0 | 191 | 100.0 |
| 1966 | 394 | 99.2 | 191 | 100.0 |
| 1967 | 414 | 104.3 | 207 | 108.4 |
| 1968 | 364 | 91.7 | 198 | 103.7 |
| 1969 | 372 | 93.7 | 143 | 74.9 |
| 1970 | 345 | 86.9 | 136 | 71.2 |
| 1971 | 377 | 95.0 | 184 | 66.3 |
| 1972 | 409 | 103.0 | 259 | 135.6 |
| 1973 | 788 | 198.5 | 423 | 221.5 |
| 1974 | 570 | 143.6 | 316 | 163.9 |
| 1975 | 779 | 196.2 | 427 | 224.1 |

Source: Stephens: 1977:129.

out at the firm level, and individual peasants and their families were not associated with any firm. The differences between regions were pronounced. In 1968 Slovenia could boast 9 percent of Yugoslavia's total land area, 8.5 percent of its population, and 15 percent of all national income. At the other extreme, Macedonia, Montenegro, Bosnia-Herzegovina, and the territory of Kosovo combined comprised 40 percent of the land, 39.5 percent of the population but only 21 percent of the national income (Kamusic 1970, 77). From 1965 to 1974, what is significant is not that interregional and intersectoral inequalities increased, but that they increased so little. The rates were only slightly higher than in the prereform era. The actual effects of Yugoslavia's entrance into the world market and the development of a labor market were minimized by state activity. These measures included loans from the central government to the poorer regions that went into consumption and "extra-budgetary" expenditures (Comisso 1979, 101).

Against growing inequalities came criticisms of market socialism. Some argued that sectoral and regional inequality along with increased concentration of capital and the growing differentiation among segments of the working class signaled the redevelopment of capitalism in Yugoslavia.[16] [17] There was increasing inequality among workers with different skills within the same sector, and among workers in different sectors. They began to demand regulation of the labor market to reduce those differences (Pasic 1970), (Matejko 1970).

The instability of the labor market prompted Yugoslav workers to take personal wage increases at the expense of capital accumulation within the enterprise. The rate of self-financing was not fixed by law; workers could take surpluses as increases in personal income. Recently privatized banks and personal savings accounts, as well as the availability of consumer durables (which only the labor aristocracy could afford), provided two alternatives to reinvestment. These alternatives had appeal for increasingly mobile laborers. Lack of central planning and the importation of new technology displaced many unskilled workers. Skilled laborers, free to change jobs as they saw fit, did so in order to maximize income. Since lifetime or even long-term employment with the same firm became an unlikely possibility, and since the amount of benefit workers accrued from investments depended upon the duration of employment, it's no wonder that they sought wages at the expense of investment and productivity.

Looking at Chile, Peru, and Yugoslavia, we can say that the rate of capital reinvestment in a firm depends upon the conditions under which the investment is to be made. Neither capital nor labor will willingly invest in an enterprise in which their ability to control their investment is limited. Capital flight occurs when nationalization threatens capitalist prerogatives. Increased private savings and consumption serve as alternatives to investment for a mobile work force.

WORKERS' PARTICIPATION AFTER THE 1965 REFORMS

Looking at survey data, it is difficult to ascertain exactly how successful self-management was in terms of real participation and in terms of benefits received by labor after 1965. Extensive research by Kamusic in 1968 revealed that a large majority of workers at all levels were in favor of further growth of self-management when growth of state authority was posed as the alternative. On the other hand, when, in the same study, workers were asked whether or not workers' councils and organizations functioned better after the 1965 reform, results were much less conclusive. Close to 30 percent of the respondents said conditions were indeed better; 45 percent thought there was no change, and 25 percent thought conditions were actually worse (1969 84). There is also evidence that indicates a growing dissatisfaction with the management of technicians and experts. The legitimacy of technocratic control declined because of growing inequalities and because workers were simply more organized and more conscious of their positions than they were in the 1950s. Strikes escalated from 1965 to 1975 as workers turned away from self-management and back to trade unions (Jovanov 1967). Trade union policies also changed. In the expanding economy of the 1960s they struggled for the introduction of market forces because wages were being depressed by the state. In the decline of the 1970s, they reversed their position, favoring more controls to keep wages from falling and to decrease growing inequality which would have been worse except for social pressure from unions which counteracted the polarizing effects of the market (Comisso 1979, 105).

## Retreat from Market Socialism

As the economic downturn got underway, workers and managers, regardless of their differences over distribution of incomes, all came to agree that more state control was necessary. They advocated state intervention at the republic level only. The regional government could be controlled. According to theory, in a market economy, downturns eliminate inefficient producers. However, less than 400 workers per year lost their jobs due to bankruptcy because of government intervention at the regional level solicited by individual enterprises (Comisso 1979, 87).

The crisis of 1972 was the product of these forces. A political stalemate had developed. Decentralization meant distribution of power among social forces with inherent conflicts of interest. Firms and republics fought over jobs and production lines. The firm was the republic's only source of revenue, and the republic served as the firm's access to credit and state aid. Interrepublic conflicts over the distribution of national wealth and intersectoral conflicts over the need for more or less state control were irreconcilable because of the lack of a strong central government.

The stalemate was finally broken by constitutional amendments in 1972, and by the new constitution in 1974. First, these documents restricted enterprise autonomy. A portion of all surplus was legally earmarked for investment. The amount that could be distributed as wages was specified. Republics were given some control over investment capital. Critical of the patterns of uneven development, in favor of more planning and less market, the constitution nevertheless promoted a weak central government. Decisions at the national level could be made only with the consent of the representatives from all the republics. With the communist party in control of arbitration, stalemates are no longer a problem. However, the new decision making process is slow and unwieldy. So many different areas and sets of interests have to be coordinated that fragmentation continues to be a problem.

Firms still have a great deal of freedom, and as long as increased prductivity continues to be the enterprise's goal, self-managment will not solve the problems Yugoslavia shares with many capitalist countries. Managers will continue to find it difficult to be both productive and community minded. The 1974 constitution specifically charges the firm with the responsibility for developing health and unemployment programs, yet the state is still the primary provider of those services. Unemployment continues to be a major problem as investment is funneled into capital-intensive projects. Since air and water are not considered production assets, they come under no one's control, and pollution is the consequence (Adizes 1978, 30).

The constitution also left unsolved many of the problems with praticipatory democracy within the enterprise. Yugoslavia is unique in that it has institutionalized the participation of the population in all spheres of life. Assemblies are elected by workers, and their organizational experience has increased as has their degree of participation. Still, the firm today is dominated by the technocracy.

Evidence indicates that workers' control programs cannot survive in nonsocialist states. But even within them, the successful implementation of a program of workers' control, by itself, will not bring about development of an egalitarian socialist state. In this regard the Yugoslav case has been informative. A social formation with a fairly well developed and, at least at the firm level, a fairly democratic system of self-management nevertheless suffers from sectoral and regional underdevelopment, regional nationalisms, stratification and fragmentation within the working class—all of which will be exacerbated by the current world economic crisis. The system of participatory democracy in Yugoslavia is not responsible for all its economic and political problems; the relationship is an interactive one. Self-management has served to fragment the working class and to encourage workers in individual firms to operate like capitalists. The "mixed" economy, in its various forms, within which these firms operate, has increased the inequalitites between sectors and regions thus supporting the fragmentation process. Meanwhile it has been only the party/state mechanism which has mitigated the inequalities that result from "market socialism." Increasingly, the party-state has been able to do very little to counteract the market, so that today some of the worst aspects of capitalism have emerged. High unemployment, increased exploitation, pollution are being repeated in the market socialism, worker managed, economy of Yugoslavia.

The process of formation of a self-management-based socialism must avoid the policy of favoring the dynamic sectors of industry and direct itself to the incorporation and activation of the class as a whole. This is the primary direction to which socioeconomic development must concern itself within the semi-industrialized countries of the Balkans and Mediterranean. To do otherwise is to attenuate the socialist commitment in society at large—especially among the large sectors of the nonworking class excluded from self-management, and among those thousands of small firms whose workers' conditions of employment are still shaped by market and entrepreneurial considerations.

## Conclusion

The emergence of a class consciousness directed toward the direct control over the productive process is not an inevitable result of class struggle, but rather the specific outcome of political leadership and organization which is actively committed to this form of social organization. The successful struggle for workers' control can be undertaken only within the broader context of a process of transformation from private to social ownership. The attempts to introduce workers' control in the context of private ownership leads to dynamic disequilibrium—

the uncertainty of power relations causes capital to disinvest and block the development of productive forces. On the other hand, workers' control allows the working class to check the operations of capital but provides little leverage to initiate new policies and to reorganize the productive relations.

The previous discussion underlies the importance of the *manner* in which collectivization and worker self-management is instituted: Changes initiated from below provide the experiences of solidarity that are so necessary for sustaining the new organs of production. Changes implemented through elite action from above impose new structures on a passive labor force, reproducing the old patterns of hierarchical authority and labor passivity. Hence, in the transition from the old form of class control to the new, only the collective action of the producers can produce an authentic transformation of social relations.

The emergence of autonomous class organizations that embrace broad sectors of the working class and that transcend the narrow or fragmented trade union structure have become the arenas within which democratic forms of collectivism have emerged. The factory council movements in Europe, the industrial belts in Chile, the workers' assemblies in Bolivia and Yugoslavia, provide the kind of open political arena within which the exercise of power from the "bottom-up" is possible.

Attempts to implement workers' self-managment through executive fiats, or through other mechanisms that do not involve the workers in the process of transformation, have generally produced negative results. The most likely outcome has been the nonparticipation of the workers and the usurpation of "representative" positions by a small coterie of former trade union officials. This top-down approach is usually accompanied by the reproduction of previous structures of hierarchial authority, now dubbed with the label "worker" something or other. The logic of this system is that the consciousness of the workers remains concerned with economistic issues, and the levels of conflict and nonresponsiveness to productivity goals remains the same as before.

The transition to self-managed socialism is first and foremost a mortal threat to the whole organization of production and political control under capitalism. For the ruling class and its state, and in the case of the Third World, its imperialist allies, the attempt by workers to seize control over the means of production is the signal for a historic confrontation. All the political, propagandistic, and coercive apparatuses are mobilized to counter this effort. The capitalist class moves to sabotage production, the bankers close off credit, the owners of transport paralyze the circulation of goods, and the military is prepared for decisive action. What is striking about this confrontation is not only the specific action taken by the ruling class but the high levels of consciousness and organization that it reflects. The repression is aimed not only at turning back the particular movement for workers' control but at obliterating the organization and consciousness in the working class. Hence, the reaction of the capitalist class to the organization of a worker self-management system frequently finds expression in historically new and deeper levels of violence and repression, to dissove the memory of self-affirming labor, and to replace it with the wage slave.

The anticipation of this historical response pattern of the capitalist state requires that the workers' movement combine local rank and file movements for self-management at the point of production with a broader social and political movement to control the financial and other networks of the economy. The movement must take control over the state or have sufficient influence to combat efforts by capital to bring the military or coercive apparatus into the struggle. Control over networks and the state becomes an essential element in allowing the self-management movement to develop.

The failure of the self-management movement to gain control over these areas can lead to the reversibility of changes. The historic experiences in Chile, Czechoslovakia, Hungary, and Poland demonstrated that even where widespread organization of workers' councils have been established, and even where they have secured the support of substantial sectors of the working class and have begun to function effectively in production, they have been reversed. The seizure of power by the capitalist class and/or by a bureaucratic elite has reversed the changes, displaced the workers in power, and either privatized or bureaucratized the self-management sector.

In the context of the transition to worker self-management, the *permeability* of a "pluralist society"—more accurately a class society verging on civil war—presents the most serious threat of destruction of the new worker institutions. The existence within a society of a class of displaced landlords, capitalists, bankers, generals, (with little to lose and everything to gain from a putsch or civil war) creates a *dangerous class* capable of and committed to the destruction of the emerging democratic foundations of the new system. In these circumstances, the diffusion of power through decentralized structure based upon open-ended political discussion is an invitation to self-destruction. In the transition period, therefore, the system must combine centralized political direction with secure democratic control from below, excluding those classes that are unwilling to accept the political boundaries of the self-managed state. Clearly there are dangers in centralized political authority, but the dangers of the decentralized pluralist state are even more transparent. The only guarantee that the tension between self-management at the level of production and centralized political rule at the national level can lead to creative results is through strict adherence to democratic procedures and to controls between the two levels.

What this discussion suggests is that self-management is an unstable form between capitalism and socialism. It threatens capitalist prerogatives, but is not securely anchored within a state structure capable of consolidating the new social power. The historical experiences cited earlier regarding the relationship between the transition from capitalism to socialism suggest that while workers' control may precede the transition, it cannot by itself insure successful consummation. Without a successful transformation of the political structure and a comprehensive restructuring of the economy, worker-controlled enterprises are likely to be undermined.

Our survey of several historical experiences demonstrates that class struggle and organization are essential in creating the political experience and social solidarity necessary for the transformation of effective self-management councils. Conversely, councils established as a consequence of parliamentary, bureaucratic, or executive efforts fail to elicit the active and sustained activity of the ostensible beneficiaries of the reforms. In summary, the institutionalization of worker self-management presupposes control over the state. The transformation of the state presupposes the existence of a revolutionary party liked to workers' councils. The realization of socialism requires councils of self managing workers.

## Notes

1. The following narrative of events makes extensive use of I. Clegg's *Workers' Self-Management in Algeria* (1971).
2. "It has been estimated that if oil and natural gas are excluded, there was a drop in overall production of 28 percent in the period 1959–1963, while in the tertiary sector there was a drop . . . of 36 percent" (Clegg 1971, 79).
3. Colonial forces removed local populations and placed them in these camps in order to make strategic locations less valuable to the FLN.
4. In agriculture, during the first year after the revolution, pre-independence production levels were met despite a 60 percent decrease in machinery. In industry, the initial blows—loss of machinery, absence of a skilled workforce, lack of capital, insecure access to supplies—were devastating, setting production figures back more than ten years. Still, there was a steady increase in production from 1963 to 1968 when 1958 levels were once again obtained. Unemployment during this period remained constant and there was virtually no investment in new technology. Salaries were not increased. The few who were employed worked harder and longer for the same amount of money.
5. CUT was formed in 1953 and controlled by the communist party aftrer 1958. The CUT program dropped the necessity of a socialist state from its platform in 1959 and was legalized in 1971.
6. If productivity is measured by the amount of crude ore extracted rather than in refined ore, then labor productivity did increase during the "honeymoon" phase of miner–government relations.
7. For a general discussion of co-participation, workers' control and co-management in Europe see also: King, C.D. et. al. (1973); Meisler (1964); and Best & Connolly (1976).
8. For a discussion of the limits of corporation see also: Stepan (1971); McClintock, C. (1977); Petras et. al. (1970) (1981).
9. His program called for the nationalization of IPC, a susidiary of Standard Oil of New Jersey, without compensation, angering the U.S. based MNC's and banks, and risking an economic blockade similar to the one applied to Chile under Allende. Less aggressively, he expropriated coastal sugar plantations and the U.S. owned Cerro de Pasco mining company, for which compensation was paid. Velasco, however, had no interest in a movement toward socialism. He was interested in promoting U.S. investment in copper as long as some of the profits could be captured for Peruvian development (Malloy 1973), (Astiz 1969), (Quijano 1971).
10. Espinosa and Zimbalist found a strong relationship between income equality within a firm and degree of workers' participation.

11. Only one IC representative was given a seat on the board initially. The number of representatives was supposed to grow in proportion to portion of total stock owned by the IC up to 50 percent and half the board of directors at which point there would be "co-determination" and the chairman of the board would be elected by simple majority.

12. See Sulmont (1974, 1975) for a discussion of the labor movement during this time.

13. A government bond program aided the transfer of private capital out of the depleted agricultural sector in an effort to foster investment in industry. However, most private investment went into real estate and the remainder was plowed back into already existing enterprises. "In 1973 76 percent of private industrial investment went into already existing enterprises, and in 1974, 66.2 percent . . . yet private investment was barely enough to cover replacement" (Stephens 1980, 148).

14. From 1958 to 1965 the percent of highly skilled workers among all industrial workers increased from 5.2 percent to 8.9 percent. The percentage of industrial workers with university degrees climbed from 6.1 percent to 14 percent (Comisso 1979, 54).

15. The government depressed the prices of resources so that these regions would profit from the inevitable rise in prices that would result from the introduction of market mechanisms.

16. There was a wave of bank mergers and from 1965 to 1967 12 percent of all firms merged.

17. For more on this see Sweezy and Hubberman (1964), Beetleheim and Sweezy (1971), and Barratt-Brown (1960).

## Bibliography

Adizes, I. (1970) "On conflict resolution and an organizational definition of self-management." In *Yugoslav Workers' Self-Management*, vol. 5, ed. M. J. Broekmeyer, pp. 17–34. Dordrect, Holland: D. Reidel.
————. (1978) *Industrial Democracy Yugoslav Style*. New York: The Free Press.
Agassi, J. (1974) "The Israeli Experience in the Democratization of Work Life." *Sociology of Work and Occupations 1* (1):52–81.
Agyris, C. (1973) "Personality and organization theory revisited." *Administrative Science Quarterly 18* (June):141–67.
Astiz, C. A. (1969) *Pressure Groups and Power Elites in Peruvian Politics*. Ithaca, New York: Cornell University Press.
Barratt-Brown, M. (1969a) "Yugoslavia revisited." *New Left Review 1* (Jan–Feb):39–43.
————. (1969b) "Workers' control in a planned economy." *New Left Review 2* (March–April):28–31.
Beetelheim, C., and P. Sweezy (1971) *On the Transition to Socialism*. New York: Monthly Review Press.
Best, M., and W. Connolly (1976) *The Politicized Economy*. Boston: D. C. Heath.
Blumberg, P. (1968) *Industrial Democracy*. London: Constable.
Boskovic, B., and D. Dasic, eds. (1980) *Socialist Self-Management in Yugoslavia 1950–1980* Belgrade: Socialist Thought and Practice.
Bourque, S. C., and D. S. Palmer (1975) "Transforming the rural sector: government policy and peasant response." In *The Peruvian Experiment*, ed. A. F. Lowenthal. Princeton, N.J.: Princeton University Press.
Bustamante, A. (1974) "La derecha frente ala comunidad industrial." In *Dinamica de la Comunidad Industrial*, ed. L. Pasara. Lima: Desco: Centro de Estudios Y Promocion del Desarrollo.
Butt, D. (1961) "Workers' control." *New Left Review 10* (July–August):24–34.
Case, J. (1972) "Workers' control: toward a North American movement." *Our Generation 8* (3):1.
Clegg, I. (1971) *Workers' self-management in Algeria*. London: Allen Lane The Penguin Press.

Cole, G.D.H. (1953) *Socialist Thought*, Vol. 1, *The Forerunners 1789–1850*. London: MacMillian.

Comisso, E. (1979) *Workers' Control Under Plan and Market*. New Haven, Conn.: Yale University Press.

Conquest, R. (1967) *Industrial Workers in the USSR*. London: The Bodley Head.

Deppe, F., et al. (1969) *Kutik der Mitbestmimmung*. Frankfurt: Suhrkamp Verlag.

Espinosa, J., and A. Zimbalist (1978) *Economic Democracy, Workers' Participation in Chilean Industry 1970–1973*. New York: Academic Press.

Flanders, A., and H. Clegg (eds.) (1954) *The System of Industrial Relations in Britian*. London.

Garcia de Romana, A. (1975) "Comportamiento germial Y politico de los empresarios industriales, 1968–1973." *Taller de Estudios Urbano Industriales*. Lima: Pontificia Universidad Catolica.

Hobsbawm, E. J. (1971) "Peru: the peculiar revolution." *New York Review of Books* (Dec. 16):33–34.

Horvat, B. (1959) "Workers' Management in Yugoslavia: a comment and a reply." *Journal of Political Economy* 67 (20):194–200.

———. (1982) *The Political Economy of Socialism*, vols. 1, 2, Armonk, N.Y.: M. E. Sharpe Inc.

Hyatt, J. (1975) "Workers" Capitalism: Free distribution of stock to employees spurred by a new tax law privision." *Wall Street Journal*. April 29.

Jaques, E. (1968) *Employee Participation and Managerial Authority* London.

Johnson, A. R. (1972) *The Transformation of Communist Ideology*. Cambridge: MIT Press.

Jovanov (1967) "Protest work stoppages' " *Socialist Thought and Practice 27* ( July–Sept.).

Kamusic, M. (1970) "Economic efficiency and workers' self-management." In *Yugoslav Workers' Self-management*, ed. M. J. Brockmeyer, pp. 76–116.

Kelly, J. (1968) *Is Scientific Management Possible?* London: Faber and Faber.

Kendall, W. (1973) "Workers' participation and workers' control: aspects of the British experience." *Participation and Self Management*, vol. 3 ed. E. Pusic, p. 57–69.

King, C. D., and M. Van de Val (1978) *Models of Industrial Democracy Consultation, Codetermination and Workers' Management*. The Hague, The Netherlands: Mouton Publishers.

Kolaja, J. (1961) "A Yugoslav workers' council" *Human Organization 20* (1):27–31.

———. (1965) *Workers' Councils: The Yugoslav Experience*. London: Travestock.

*Latin American Economic Report*, (1967) 18.

Lorwin, V. R. (1954) *The French Labor Movement*. Cambridge, Mass.: Havard University Press.

Macesich, G. (1964) *Yugoslavia: The Theory and Practice of Development Planning*. Charlottsville: University Press of Virginia.

McClintock, C. (1977) "Self-management and political participation in Peru 1967–1975: the corporatist illusion." *Sage Professional Papers*, Contemporay Sociology Series.

Maloy, J. (1973) "Dissecting the Peruvian Military: Review Essay." *Journal of Inter American Studies and World Affairs*. 15 (3):375–82.

Mandel, E. (1967) "Yugoslav economic theory." *Monthly Review 18* (April):40–49.

Matejko (1970) "The socialist principles of workers' control." In vol. 3, *Participation and Self Management*, ed. E. Pusic, pp. 25–55.

———. (1971) "From peasant to worker in Poland. "*International Review of Sociology*. 7 (3).

Matos Mar, J. et al. (1970) *El Peru Actual: Sociedad y Politica*. Mexico: Universidad Nacional Autonoma de Mexico, Instituto de Investigacions Sociales.

Meisler, A. (1964) *Socialism et Autogestion*. Paris: Editions du Seuil.

Milenkovitch, D. (1971) *Plan and Market in Yugoslav Economic Thought*. New Haven: Yale University Press.

Nash, J. (1972) "Workers' participation in nationalized mines of Bolivia 1952–1972." In *Participation and Self management*, vol 3, ed. M. E. Pusic, pp. 157–72.

Obradovic, J., and W. Dunn (eds.) (1978) *Workers' Self-management, Management and Organizational Power in Yugoslavia.* Pittsburg: University of Pittsburg Center for International Studies.

Pasic, N. (1970) "Self management as an integral political system." In *Yugoslav Workers' Self Management*, vol. 4, ed. M.J. Broekmeyer, pp. 1–29.

Payer, C. (1975) *The Debt Trap.* New York: Monthly Review Press.

Pejovich, S. (1966) *The Market Planned Economy of Yugoslavia.* Minneapolis: University of Minnesota Press.

Petras, J. (1970) *Politics and Social Structure in Latin America.* New York: Monthly Review Press.

Petras, J., and M. Morley (1975) *The United States and Chile: Imperialism and the Overthrow of the Allende Government.* New York: Monthly Review Press.

Petras, J., E. Havens, M. Morley, and P. DeWitt (1981) *Class, State and Power in the Third World.* London: Zed Press.

Pusic, E. (ed.) (1972) *Participation and Self Management*, (6 vols.). Zagreb: Institute for Social Research, University of Zagreb.

Quijano, A. (1971) "Nationalism and Capitalism in Peru: a study of neo-imperialism." *Monthly Review 23* (3).

Ramos, S. (1972) *Chile: Una Economia de Transicion?* Santiago: Editorial Prensa Latino-americana.

Ross, A. M., and P. T. Hartman (1960) *Changing Patterns of Industrial Conflict.* New York: Wiley.

Sawer, M. (1976) "Income distribution in OECD countries." *OECD Economic Outlook Studies*, July, Paris.

Stepan, A. C. (1978) *The State and Society: Peru in Comparative Perspective.* Princeton: Princeton University Press.

Sulmont, D. (1972) "Dinamica Actual del movimiento obrero Peruano." *Taller de Estados Urbanos Industriales.* Lima: Pontificia Universidad Catolica.

Sweezy, P., and L. Huberman (1964) "Peaceful transition from socialism to capitalism?" *Monthly Review 14* (March):569–89.

Singleton, F., and T. Tapham (1964) "Yugoslav workers' control: the latest phase." *New Left Review 8* (Jan.):73–86.

Stallings, B. (1978) "Peru and the US banks: Who has the upper hand.?" Paper prepared for a conference on U.S. foreign policy and Latin American and Caribbean regions: Joint Committee in Latin America, Studies of the Social Science Research Council. Wash. D.C., March 27–31.

Stephens, E. H. (1980) *The Politics of Workers' Participation: The Peruvian Approach in Compartive Perspective.* New York: Academic Press.

Supeck, R. (1970) "Problems and perspectives of workers' self-management in Yugoslavia." In *Yugoslav Workers' Self Management*, ed. M. J. Broekmeyer, pp. 216–41.

Tornquist, D. (1975) "Strikes in Yugoslavia." *Working Papers for a New Society 3* (Spring): 51–62.

Vaneck, J. (1971) *The Participatory Economy: An Evolutionary Hypothesis and a Strategy for Development.* Ithaca: Cornell University Press.

————. (1977) *The Labor Managed Economy.* Ithaca: Cornell University Press.

Vos, A., and M. Brzoska (1970) "Peasant Participation and self-management in the development of Polish Agriculture." *Participation and Self Mangement*, vol. 5, ed. E. Pusic, pp. 203–15.

World Bank. (1975) *Yugoslavia: Development with Decentarlization.* Baltimore: The Johns Hopkins University Press.

# Part IV

## Development and Crisis

# 9

# Economic Expansion, Political Crisis, and U.S. Policy in Central America

JAMES F. PETRAS
MORRIS H. MORLEY

## Introduction: Overview

Central America is in the center of conflict between social revolutionary
and counterrevolutionary forces. An unprecedented level of right-wing
governmental and paramilitary repression is matched by the most
inclusive, far-reaching left-wing mobilization in recent history. This
historic confrontation which is unfolding before us at the present moment
is the product of 25 years of rapid and uneven capitalist growth and
transformation, which have unmercifully exploited and uprooted millions
of peasants and workers and destroyed locally anchored communal
productive systems. Trade expansion, industrial growth, the commercialization of agriculture, and the extension of urban space are testaments
to both a period of sustained economic expansion and a process which
has left in its wake a vast army of underpaid and unrepresented wage
laborers. The predominant "outside and above" capitalist development
model has also led to the creation of a mass of semi-employed and
unemployed workers in urban and rural Central America. According
to a recent study under the auspices of the United Nations' Economic
Commission for Latin America, "a significant segment of the Central
American population—possibly over 50%—lives in what could be described as extreme poverty by any reasonable criteria."[1] Open unemployment in the region as a whole currently stands at between 8% and

This essay originally appeared in *Revolution and Intervention in Central America,*
edited by Marlene Dixon and Susanne Jonas, as part of the CONTEMPORARY MARXISM
SERIES published by Synthesis Publications, San Francisco, © 1981. Reprinted by
permission.

15%, while underemployment is estimated as approaching 50% of the economically active population.[2]

Capitalist growth in the region has occurred within a socioeconomic and political framework which includes: 1) the continuity of the traditional ruling class increasingly diversifying its holdings, but retaining its family-based source of political and economic power;[3] 2) rulership through military or civilian-police state regimes with familial and economic ties to the ruling class and to military and police agencies of the U.S. imperial state; and 3) multinational corporations, primarily from the United States, but increasingly from Western Europe and Japan, with links to traditional ruling class groups, as well as to the economic and political agencies of the U.S. imperial state.[4] This Triumvirate of traditional family-based capitalism, multinational corporations and military rulers has provided the framework for capitalist growth for almost a half-century in the Central American countries of Nicaragua, El Salvador, Honduras and Guatemala.

The growth of capitalism in Central America and the transformation of the social structure have had differential effects on the region's class structure. On the one hand, growth has been accompanied by the concentration of capital, as evidenced by the activities of the Somoza family in Nicaragua. The "clan" fortune increased from around $60 million in the mid-1950s to an estimated $400–$500 million in the mid-1970s—encompassing estates and agricultural businesses, processing industries, industrial enterprises, communications and banking, and foreign investments.[5] On the other hand, repression of wage and salary demands has contributed mightily to the process of steady economic expansion. In turn, these twin processes of wealth concentration and sustained levels of repression have induced the growth of radical popular movements which link their demands for immediate improvement with a transformation of the social structure.

The social movements in Central America have grown in the past decade from small, urban-based groups of skilled workers and intellectuals to broad-based mass organizations. These include an extremely wide range of wage and salaried workers, extending to practically all major industries and services, landless rural wage workers, smallholding peasants and, significantly enough, a growing number of indigenous communities.

The dynamic growth of capital, with its voracious appetite for new sources of land, labor and resources has drawn into its vortex practically every segment of society. The expanded accumulation process which has fueled economic expansion has at the same time provoked the most comprehensive opposition. By subordinating a great variety of social classes to the common yoke of repression and exploitation, by monopolizing all mechanisms of legality and representation, the process of capitalist development has *homogenized the conditions of heterogeneous social classes* (salaried, wage, unemployed, smallholders, etc.)

and has *created the basis for a broad unified social revolutionary movement.*

U.S. political and economic policy must be analyzed within this process of growth, repression and popular mobilization. Decades of financial assistance and military aid were geared essentially to *promoting* and *supporting* the capitalist development programs and the repressive regimes which preceded the current period of unrest. Through public and private loans and investments, through direct governmental programs, and through their influence in shaping the policies of the so-called international banks (World Bank, Inter-American Development Bank, etc.), Washington policymakers sought to promote the economic infrastructures, financial institutions and industries of Central Ameria. At the same time, U.S. military assistance, arms sales and training programs were directly linked to the maintenance of dictatorial regimes supportive of U.S. policy goals in the area. In other words, the efforts of imperial state agencies and personnel were directed toward "building," protecting and nurturing state regimes that undertook to free markets, control labor and incarcerate trade union leadership.

Beginning in the early to mid-1950s, U.S. policy became increasingly linked with those sectors of the Central American ruling class involved in industrial and financial institutions and less tied to the direct ownership of land. The shift in economic activity did not, however, lead to any change in policy toward the political and social status quo. The convergence of U.S. policy and investor interests with those of the Central American ruling classes thus led to a historic compromise in which successive U.S. administrations sacrificed democratic rights in exchange for capitalist economic opportunity and U.S. strategic interests. For the rulers of these countries were not only willing to promote "open" economies in the interests of foreign capital accumulation; they were also agreeable to direct involvement in U.S.–promoted operations against nationalist and/or anti-capitalist states in the region (the overthrow of the Arbenz government in Guatemala in 1954, the invasions of Cuba in 1961 and the Dominican Republic in 1965, the counterrevolutionary activity currently being directed against the present Nicaraguan government).

The fundamental challenge to this long-standing U.S. policy came with the military defeat of the Somoza dictatorship in Nicaragua in July 1979. The overthrow of an erstwhile American ally by a mass-based, poly-class movement under the leadership of the Sandinista guerrillas and the initiation of a democratic-revolutionary process in Nicaragua sent shock waves throughout Central America, which had immediate reverberations in Washington. The Carter Administration, fearful of a new wave of revolution in the region, embarked upon a series of political maneuvers designed essentially to sustain U.S. economic and strategic interests, and to prevent the success of new revolutionary struggles.

Table 9.1   Gross National Product Average Annual Growth Rate, 1960–1978 (percentage)

| Honduras | 4.20 |
|---|---|
| El Salvador | 5.55 |
| Guatemala | 5.80 |
| Nicaragua | 6.50[a] |
| Mexico[b] | 6.10 |
| Panama | 5.60 |
| Costa Rica | 6.25 |

[a]1960–1977.

[b]For the purposes of this study, Mexico has been included.

Source: World Bank, World Development Report (August 1980), pp. 112–13.

## Capitalist Growth and Political Crisis

The political crisis in Central America is the product of capitalist expansion and the consequently increasing class polarization which has put the issue of a class-anchored social revolution on the historic agenda. The crisis is not the result of "stagnation and underdevelopment," the incapacity of capitalism to transform society, but is rather the social consequence and political framework within which the transformation is taking place.[6]

The last two decades provide abundant evidence of the capitalist transformation of the economies and class structure of the region. Autocratic rule created optimal conditions for capitalist expansion, as reflected in the growth rate in the Gross Domestic Product during the period 1960 to 1978.

The growth of diversified economies, as multinational and local capital increasingly invested in industrial enterprises, is rather strikingly illustrated by the changing pattern of U.S. investments in Central America, especially between 1970 and 1979. Whereas in 1970, manufacturing accounted for approximately 12% of total U.S. investments, by 1979 this figure had grown to more than 33%—clearly indicating the extent to which manufacturing had become one of the preferred areas of investment for metropolitan capital.

Between 1960 and 1978, all countries in the region experienced steady rates of industrial growth, despite variations between economies and over time.

The increase in Central America's agricultural production and the parallel rise of its role in world trade has essentially been a function of mechanization of the rural sectors. This process of mechanization is indicated by the tremendous increase in the use of tractors and the expansion of irrigated land. Nicaragua, for example, as the following tables show, experienced an almost fourfold increase in both the amount

Table 9.2   U.S. Direct Investment in Central America Excluding Mexico and Panama ($ millions)

|                        | 1970 | 1979 |
| ---------------------- | ---- | ---- |
| All industry           | 624  | 895  |
| Mining and smelting    | 10   | 24   |
| Petroleum              | 160  | 72   |
| Manufacturing          | 74   | 304  |
| Transport              |      | 75   |
| Trade                  |      | 102  |
| Finance and insurance  | 380  | 56   |
| Other industries       |      | 262  |

Source: U.S. Department of Commerce, Survey of Current Business, Vol. 52, No. 11 (November 1972), pp. 30–31; Vol. 60, No. 8 (August 1980), p. 27.

of land under irrigation and the number of tractors in operation in the agricultural sector.

The agricultural sector has also continued to expand since 1960, though at a slightly slower rate than industry; and, as one would expect, the growth has not been in food production.

A major consequence of this mechanization process has been an accelerated rate of displacement of landless laborers from the countryside into the large population centers, where they have swelled the ranks of the unemployed and underemployed urban poor. The agricultural work force as a percentage of the total work force has declined significantly in every Central American country since 1960.

While Central American agriculture has mechanized and increased its role as an exporter of rural commodities, the pattern of land ownership, highly concentrated in a few hands, has not changed at all. In Guatemala, 2% of the landholders own 70% of the land (1980); in Honduras, 0.3% of the landholders own 27.4% of the land (1975); in El Salvador, 1%

Table 9.3   Growth of Production: Industry (in percentages)

|             | 1960–70 | 1970–78 |
| ----------- | ------- | ------- |
| Honduras    | 5.2     | 5.9     |
| El Salvador | 8.5     | 7.0     |
| Guatemala   | 7.8     | 7.6     |
| Nicaragua   | 11.0    | 7.3[a]  |
| Mexico      | 9.1     | 6.2     |
| Panama      | 10.1    | .7      |
| Costa Rica  | 9.4     | 9.1[a]  |

[a] 1977.

Source: World Bank, World Development Report (August 1980), pp. 112–113.

Table 9.4    Growth of Production: Agriculture (in percentages)

|           | 1960–70 | 1970–78 |
|-----------|---------|---------|
| Honduras    | 5.7 | 0.8 |
| El Salvador | 3.0 | 2.7 |
| Guatemala   | 4.3 | 5.3 |
| Nicaragua   | 6.7 | 5.4[a] |
| Mexico      | 3.8 | 2.1 |
| Panama      | 5.7 | 2.4 |
| Costa Rica  | 5.7 | 2.5 |

[a]1977.
Source: World Bank, World Development Report (August 1980), pp. 112–113.

of the landholders own 57% of the land (1978); and in Nicaragua under Somoza, 1.4% of the landholders owned 41.2% of the land.[7]

One of the more notable features of the region's economic development since 1960 has been the central role of the so-called service sector. While agriculture's contribution to the Gross Domestic Product has declined to less than 30% in every country with the exception of

Table 9.5    Irrigated Land, 1961–1976 (in thousands of hectares)

|             | 1961–65 | 1976 |
|-------------|---------|------|
| Costa Rica  | 26 | 26 |
| El Salvador | 18 | 33 |
| Guatemala   | 38 | 62 |
| Honduras    | 60 | 80 |
| Nicaragua   | 18 | 70 |
| Panama      | 15 | 23 |

Table 9.6    Tractor Use, 1961–1976

|             | 1961–65 | 1976 |
|-------------|---------|------|
| Costa Rica  | 4,311 | 5,700 |
| El Salvador | 1,800 | 3,000 |
| Guatemala   | 2,250 | 3,750 |
| Honduras    | 331   | 1,050 |
| Nicaragua   | 450   | 1,316 |
| Panama      | 789   | 3,800 |

Source: James W. Wilkie, ed., Statistical Abstract of Latin America, Volume 20 (University of California at Los Angeles: Latin American Center, 1980), p. 39.

Table 9.7   Sectoral Distribution of Labor Force: Agriculture (in percentages)

|  | 1960 | 1978 |
|---|---|---|
| Honduras | 70 | 64 |
| Guatemala | 67 | 57 |
| El Salvador | 62 | 52 |
| Nicaragua | 62 | 44 |
| Mexico | 55 | 39 |
| Panama | 51 | 31 |
| Costa Rica | 51 | 29 |

Source: World Bank, World Development Report (August 1980), pp. 146–47.

Honduras, and while industry's contribution has grown steadily, "services" still account for the greatest share of Gross Domestic Product in each Central American economy (approximately 50%). The capacity of this sector to maintain its position within these economies over time reflects a pattern of economic growth characterized by large-scale, nonproductive investments. The entrepreneurial activities of high military figures, bankers and family elites, in the form of heavy investments in high-rise offices, luxury housing, commercial buildings and other urban real estate, have directly shaped and promoted this type of development.

Central America's economic expansion has been, in large measure, export-based. The following table shows that during the 1960s, the region experienced a dynamic upsurge in trade, with an average annual growth rate in excess of 8%. During the 1970s, exports continued to

Table 9.8   Sectoral Distribution in Gross Domestic Product (in percentages)

|  | Agriculture | | Industry | | Services | |
|---|---|---|---|---|---|---|
|  | 1960 | 1978 | 1960 | 1978 | 1960 | 1978 |
| Honduras | 37 | 32 | 19 | 26 | 44 | 42 |
| El Salvador | 32 | 29 | 19 | 21 | 49 | 50 |
| Nicaragua | 24 | 25.2 | 21 | 26[a] | 55 | 51[a] |
| Mexico | 16 | 11 | 29 | 37 | 55 | 52 |
| Panama | 23 | 16.1 | 21 | — | 56 | — |
| Costa Rica | 26 | 18.6 | 20 | 27[a] | 54 | 51[a] |
| Guatemala | 30[b] | 25.9 | — | — | — | — |

[a]1977.
[b]1960–1964 annual average contribution.

Source: World Bank, World Development Report (August 1980), pp. 114–15; Inter-American Development Bank, Economic and Social Progress in Latin America, 1979 Report, pp. 15, 21.

Table 9.9    Growth of Merchandise Trade Average Annual Growth Rate of Export (in percentages)

|              | 1960–70 | 1970–78 |
|--------------|---------|---------|
| Honduras     | 11.1    | 2.9     |
| Nicaragua    | 9.7     | 5.6     |
| El Salvador  | 5.6     | 0.6     |
| Guatemala    | 9.0     | 3.4     |
| Mexico       | 3.3     | 5.2     |
| Panama       | 10.4    | 2.2     |
| Costa Rica   | 9.4     | 5.9     |

Source: World Bank, World Development Report (August 1980), pp. 124–25.

grow, although at a slower rate in all countries with the exception of Mexico.

While primary products still make up a significant proportion of exports, the shifting pattern of foreign investments, into economic sectors apart from the traditional agro-mining centers of production, indicates that the countries of the region can no longer simply be referred to as "banana republics." In 1950, a single primary commodity accounted for 80% to 90% of total exports; by the late 1970s, no country was dependent on any one product for more than 50% of its export trade.[8] The growth of industrial investments has stimulated the expansion of nontraditional exports throughout the region. Even though the local economic elites continue to invest heavily in commercial agriculture, and primary commodities are still the predominant exports, they are less central than in the past.

The Central American development "model" has been substantially dependent on large-scale inflows of finance and investment capital, principally from U.S. sources and the international banking community. Overall U.S. private investment in Guatemala, Honduras, Costa Rica, El Salvador and Nicaragua, for example, grew steadily between 1963

Table 9.10    Merchandise Exports: Primary Commodities (percentage share of total)

|             | 1960 | 1977 |
|-------------|------|------|
| Honduras    | 98   | 90   |
| El Salvador | 94   | 80   |
| Guatemala   | 97   | 83   |
| Nicaragua   | 98   | 83   |
| Mexico      | 88   | 71   |
| Costa Rica  | 95   | 76   |

Source: World Bank, World Development Report (August 1980), pp. 126–27.

Table 9.11   U.S. Private Investment in Central America, 1980

| | |
|---|---|
| Guatemala | $260 million |
| Honduras | $250 million |
| Costa Rica | $210 million |
| Nicaragua | $160 million |
| El Salvador | $145 million |

Source: New York Times (July 9, 1980), p. 10.

and 1970, rising from $539 million to $624 million.[9] During the 1970s, however, the total American investment "stake" increased in size by approximately 40%.

At the same time, finance capital from metropolitan and private banking institutions began to assume a commanding role in a number of countries in the region. Between 1970 and 1978, gross inflows of medium and long-term loans jumped approximately threefold in Guatemala and Nicaragua, tenfold in El Salvador, almost elevenfold in Mexico, over thirteenfold in Costa Rica and around fifteenfold in Panama.

This accelerated dependence on external sources of financing was accompanied by a massive growth in the region's external debt. In Panama, the external public debt as a percentage of the Gross National Product grew from 19.0% in 1970 to 84.1% in 1978. Over the same time span, it rose from 20.6% to 45.8% in Nicaragua, from 12.9% to 34.9% in Honduras, and from 13.8% to 29.3% in Costa Rica. Comparable trends were also evident with regard to the debt-exports ratio. Between 1960 and 1978, Panama's external debt rose from 7.6% to 62.0% of the value of its exports, Mexico's grew from 24.1% to 59.5%, Costa Rica's increased from 10.0% to 23.4%, and Nicaragua's moved from 10.6% to 17.3%.

Table 9.12   Public and Publicly Guaranteed Medium and Long-Term Loans, Gross Inflows ($ millions)

| | 1970 | 1978 |
|---|---|---|
| Honduras | 29 | 163 |
| Guatemala | 37 | 107 |
| El Salvador | 8 | 80 |
| Nicaragua | 44 | 142 |
| Mexico | 782 | 8,606 |
| Panama | 67 | 986 |
| Costa Rica | 30 | 396 |

Source: World Bank, World Development Report (August 1980), pp. 136–37.

Table 9.13    External Public Debt Outstanding and Disbursed

|  | $ millions | | % of GNP | |
|---|---|---|---|---|
|  | 1970 | 1978 | 1970 | 1978 |
| Honduras | 90 | 591 | 12.9 | 34.9 |
| El Salvador | 88 | 333 | 8.6 | 11.0 |
| Guatemala | 106 | 374 | 5.7 | 6.0 |
| Nicaragua | 155 | 964 | 20.6 | 45.8 |
| Mexico | 3,238 | 25,775 | 9.8 | 28.7 |
| Panama | 194 | 1,910 | 19.0 | 84.1 |
| Costa Rica | 134 | 963 | 13.8 | 29.3 |

As a result of these developments, a number of regimes increasingly came to view access to overseas financial capital as crucial to their continued ability to refinance existing foreign debt structures.

Over time, and in the absence of state structures seeking to promote redistributive socioeconomic programs in the context of nationally anchored development strategies, these parallel processes—the commercialization of agriculture, the growth of industry, urbanization, and the permeation of Central American economies by foreign capital—have had a profound impact in creating the social movements and class conflicts that more and more dominate the political horizon in the region.

## Class Transformation and Class Struggle

The nature of Central American economic development has rendered major changes in the class structures of the region. Accompanying these shifts has been a massive concentration of population in the cities: in most countries between one-third and one-half of the population is now located in major urban centers.

Table 9.14    Ratio of External Public Debt to Value of Exports of Goods and Services (in percentages)

|  | 1970 | 1978 |
|---|---|---|
| Honduras | 3.0 | 8.6 |
| El Salvador | 3.5 | 3.1 |
| Guatemala | 7.4 | 1.8 |
| Nicaragua | 10.6 | 17.3 |
| Mexico | 24.1 | 59.5 |
| Panama | 7.6 | 62.0 |
| Costa Rica | 10.0 | 23.4 |

Source: World Bank, World Development Report (August 1980), pp. 138–39.

Table 9.15    Urban Population as a Percentage of Total Population

|  | 1960 | 1980 |
|---|---|---|
| Honduras | 23 | 36 |
| Guatemala | 33 | 39 |
| El Salvador | 38 | 41 |
| Nicaragua | 41 | 53 |
| Mexico | 51 | 67 |
| Panama | 41 | 54 |
| Costa Rica | 37 | 43 |

Source: World Bank, World Development Report (August 1980), pp. 148–49.

In rural Central America, the commercialization of agriculture has increased the number and importance of rural wage workers; at the same time it has uprooted peasant populations, depressed the conditions of production of the petty commodity producers, and maintained large segments of the population at the margins of economic life. The Mexican experience well illustrates the exclusionary nature of these development schemas. Between 1953 and 1975, according to a World Bank study, changes in the country's highly unequal income distribution were "small or non-existent." The number of "poor" families in the agricultural sector declined by a mere 2% (54% to 52%) over this 22-year period. In 1975, the World Bank still categorized as "poor" some 1.5 million landowning families and 850,000 landless families—or 76% of all families residing in rural Mexico.[10] El Salvador, on the other hand, presents a striking example of rapid and massive proletarianization of the agricultural population: from 11% of the total number of peasants in 1961 to 29% in 1971, to 40% in 1975, to an estimated 65% in 1980.[11] Similarly, in Guatemala the growth of a landless or near-landless peasantry (owning insufficient land to maintain a subsistence living) had reached enormous proportions by the early 1970s.[12]

The transformation of the class structure in the countryside has led to wider and deeper involvement of rural populations in agrarian social movements and in struggles for unionization. In Guatemala, following a period (1966-1972) of violent rural repression by the state, guerrilla movements reemerged in the countryside, where a great deal of their efforts were focused on the development of labor and peasant unions. At the same time, ongoing land conflicts and government terrorism (e.g., the massacre of at least 100 Kekchi Indians by the army of Panzós, Alta Verapaz in May 1978) have contributed to a growing militancy on the part of the peasants and have increased their openness to the political and economic appeals of the guerrillas. In the northern province of Quiché, a center of operations of the Ejército Guerrillero de los Pobres (Guerrilla Army of the Poor), many villages have been under military occupation since the mid-1970s.[13]

Table 9.16   Sectoral Distribution of Labor Force (in percentages)

|              | Industry | | Service | |
|              | 1960 | 1978 | 1960 | 1978 |
|--------------|------|------|------|------|
| Honduras     | 11   | 14   | 19   | 23   |
| Guatemala    | 14   | 20   | 19   | 24   |
| El Salvador  | 17   | 22   | 21   | 26   |
| Nicaragua    | 16   | 15   | 22   | 41   |
| Mexico       | 20   | 26   | 25   | 35   |
| Panama       | 14   | 18   | 35   | 47   |
| Costa Rica   | 19   | 23   | 31   | 48   |

*Source:* World Bank, *World Development Report* (August 1980), pp. 146–47.

In El Salvador, since the announcement of the so-called agrarian reform in March 1980, the army, security forces and right-wing death squads (operating in concert) have stepped up the level of repression and counterinsurgency operations in the countryside—especially in the most impoverished rural areas (Chalatenango, Aguilares, etc.) where peasant political origanization is strongest.[14]

Even in "stable" Costa Rica, rural wage workers have begun to organize in pursuit of social and economic demands. In February 1979, for instance, some 4,200 banana plantation laborers, around 80% of whom were represented by the Unión de Trabajadores de Golfito, went on strike against their imperial-capitalist employer, United Brands, over management's continued refusal to negotiate a new collective labor contract. The workers' demands encompassed salary increases, improved holiday and social benefits, and a reduction in the workday from eight to six hours. Their strategic location in the economy—bananas are the second most important export crop—at a time of decline in Costa Rica's foreign trade position forced the Carazo government to intervene directly in the dispute. An official mediator granted immediate wage increases ranging up to 30%, with the understanding that the social demands would be incorporated into the eventual new labor contract.[15]

In urban Central America, the growing concentration and centralization of industry has led to an increasing concentration of labor which, in turn, has facilitated organization and struggle. The proportion of industrial workers has been steadily growing over the past two decades—though their proportion in the labor force in 1978 varied from 14% in Honduras to 26% in Mexico. More significantly, the proportion of "service" workers, largely underemployed or unemployed workers, has jumped tremendously since 1960. In Nicaragua, for example, the following table shows that, while the percentage of industrial workers actually declined between 1960 and 1978 from 16% to 15%, the "service sector" almost doubled in size, going from 22% to 41%.

The integration of a significant proportion of rural migrants into the factory system has provided them with a class-anchored frame of reference through which to act politically. The mass of migrants, however, excluded from stable wage employment, are systematically concentrated in urban slums, as a result of the organic ties between the state and the real estate investors: state subsidies, expenditures and loans facilitate the expansion of big real estate interests and the eradication of lower class communities. The state links to expanding real estate capital have, in recent years, provoked mass opposition among squatter settlements throughout the region.

The region-wide growth model, based on economic incentives for those "above and outside," has not only produced changes in the class structure but also led to precipitous declines in the standard of living for wage and salaried groups—especially salaried employeees within the public service sector. Real wage levels fell by 25% in Nicaragua between 1967 and 1975 and by 30% in Honduras between 1972 and 1978.[16] In El Salvador, workers experienced a substantial decline in real wages during the decade of the 1970s, while the value of the minimum wage in Mexico declined during 1977, 1978, and 1979 as inflation continued to outstrip wage gains.[17] In Costa Rica, inflation and the erosion of living standards among industrial workers and public employees translated into increased strike activity by these groups beginning in late 1979.[18] In fact, spiraling prices for goods and commodities were a feature of most area economies during the 1970s. While the average price index for the region rose by only 13% between 1950 and 1970, it increased by 74% during the 1970 to 1977 period.[19]

The general and chronic deterioration in economic conditions served to unite adversely affected fractions of salaried and wage groups. The combined impact of externally induced inflation, declining standards of living, and autocratic-predatory states has led to united actions across class and occupational lines against the existing regimes. In Nicaragua, a broad-based anti-dictatorial movement incorporating multiple class participants succeeded in overthrowing the Somoza dictatorship in July 1979.[20] In El Salvador, workers, peasants, urban slum dwellers, university students, independent professionals and churchpeople, under the aegis of more than 20 popular organizations, poltical parties and labor federations, have coalesced (and allied themselves with rurally based guerrilla movements) to pursue the struggle to oust the military-dominated junta currently in control of the Salvadorean state.[21] In the late 1970s, the resurgence of rural struggle in Guatemala was accompanied by a growing urban labor militancy, principally among public sector employees, as the military regime sought to contain demands for union recognition, growing inter-union activity in the form of solidarity strikes, and opposition to rising inflation and lowered standards of economic life.[22]

The expansion of capital in the region has not been a linear upward progression, but rather has followed a cyclical pattern. The fluctuations have led to the incorporation of labor into the work force at low wages during the upswing, and the explusion of labor in the downswing, undermining the limited gains and the possibility of cumulative incremental gains. The introduction of the workers to factory or plantation organization preceding the layoff provides them with a class perspective through which to challenge the social order. The "disorder" generated by capitalist instability on workers' lives forces them to seek to "reorder" the class system.[23]

The diversification of capital beyond the agro-mining-export centers of production has led to the proliferation of points of class contestation within the economies of Central America. The overwhelming majority of worker strikes in El Salvador during 1977 and 1978, for example, were concentrated in the construction and manufacturing sectors of the economy.[24] In sum, the growth of state-local-multinational capital has created new class formations and new class conflicts.

Generalized class conflict and multiple class demands challenging the old paternalistic and personalistic forms of domination go beyond the collective bargaining framework, laying claims for a new social and political order. Emerging from the sometimes turbulent movements in opposition to existing state regimes is a fourfold challenge: 1) to the forms of rulership; 2) to the social order; 3) to the external linkages; and 4) to the economic development model.

The attempts by the autocratic regimes to contain the growth of proletarian class consciousness through the promotion of state-controlled bureaucratic organizations (sometimes described as "corporatism") undermine the reformist organization which attempts to mediate the struggles between the state and "society." The lack of reformist representation within the state is combined with economic and political struggle. Even the immediate issues of contention—salaries, wages, working conditions—are set by the state. The resolution of the immediate issues requires resolving the issue of the forms of rulership. The quasi-political monopoly exercised by the Triumvirate mentioned above and the development strategies pursued (free market, cutbacks in public spending, state penetration of private organizations, etc.) marginalize small local capital, pauperize public employees, and undermine the prerogatives of church and civic association leaders—forcing them to go beyond criticism of specific policies and to question the economic model in its totality.

The mobilization of multiple strata and classes in society, and the opposition to the social order, external linkages and economic model, move toward a low level of civil war. One major consequence is the drying up of investment funds, as factories are closed and large amounts of capital are shipped out of the country ($90 million from Nicaragua during July–Decemeber 1977, $300 million from El Salvador during 1978, $100 million from Honduras during 1980).[25] The crisis of the regime is manifested by internal divisions between those who seek to make "concessions" and those who want to "go to war." In society, alternative sources of authority are created—a pre-revolutionary situation emerges. In the crisis, the multinationals and their states seek to substitute new partners—replacing the military dictators and plantation owners with representatives of local industrialists and small and medium-size firms. In turn, the local members of the Triumvirate may lay claims to "nationalism" by attacking foreign intrusions, while simultaneously accelerating the outward flight of capital ($315 million left Nicaragua during January–June 1979, $1.5 billion fled El Salvador during 1979–1980).[26] The common fear of social revolution, however, prevents any decisive breaks within the Triumvirate and, in the end, it unites to attempt to prevent the new mass-based movements from taking power.

## U.S. Aid Policy Toward Central America

The crisis in Central America is a very complex, multi-layered phenomenon that touches every aspect of society and polity. It cannot be reduced to either a "political" crisis, a problem of underdevelopment, or to a set of discrete social problems. This is a "constitutional" crisis, in the sense that what is at stake is the very foundation of the social order. The challenge posed is one that involves reversing historical relationships, transforming the social order and sustaining the development of the productive forces. This is no easy task, given the central position of the U.S. within the region. The U.S. government is attempting to cope with this revolutionary challenge through a combination of repression and reform, with the former clearly in ascent.

The U.S. government's support for Central American dictatorships has been manifested through a vast program of bilateral and multilateral economic aid and various forms of military assistance. Between 1953 and 1979, Washington provided the ruling classes of El Salvador with $218.4 million in economic aid and $16.8 million in military loans and credits. This sum was more than matched by the World Bank, Inter-American Development Bank and other U.S.-influenced multilateral banks to the tune of $479.2 million. The Guatemalan oligarchy received $526.0 million in U.S. economic aid and $41.9 million in military assistance, in addition to some $593.0 million from the "international" financial institutions. The Somoza clan in Nicaragua was the recipient of $345.8 million in U.S. economic aid and $32.6 million in military assistance, while the "international" agencies channeled $469.5 million into its coffers. In Honduras, the ruling political and economic elites benefited significantly from these same sources: $305.1 million in U.S. economic aid, $28.4 million in U.S. military assistance, and $688.0 million from the "international" banks.

The long-term, large-scale involvement of the U.S. in Central America, both economically and militarily, has been to a considerable degree responsible for sustaining in power repressive, autocratic regimes which refuse to deal with underlying social and economic problems persisting into the present period. Economic assistance largely benefited the entrenched oligarchies who, in turn, utilized much of these funds not for developing the productive forces but rather for speculative investments, luxury puchases, or for transferral to foreign bank accounts. The military assistance and training programs acted to enhance the repressive capabilities of these state regimes wedded to development strategies based on "open" economies and coerced labor forces.

Even the much vaunted Carter "human rights" policy did not change the preexisting economic relations between the U.S. and Central America that were, in large measure, responsible for creating the social and political unrest. U.S. economic assistance to the military juntas in Honduras, Guatemala and El Salvador during 1980 totaled more than $125 million, notwithstanding the enormous rise in the number of government opponents assassinated and tortured by the armies, security forces and paramilitary "death squads" of these countries over this 12-month period.[27] According to the El Salvador Human Rights Commission, more than 13,000 deaths were recorded in 1980, the overwhelming majority at the hands of the security forces and the paramilitary groups.

In Guatemala, the growth of mass popular trade union movements, the radicalization of the highland Indian communities and the growing effectiveness of the guerrillas did cause the Carter White House to apply some pressures, largely in the form of a temporary cutback in military credits. This was an effort to force the regime to modify its repressive policies: to be more selective in their application and to combine state control with limited social reforms. The refusal of the military-landlord ruling class to modify its rulership led to some friction between Washington and Guatemala City but did not stop the flow of economic assistance.[28]

Continuing its government-to-government economic assistance, the Carter Administration at no point exercised its economic "muscle" in the multilateral banking institutions to limit the gross human rights violations in the region. During 1979 and 1980, it supported International Monetary Fund loans of $65 million and $77 million to Somoza in Nicaragua and the Salvadorean junta respectively.[29] Furthermore, in December 1980, Washington did successfully flex its economic "muscle" in the Inter-American Development Bank *in support of* a $45.4 million agrarian reform loan to El Salvador, to be drawn from the Bank's special operations fund, in which the U.S. holds 62% of the capital.[30]

While U.S. *economic* policy remained consistent under Carter, there were, as previously noted, some cutbacks in military aid, notably in respect to El Salvador, Nicaragua and Guatemala. Yet these were essentially conjunctural responses over discrete issues at particular moments in time, and did not denote a defined, consistent opposition to repressive military regimes in that area. The government of General Romeo Lucas García in Guatemala, for example, continued to make cash purchases of American weaponry between 1977 and 1980 worth

Table 9.17   U.S. Economic and Military Assistance to Central America, 1953–1979
            ($ millions)

|  | 1953–61 | 1962–69 | 1970–79 | Total 1953–79 |
|---|---|---|---|---|
| Mexico |  |  |  |  |
| economic | 342.1 | 518.4 | 1,672.1 | 2,352.6 |
| military | 3.6 | 4.0 | 7.2 | 14.8 |
| Nicaragua |  |  |  |  |
| economic | 46.2 | 116.2 | 183.4 | 345.8 |
| military | 1.9 | 10.4 | 20.3 | 32.6 |
| Panama |  |  |  |  |
| economic | 67.9 | 173.4 | 341.9 | 583.2 |
| military | 0.1 | 3.0 | 11.8 | 14.9 |
| Costa Rica |  |  |  |  |
| economic | 71.5 | 115.7 | 118.0 | 305.2 |
| military | 0.1 | 1.7 | 5.1 | 6.9 |
| El Salvador |  |  |  |  |
| economic | 14.3 | 115.1 | 89.0 | 218.4 |
| military | 0.1 | 6.5 | 10.2 | 16.8 |
| Guatemala |  |  |  |  |
| economic | 134.7 | 170.8 | 220.5 | 526.0 |
| military | 1.5 | 18.3 | 22.1 | 41.9 |
| Honduras |  |  |  |  |
| economic | 37.9 | 75.9 | 191.3 | 305,1 |
| military | 1.1 | 8.0 | 19.3 | 28.4 |

*Note:* Includes U.S. Export-Import Bank and other U.S. government loans.

$4.7 million, under the Foreign Military Sales program.[31] Selectivity was the byword—in some countries and respects, military assistance was cut back for limited durations of time and in others it was not. Beyond that, the real impact of U.S. arms sales policy was substantially minimized by the emergence of Israel—a strategic Washington ally and "regional policeman" in the Middle East—as a major exporter of military supplies to the Central American dictatorships during the 1970's. Israel supplied 81% of El Salvador's foreign arms purchases between 1972 and 1977, and 98% of Somoza's arms imports during the final year of his rule.[32] The following table presents a detailed breakdown of major Israeli military sales to El Salvador between 1974 and 1978.

The largest single Israeli arms exporter to Central America has been the state-owned Israel Aircraft Industries (IAI), which has found a ready market for its products—especially the ARAVA, a tactical transport aircraft particularly suited to counterinsurgency warfare.

In late 1979, in the context of a heightened social class struggle in El Salvador and the growing consolidation of the Nicaraguan Revolution under Sandinista leadership, the Carter Administration decided to terminate its policy of selective arms constraints in favor of a policy of directly arming the terrorist juntas in Central America. Between the

Table 9.18    Economic Assistance From International Financial Institutions, 1953-1979
              ($ millions)

|  | 1953-61 | 1962-69 | 1970-79 | Total 1953-79 |
|---|---|---|---|---|
| Mexico | 153.6 | 971.8 | 4,746.7 | 5,872.1 |
| Nicaragua | 33.8 | 86.3 | 349.4 | 469.5 |
| Panama | 15.4 | 37.8 | 535.5 | 588.7 |
| Costa Rica | 18.8 | 75.9 | 587.7 | 682.4 |
| El Salvador | 24.7 | 57.4 | 397.1 | 479.2 |
| Guatemala | 21.6 | 76.1 | 495.2 | 593.0 |
| Honduras | 32.5 | 85.7 | 569.8 | 688.0 |

Source: U.S. Agency for International Development, Statistics and Research Division, Office of Program and Information Analysis Services, U.S. Overseas Loans and Grants and Assistance From International Organizations, July 1, 1945–September 30, 1976, pp. 43, 47–48, 53–55, 183–85; U.S. Agency for International Development, Office of Planning and Budgeting, Bureau for Program and Policy Coordination, U.S. Overseas Loans and Grants and Assistance From International Organizations, July 1, 1945–September 30, 1979, pp. 45, 49–50, 53, 55–57, 218–22.

---

military coup of October 1979 and the resignation of the first civilian-military government in January 1980, Washington shipped $205,541 worth of riot control equipment and reprogrammed (with Congressional assent) some $300,000 in International Military Education and Training funds to El Salvador.[33] In April 1980, the U.S. government reprogrammed $5.7 million in military aid for El Salvador and submitted a request for an additional $5.5 million for the junta in Fiscal Year 1981.[34]

At the same time, Carter also obtained Congressional support for the reprogramming of $3.53 million in Foreign Military Sales credits to the Honduran regime and for an increase of International Military Education and Training funds from the budgeted Fiscal Year 1980 of $225,000 to $347,000. The Honduran military was further permitted

---

Table 9.19    Major Israeli Arms Sales to El Salvador, 1974-1978

|  | Deliveried |
|---|---|
| 25 IAI-201 Arava STOL transport aircraft | 1974–79 |
| 200 9mm UZI submarine guns | 1974–77 |
| 200 80mm rocket launchers | 1974–77 |
| 18 refurbished Dassault Ouragan fighter bombers | 1975 |
| 6 IAI Fouga Magister trainer aircraft | 1975 |

Source: Institute for Policy Studies, Background Information on the Security Forces in El Salvador and U.S. Military Assistance (March 1980), p. 12.

Table 9.20 Israel Aircraft Industries Sales in Central America, 1973–1979

|  | Equipment |
|---|---|
| El Salvador | 18 Ouragan, 6 Fouga, 5 Arava |
| Guatemala | 8 Arava |
| Honduras | 12 Super-Mystere, 3 Arava, 1 Westwind |
| Mexico | 25 Arava |
| Nicaragua | 14 Arava |
| Panama | 1 Westwind |

Source: "Problems From the Barrels of Israeli Guns," Latin American Weekly Report WR-80-19 (May 16, 1980), p. 9.

to lease at least 10 U.S. Bell Huey helicopters, while welcoming dozens of U.S. military advisers who entered the country during 1980.[35] In Fiscal Year 1981, the White House and the Pentagon expected the Guatemalan junta to expand its purchases of military hardware through the Foreign Military Sales cash program.[36]

The long-term continuity in U.S. economic assistance—despite changes in political administration—mirrors the long-term capitalist interests in Central America and the basic support for local ruling groups by all U.S. Presidents, whether Republican or Democratic, liberal or conservative. The limited change in military aid policy under Carter reflected a variety of factors: the relative importance of the human rights lobby within the Executive branch; the shifting nature of the bureaucratic debate over tactics and strategy; and the political changes taking place within the Central American countries.

The human rights lobby was strongest in the early part of the Carter Administration. In the years between 1976 and 1978 it was able to push legislation which successfully limited U.S. military support for specific regimes (Guatemala, El Salvador). By 1979, however, the more conservative forces within the State Department and the National Security Council had effectively isolated the human rights proponents within the foreign policy bureaucracy. This, in turn, was followed by a reopening of the military aid "pipelines" as the U.S. government moved to actively support repressive pro-capitalist military regimes in Central America (as well as in other parts of Latin America and the Third World).

The major change in Washington's policy was the recognition, in the aftermath of Somoza's overthrow in July 1979, that a major effort had to be made to forge a coalition of civilian business groups and the army to provide a political, as well as a military, solution in other Central American countries experiencing a resurgence of anti-dictatorial and class struggle. The central concern of U.S. policy was first and foremost to undermine the revolutionary popular movements and preserve the existing armed forces. Irrespective of whether these armed forces engaged in declared wars on their own populations, Washington's pressure for reforms has always been subordinated to that intent.

In the first instance, the effort was made by the White House to forge an alliance between the right-wing armed forces and reformist social democratic groups in El Salvador following the October 1979 coup which ousted General Carlos Humberto Romero from office. The effort was doomed to failure. The social democratic representatives in the junta could not generate any significant support for reform programs, while the armed forces were killing scores of workers and peasants— literally on a daily basis. As the reformers abandoned the coalition government, U.S. policy shifted speedily to the political right.

With the collapse of the civilian-military junta in January 1980, new, more malleable Christian Democratic politicians were brought into the regime to maintain the illusion of civilian authority within the ruling coalition. The sudden increase in U.S. military aid now reflected an attempt to combine repressive policies against the popular movement with limited economic reforms. The locus of economic change was in Washington's attempt to benignly sacrifice the short-term interests of segments of the local landowning class—through land reform—in order to reformulate a political bloc that subordinated peasant property owners to multinationals. The refusal of landowners to submit to U.S. tatical maneuvers and their desire to exclude the new U.S. political clients from a share in effective governmental responsibility set the stage for the new triangle. By mid-1980, at least 10 Cabinet members or high-ranking civilian officials had resigned from the government, as the U.S. government became forcibly allied with the terror of the military, security forces and paramilitary organizations such as the 50,000 to 100,000 member ORDEN. At the same time, Washington attempted to convince the ultra-right to share power with its increasingly compromised, impotent and isolated middle-sector client groups.

U.S. policymakers still proclaimed the viability of the regime, while the Salvadorean ruling class withdrew $1.5 billion in the midst of the 1979-1980 political crisis. U.S. Agency for International Development officials continued to insist that the junta's agrarian programs were designed to help the poor, while economic resources were channeled to a government controlled by large landholders and financial groups who siphoned off the bulk of the funds for their own use. During 1980, according to Socorro Jurídico (Legal Aid Office of the Archbishop of El Salvador), some 8,062 peasants, workers, students, trade unionists, professionals and churchpeople were assassinated in *nonmilitary* confrontations with the security forces, paramilitary groups and Salvadorean troops commanded by U.S.-trained officers.[37] Hundreds more opponents of the regime "disappeared" after being arrested.[38]

Meanwhile, in the absence of the prosecution of a single military official, the Carter Administration perversely continued to label the regime a "moderate," "reformist" and centrist government and to engage in a determined effort to focus the blame for the violence on nongovernmental paramilitary organizations. Select cutbacks in U.S. military aid were in no way designed to undermine the internal discipline and cohesion of the armed forces. While on occasion condemning the "extremists on the right," the "human rights" Administration continued to support the military which practiced the violence and provided the recruits for the right-wing terrorist groups.

Washington's formula for reviving military aid to the Salvadorean armed forces in late 1979 was the same as in the past: the defense of economic privilege, support for the "integrity of the military" and opposition to social revolution. What was different was the attempt to forge a coalition between the military and the civilian middle class liberals to undercut the polarization emerging from past and present economic policies.* Through the facade of a controlled civilian regime, token reforms and an intact military, U.S. policymakers hoped to defuse public criticism at home and abroad, without endangering corporate economic and strategic interests. By December 1980, this policy had led neither to reform of the underlying conditions generating mass discontent, nor to a lessening of the level of repression by the regime. What it left was basically an escalating civil war and the threat of new U.S. interventions in the region.

Washington's attempt to defend traditional economic interests and sustain the Central American armed forces by creating a new set of civilian-military coalitions, through controlled and restricted elections, was the other side of the coin of its policy of continuing economic support to a military intent on physically destroying the revolutionary popular organizations and their supporters. Both the so-called "moderate civilians" and the extremist military were wedded to the same destructive ends. A brief survey of recent U.S. policy in the post-Somoza period is useful in demonstrating this approach and the extent to which it has, or has not, been incorporated into the foreign policy outlook of the Reagan Administration.

## From Carter to Reagan: U.S. Policy in The Post-Somoza Period

By the fall of 1979, all of Carter's campaign promises of 1976 had vanished: contrary to the earlier human rights commitments, global arms sales and the overall military budget were on a pronounced upward spiral. Among the primary recipients of new "security assistance" aid programs were an array of military and autocratic regimes in Central America, the rest of Latin America and other parts of the Third World

---

*A similar strategy was followed in Honduras, as the Carter Administration sought to defuse a burgeoning mass movement by enlisting traditional conservative and liberal civilian politicals to participate in elections—while the military excluded leftists, social democrats and even Christian Democrats.

which had previously been criticized for widespread violations of human rights. The appearance of a new aggressive U.S. posture toward the Third World, which went hand-in-hand with the armaments build-up, also served to distract attention from internal U.S. problems (inflation, unemployment, declining standards of living and the energy crisis) which were themselves transformed by Carter into instruments for external confrontation. Hostility toward OPEC, ect., became a tool for sustaining internal cohesion within the U.S. and avoiding potentially divisive cleavages between consumers and corporations.

The first major step toward reactivating the Marines was the effort by the U.S. government in June 1979 to secure passage of a resolution in the Organization of American States calling for the creation of a hemispheric military force to intervene in Nicaragua to prevent a Sandinista victory.[39] The failure of the resolution to gain support within the regional body, and the fact that Washington was not in a position to intervene unilaterally in Nicaragua, should not obscure the profound shift that had taken place in U.S. policy and its consequences for the immediate future.

In the fall of 1979, the Carter Administration accelerated efforts to create a 100,000-person Rapid Deployment Force capable of intervening within hours in any area of the world. The "new interventionists" also proposed the creation of a hemispheric military "peacekeeping" force—which would have required a complete conciliation with the worst dictatorships in Latin America. The efforts to reconstitute a post-Vietnam domestic constituency that would support the "new interventionist" policy reached a hysterical pitch with the effort by Carter and his National Security Adviser Brzezinski to fabricate a Soviet military threat in Cuba—an effort so transparently fraudulent that even the Washington political establishment was soon forced to reject it. Nonetheless, the incident was part of a singular bellicose pattern—a drift toward "direct action." In fact, out of the non-threat of Soviet troops in Cuba, Carter was able to set up a Caribbean Joint Task Force in Florida to police the area and prepare for possible interventionary actions.

In summary, military resources and public opinion were again being mobilized to defend imperial interests under the ideology of "defending ourselves against aggression," i.e., national security. U.S. policy had come full circle since 1976: the policies, rhetoric and instrumentalities of the 1960's and early 1970's are being refurbished for the 1980's.

The transition from Carter to Reagan has been accompanied by a remarkable degree of continuity in the area of foreign policy. While the "new interventionist" framework undergoes further elaboration and extension, however, some shifts in strategy are already clearly discernible as regards Central America and other parts of the Third World.

As part of its overriding goal to revitalize U.S. capitalism both at home and abroad, the incoming Administration intended to further downplay human rights considerations in the execution of foreign policy, and to seek closer ties with autocratic military regimes in the Third

World—regimes that supported U.S. political-strategic interests and accorded foreign capital a central role within their development schemas. One of the major recommendations contained in a report prepared by Reagan's State Department Transition Team on Latin America was the following: "Internal policy-making procedures should be structured to ensure that the Human Rights area is not in a position to paralyze or unduly delay decisions on issues where human rights concerns conflict with other U.S. interests."[40] Subsequently, the head of the Transition Team, Ambassador Robert Neumann, put it more bluntly in an address to a group of Foreign Service Officers, declaring that such "abstractions" as human rights had no central place in a foreign policy that wished to pursue "American national interests."[41]

The other side of this coin was the new rhetoric that defined support of pro-capitalist, pro-U.S. "moderately repressive [sic!] autocratic governments" as compatible with the "national interest."[42] In language that recalled the Johnson Administration's "Mann Doctrine"* (which formalized U.S. support of military dictatorships in Latin America and described them as "pre-democratic" phenomena), a senior Reagan foreign policy adviser on Latin America was quoted, in part:

> "We must maintain our interest in promoting democracy without getting disillusioned because there's a military coup in Honduras and the generals didn't respond the way we wanted. . . ." A Reagan administration, he said, would structure Latin American policy on the idea that democracy and not military dictatorship is the best protection against Communism, but it would recognize that democracy in some cases can be instituted too rapidly.[43]

At the operational level, the new policy is currently focused largely on the Central American region, with particular attention to El Salvador.

In late November 1980, Reagan's Latin American policy advisers personally "assured" leading representatives of El Salvador's business community "that the new administration will increase military aid, including control equipment, to security forces fighting leftist guerrillas."[44] On January 17, 1981, the outgoing government, utilizing special executive powers that circumvented the need for Congressional assent, authorized an emergency $5 million package of lethal military assistance for the Salvadorean junta.[45]

In early March, the Reagan White House announced its intention to provide a further $25 million in new military aid and increase the number of American military advisers in El Salvador from 25 to 45.[46] By the end of the same month, total Fiscal Year 1981 U.S. military appropriations for the junta had risen to $35.4 million.[47] In Congressional testimony at the end of March, acting Assistant Secretary of State for

---

*Named after Thomas Mann, Under Secretary of State for Economic Affairs, 1965-66.-Ed.

Inter-American Affairs John Bushnell stated that the Administration would authorize the dispatch of 56 Pentagon advisers to El Salvador, including a number of Special Forces personnel experienced in counterinsurgency warfare.[48]*

For Fiscal Year 1982, the Administration has requested $26 million in direct military aid to El Salvador and an additional $40 million from the misnamed "Economic Support Fund" which, in practice, operates as a weapons assistance "support fund."[49] These current and projected increases in military aid to the regime in San Salvador in part reflect Reagan's decision to forego the Carter strategy of attempting to disassociate the junta from responsibility for the terror—preferring, instead, to support the militarization of civil society, if that is what is required to defeat a revolutionary popular movement which has put the issue of state power on the immediate agenda.

Like his predecessor, Reagan is continuing the program of large-scale economic assistance to what is now pictured as "a moderate government . . . looking forward [sic!] to legitimate elections. . . ."[50] Bilateral aid from the U.S. Agency for International Development for the current Fiscal Year stands at $63.5 million, but will be doubled if Congress can be persuaded to support a further $63.5 million in "emergency" economic assistance.[51] Of even greater (potential) significance is the reported Administration plan, utilizing various imperial state agencies and the multilateral financial institutions (World Bank, Inter-American Development Bank, International Monetary Fund), that would channel an estimated $429.5 million in economic assistance to El Salvador before the end of the present Fiscal Year. In pursuit of this goal, Washington has apparently let it be known that it is prepared to apply considerable pressure on allied governments in Western Europe, Japan and Canada to contribute a substantial proportion of the total amount under the aegis of the "international banks."[52]

The military juntas in Honduras and Guatemala have been visibly encouraged by the advent of a staunchly anticommunist "business" Administration in Washington and the shifts in Central American policy that have followed in its wake. Honduras will receive $5.4 million in military assistance during Fiscal Year 1981 and a proposed $10.7 million (the third-highest appropriation for the entire region, exceeded only by the requests for El Salvador and Colombia) during Fiscal Year 1982.[53] While Guatemala is not expected to receive any direct U.S. military aid before the end of Fiscal Year 1982, the new U.S. "policy line" has coincided with an acceleration of the terror campaign against urban and rural opponents of the regime. In January 1981, for example, almost 400 people were killed by the military. In the first week of February,

---

*Apparently, some 20 to 30 Israeli military advisers are also currently involved in training Salvadorean government forces in anti-guerrilla warfare tactics. See "Latin Letter," Latin American Weekly Report WR-81-13 (March 27, 1981), p. 8.

at least another 85 peasants were assassinated in a "scorched earth" attack on two villages in an area northwest of Guatemala City, by army units reinforced by helicopter gunships.[54] Later that same month, *Amnesty International* released a detailed report on the repression which documented in great detail the regime's role as the only author and practitioner of the "official" and "unofficial" terror:

> people who oppose or are imagined to oppose the government are systematically seized without warrant, tortured, and murdered, and . . . these tortures and murders are part of a deliberate and long-standing program of the Guatemalan government. This report contains information, published for the first time, which shows how the selection of targets for detention and murder, and *the deployment of official forces for extra-legal operations*, can be pinpointed to secret offices in an annex of Guatemala's National Palace, under the direct control of the president of the Republic.[55]

Toward the revolutionary government in Nicaragua and its devastated economy, on the other hand, the Reagan Administration has adopted a policy of diplomatic hostility and cutbacks in previously authorized economic assistance. In a verbal message relayed to Managua in February, and supposedly originating from a staff member of the National Security Council, the American Embassy was informed that "the question is not whether U.S.-Nicaraguan relations were good or bad, but whether there will be any relations at all."[56] Subsequently, the White House announced that it was withholding disbursement of the final $15 million of a $75 million economic aid package authorized and released by the Congress in late 1980.[57] At the same time, an official of the Agency for International Development acknowledged that a $9.6 million shipment of vitally needed food supplies (wheat) could not be completed until approval had been given at "the political level."[58]

Secretary of State Alexander Haig justified the aid suspension on the grounds that Nicaragua was providing arms to the guerrillas in El Salvador. Although, according to the State Department, the arms flow has since been halted, the economic funds remain frozen.[59] Furthermore, the Reagan Administration has drastically cut the level of proposed U.S. economic assistance to Nicaragua during Fiscal Year 1982 (via the Agency for International Development): from $33.2 million proposed by the Carter White House to a mere $13.4 million.[60] Nicaraguan officials have recently expressed growing concern that this policy of economic denial might soon be expanded by Executive branch policymakers to include efforts to prevent possible large-scale international banking credits from reaching Managua.[61]

*Conclusion*

In retrospect, the limits on U.S. intervention in the mid and late 1970's in Central America reflected several conjunctural factors. In the case of Nicaragua, to take the most striking example, the extent of mass internal support for the Sandinista regime increased the cost of direct involvement, threatening to bog down the U.S. in an endless policing operation. Diplomatic efforts in the Organization of American States failed to secure regional support for military intervention, while the opposition of Western European and Latin American social democratic and liberal governments (and parties) to U.S. policy threatened to destroy the efforts to reconstruct alliances within the Western world. Given these conjunctural constraints, U.S. policymakers were unable to work in a single channel (direct intervention) or with a simple set of alliance partners: the circumstances dictated flexible, political tactics in pursuit of rigidly set economic imperatives that continue to characterize and shape Executive branch decision-making.

U.S. policy tactics will vary substantially with contexts in which Washington will not always be able to control and dictate its optimal solution. U.S. policymakers will continue to support *viable* dictators: those firmly in control over the population and state apparatus and promoting American economic interests. In periods of *emerging instability*, Washington may support conservative (civilian) factions of the opposition or "reform" military groups *if available*. In highly polarized situations, the U.S. will support reformist-liberal coalitions against revolutionaries *if necessary*. Finally, in strategic areas, the U.S. will directly intervene to prevent social revolution, when lacking any of the previous alternatives. As the cases of Nicaragua and El Salvador illustrate, the forms of U.S. interventionism do not always take the most direct (military occupation) or reactionary (in any absolute sense) direction, but rather reflect the *relatively most reactionary position*, depending on the context.

In Nicaragua, the U.S. attempted to substitute conservative opposition figures for Somoza, preserving the National Guard and preventing a Sandinista victory. This move occurred, however, on the eve of Somoza's overthrow, when virtually all of the major urban centers were under the control of the revolutionary forces. Hence, U.S. policy shifted after July 1979 toward an effort to support and bolster anti-Sandinista and reformist elements within the governing coalition and the society at large—a strategy that is still in operation. The $75 million economic aid package passed by the U.S. Congress and finally released, after months of delay, in September 1980 exemplified the Carter Administration strategy. Nearly two thirds of the funds were stipulated for use by the private sector—reflecting an obvious effort to improve the position of the conservative propertied groups in Nicaraguan society. With the advent of the Reagan presidency, the continuing application of external economic pressures on the Nicaraguan government has been complemented by the provision of increased U.S. military assistance to area dictatorships hostile to the Nicaraguan Revolution.

In El Salvador, the U.S. attempted a preemptive coup: in the face of a profound polarization in which practically all of civil society was ranged against the Romero regime, Washington promoted a center-right coalition in late 1979, coopting liberal Catholics, social democrats and reformist military officials, while maintaining intact the existing state apparatus. The timing of the change in El Salvador was a response to the lesson learned in Nicaragua, where it was impossible to create alternatives in an open insurrectionary situation. Nevertheless, after three months the Salvadorean reformers realized their ineffectiveness and withdrew from the government, forcing the U.S. to call upon the most reactionary wing of the Christian Democratic Party to maintain the ficiton of a coalition government. The shift from inflexible dictatorial rule to conservative but "flexible" military control (including openings to conservative civilian politicians) clearly reflected the growing recognition in Washington of the importance of timing its political tactics in gauging its activities vis-à-vis the emerging political and social struggles in the Third World. The current Reagan strategy of promoting the militarization of civil society in order to defeat the popular movement is further evidence of this new tactical sophistication on the part of the imperial state.

A proper conception of U.S. policy toward Central America must follow the multiple tracks which it pursues, as well as its capacity to shift tracks depending on the contextual situation, and depending specifically on the scope and depth of the class struggle. In periods of individual protest, Washington will continue to collaborate with the regime, with occasional public criticisms of its "excesses." In situations of incremental growth of the opposition, where collective conflicts are local and uncoordinated, it will continue to work with the regime, criticize the lack of tactical flexibility, maintain ties with the civilian conservative opposition and support repression of the revolutionary left. In periods of mass mobilization, U.S. policy will be to strengthen the conservative, electoral opposition forces and promote alliances with sectors of the military—and even try to entice opportunistic and unprincipled sectors among the social democrats to isolate the revolutionary left. A coup against the incumbent power holder may be encouraged, and foreign aid and support of reformist policy declarations may accompany the switchover, as long as the revolutionary left is kept out of power and effectively repressed. If these political maneuvers fail and there exists the imminent likelihood of a politico-military victory by a movement led by social revolutionaries—especially in a country designated as "strategic"—the use of a Rapid Deployment Force, or some variation thereof, by the United States cannot be discounted.

Given the rising mass governments, especially in Central America and the Caribbean, and given the increasingly interventionist orientation in the U.S. government, the 1980's promise to be a period of growing confrontation. U.S. interests in preserving or only marginally changing the repressive state apparatuses, and wholehearted U.S. support of the "free market" economic policies in the region, are inevitably in conflict with the broad-based pressure for dismantling the same repressive state structures, nationalizing multinational properties, and redistributing income and other forms of wealth. As the populations of the region change from being passive human rights victims to active protagonists of revolution, the U.S. government shifts from being a "critic of repression" to a promoter of intervention.

## Notes

1. Gert Rosenthal, "Economic Trends in Central America," *CEPAL REVIEW, Second Half of 1978*, p. 47.

2. Ibid.

3. For a discussion of family-based corporate capitalism in Latin America, see Maurice Zeitlin and R. E. Ratcliff, "Research Methods for the Analysis of the Internal Structure of Dominant Classes: The Case of Landlords and Capitalists in Chile." *Latin American Research Review* X, 3 (Winter 1965), pp. 5-61.

4. For a detailed analysis of the U.S. imperial state, see James F. Petras and Morris H. Morley, "The U.S. Imperial State." *REVIEW* (Fernand Braudel Center for the Study of Economies, Historical Systems, and Civilzations) IV, 2 (Fall 1980), pp. 171-222.

5. See "Nicaragua: How the Local Boys Made Good." *Latin American Economic Report* VI, 4 (January 27, 1978), p. 27.

6. See, for example, Edelberto Torres-Rivas, "The Central American Model of Growth: Crisis for Whom? *Latin American Perspectives* VII, 2&3 (Spring and Summer 1980), pp. 24-44.

7. See Clifford Draus, "Gautemala's Indian Wars," *The Nation* (March 14, 1981), p. 306; "Honduras: Land Seizures." *Latin America* IX, 21 (May 30, 1975), p. 165; data from Amnesty International as reprinted in Institute for Policy Studies, *Background Information on the Security Forces in El Salvador and U.S. Military Assistance* (March 1980), p. 2; Inter-American Development Bank, *Nicaragua: Proposed Loan for an Agricultural Recovery Credit Program.* Internal Document, No. PR-1083 (November 25, 1980), p. 5.

8. Gert Rosenthal, op. cit., p. 49.

9. U.S. Department of Commerce, *Survey of Current Business* 45, 8 (September 1965), p. 24, and 52, 11 (November 1972), p. 30.

10. World Bank, Latin America and the Caribbean Regional Office, *Income Distribution and Poverty in Mexico.* Staff Working Paper No. 395 (Washington, D.C., June 1980), pp. 20-22.

11. "El Salvador: One Hundred Years of Crisis on the Land." *Latin American Regional Reports: Mexico & Central America* RM-80-03 (March 21, 1981), p. 5; "El Salvador: Reform Imposed From Above." *Latin American Weekly Report* WR-81-10 (March 6, 1981), p. 10.

12. See Edelberto Torres-Rivas, "Guatemala—Crisis and Political Violence." *NACLA Report on the Americas* XIV, 1 (January-February 1980), p. 20.

13. See "Guatemala: Peasant Massacre." *Latin American Political Report* XII, 22 (June 9, 1978), p. 175; "Guatemala Massacre Points to Growing Peasant Resistance." *Latin American Regional Reports: Mexico & Central America* RM-80-02 (February 15, 1980), pp. 1, 3; "Guatemala: Guerrillas Put the Military in a Sweat." *Latin American Regional Reports: Mexico & Central America* RM-81-01 (January 9, 1981), pp. 5-6.

14. See "El Salvador: Counter-Insurgency Moves Into Overdrive." *Latin American Regional Reports: Mexico & Central America* RM-80-06 (July 11, 1980), p. 5.

15. "Costa Rican Banana Workers Win Big Pay Increases." *Latin American Economic Report* VII, 9 (March 2, 1979), p. 72.

16. "Deepening Crisis Alarms Nicaragua Private Sector." *Latin American Economic Report* VII, 17 (May 4, 1979), p. 133; "Spotlight on Honduras." *Latin American Regional Reports: Mexico & Central America* RM-80-05 (June 6, 1980), p. 8.

17. World Bank, *El Salvador: An Inquiry Into Urban Poverty.* Internal Document, Report No. 2945-ES (November 5, 1980), p. iii; Harold Jang, "Civil War in El Salvador." *New Left Review* 122 (July-August 1980), p. 15; "Mexico Fall in Real Wages Threatens Labour Unrest." *Latin American Regional Reports: Mexico & Central America* RM-80-01 (January 11, 1980), p. 5.

18. "Costa Rica: Grapples With Inflation and Labor Problems." *Latin American Economic Report* VII, 33 (August 24, 1979), p. 26.

19. Gert Rosenthal, op. cit., pp. 51-52.

20. See James Petras, "Whither the Nicaraguan Revolution?" *Monthly Review* 31, 5 (October 1979), pp. 1-22; Harold Jang, "Behind the Nicaragua Revolution." *New Left Review* 117 (September-October 1978), pp. 69-89; William M. LeoGrande "The Revolution in Nicaragua: Another Cuba? *Foreign Affairs* 58, 1 (Fall 1979), pp. 28-50.

21. See, for example, Harold Jang, "Civil War in El Salvador," op. cit., pp. 3-25.

22. See "Guatemala: Labour Challenge," *Latin American Political Report* XII, 34 (October 6, 1978), pp. 308-09; "Guatemala: Bus Fare Crisis," *Latin American Political Report* XII, 40 (October 13, 1978), pp. 314-15; "Growing Militancy Provokes Clampdown in Guatemala." *Latin American Economic Report* VI, 46 (November 24, 1978), p. 368.

23. For a well-documented and convincing study of this process in another context, see Maurice Zeitlin, *Revolutionary Politics and the Cuban Working Class* (Princeton, New Jersey: Princeton University Press, 1967).

24. International Labor Organization, *Yearbook of Labor Statistics* 1979 (Geneva), p. 616.

25. Harold Jang, op. cit., p. 18; "Deepening Crisis Alarms Nicaraguan Private Sector," op. cit., p. 133; "Spotlight on Honduras," op. cit., p. 8.

26. Karen de Young, "Somoza Legacy: Plundered Economy," *Washington Post* (November 30, 1979), p. A30; "Common Market: Little to Spare in the CACM's Money Box." *Latin American Regional Reports: Mexico & Central America* RM-81-02 (February 13, 1981), p 8.

27. See U.S. Agency for International Development, *Congressional Presentation. Fiscal Year 1982, Main Volume* (United States International Development Cooperation Agency), pp. 235, 243, 251.

28. On the terror in Guatemala, see, for example, Jean-Pierre Clerc, "Bananas and Death Squads." Le Monde Supplement of the *Manchester Guardian Weekly* (August 10, 1980), pp. 12, 14; Clifford Kraus, op. cit., pp. 303-07.

29. See James Nelson Goodsell, "IMF Loans to Nicaragua Give Somoza Breathing Space." *Christian Science Monitor* (May 16, 1979), p. 7; Hobart Rowen, "Blumenthal Supports Loan to Nicaragua." *Washington Post* (June 14, 1979), p. D1; Institute for Policy Studies, *Update #2: Background Information on El Salvador and U.S. Military Assistance to Central America* (November 1980), p. 8.

30. See "El Salvador: U.S. Ready to Put Pressure on the Aid Donors," *Latin American Regional Reports: Mexico & Central America* RM-81-03 (March 20, 1981), p. 2.

31. Institute for Policy Studies, op. cit., p. 4.

32. "Problems From the Barrels of Israeli Guns," *Latin American Weekly Report* WR-80-19 (May 16, 1980), p. 9.

33. Institute for Policy Studies, *Update: Background Information on El Salvador and U.S. Military Assistance to Central America* (June 1980), pp. 6-7.

34. Ibid., p. 7.

35. Ibid., p. 8; Institute for Policy Studies, *Update #2* . . . , op. cit., p. 2; Christopher Dickey, "Political Violence Spreads to Once-Peaceful Honduras, Costa Rica." *Washington Post* (March 29, 1981), p. A16.

36. Institute for Policy Studies, *Update #2* . . . , op. cit., p. 4.

37. Socorro Jurídico (Legal Aid Office of the Archbishop of El Salvador), *El Salvador* (February 1981), p. 9.

38. Ibid., p. 22.

39. James Petras, op. cit., p. 17.

40. Office of the President-Elect, Washington, D.C., Memorandum to: Ambassador Robert Neumann. From: Pedro A. Sanjuan, State Department Transition Team. *Subject:*

*Interim Report on the Bureau of Inter-American Affairs and Related Bureaus and Policy Areas*, Department of State.

41. Quoted in John M. Goshko, "Reagan State Department Aide Sees 'Nationalistic' Policy." *Washington Post* (December 18, 1980), p. A1.

42. Jeane Kirkpatrick, United Nations Ambassador-designate, quoted in Philip Geyelin, "Human Rights Turnaround." *Washington Post* (December 12, 1980), p. A23.

43. Roger Fontaine, quoted in Warren Hodge, "Reagan Aides, in South America, Say He Would Not Favor Dictators." *New York Times* (September 22, 1980), p. 12.

44. Juan de Onis, "Reagan Aides Promise Salvadoreans More Military Help to Fight Rebels," *New York Times* (November 29, 1980), p. 1.

45. Institute for Policy Studies, *Update #3: Background on U.S. Military Assistance to El Salvador* (January 1980).

46. John M. Goshko and Don Oberdorfer, "U.S. to Send More Aid, Advisers to El Salvador." *Washington Post* (March 3, 1981), pp. A1, A11.

47. Edward Walsh, "Policy on El Salvador Narrowly Survives First Hill Test, 8 to 7." *Washington Post* (March 25, 1981), p. A14.

48. See Edward Walsh, "El Salavdor Protests Called 'Orchestrated' Communist Effort." *Washington Post* (March 24, 1981), p. A3. Also see Judith Miller, "15 U.S. Green Berets to Aid Salvadorans." *New York Times* (March 14, 1981), pp. 1, 8.

49. See Ibid.; "Reagan Seeks Big Rise in Military Aid to Latin America." *Latin American Weekly Report* WR-81-14 (April 3, 1981), p. 5.

50. Excerpts from Transcript of an interview with President Reagan by Lou Cannon and Lee Lescaze, *Washington Post* (March 29, 1981), p. A6.

51. Edward Walsh, "Policy on El Salvador Narrowly Survives First Hill Test, 8 to 7," op. cit., p. A14; "Reagan Seeks Big Rise in Military Aid to Latin America," op. cit., p. 5.

52. See "El Salvador: U.S. Ready to Put Pressure on the Aid Donors," op. cit., p. 2.

53. Alan Riding, "Ally of Honduran Army Expects U.S. Right-Face." *New York Times* (April 15, 1981), p. 2; "Reagan Seeks Big Rise in Military Aid to Latin America," op. cit., p. 5.

54. See "Guatemala: Army Steps Up Its Terror," *Latin American Regional Reports: Mexico & Central America* RM-81-03 (March 20, 1981), p. 3.

55. "Guatemala: A Government Program of Political Murder—The Amnesty Report (Extracts)." *The New York Review of Books* (March 19, 1981), p. 38.

56. Quoted in Alan Riding, "Nicaragua Seeking Accord in El Salvador." *New York Times* (February 12, 1981), p. 11.

57. See Juan de Onis, "U.S. Halts Nicaraguan Aid Over Help for Guerrillas." *New York Times* (January 23, 1981), p. 1.

58. Quoted in Juan de Onis, "Wheat Sale to Nicaragua Delayed." *New York Times* (February 11, 1981), p. 4.

59. See "U.S. Halts Economic Aid to Nicaragua." *New York Times* (April 2, 1981), p. 3; Edward Walsh, "U.S. Economic Aid to Nicaragua Suspended But May Be Resumed." *Washington Post* (April 2, 1981), p. A2.

60. See "Reagan Seeks Big Rise in Military Aid to Latin America," op. cit., p. 5.

61. See, for example, "Nicaraguans Prepare Themselves for the Gathering Storm." *Latin American Weekly Report* WR-81-15 (April 10, 1981), pp. 1-2.

# 10

## Petrodollars and the State: The Failure of State Capitalist Development in Venezuela

JAMES F. PETRAS

MORRIS H. MORLEY

### The State in Venezuelan Development

The state capitalist development project elaborated by the Acción Democrática (AD) government of Carlos Andrés Pérez (1974–8) sought to regulate foreign capital operations in order to create 'economic space' for accelerated indigenous private capital accumulation and growth. The expanding presence of the state in the Venezuelan economy coincided with the pre-1974 emergence of a private capitalist class that increasingly looked to the state's oil-derived financial/economic resources to sustain and strengthen its position within the national economy. Essentially, the Pérez government articulated and operationalised a two-pronged strategy: sectoral nationalisation (iron ore and petroleum) and massive investments in low profitability 'up-stream' sectors of the economy (steel, *etc.*); and the re-direction of foreign investment into 'downstream' non-oil economic activities, which included support of 'partnership' ventures between multinational and peripheral capitalists.

The popular and redistributionist phase of the Pérez government was of limited duration and terminated in favour of an economic policy that emphasised notions of 'efficiency', increased production and capitalist entrepreneurship. The state increasingly performed as a redistributive organ of this rising entrepreneurial bourgeoisie who preferred to recycle the wealth into 'services', imports, commerce, real estate, and liquid bank deposits, rather than undertake investments in long-term,

---

This article was first printed in *Third World Quarterly* 5, no. 1 (January 1983), pp. 7–27. Reprinted with permission.

large-scale productive enterprise. In addition to financing a capitalist class that lacked a commitment to dynamic industrial growth, state petroleum income funded an ever-expanding and unproductive state sector which rapidly became the focal point of widespread corruption in society. In large part, corruption resulted from the close ties between the national bourgeoisie and the state, a relationship that led to the massive allocation of resources toward private capital accumulation and profitmaking.[1]

The Social Christian Party (COPEI) administration of Luis Herrera Campins (1979 to present) outlined an economic strategy that was intended to reinvigorate this statist development 'model'. In practice, however, it diverged little from that of the Pérez period. The most striking features of the prior years have persisted throughout Herrera's tenure in office: low and declining rates of overall economic growth; stagnant industrial growth and agricultural production; massive capital losses in the state industrial sector; the continued failure of the entrepreneurial strategy to deal adequately with the major social and economic problems (inflation, employment, prices, welfare, housing, etc.); deepening financial dependence on external (banking) sources; and virtually no growth in secondary (non-oil) exports to provide the basis for a more diversified economy.

The continuing dependence on petrodollar financing and the increasing role of the state have been the two most prominent features of the national capitalist development strategy promoted by successive Venezuelan governments since the early 1970s. Annual revenues from oil exports averaged around 95 per cent of total export earnings.[2] While the contribution of petroleum revenues to the Gross National Product (GNP) fell from nearly 40 per cent in 1974 to 21.5 per cent in 1978, and while the percentage of total government income derived from petroleum sales dropped from 71.6 per cent in 1976 to 49.6 per cent in 1978, oil income continued to sustain the major role of the state in the economic development programme.[3] To the degree that central, state and municipal government expenditures still absorb more than 50 per cent of total national income, the crucial importance of petrodollar earnings remains undiminished.[4] The dramatic upsurge in the value of Venezuela's oil exports from approximately $8.6 billion in 1978 to around $18.0 billion in 1980 merely served to emphasise this state of affairs.[5]

To appreciate how extensive the role of the Venezuelan state has been in shaping the new development project, one need only observe that by mid-1977 it accounted for 60 per cent of the country's GNP.[6] The authoritative *Business Latin America* estimated that by that year's end (given the realisation of projected investment plans) the state would be responsible for 72 per cent of capital formation as compared with 33 per cent during the early 1970s.[7] The predominant role of the state in the economy is reflected by the fact that six of the ten largest enterprises are state-owned, while the nationalised petroleum industry is 17 times larger than the second biggest economic enterprise (the state-owned public works company). A 1980 study of the one hundred key financial institutions in the Venezuelan economy concluded that the state's superiority in terms of total assets has allowed it to wield a primary role in shaping and directing the activities of the sector as a whole.[8]

### Acción Democrática: The Pattern of Social and Economic Development

Venezuelan economic growth between 1974 and 1978 was characterised by an uneven performance on the part of the priority sectors, a failure to reach annual projected growth goals and a generally low overall economic rate of growth. The dynamic 'growth' sectors were not industry or agriculture but construction and the basically non-productive tertiary or service sector.[9] During 1976, for example, pressures created by speculative capitalist class investments and uncontrolled increases in property values resulted in a construction boom that produced a growth rate of more than 3 per cent above the desired government goal.[10] By contrast, the growth rate in manufacturing declined from a high of 12 per cent in 1976 to 3.5 per cent in 1977, rising slightly to 4.4 per cent in 1978.[11] In agriculture, the landlord's footdragging had even more disastrous consequences. The rural sector under Pérez experienced stagnant or low overall rates of growth, minimal efforts at agrarian reform, almost non-existent increases in per capita food production, a growing dependence on the import of basic foodstuffs, and a state funding policy that benefited an agro-entrpreneurial class at the expense of debt-burdened small farmers who owned their own properties. The agricultural sector's average annual contribution to the Gross Domestic Product (GDP) declined from 7.0 per cent between 1961 and 1970 to 6.6 per cent between 1971 and 1975 to 6.1 per cent between 1976 and 1980.[12]

In the area of foreign trade, the administration goal of a rapid expansion of non-petroleum exports failed to materialise. By December 1977, non-traditional exports did not exceed 2 per cent of the volume of total exports.[13] Expectations that export income would remain substantially in excess of import costs were dramatically undermined by the 'unchecked appetitite' of the Venezuelan bourgeoisie, so much so that the huge amounts of foreign exchange accumulated through oil sales could not prevent the beginnings in 1977 of a serious external sector deficits problem.[14]

The quadrupling of oil price increases in 1974 generated 'a veritable explosion' in the quantity and value of Venezuelan imports.[15] Between 1974 and 1978, the value of import purchases almost tripled from $3.9 billion to $11.2 billion.[16] During this same period, the ratio of imports to GDP rose from 17 per cent to 37 per cent while the ratio of exports to GDP dropped sharply from 44.7 per cent to 25.6 per cent.[17] These

Table 10.1    Venezuela: Announced Euro-currency Credits and Foreign and International
Bond Issues ($ billion approx.)

|         | 1973 | 1974 | 1975 | 1976 | 1977 | 1978 |
|---------|------|------|------|------|------|------|
| Credits | 0.1  | 0.1  | 0.2  | 0.1  | 1.7  | 2.1  |
| Bonds   | negl.| negl.| —    | —    | 0.4  | 0.7  |

parallel trends—booming imports and stagnating exports—caused a
pronounced decline in the trade account surplus from $7.2 billion in
1974 to $3.5 billion in 1975 to $2.1 billion in 1976.[18] By 1978, both
the trade and current accounts were in deficit to the tune of $1.8 billion
and $5.4 billion respectively.[9] The last year of Pérez's rule witnessed
a decline of 21 per cent in Venezuela's foreign reserves.[20] The institution
of a government ban on the purchase of a substantial number of luxury
goods, vehicles and machinery, and the application of quotas on other
consumer items failed to reverse significantly the decline due to the
massive capital goods-technology-raw materials demands generated by
the development programme. Only major external financial borrowings
by the state and its various agencies prevented trade and current account
deficits of even greater magnitude.[21]

Table 10.1 shows the growing dependence of the Fifth National Plan
(1976–80) on foreign financing to sustain the industrial effort.[22] While
the total public debt increased by more than 50 per cent under Pérez,
foreign capital borrowings in the international capitalist money markets
exceeding $6 billion added to an external sector debt that almost
quadrupled during the 1974–8 period.[23]

### The Pérez State in Industry and Agriculture

In 1974, the new administration created the Fondo de Inversiones de
Venezuela or Venezuelan Investment Fund (FIV) to adminster and
oversee the expenditures of surplus oil revenues for an ambitious
programme of industrial development. During its first three years of
existence, the FIV was allocated some $23 billion or almost 20 per
cent of total government revenues. The implementation of the industrial
programme, however, was accompanied by enormous waste, corruption,
cost overruns and financial mismanagement that resulted in the growth
of a serious public debt problem despite the multibillion annual oil
revenues.[24] Between 1974 and 1975, the public (internal and external)
debt almost doubled, while debt service as a percentage of the total
budget increased from 6 per cent in 1975 to 15 per cent in 1977.[25]
During 1976, the government negotiated Eurocurrency credits that
exceeded $1 billion primarily 'to refinance the short-term debts of the
autonomous public agencies.'[26]

Table 10.2    Venezuela: Indices of Per Capita Food Production (1969–71 = 100)

| 1971 | 1972 | 1973 | 1974 | 1975 | 1976 | 1977 | 1978 |
|------|------|------|------|------|------|------|------|
| 100  | 97   | 99   | 103  | 109  | 103  | 116  | 116  |

Against this background, the Venezuelan auditor-general's 1976 annual report was notable for its harsh criticism of the planning and budgetary policies of the government ministries. The report further concluded that the performance of the autonomous institutes and state companies in the area of finance, administration and organisation were at least as disappointing if not more so. The 16 state companies, with a combined operating budget more than double that of the government ministries, were principally taken to task over the absence of satisfactory accounting controls and their inadequate procedures for the dispersal of funds. The Corporación Venezolana de Fomento (CVF), for example, completed only 42 per cent of the credit operations budgeted for it, while the FIV paid out barely more than one-third of capital allocations approved for the state enterprises.[27] During 1977, approximately 40 per cent of all state enterprises operated at a financial loss and had to be subsidised by major contributions from the FIV and the Central Bank. The aggregate surplus of the public companies declined by 20 per cent compared with 1976, and the resultant surplus was largely a function of profitable FIV investments at home and abroad, and a Central Bank Surplus of Bolivars (Bs) 1.5 billion.[28] The multi-million dollars in accumulated losses sustained by the state enterprises centred around the $52 billion integrated industrial complex in Ciudad Guayana. Its operations were characterised by 'chronic delays in some cases a complete absence of long-range financial planning'. In addition, it negotiated a number of highly disadvantageous construction and technology contracts with foreign companies.[29]

Between 1974 and 1978, government expenditures in the agricultural sector exceeded $5 billion in the context of the Fifth National Plan which envisaged a 9 per cent annual growth rate in the rural economy. In real terms, however, the sector grew at an annual average rate of only 4.7 per cent.[30] Furthermore, the annual average contribution of agriculture to the GDP declined from 6.6 per cent in the 1971–5 period to approximately 5.9 per cent in the 1976–8 period.[31] In the area of per capita food production, the failure of the Pérez agrarian reform was even more pronounced, as shown in Table 10.2.[32]

The 'explosion' of food imports underscored the persistence of stagnation in the agricultural sector. Although the amount of land under cultivation increased during 1974 and 1975, the failure to engage in meaningful agrarian reform and the decline in yields culminated in a contraction in the real value of agricultural production (1.8 per cent) for the first time in decades. The value of total food imports increased from Bs.2,021 million in 1973 to Bs.3,500 million in 1976, excluding the vast illegal smuggling of cattle, coffee, *etc.* across the Colombian border into Venezuela. Between 1974 and 1976, imported foodstuffs increased from 11 per cent to approximately 20 per cent of total food requirements. Instead of movement toward greater self-sufficiency in food production, Venezuela imported 20 per cent of beef consumption, 24 per cent of milk consumption, 49 per cent of maize and 68 per cent of sorghum needs, and 100 per cent of wheat and soya needs in 1976. Emergency food shortages in early 1977 forced the government to lift restrictions on the importation of a number of basic food products in May for a provisional three-month period. For the remainder of the year, however, the whole country 'was plagued by continual shortages of items such as rice, sugar, milk and coffee . . .'. More alarming still, the value of food imports had increased tenfold in little over a decade.[33]

The divergence between the government's 'populist' rhetoric and public practice was never more evident than in relation to its stated goal of eliminating debts accumulated by the small property-holding agricultural class who were singled out to be the major beneficiaries of the state's financial investments in the countryside. The Agricultural Investment Fund channelled the bulk of its loans and grants to the politically influential, high-capitalised, large-scale commercial cattle ranchers. The result was a situation in which the small-farming class continued to labour under the weight of financial debts with minimal relief in sight. For their part, the agro-entrepreneurial recipients of state funds used part of their 'windfall' to pay off accumulated debts, and even diverted some of these monies into more profitable non-agricultural investments or into private overseas bank accounts.[34]

## The 'Development' State: Private Accumulation over Socioeconomic Redistribution

The Venezuelan economy under Pérez was characterised by uneven industrial growth, agricultural stagnation and the enormous expansion of the service sector. These features were paralleled by a significant inflation problem and a steady rise in the cost of living (especially in the urban centres outside Caracas), a fall in the value of real wages and salaries, large-scale unemployment and underemployment, periodic food shortages, a decline in the levels of social welfare, and the growth of urban slums.

Between 1974 and 1977, the cost of living index indicated an average annual increase of 15 per cent to 18 per cent, while the growth rate of real wages and salaries declined from 17.8 per cent to 9.3 per cent.[35] According to a United Nations study prepared in 1977, the cost of living index in the principal interior cities of Ciudad Guayana, Mérida, Maracaibo, Valencia and Puerto La Cruz-Barcelona increased at a greater rate than was recorded in the capital city of Caracas.[36] The modest efforts of the Pérez government to implement an anti-inflation strategy were vigorously and, in large part, successfully opposed by a private sector intent on maximising profits. In July 1977, the regime enacted a 'package' of austerity legislation designed to grapple with the primary causes of the inflationary problem—a booming property market and a spiralling money supply. Controls were placed on bank liquidity, available lines of credit were reduced, measures were instituted to curb real estate speculation, administrative costs were pared, and price controls were imposed on a number of goods and services. The predictably hostile response from the business community in general and the Venezuelan Federation of Chambers of Commerce and Industry (FEDECAMARAS), especially over the issue of price controls, led Pérez to modify those actions taken in regard to real estate financing and sales.[37] Private sector opposition also manifested itself in the form of capital flight which, combined with the high level of imports, reduced Venezuela's international reserves by nearly $1.2 billion during August and September 1977 alone.[38] The government, in an effort to mollify this internal opposition, ordered the Central Bank to ease the restrictions on liquidity and thereby provide greater local capitalist class access to the lines of financial credit.[39] During the final months of the Pérez presidency, the Central Bank lifted interest rates in an attempt to stem the still substantial outflow of private capital enticed by higher investment yields abroad, especially in the United States.[40]

The government also bowed to private sector opposition to its proposed anti-inflation tax reform programme during late 1977 and the first half of 1978.[41] Although the average per capita tax payment was a mere $82, and taking into account the fact that the rate did not reach 45 per cent on taxable income below $1.8 million, the FEDECAMARAS (as well as Acción Democrática and the Social Christian Party) rejected any idea for fighting inflation through changes in income-tax rate structure.[42] Four of the eight bills introduced into the Congress to change the fiscal tax system were eventually dropped while the others were drastically weakened in comparison with their original aims. The emasculation of these latter bills was the direct outcome of Pérez's decision to establish a tripartite commission composed of government, business and labour representatives for the express purpose of diluting the envisaged impact of the tax legislation. 'Initial fears,' commented one economic analyst, 'that the reform was a purely fiscal measure aimed at soaking the relatively undertaxed Venezuelans have now abated . . .'[43]

The extent of improvement in the areas of health services, public housing and social services under Pérez was minimal. Between 1974 and 1977, incremental gains were registered in the infant mortality rate per thousand which declined from 45.7 to 42.0 and in the number of hospital beds which rose from 36,207 to 41,967.[44] Despite a 60 per cent increase in construction activity during the same period, the growth in new low-cost public housing was far outstripped by the demand for such dwellings. What the building boom did produce, however, was a proliferation of 'modern shopping arcades crammed with imported luxuries, glass office towers and expensive apartment buildings [which were] sprouting all over Caracas.'[45] The Venezuelan bourgeoisie also invested heavily in luxury dwellings in the United States, channelling an estimated $2.3 billion in 1977, for example, into the purchase of weekend houses and condominiums in southern Florida.[46] Meanwhile, even conservative estimates agreed that at least 25 per cent of the population lived in substandard housing. The large urban centres also experienced a decline in public services, water and electricity shortages, inadequate educational facilities, serious and persistent unemployment, and a notable contraction in available state-funded health facilities.

The low purchasing power of the mass of the Venezuelan population contributed to the inability of the economy to absorb the petrodollar wealth. Instead, the government acted to channel the surplus financial resources abroad in the form of interest-bearing loans and investments which would also provide increased trade-investment opportunities for the private bureaucratic bourgeoisie and establish raw materials enterprises to 'feed into' the state industrial experiment. At the end of 1978, approximately 40 per cent of the FIV's monies were invested in money market instruments 'denominated primarily in US dollars', foreign medium- and long-term securities, and government loans abroad while just over 60 per cent was allocated to national projects.[47]

## The Herrera Development Strategy: Continuity over Change

The transition from Pérez to Herrera did not create the basis for the emergence of a dynamic growth oriented agro-industrial strategy. The Herrera administration has presided over a stagnant economy, little or no growth in the non-oil economy, sustained losses in the state industrial sector, high-level import expenditures, massive increases in the public and foreign debt, rising inflation, and declining living standards for the bulk of the population. The rate of growth in GDP, which had dropped from 8.4 per cent in 1976 to 6.8 per cent in 1977 to 3.2 per cent in 1978, expanded by an infinitesimal 0.7 per cent in 1979. All the strategic non-oil sectors—manufacturing, agriculture, construction, motor vehicles, textiles, capital goods—experienced declining rates of growth during Herrera's first year as President compared with the last year of the Pérez government.[48] This state of affairs worsened in 1980 when a negative GDP growth rate of −1.2 per cent was recorded, improving only marginally to 0.3 per cent in 1981.[49] These were the lowest growth rates in decades and indicated the extent to which the economic recession had taken root within the oil-rich society. Finally, in August 1982, a report prepared by the American Embassy in Caracas stated that 'Venezuela seems headed for its fourth consecutive year of little or no growth in the national economy.'[50] In the external sector, imports remained at, and even exceeded, the high levels attained during the

Pérez period. Following a decline in the total value of import purchases from $11.2 billion in 1978 to $10.8 billion in 1979, with a marginal rise to $10.9 billion in 1980, the cost jumped to $12.4 billion in 1981— and is expected to at least equal, if not surpass, this total during 1982.[51] Initially, Herrera proposed a threefold shift in the thrust of the overall economic programme: 'stabilisation' of the industrial development enterprise through a slow-down of state investments in steel, aluminium, hydroelectric and other operations; a general contraction in public sector spending as the primary means of controlling inflation; and increased 'flexibility' for private (national and foreign) capital participation in the development plan. In late 1979, to assuage growing private capitalist class 'unease' over the operational aspects of the 'new economic policy,' the new administration began to dismantle the system of price controls instituted by the previous regime. Approximately 200 products were no longer subject to price regulation, while an additional 60 or more basic products were now 'flexibly' regulated such that their prices were no longer 'frozen'. Tariffs on a large number of imported household goods were reduced by an average of 50 per cent of existing levels, and import prohibitions and licensing restrictions were removed from other products.[52] This concerted effort to accommodate capitalist class interests extended to a decision to oppose legislation before Congress favouring across-the-board wage increases. The government's threatened use of its veto power in this regard was withdrawn in November only under the pressure of major working-class demonstrations in Caracas and the other industrial cities organized under the aegis of the Confederación de Trabajadores de Venezuela (CTV).[53]

With the promulgation of the Sixth National Plan (1981–6) in mid-1980, state-private sector relations began to experience renewed strains. The development strategy outlined in the Plan implied a shift away from the economic 'deceleration' rhetoric of the immediate past. Gross fixed investment under the Plan was projected to exceed the amount absorbed during the 'expansionist' Pérez years. While this new growth strategy prefigured a likely boom period for foreign suppliers of equipment in the Venezuelan market, local capitalist class opposition preferred to focus on what it viewed as the Plan's limited support of 'national' industry and particularly Herrera's proposed greater allocation of financial resources for use in social programmes (housing, education, public services, etc.).[54] In August 1980, the FEDECAMARAS issued a major policy position in which it juxtaposed an indiscriminate and extensive state involvement in the economy against alternate state actions that could 'positively direct the country. . . .'[55] High economic growth rates, the position paper argued, could only be attained if the administration was reorganised and streamlined, if further reductions in state spending were put into effect, and if the price decontrol process was accelerated. At the same time, while fundamentally sympathetic to the use of import duties as a useful price-regulating mechanism, the document still emphasised the importance of the state in providing the necessary tariff protection for infant domestic industries until they had evolved a capacity to compete within a 'free-market' context. Therefore, the administration decision to loosen the state protectionist programme was opposed by 'a powerful element within the business organisation [that] still expects government protection from cheaper imports.'[56] The FEDECAMARAS statement generally sought to differentiate between state participation in the economy that directly benefited specific sectors of local capital and state initiatives that contracted the possibilities for private accumulation and exploitation. In December 1980 Herrera announced that sixty state-owned companies would be sold off to private shareholders. This decision was interpreted within the local business community as signalling Herrera's concern 'that the time has come to mend some fences with the private sector'.[57]

Throughout 1981 and the first half of 1982, nonetheless, local capitalists remained at odds over specific government actions, such as its pricing policies, and were not predisposed to make large-scale productive investments in the domestic economy.[58] Instead, they channelled their capital resources into more profitable ventures abroad, the preferred destination being foreign banking institutions. The significant interest rate differentials between American and Venezuelan money markets generated a flight of capital which reached an estimated $100 million per day during June to September 1981.[59] In September, the Central Bank was forced to decontrol local interest rates in an effort to stem this haemorrhage of funds which had begun to make an impact on the country's foreign reserves and even threaten the stability of the bolivar. During 1981, private capital flows out of Venezuela exceeded inflows by $2.3 billion, approximately double that of the previous twelve-month period.[60] Whatever initial success this and subsequent government actions to adjust interest rates may have achieved, the 'leakage' of capital was once again in full swing by early 1982. In March, *Business Latin America* reported that an estimated $133 million was being sent abroad on a daily basis.[61]

Depite Herrera's talk of lowering state expenditures in the industrial sector, the latter continued to receive priority treatment in comparison with the rural economy. The generally meagre allocation of financial resources to agriculture in association with the lack of technical and managerial expertise, the absence of proper coordination and planning, labour shortages and the endemic problem of misallocation of funds, virtually ensured a widening of the gap between available food supplies and Venezuela's domestic requirements.[62] Between 1975 and 1979, net agricultural investments in constant 1968 prices declined from approximately Bs.1.3 billion to Bs.562 million while the importation of foodstuffs and live animals skyrocketed from 1,695,000 tons to 3,079,000 tons.[63] The value of food imports, which continued to account for 40 to 50 per cent of domestic consumption increased from $1.1 billion in 1979 to $1.7 billion in 1981.[64] Although food self-sufficiency is a major target of the Sixth National Plan, policymakers concede that the trend in food imports will persist through the mid-1980s. Under Herrera, the increase in per capita food production has been negligible or non-existent. Taking 1969–71 as the base period of 100, there was a marginal increase from 116 in 1978 to 119 in 1979, only to be followed by a return to the 1978 level in 1980.[65] According to a statement issued by the private sector organisation FEDEAGRO in early 1981, there was also a process under way of shrinkage both in sown areas and yields in the agricultural sector.[66] Between 1980 and 1981, the growth rate in agricultural production dropped from 4.2 per cent to 2.8 per cent— indicative of the overall stagnation in the rural sector during the era of state capitalist development.[67]

In his inaugural speech, Herrera called Venezuela 'a mortgaged country' and promised to restructure the foreign debt during his period in office.[68] By the end of 1981, however, the country's short-term debt had risen from $7.2 billion to $14 billion while the long-term debt had increased from $12 billion to $15 billion.[69] The administrative and financial problems that continued to bedevil the major industrial complex in Ciudad Guayana (operating difficulties, poor management, project delays, escalating costs, etc.) was a direct contributor to this rising external indebtedness.[70] The Guayana steel corporation, Sidor, for instance, lost an estimated $232 million in 1980 and probably well in excess of that amount during 1981.[71]

Unlike the cases of Brazil and Peru, however, the international financial community did not see fit to elevate the Venezuelan debt to an issue of pressing importance. As one American banker who participated in an $850 million syndicated loan to the state agencies in December succinctly put it, Venezuela's oil wealth still made it 'the best place to lend your money in Latin America. . . '[72] Although concern was expressed over the failure of a number of the state corporations to meet interest payments on short-term loans at the appropriate time, this did not dissuade a consortium of European and American banks in June 1980 from providing a $1.2 billion loan to refinance a large portion of the foreign debt.[73] The government's decision to utilise the resources of the private Banco de las Trabajadores de Venezuela to repay some of the approximately $2 billion in accumulated debts of the state sector assuaged whatever doubts may have existed regarding the country's 'international creditworthiness'. In August 1980, some 85 Western banks agreed to extend a further $1.8 billion Eurocredit to Venezuela at very favourable rates.[74] During 1979 and 1980, the Herrera government negotiated more than $6 billion in new Eurocurrency credits—which represented a substantial deepening of Venezuela's foreign financial dependence when compared with the $2.1 billion obtained during Pérez's last year in office.[75]

The decline in foreign borrowings since 1981 might well be succeeded by a new series of interventions into the international money markets in the immediate future.[76] The revised version of the Sixth National Plan issued in September 1981 was premissed on an annual average petrodollar income of more than $20 billion, notwithstanding the emergence of a world oil glut and the failure of OPEC to maintain its production quota system intact. As a result of these industry developments, however, Venezuela's 1982 petroleum shortfall could amount in value to more than $4 billion.[77] The state oil company did not make a profit in 1982 for the first time since its founding in 1976, and has been forced to draw on its investment reserve which underpins the country's international credit standing—thereby raising the spectre of lowered global confidence in the strength of the Venezuelan currency.[78] This contraction in oil earnings has had significant repercussions in the external sector where the balance of payments surplus on current account of $3.9 billion in 1981 is projected to shift to a $2 billion deficit by the end of 1982.[79] In addition, the International Monetary Fund estimates that the trade surplus is likely to decline from $7.7 billion in 1981 to only $1.5 billion in 1982.[80]

The oil-rich Venezuelan state under Herrera's leadership has thus far failed to perform as a meaningful mechanism for social and economic redistribution. The decontrol of prices in 1979 fuelled an inflation rate of more than 22 per cent which undermined the modest wage and salary gains passed by Congress during the latter part of that year.[81] According to authoritative Venezuelan sources, the inflation rate in 1980 rose to 30 per cent and climbed again in 1981 reaching 32 per cent by the year's end.[82] Furthermore, these figures underestimated the disproportionate impact of this spiralling upsurge in the cost of living borne by the working class, because the main burden of the price increases fell on such basic consumer items as food, clothing and other household goods. In the public works and social welfare areas, the government's policies had 'little or no impact' in ameliorating existing conditions.[83] Meanwhile, unemployment among the urban work force remained at well above 20 per cent as industry proved itself manifestly incapable of absorbing the growing numbers of people leaving the countryside in search of jobs and economic security.[84] The crisis in housing is particularly acute, with the average annual number of new units between 1976 and 1980 accounting for only half of the government's announced target.[85] While the inflation rate did fall during 1982 this was largely achieved through the application of tight monetary controls and as a result of the absence of significant all-round economic growth.[86]

### The Role of Foreign Investment under Pérez and Herrera

The Pérez government sought to maintain an important role for foreign investment in the new development scheme both independently of, and in association with, national capital. In redefining the terms of overseas capital participation in the Venezuelan economy, new concessions co-existed with new constraints as external investors were encouraged to relocate into the non-enclave, non-extractive 'downstream' sectors of the economy. During 1976 and 1977, however, the largely state-financed heavy industry (petrochemicals, steel, aluminium, *etc.*), manufacturing and construction sectors experienced a period of stagnation. In an effort to restore the 1974–5 'dynamism' of these sectors so critical to the overall industrial development programme the regime '[began] softening its attitude towards foreign investment. . .'[87]

The gradual unravelling of existing controls on foreign investment was most immediately noticeable with regard to the construction industry. In July 1977, the government declared that, henceforth, foreign capital located in this sector would be confined to investment in 'social interest' housing. In September, the regulation was substantially diluted 'to allow investments intended for the construction or purchase of offices outside Caracas and Maracaibo, industrial buildings that met the requirements of official decentralisation policies, shopping centres and medical, tourist and educational facilities.'[88]

Another indication of this shifting government attitude on foreign investment was the decision to forego its intention to assume full ownership of the Zulia steel complex in favour of allocating a 49 per cent minority share to multinational capital on the basis of competitive bidding.[89]

The action of Pérez in shelving the foreign investment law (Decree No 52) enacted in 1974 was interpreted by US corporate investors in Venezuela as indicating the appearance of a more 'pragmatic' attitude on the part of a regime that was highly dependent on imported technology for its industrial development programme. These capitalists also interpreted this government decision as part of its growing disposition to 'fall into line' with the general Andean Pact trend toward devolution of foreign investment controls. The new proposed foreign investment law 'provide[d] for sweeping exemptions from fade-out regulations and also extend[ed] the deadline for formalising divestment intentions for marketing firms. . . '[90] The legislation (Decree No 2442) passed through Congress and was promulgated during October–November 1977. Under what *Business Latin America* called the government's 'definitive position on foreign investment'[91], dividend remittances and reinvestment ceilings were raised and national companies (at least 80 per cent locally-owned) were allowed to revert to mixed status (52 per cent to 80 per cent locally-owned) through capital increases.[92]

This further unravelling of 'constraints' on foreign capital generated a notable, if not dramatic, growth in new authorised direct overseas investment: from $50.6 milion in 1976 to $156.6 million in 1977 to $242 million in 1978.[93] American multinationals continued to account for almost 60 per cent of all foreign investments, concentrated primarily in the financial, insurance and manufacturing sectors of the economy.[94] While US direct investment in Venezuela grew at one of the lowest rates in the region during 1977 and 1978 (25.9 per cent and 15.1 per cent respectively), the rate of return on investments (15.1 per cent and 17.4 per cent respectively) was the second highest in Latin America.[95]

The inflow of foreign capital (including external credits) into Venezuela rose by 20 per cent in 1978. Of the 91 new capital projects initiated during this twelve-month period, 25 represented 'national companies', 54 were joint ventures, and 10 were foreign companies. This emphasis on mixed ventures and government projects, and the use of new investments to increase capital in existing companies (stemming from a change in the Andean Pact legislation which raised the automatic reinvestment of profits level from 5 per cent to 7 per cent), was indicative of a still cautious attitude on the part of foreign investors in their desire for increased 'clarification' of the investment 'rules of the game'.[96] During 1978, nonetheless, a number of companies began to negotiate some highly favourable contracts with the Pérez government including, in some cases, guarantees against losses. The Spanish-based corporation, Astilleros Españoles, for example, was offered just such a guarantee to build a Bs.2.8 billion shipyard. This particular arrangement apparently committed the incoming Herrera administration to providing an annual subsidy of Bs.300 million until completion of the project.[97]

The new COPEI government confronted a multinational business community that was wary of large-scale financial commitments because of what it described as the 'arbitrary interpretations' of existing regulations that occurred under Pérez.[98] Herrera's pro-foreign investment orientation and his price decontrol policies failed to erase completely foreign capital's concern over what it viewed as the regime's 'economic vagueness' and its ability, or inclination, adequately to 'discipline' the labour force in the interests of capital accumulation and expansion.[99] Direct registered foreign investment in Venezuela grew by only $83 million in 1979, most ot it reinvestments in on-going operations.[100] At the same time, a *Business Latin America* survey of foreign companies in mid-1979 found that most expected to exceed their 1978 profit levels by more than 10 per cent.[101] Such gains, however, served to generate increased multinational pressures on the regime to provide new concessions and intensify existing rates of labour exploitation: 'The most frequent complaints concern the Herrera administration's confusing economic policy, the high costs of doing business in Venezuela and a lack of incentive for new investment.'[102]

In early 1980, as part of a general effort to accommodate foreign investor concerns, Herrera appointed a businessman-economist, Alfredo Gonzalez Amare, as the acting director of the office of the Superintendent of Foreign Investment (SIEX). In one of his first post-appointment interviews, Gonzalez defined the new approach: 'We have an open policy to foreign investment . . . We're recognising our need for foreign capital and technology, our need to make the Venezuelan economy more efficient.'[103] The *Journal of Commerce* reported that, during his first four months as acting director, Gonzalez 'has been making the rounds of embassies and chambers of commerce, trying to encourage investment.'[104] Increasingly, SIEX was being divorced from its original regulatory function to serve, first and foremost, as a promoter of foreign capital participation in the national economy. Gonzalez described multinational investment as 'a strategic element' in the forthcoming Sixth National Plan.[105]

Herrera's efforts to promote foreign capital accumulation were not confined to SIEX but also included the elimination of price controls on 200 products,[106] the reduction of import restrictions on some additional products, the termination of discriminatory rates against foreign companies, and the institution of a more flexible interest-rate structure. These multiple concessions served to encourage an 11 per cent increase in direct foreign investment in the first half of 1980 compared with the same time period in 1979.[107] Not content, however, the multinationals and their representatives called for a further dismantling of investment controls: '. . . the drug, auto, rubber and some foodstuffs industries are still squeezed by price controls, a number of products are still subject to stiff import duties and investors remain wary of Venezuela.'[108] In another conciliatory gesture, the Finance Ministry announced in September 1980 that foreign enterprises would be allowed to reinvest in excess of the Andean Pact limit of 7 per cent of registered capital 'if they show that the investment will increase economic activity in priority areas.'[109]

The initial response of American investors to this change in the 7 per cent investment ceiling was favourable although they did not view it as representing 'a significant shift in the country's generally restrictive foreign investment policy.'[110] But, within the new guidelines, the companies were able to expand their productive capacities, use a greater capital base to calculate their profit remittance ceilings 'and, in effect, decrease the overall amount of taxable profits.'[111] Almost immediately following the SIEX announcement regarding the investment ceiling modification, requests for new investments totalling some Bs.300 million were received. A foreign investment consultant in Caracas assessed the likely medium-term consequences of this government measure: '[It] will definitely stimulate foreign investment. A number of reinvestment projects that had been held back are now going through because firms will not have to pay 20 per cent tax on those funds.'[112] In fact, most of the foreign investment that entered the country during 1981 went into expenditures, or to offset losses, in existing operations.[113] The fall in oil income beginning in 1981 has led to a further erosion of the government's foreign investment constraints. According to Gonzalez Amare of SIEX, 'practically all the projects we get' during 1982 will be authorised irrespective of whether they dovetail with the goals of the Sixth National Plan. 'All areas', he declared, 'have priority billing.'[114] While the administration continues to voice support for the Andean Pact foreign investment code (Decision 24), officials admit that investment legislation is being applied 'as loosely as possible.'[115]

The American economic presence has remained the single most important external factor in the Venezuelan economy despite the nationalization of the US-owned iron ore and oil interests during the early Pérez period. This negotiated transfer of ownership of these extractive industries to the Venezuelan state accounted for a decline in total US direct investment from $1.9 billion in 1975 to $1.5 billion in 1977. Thereafter, American investments experienced a slow but steady growth throughout the local economy, reaching approximately $2.2 billion by the end of 1981. The more diversified US capital 'stake' is reflected in the fact that whereas manufacturing only accounted for $668 million of total US direct investment in 1975, by 1981 this figure had more than doubled to around $1.2 billion. This same period also witnessed a three-fold increase in the value of US investments in the financial-insurance-real estate sector of the Venezuelan economy.[116]

While American capital inflows renewed their upward trend following the extractive sector nationalisations of the mid-1970s, it was trade and commerce that stood out as the single most important area of profit-making for those fractions of the US capitalist class involved in the Venezuelan economy. Despite low growth rates, the total value of US exports to Venezuela increased from $2.2 billion in 1975 to $3.7 billion in 1978. Under Herrera, Venezuela became an even more lucrative market as the value of imported US goods and services rose from $3.9 billion in 1979 to $4.6 billion in 1980 to $5.4 billion in 1981.[117] Between 1980 and 1981, the US share of the import market rose from 48 per cent to round 50 per cent, and is expected to climb even further by the end of 1982 as a result of new large-scale government capital investments in petroleum and industry, the continuing demand for agriculture commodities and projected improvements in the electric, transportation and telecommunications sectors. In February 1982, the American Embassy in Caracas prepared an analysis of the Venezuelan economy which described the country's market as 'one of the world's most attractive targets for US exporters.'[118]

## Conclusion

The state in the periphery, as the Venezuelan experience illustrates, plays a major role in all aspects of economic development. The increasing willingness of the peripheral state to nationalise basic resources and to promote economic growth, however, requires that one look beyond the state apparatus to identify the social configuration that controls the state and benefits from its policies. The principal beneficiaries of state ownership have been the big manufacturers, large commercial farmers and ranchers, bankers, construction contractors and real estate interests and the large export-importers who have received the bulk of investment funds and credits. Moreover 'state ownership' and nationalisation in some areas is perfectly compatible with the promotion of foreign capital in other areas. In word, state ownership serves as a mechanism for redistributing economic surplus among segments of the national and foreign bourgeoisie, increasing their profit opportunities but not necessarily expanding the productive forces in either industry or agriculture.

The growing gap between expanding public ownership and declining public services is explained by the lack of any democratic control from below over the allocation and direction of surplus accumulated in the public sector. Likewise, the gap between the growing allocation of investment funds toward industry and agriculture and the limited growth thus far experienced is explained by the channelling of funds into non-productive areas, a result of the incapacity (or unwillingness) of the state to supervise its credit and investment policies. Behind the statist facade, there is a *laissez-faire* reality in which private capital determines the purposes and ultimate distribution of state accumulation resources—independently of government plans and electoral promises. The state-owned firms, rather than ameliorating class and regional differences, have reflected and reinforced them. Moreover, within the publicly-owned firms, the organisational structure has merely reproduced the same income, status and power relations that are present in the private sector. It appears that the horizontal links between the hierarchies of both the private and public enterprise are stronger than the vertical links within each type. It is not surprising then that the growth of state enterprise has neither changed the class basis of society nor the class cleavages which are manifest throughout the society. State ownership and growth has served as a means of increasing employment opportunities for the employee and professional groups (*petite bourgeoisie*). It has also served to provide opportunities for upper-echelon bureaucrats to accumulate private wealth and contacts with the private sector, thus facilitating the conversion of wealth and position into capital and property.

Within the capitalist class, the most powerful tendencies seem to be located among the export-import segments and the financial, real estate and construction interests which accounts for the hypergrowth of luxury imports and buildings, resulting in spiralling commercial profits and rent income at the expense of industry and agriculture. The growing imbalances in trade deficits and budgets, the growing interest payments and foreign loans, reflect the incapacity of the state to base itself on an entrepreneurial class with a vocation toward increasing the productive forces. Rather, the powers situated to benefit from the expanding state apparatus are largely *rentier* and commerical groups. While the petro-dollars have papered over the cleavages in Venezuelan society, it is clear that neither oil wealth nor state ownership have laid the basis for a more equitable and productive society. In addition, the vaunted economic independence which the oil wealth was supposed to have bestowed has turned into a chimera; Venezuela has now become as dependent on finance capital as it was earlier on investment capital.

## Notes

1. For a detailed analysis of the origins of statist-bureaucratic rule in Venezuela and the first half of the Pérez presidency, see James Petras, Morris Morley, and Steven Smith, *The Nationalisation of Venezuelan Oil*, New York: Praeger, 1977.

2. See *Bank of London & South America Review* (hereafter *BOLSA Review*), 11(6), June 1977, p 333; 'Venezuela's search for balanced development', *Latin American Economic Report* (hereafter *LAER*) 4(14), 2 April 1976, p 54; US Congress, Joint Economic Committee, Subcommittee on Energy, *Outlook on Venezuela's Petroleum Policy: a study*, 96th Congress, 2nd Session, February 1980, Washington DC: US Government Printing Office, 1980, pp 37–8, 40–41; 'Latin America: After the Oil Crises', *BOLSA Review* 13(12), December 1979, p 719.

3. US Congress, *op cit.*, pp 40–41.

4. ibid., p 40.

5. Inter-American Development Bank, *Economic and Social Progress in Latin America: 1980–81 Report* Washington, DC, 1982), Tables 1–19, p 34. See also 'Extra oil income likely to overheat Venezuelan economy', *LAER*, 8(36), 14 September 1979, p 287.

6. See 'Inflation and budget strains still limit Venezuelan growth', *LAER*, 5(32), 19 August 1977, p 126.

7. See *Business Latin America* (hereafter *BLA*) 5 October 1977, p 317.

8. See 'The rich and super-rich in Venezuela', *Latin America Weekly Report* (hereafter *LAWR*), 4 July 1980, p 10.

9. Inter-American Development Bank, *Economic and Social Progress in Latin America*: 1979 Report (Washington, DC, 1980) p 386.

10. See ibid., p 20, 'Latin America Special Report: Venezuela', Supplement to *LAER*, January 1978, p 3.

11. Inter-American Development Bank, *Economic and Social Progress in Latin America: 1980–81 Report, op. cit.*, Tables 1–12, p 25.

12. ibid., Tables 1–6, p 16.

13. Inter-American Development Bank, *Economic and Social Progress in Latin America: 1978 Report* (Washington, DC, 1979), p 409.

14. 'Focus on Venezuela: the easy life may need some tending to', *BLA*, 23 March 1977, p 96.

15. Economic Commission for Latin America, *Economic Survey of Latin America 1977*, Santiago, Chile: United Nations, 1978, p 479.

16. Inter-American Development Bank, *Economic and Social Progress in Latin America: 1980–81 Report, op. cit.*, Table 44, p 426.

17. Inter-American Development Bank, *Economic and Social Progress in Latin America: 1979 Report, op. cit.*, p 385.

18. *ibid.,* p 431.

19. ibid., pp 38–40.

20. See Joseph A Mann Jr., "Venezuela: Economic Star Dims', *New York Times*, 22 January 1979. p D4.

21. See *BOLSA Review*, 12 (8), August 1978, p 441; 'Business Outlook: Venezuela', *op. cit.*, p 318; Joseph A Mann Jr., *op cit.*, p D4.

22. Inter-American Development Bank, *Economic and Social Progress in Latin America: 1980–81 Report, op. cit.*, Tables 111–15, p 90; World Bank, *Annual Report 1979*, (Washington, DC, 1979), p 148.

23. See 'Venezuela Ends' 77 With Payments Gap', *New York Times*, 2 January 1978, pp 32–3.

24. See 'Venezuela: The changing fortunes of FIV', *Latin America Regional Report*: (hereafter *LARR: Andean Group*) 11 December 1981, p 7; David Vidal, 'Venezuela Finding That Problems Come with Oil Wealth', *New York Times*, 3 August 1978, p 8; Joseph A Mann Jr., 'Venezuela Woos Investors', *New York Times*, 15 July 1980, p D1.

25. 'Current spending soars in Venezuelan Budget', *LAER*, 6(44), 12 November 1976, pp 174, 176; 'Venezuela ready to launch foreign borrowing drive', *LAER*, 5(1), 7 January 1977, p 2.

26. 'Venezuela secures better terms for eurodollar loan', *LAER*, 5(5), 4 February 1977, p 17.

27. See 'Venezuelan audit highly critical of public spending', *LAER*, 5(20), 27 May 1977, p 79.

28. 'Venezuelan candidates aim to sell state companies', *LAER*, 6(40), 13 October 1978, p 313.

29. 'Debt and delay hit Guayana project', *LARR: Andean Group*, 3 October 1980, p 6; 'Plans for big shake-up of Venezuela's projects', *LAER*, 111(32), 17 August 1979, p 249.

30. *BOLSA Review*, 13(11), November 1979, p 688.

31. Inter-American Development Bank, *op. cit.*, Tables 1–6, p 16.

32. ibid., Tables 1–9, p 21.

33. 'Venezuela's search for balanced development', *op. cit.*, p 54; 'Spending fails to solve Venezuelan food shortages', *LAER*, 4(18a), 7 May 1979, p 71; 'Real problems of Venezuelan Agriculture still unresolved', *LAER*, 5(21), 3 June 1977, p 82; 'Latin American Special Report: Venezuela', *op. cit.*, p 10; 'Heavy rains wreak havoc with crops in Venezuela', *LAER*, 6(20), 26 May 1978, p 159; Alan Riding, 'Full Coffers But Empty Pledges Irk Venezuelans', *New York Times*, 10 December 1978, p E2.

34. See 'Venezuela's search for balanced development', *op. cit.*, p 54; 'Spending fails to solve Venezuelan food shortages', *op. cit.*, p 71; 'Real problems of Venezuelan agriculture still unresolved', *op. cit.*, p 82.

35. See 'Focus on Venezuela: The Easy Life May Need Some Tending To', *op. cit.*, p 95; *BOLSA Review*, 11(6), June 1977, p 333; 'Focus on Venezuela: numerous problems and no clear solutions', *BLA*, 22 February 1978, p 62; Economic Commission for Latin American, *op. cit.*, p 499; Everett G. Martin, 'Spending Spree PUts Venezuela in the Red After Oil Price Rise', *Wall Street Journal*, 2 May 1978, p 34.

36. Economic Commission for Latin America, *op. cit.*, p 498.

37. See 'Inflation and budget strains still limit Venezuelan growth', *op. cit.*, p 126.

38. *BOLSA Review*, 12(1), January 1978, p 39.

39. See ibid., pp 39–40; 'Venezuela relaxes financial restrictions after budget', *LAER*, 5(43), 4 November 1977, p 198; 'Venezuela eases credit in effort to stave off recession', *LAER*, 6(23) 16 June 1978, p 177.

40. See 'Venezuela lifts rates to slow flight of capital', *LAER*, 7(2), 12 January 1979, p 9.

41. See 'How Venezuela Shapes Up: operating problems and industrial outlook', *BLA*, 13 July, 1977, p 219.

42. Everett G Martin, *op. cit.*, p 34.

43. 'Weakened tax reform approved in Venezuela', *LAER*, 6(20) 26 May 1978, p 158.

44. Economic Commission for Latin America, *op. cit.*, p 490.

45. Everett G Martin, *op. cit.*, p 34.

46. Ibid.

47. 'Latin America: After the Oil Crisis', *op. cit.*, p 720.

48. See Economist Intelligence Unit (UK), *Quarterly Economic Review of Venezuela*, No. 1, January 1981, pp 7–8; Inter-American Development Bank, *op. cit.*, pp 380–2.

49. 'Venezuela: Herrera Campins treads a tightrope', *LARR: Andean Group*, 22 January 1982, p 7.

50. US Department of Commerce, International Trade Administration, *Foreign Economic Trends and Their Implications for the United States: Venezuela*, August 1982, FET 82–075. Prepared by the American Embassy, Caracas, p 3.

51. See *BLA*, 21 May 1980, p 166; Inter-American Development Bank, *op. cit.*, Table 44, p 426. Figures for 1980 and 1981, and 1982 projections provided by the Venezuelan Economic Desk, International Monetary Fund, Washington, DC, August 1982.

52. 'Venezuela lifts price controls', *LAER*, 8(33), 24 August 1979, p 258. See also 'Venezuelan Government Eases Price Controls and Lowers Tariffs', *BLA*, 15 August 1979, p 258.

53. See 'Venezuela's unions flex their muscles', *LARR: Andean Group*, 30 November 1979, p 7.

54. 'Venezuela: the road to 1985', *LARR: Andean Group*, 25 July 1980, p 7; 'Herrera Government Makes Big Spending Plans for 1980–85 Period', BLA, 23 January 1980, p 25.

55. ibid., 'Venezuelan Officials Integrate Social Goals into Industrial Policy', BLA, 11 June 1980, p 190; 'Venezuela: the road to 1985', *op. cit.* p 7. In addition, higher interest rates abroad continued to entice substantial amounts of private capital out of the country. Quoted in Juan de Onis, 'Venezuela's Problems Erode President's Popularity', *New York Times*, 17 March 1980, p 3.

56. See 'Venezuelan Business Makes Recommendations for National Development', *BLA*, 3 September 1980, pp 281–2. See also 'Herrera clashes with business', *LARR: Andean Group*, 29 August 1980, pp 3–4.

57. 'President offers olive branch', *LAWR*, 24 October 1980, p 3.

58. See *BOLSA Review*, 16(1), February 1982, p 49.

59. Jackson Diehl, 'Oil Wealth Isn't Lubricating Venezuela's State Industries', *Washington Post*, 7 October 1981, pp A8, A9; 'Venezuela: Capital flight causes dissension in the government's ranks', *LAWR*, 10 July 1981, p 5; *BOLSA Review*, 16(1), February 1982, p 50.

60. 'Venezuela: Herrera Campins treads a tightrope', *op. cit.*, p 8.

61. 'Odds for a Devaluation Rise in Venezuela As Oil Income Falls', *BLA*, 24 March 1982, p 89. In a subsequent discussion, the same source estimated that close to $1 billion left the country during the first half of 1982. See *BLA*, 11 August 1982, p 25.

62. 'Food Self-Sufficiency Remains Elusive Target for Venezuelan Economy', *BLA*, 2 December 1981, pp 377–8.

63. Economist Intelligence Unit (UK), *Quarterly Economic Review of Veneuzela*, No. 2, March 1981, p 10.

64. See BLA, 21 May 1980, pp 164–5; Inter-American Development Bank, *Economic and Social Progress in Latin America: 1979 Report*, *op. cit.*, p 16; US Department of Commerce, *op. cit.*, p 8.

65. Inter-American Development Bank, *Economic and Social Progress in Latin America: 1980–81 Report*, *op. cit.*, Tables 1–9, p 21.

66. *BOLSA Review*, 15(5), May 1981, p 109.

67. US Department of Commerce, *op. cit.*, p 8; 'Venezuela: Herrera Campins treads a tightrope', *op. cit.*, p 8.

68. *BOLSA Review*, 13(4), April 1979, pp 250–51; Joseph A Mann Jr., 'Caracas Unveils Economic Plan', *New York Times*, 28 May 1979, p D4.

69. 'Venezuela's jumbo turns into a white elephant,' *LARR: Andean Group*, 18 June 1982, p 1. See also 'Venezuela Banks Eye Overseas Loans', Special Supplement on Venezuela in *Journal of Commerce*, 28 July 1980, p 20.

70. See, for example, 'Venezuela: blowing hot and cold for steel', *LARR: Andean Group*, 3 April 1981, p 7.

71. Jackson Diehl, *op. cit.*, p A9.

72. See Juan de Onis, *op. cit.*, p 3.

73. 'Venezuelan enigma puzzles bankers', *LAWR*, 27 June 1980, p 6.

74. 'Prompt payment of debt reassures the bankers', *LAWR*, 8 August 1980, p 4; 'Firms in Venezuela Remains Confused by Muddled Policies, *BLA*, 27 August 1980, p 275.

75. Inter-American Development Bank, *op. cit.*, Tables 111–15, p 90.

76. On the decline in Venezuelan borrowings in the eurocurrency market, see 'Latin America Steps Up Borrowing on Eurocurrency Market', *BLA*, 18 November 1981, pp 361, 368.

77. 'Focus on Venezuela: Trying Times Ahead as Oil Income Shrinks', *BLA*, 31 March 1982, p 97.

78. ''Venezuela: economy cools to freezing point', *LARR: Andean Group*, 23 July 1982, p 6.

79. ibid.

80. ibid.

81. *BOLSA Review*, 14(111), August 1980, p 213; 'Regional Outlook: Latin America', *Business International*, 17 October 1980, p 334.

82. Economist Intelligence Unit (UK), *Quarterly Economic Review of Venezuela*, No. 4, September 1980, p 8 & No. 2, March 1982, p 8.

83. 'Despite its Wealth, Caracas Sits in Garbage and Smog', *New York Times*, 17 March 1980, p 3.

84. Economist Intelligence Unit (UK), *Quarterly Economic Review of Venezuela*, No. 1, January 1981, p 8.

85. See 'Venezuela: No shelter for the homeless', *LARR: Andean Group*, 28 August 1981, p 8.

86. See 'Companies in Venezuela Begin to Take a Hard Look At Changing Market Forces', *BLA*, 2 June 1982, p 175; 'Venezuela: Economy cools to freezing point', *op. cit.*, p 6; 'Venezuela: Herrera Campins treads a tightrope', *op. cit.*, p 7. Recent public opinion polls (late 1982) show the Acción Democrática (AD) with a convincing lead over the Social Christian Party (COPEI) for the December 1983 presidential election—largely as a result of the disastrous economic performance of the Herrera government. The AD presidential candidate, Jaime Lusinchi, was nominated with strong backing by organised labour. He has promised a return to the populist policies of 1974–5 and to make the revival of the agricultural economy a priority objective of his administration. As of September 1982, COPEI remained in considerable internal disarray and had not yet chosen a presidential candidate.

87. 'Focus on Venezuela: numerous problems and no clear solutions', *op. cit.*, p 62.

88. 'Venezuela Relaxes Stance on Foreign Investment in Construction Sectors', *BLA*, 29 March 1978, p 104.

89. 'Focus on Venezuela: numerous problems and no clear solutions', *op. cit.*, p 62.

90. 'New Venezuelan Decree Shows Changes in Attitude Toward Foreign Investors', *BLA*, 9 March 1977, p 75. See also 'Venezuelan decree softens foreign investment rules', *LAER*, 5(8), 25 February 1977.

91. 'Venezuelan Foreign Investment Law', *BLA*, 18 January 1978, p 19.

92. See 'Important Changes Coming in Venezuela's Foreign Investment Law, 19 October 1977, p 329.

93. *BOLSA Review*, 11(6), June 1977, p 335; 'Foreign investors wait for Venezuelan policy moves', *LAER*, 11(8), 23 February 1979, p 58: 'Venezuelan Foreign Loans and Investment', *BOLSA Review*, 13(3), March 1979, p 195.

94. *BOLSA Review*, 11(6), June 1977, p 335; 'Investment Lags in Venezuela', *BLA*, 13 June 1979, p 191.

95. 'New US Enthusiasm for Latin America', *LAWR*, 16 November 1979, pp 32–3; 'US Investment in Latin America Is Up Sharply, Profits Are Off Slightly', *BLA*, 11 October 1978, p 322.

96. 'Foreign investors wait for Venezuelan policy moves', *op. cit.*, p 58; 'Venezuela: foreign loans and investments', *BOLSA Review*, 13(3), March 1979, p 195.

97. See 'Plans for big shake-up of Venezuela's projects', *op. cit.*, p 249.

98. 'Investment Lags in Venezuela', *op. cit.*, p 191.

99. 'Companies in Venezuela Are Disconcerted by Lack of Guidelines', *BLA*, 1 August 1979, p 247. The Herrera government also became embroiled in a dispute with foreign oil multinationals over the renegotiation of a number of sales and technology contracts that were due to expire at the end of 1979. See 'Venezuela faces deadlock with oil transnationals', *LARR: Andean Group*, 30 November 1979, p 1.

100. Joseph A Mann Jr., *op. cit.*, p D11.

101. 'Companies in Venezuela Are Disconcerted by Lack of Guidelines', *op. cit.*, pp 247–8.

102. Joseph A Mann Jr., *op. cit.*, p D11.

103. Quoted in *ibid.*

104. 'Venezuela Seeks More Investment from Overseas', Special Supplement on Venezuela in *Journal of Commerce*, *op. cit.*, p 26.

105. Quoted in 'Venezuela's Siex Chief is a Positive Force in Investment Climate', *BLA*, 13 August 1980, p 259.

106. See Footnote 52.

107. 'Firms in Venezuela Remain Confused by Muddled Policies', *op. cit.*, p 275.

108. *ibid.*

109. 'Siex Softens Reinvestment Limit', *BLA*, 24 September 1980, p 310.

110. 'Firms in Venezuela Welcome Siex Changes But Remain Sceptical', *BLA*, 8 October 1980, p 322.

111. *ibid.*

112. Quoted in *ibid.*

113. See *BLA*, 13 January 1982, p 13; 11 August 1982, pp 253–4.

114. Quoted in 'Venezuela's Money Woes Augur Warmer Welcome for Foreign Investment', *BLA*, 17 March 1982, pp 85–6. The Sixth National Plan had formally upgraded foreign investment from a 'marginal' to a 'strategic' investment in the development programme in mid-1981. See 'Sixth National Plan Charts Ambitious Course for Venezuelan Economy', *BLA*, 3 June 1981, p 171.

115. Quoted in 'Venezuela's Money Woes Augur Warmer Welcome For Foreign Investment', *op. cit.*, pp 85–6.

116. See US Department of Commerce, Bureau of Economic Analysis, *Survey of Current Business*, 57(8), August 1977, p 44; 58(8), August 1978, p 27; 61(8), August 1981, p 37. Investment figures for 1981 were provided by the International Investment Division, US Department of Commerce, August 1982.

117. Inter-American Development Bank, *op. cit.*, Table 44, p 426.

118. US Department of Commerce, International Trade Administration, *Foreign Economic Trends and Their Implications for the United States: Venezuela*, February 1982, FET 82–014. Prepared by the American Embassy, Caracas, p 12. In February 1982, the government announced a new strategy, based on a series of fiscal, financial and tariff incentives, to give locally based manufacturers a bigger share of the massive capital goods business. But *Business Latin America* estimated that, on the basis of then current government spending targets in this area, the new programme would only increase local industry's percentage of the market by an extra 10 per cent to a total of 25 per cent. See 'Capital-Goods Decree May Mean More Business For Venezuela-Based Firms', *BLA*, 17 February 1982, pp 54–5.

# 11

## The Eritrean Revolution and Contemporary World Politics

JAMES PETRAS

The incapacity of the Ethiopian regime to conquer Eritrea, and its growing dependence on Eastern bloc and Cuban military supplies, advisers, and logistical support has deep historical roots in the particular relations which defined empire–colonial relations. The particularities of this relationship are grounded in the fact that the Eritrean colony was, and is, *more advanced* economically and socially than the imperial regime. Haile Selassie imposed imperial domination through a bureaucratic-feudal state upon an Eritrean social formation which had already established a relatively more advanced form of commodity production, including capitalist plantations, and industry linked through a developed mercantile network. Feudal bureaucratic colonial domination blocked further growth of the more advanced Eritrean social formation, stunting the development of the productive forces, limiting market production, absorbing skilled labor and "pillaging" the advanced units of production. The numerically superior Ethiopian state's incapacity to colonize Eritrea effectively was based on the latter's qualitatively higher level of cultural achievement, rooted in the more advanced forms of social production. Ethiopia's initial annexation and occupation of Eritrea did not immediately bring to bear the substantive inequality of development: yet the ingredients for underdeveloping Eritrea were present from the beginning. The willingness of sections of the Eritrean compradore bourgeoisie and sections of the petty bourgeoisie to "trade off" political freedom for "economic opportunity" within a federated framework proved to be illusory. The feudal-bureaucratic state used its politico-military apparatus to harness the economic resources of Eritrea to sustain the decaying imperial power. The systematic disintegration of Eritrean socioeconomic structures under the feudal-bureaucratic regime tended to impoverish and block opportunities for continuing reproduction of Eritrean capital externally and internally. This pattern of "regressive underdevelopment" set in motion a chain reaction of opposition which linked together all classes tied to the previously developed productive and distributive networks. The generalized constraint imposed by the bureaucratic feudal empire homogenized Eritrean discontent: all classes faced the imminent stagnation imposed by the deadhand of the decrepit emperor. The initial national protest by the workers' movement in the advanced economic centers (culminating in the general strike of 1958) reflected their greater sensitivity to the disintegrating effects of feudal control. The spread of the national liberation struggle from the cities to the countryside, and the subsequent reciprocal relationships that emerged between town and country, describes the process by which the colonial regime's initial selective political repression became massified, engulfing all sectors and levels of Eritrean society, from the workers and professionals in Asmara to the subsistence producers and nomadic pastoralists in the hinterland.

The strategic superiority of the Eritrean liberation movement is rooted in the particular colonial experiences that set Eritrean development apart from the Ethiopian feudal empire. In particular, Italian colonial occupation and later British administrative control more fully developed the productive forces and political institutions in Eritrea than did the bureaucratic-feudal regime of Selassie. This anomalous outcome, of colonialism contributing to growth while an independent state perpetuated backwardness, must be examined in its historical and class specificities lest we be drawn to the pernicious doctrine of the neo-colonial Warren school which trumpets the universally and historically progressive nature of imperial exploitation.

Italian imperialism in Eritrea had two faces: On the one hand, it was an oppressive colonial power; on the other, it developed the productive forces. In particular, Italian colonialism envisioned Eritrea as a *special colony*—a *jumping-off spot* to establish an Italian empire in Africa. Being the initial point, the Italian state invested heavily in the development of infrastructure and financed the development of an Italian settler-colony which, in turn, was influential in drawing further resources from the metropolitan country to the colony. In the case of the Italian-Eritrean relation, the flow of capital from the center to the periphery greatly exceeded the return of profits.

The settler colony also placed demands on the "mother-country" which a common "exploitation colony" could not have exercised. The Italian state rationalized the unprofitability of the particular Eritrean colony in terms of the larger empire and profits it envisioned as part of its continual conquest. Hence the Italian-promoted infrastructure developed in Eritrea was seen as a means of conquering Ethiopia— hence the specific unevenness in development between the two regions in transport, development, and market relations.

The second source for the greater development of Eritrea was the role that Eritrea played during World War II as a supply depot for the Allied forces. Under British administrative control, and due to its strategic position, Eritrea was able to develop industry and expand its commerce. Because of wartime constraints on the developed industrial countries, local Eritrean enterprises flourished. At the same time under the relatively "liberal" political climate that was tolerated by British rulers (relative to political conditions under the Selassie regime) the new wage, entrepreneurial, and employee groups were able to participate openly in political life, forming civic, trade union and political associations. The combined impact of Italian colonial investment, and the stimulation of production and distribution during World War II, created very substantive unevenness in development between Eritrea and Ethiopia—and became a major source of conflict: having experienced economic expansion and political liberalization, the Eritreans experienced the Ethiopian occupation as a backward and downward push. The growth of Eritrean national and cultural consciousness is intimately linked with the collective experience of sharing a common decline in socioeconomic status and political freedom. To the common experience of resisting European oppression was added the degradation of being subject to a stagnant feudal empire. The World War II boom that saw aircraft assembly plants, increasing commercial and transport activity, growing administrative experience, was initially undermined by the reassertion of world capitalist penetration of local markets after the war and by the Ethiopian occupation. The rising Eritrean petty bourgeoisie and working class associated with the previous growth increasingly came into conflict with the feudal political and social fetters that increasingly restricted their capacity to control the state and direct it toward promoting the productive forces in Eritrea. The economic decline precipitated by Ethiopian domination had the increasing effect of homogenizing the Eritrean population—in poverty. In the 1970s the increased repression and destruction leveled the distinctions between property and propertyless classes, creating displaced masses without ties to traditional patterns, who became available for and increasingly provided the basis for the further radicalization of the Eritrean liberation movement. The combined effects of pillage, oppression, repression, and displacement led the most advanced sectors of the national liberation movement to combine the struggle for national liberation with the socialization of production.

## Soviet Policy and the Ethiopian Regime

The growth and deepening of Soviet ties to Ethiopian military dictatorship is not a result of its so-called radical social reforms nor of its anti-imperialist foreign policy. Nor is it a reflection of growing Soviet "social imperialism." The Soviet Union's deep involvement in Ethiopia is the result of its *declining* position in the region and its relative weakness vis-à-vis the United States and the conservative Arab state. A brief examination of the context of Soviet involvement in Ethiopia will bring the issues into focus. The major Soviet push in Ethiopia occurred after the USSR was ousted in the Sudan and Egypt, which, in turn, was preceded by the jailing and assassination of pro-Soviet communist supporters in each of these countries. The defeats of the communist party in both countries and Soviet political defeats and diplomatic isolation were compounded by the shift in Somolia toward Saudi Arabia and the expulsion of the Soviets in November of 1977. It was only after these political losses that the USSR made a massive commitment to the Menghistu regime, and then only after the dictatorship demonstrated a capacity to consolidate its rulership and after it had weakened its ties with Israel and the United States. Up until then Soviet policy had been more concerned with retaining its right-wing regional allies than with any of the "land reforms" undertaken by the regime. *Soviet policy was conditioned by the shifts in state-to-state relations* and its concern with retaining political and diplomatic leverage. This belies the contention that the Kremlin's support of Ethiopia was based on internal social changes, most of which took place much earlier. If it were not for the hostile policies initiated by the neighboring countries in expelling the Soviets and aligning with the United States, it is doubtful whether the USSR would have made its big move to bolster the sagging Menghistu regime, at least not in the scale and scope that it did. More basically, the Soviet ties to Third World regimes, like the Menghistu regime, are "extensive" at the state-to-state level but don't penetrate deep into the society, nor are they linked to any revolutionary class forces. Ethiopia's economic ties continue basically with the West. In fact, its exports to the Western industrial markets increased from 69 percent to 72 percent between 1960 and 1978. Capitalist and precapitalist relations of production operate as a sea around the islands of nationalized enterprise. These state-to-state ties at the apex of society are designed by the Soviets to carve out outposts of political influence and strategic advantages (e.g., a military base, a naval port) and are extremely vulnerable to being reversed with shifts within the governing clique. Massive Soviet support has not changed Menghistu into a Soviet-style communist of the Eastern European variety. On the contrary, there is a high probability of the Soviets being ousted as they were in Somalia, Egypt and Sudan, if and when the bureaucratic dictatorship deems it to its interest.

The major impact of the Soviet intervention was fundamentally to shift the balance of struggle against the Eritrean liberation struggle and in favor of the Menghistu regime. In this regard, Halliday and Molyneaux's discussion of the Ethiopian revolution is deeply flawed and contradictory. At one point they argue that the provision of Soviet arms and Cuban troops merely enabled the Ethiopians to achieve a more rapid and decisive victory than would otherwise have been possible. They argue that the "demographic preponderance" of Ethiopia, the fact that it "felt itself invaded," would have led it to reassert its "strategic predominance" over Eritrea. This is one of the more specious arguments that they raise. First, mere population size is no determining factor in modern or ancient conflicts. In particular, the qualitative advantages discussed above certainly were decisive in the Eritrean victories in the mid-1970s. Secondly, empirical evidence suggests that it was the Eritreans who felt themselves invaded (and not only "felt" it but experienced it in bombed-out villages and razed cities) and who therefore developed the will to struggle to the end. In contrast, the forced conscripted peasant armies felt no such commitment; they were fighting far from their land and family and frequently deserted or fought very poorly. In sum, the Halliday-Molyneaux assertion that the Ethiopian dictatorship would have eventually conquered Eritrea without Soviet assistance is not at all convincing. Paradoxically, in an offhand statement they later observe, more accurately, "Overall, the Ethiopian military campaign in Eritrea would have been impossible without the initial and continuing agreement of the Russians." Apparently and fortunately, consistency is not one of their virtues.

Soviet support was directed at maintaining a political foothold in the Horn of Africa to compensate for declining influence in world politics and, in particular, in the Middle East and Northern Africa. The Ethiopian regime opening to the Soviets was to harness military aid to prevent it from military and political disintegration and to retain control of its colonial possessions. The Soviet-Ethiopian alliance's ideological affinity with socialist values is minimal. Soviet ideologists and the defenders of the Ethiopian regime claim that the alliance is an expression of revolutionary solidarity. There is better reason to think that it is based on conjunctural congruence of state interests. Those who argue that it is a question of solidarity presume that we are dealing with a social revolutionary regime when in fact it is a dictatorship over, not by, the proletariat. Apart from the systematic exclusion of workers and peasants and their representatives from all decision-making bodies, the regime's policies and intervention are directed against all expressions of independent working-class action. The question that proponents who argue that Ethiopia has experienced a social revolution have to answer is whether there can be a *revolutionary* class in the modern world that is not only nonworking class or peasant but rather acts in a systematic and violent fashion to destroy their independent class organizations. If so, the proponents must demonstrate how and where this new revolutionary class emerges, and they must specify the substance and nature of the society that this "revolution" produces. The political institutionalization of bureaucratic-military rulers—the Dergue—not workers' councils, defines the class nature of the state as a highly centralized and authoritarian state capitalist regime.

Despite the claims of the military rulers, the dictatorship over the workers and peasants controls all political life and subordinates all classes to the state. This is not a case of socialism but of dictatorial statism. The Soviet characterization of it as a "noncapitalist road" type of regime is not convincing. It is not a way station between reaction and socialist revolution, but rather a form of dictatorial state capitalism that attempts to usurp political space from both the masses and imperialism; it nationalizes imperial property and appropriates the workers' surplus. The proponents of the "noncapitalist regimes" are defined by what they *deny* more than by what they *affirm*, by the classes they *repress* rather than the classes they represent. The advocates of the "noncapitalist way" have formulated a regime in search of political perspective—one that substitutes demagogic maneuvers for political principles, which improvises radical rhetoric precisely when it denies the oppressed class the means to institutionalize class power. The style of the regime reveals its content: Their revolutionary manifestos fill the squares with demonstrators while their broken promises empty the streets and fill the morgues. Historical experience teaches us that sooner or later space for maneuver shinks and time runs out. The continual internal and external pressures (class, national, imperial) exhaust the regime's options and it turns against itself. A military coup sets the stage for the resurgence of neocapitalist restoration. The imprisoned workers, repressed intellectuals, the militants from the national movements are in no position to deepen the process; only the military officials next in line execute change, and not infrequently in collaboration with imperial intelligence agencies and with the promises of the international bankers. There is no reason to believe that the road of the Ethiopian regime will be any different. And Soviet "Marxists" can overlook another example of a noncapitalist regime which returns to the capitalist road.


## Nationalization Class Relations and the Ethiopian State

Soviet, Cuban, and Western defenders of the Ethiopian regime cite the growth of the state sector—nationalization of property—as the key issue in defining its "revolutionary" character. No doubt there have been very basic shifts in the forms of property ownership. The old feudal landlords, the Church, and the absolutist monarchy have been replaced. The fundamental question, however, is By whom and for what? We cannot assume that what is not landlord is peasant; what is not capitalist is worker; what is not absolutist rule is popular-democratic government. The nationalization establishes a new bureaucratic military class power that is neither feudal nor social revolutionary: it has destroyed one set of hierarchical exploitative relations and raised another. Insofar as the direct producers are concerned, it has not ended the appropriation of surplus, nor has the regime even proven that it can utilize the surplus exploited from labor to develop the productive forces. Nationalization can be viewed as progressive when it serves to develop the productive forces (not develop the forces of destruction), to develop internal markets (not to conquer external markets). Thus far the empirical evidence demonstrates that the statification of the Ethiopian economy has been harnessed to a military caste intent on pillaging a more advanced social formation (Eritrea), and it is these military-political goals and activities that define the function and meaning of nationalization, not the professions of socialism mouthed by regime publicists.

Ethiopia's regimes' and society's backwardness preclude any neo-colonialist style "federation" solution to the Eritrean question. The Ethiopian ruling class lacks the economic resources and financial power to establish strong economic links. Without Soviet-backed Ethiopian political-military domination, Eritrean society would soon develop links to those developed economies and societies that complement its own development needs. Secondly, the Ethiopian regime lacks collaborator classes within Eritrea capable of sustaining a neocolonial federated state: The advance of the class-national struggle has progressively eliminated those groups and individuals who earlier might have played this role.

### Soviet-Ethiopian Relations in World Historic Perspective

The Vietnam revolution disarticulated the U.S. imperial state. In the immediate aftermath of the U.S. defeat, the armed forces, the American public, and U.S. allies were not willing or able to intervene effectively in Third World revolutionary struggles. Simultaneously with the disarticulation of the U.S. state, Soviet influence continued to decline both in the Third World and among its former allies. The development of revolutionary movements independent and frequently in opposition to the two dominant powers defined the new reality.

Within the Third World where the superpowers were no longer controlling events, there emerged several strands of "anti-imperialism," each reflecting its unique social-political characteristics and a different set of dominant forces.

In Nicaragua and Angola, "nationalist-socialist" regimes emerged; in Iran a clerical-feudal, anti-imperialism that sought to restore precapitalist relations gained hegemony; in Afghanistan a pro-Soviet elite attempted to impose "socialism" from above on a precapitalist society; in Ethiopia the bureaucratic-military regime attempted to forge a state-capitalist society while retaining its colonial framework. The crises of U.S. hegemony produced a variety of responses; the results were not all "progressive." The Soviet response, however, was not predicated on how "progressive" the regime was from the point of view of internal class relations, but on how it reacted at the state level—did it weaken U.S. imperialism?

What the Soviet state sought to obtain was political and military influence at the level of the state, not the promotion of social revolution. Soviet intervention was based on obtaining "spheres of influence." It does not penetrate deeply into society. It is precisely for that reason that what some describe as Soviet "client states," "surrogates," and so on, are able to dislodge the Soviets with such ease. In pursuit of strategic locations, bases, ports, and diplomatic support, Soviet civil and military missions have no deep ties with important collaborator classes in Ethiopia. Unlike Western imperialism, which develops long-standing, deep-structural relations with capitalists, landowners, and the like, the Soviets lack organic ties with old oppressors and new exploiting classes.

Soviet policy support regimes that weaken imperialism but do not threaten Soviet-style socialism by raising the issue of democratic control. Soviet policy-makers' reliance on military-political influence at the level of the state is designed to avoid involvement in revolutionary mobilization that might break out of the boundaries of bureaucratic-statist regime-states. For Soviet strategists, state-capitalist regimes are more compatible with their internal class and ideological interests, as well as for international reasons. This combination of internal and external reasons explains why Soviet policy-makers continually reiterate their support for "noncapitalist regimes" despite the frequency with which they turn against the USSR.

## The United States: Declining Hegemony and the Revival of the Cold War

The decline of U.S. imperial state and the upsurge of anti-imperialist revolts revealed that no substitute imperial state could replace the role played by the United States. The proliferation of regional power centers and the growth of intra-Third World wars was one symptom of the new fragmentation of power. Most clearly the expansionist efforts by Indonesia in East Timor, Turkey into Cyprus, Iraq and now Iran in the Persian Gulf, Israel into Lebanon and Ethiopia in Eritrea, defined new conjunctural phenomena: the attempts by local Third World regimes to resolve the crisis of legitimacy through external conquest. The rise and demise of bourgeois nationalism in Ethiopia stands as a clear example, a regime which simultaneously promoted "national liberation" and national oppression. The contradiction between its economic backwardness and political hegemonic aspirations was temporarily resolved through massive external dependence (on the USSR). The Ethiopian regime lacked an underlying strategic predominance to carry off its dual goal; its very backwardness in material life undercut any appeals it might make to the Eritrian masses. Ethiopia's high rates of illiteracy, technical backwardness, and dictatorial regime, and its general low level of economic development did not provide for a kind of "Napoleonic liberation" from above and the outside. Without Soviet intervention, the strategic historical advantage was clearly in Eritrean hands—a more developed society, with higher skills, and the motivation of an invaded country. It is in this context of declining U.S. hegemony that we can best understand the effort by the Reagan administration (and before it, Carter) to revive the Cold War. Essentially it represents an effort to reestablish the power and supremacy that it possessed in the 1950s. In the following section we will discuss the nature and strategy of the Reagan administration in pursuing this new policy and its implications for Third World liberation struggles.

## Confrontation on a Global Scale: Components and Strategies

The most salient feature of the revival of the Cold War has been the massive military buildup undertaken by the Reagan administration. The military program is a wide-ranging and comprehensive effort. Multi-purposed and multi-pronged, it is directed at strengthening U.S. military interventionary capacity, bolstering clients, and bludgeoning European and Japanese allies into sharing the military costs commensurate with the benefits that they derive from the imperial system. The military buildup is manifested in several interrelated areas: (1) the development of new weapons systems and their location in forward positions; (2) the development of new military bases and the increasing effort to integrate "host" nations in overall U.S. strategy; (3) the strengthening of old military alliances, including demands that allies increase their military spending, including new weapon systems, and (4) developing new military alliances, especially with former pariah regimes (colonial settlers, such as Israel and South Africa) that can serve as "regional police forces" sharing in the destabilization of zones of revolutionary mobilization.

The overarching commitment of the Reagan administration is to out-muscle the Soviet Union.

The build-up of the naval and air forces is intended to intimidate Third World regimes in the process of transforming their society and to inhibit the transfer of material supplies to liberation movements. Equally important, the military buildup is a form of "armed propaganda," putting recalcitrant democratic allies on notice of the centrality of the United States in the Western scheme of things, as well as providing moral support to dictatorial clients in the Third World that the armed might of Washington stands ready to protect regime stability. The new weapons system, then, is as much a propaganda symbol, signaling a new policy of confrontation, as it is an outcome of the Reaganites' drive to substitute military solutions for the political, diplomatic, and economic failures of U.S. policy. Unable to construct a meaningful political-economic approach to revolutionary upheavals and North-South conflicts, Washington seeks, through its military power, to re-organize the agenda, establish new political boundaries, impose solutions that basically reflect overwhelming U.S. economic interests.

The military bases are physical extensions of the new military definitions of foreign policy: the military presence and "exercises" give little meaning to the "projection of power" policy currently enunciated in Washington. Psychologically it reassures local clients that U.S. intervention to save tottering regimes is a credible policy. The bases are not concerned primarily with external Soviet expansion, but are seen mainly as points of departure to intervene in critical Third World countries, in which vital U.S. corporate interests are being adversely affected. The argument of "deterrence" against the USSR becomes a means for preemptive action against internal revolutionary forces. Nevertheless, the political costs of a U.S. military presence in delegitimizing a regime has precluded some ruling groups from openly embracing the U.S. proposal; large-scale training missions and bases in adjoining areas serve the same purpose.

Complementing the military buildup is a policy of strengthening old military alliances and developing new ones. The tacit alliances with South Africa and Israel are being upgraded to strategic ones; the de facto collaboration with the right-wing dictatorships in Chile and Argentina is being revived; efforts to promote a South Atlantic Treaty Organization to dominate the region are being pursued.

The most serious efforts, however, are concentrated in pressuring the NATO countries to increase their weapons procurement policies, to build up their armed forces and share the military cost of defending the imperial system. Long-standing tensions have emerged between the United States, Europe, and Japan over the fact that the United States pays the military bill for sustaining Third World regions in which their competitors are extracting high profits. The U.S. program is to pressure all its regional allies to accelerate and expand their military programs within a basically United States-centered global alliance. In Europe, the effort of the Reagan administration is to implicate the NATO members in U.S. policy through new military deployment. The stationing of new missiles and weapon systems controlled by the United States underlines the very real loss of sovereignty that this implies in the control over foreign policy—and the terms of negotiation with the Soviet Union. The added leverage obtained by U.S. policymakers enhances their capacity to disregard European initiatives, reverting United States–European relations back to the 1950s. The policies toward the Third World are in major agreement with the direction of this approach; arms sales and "strategic agreements" are being hammered out with Turkey, Pakistan and South Korea, South Africa, and Egypt at each end of Africa and the promotion of Somalia as a military outpost at the Horn. The military bases and the joint military activities within these regions serve to bolster the status quo regimes and directly involve the U.S. armed forces in the role of defending incumbent dictators against popular opposition movements. The military buildup of the United States and its extension abroad has the general political effect of strengthening the coercive apparatus of incumbent regimes, and marginalizing democratic and reformist forces from any institutional role.

## New Strategies for Direct Intervention

Above we have been discussing the new patterns of arms buildup and the patterns of military alliances that are emerging. In this section we would like to focus on the likely policies to be pursued in accordance with these developments. The overarching reality that emerges is the growing willingness by U.S. policymakers to sanction and approve a "regional policeman's" role for its strategic allies. The explicit relations with South Africa, the strategic alliance with Israel, and the reestablishment of ties with Pinochet in Chile, Viola in Argentina, the reconsolidation of relations with Marcos in the Philippines, and the South Korean regimes are directed at forestalling any new changes in the Third World, as well as reversing processes of change already under way. The U.S. defense of the South African invasion of Angola is in accordance with the Reagan administration's policy of defending South Africa, of destabilizing Angola, and of creating a client regime in Namibia. The invasion reflected the convergence of interests between the Botha and Reagan regimes. The disregard of African bourgeois nationalist and Western European opinion suggests the centrality of the South African connection for U.S. policy. Likewise in the Middle East, the U.S. agreement to deepen its ties with Israel, the doctrine of strategic collaboration including military ties on land, sea, and air, involves efforts by Washington policymakers to police the whole Middle East. The growth of radical anti-imperialist forces, the fragility of oil-rich regime, and the absence of Arab-based forces with a capacity to intervene has led the Washington administration to seek to increase the role of Israel, despite the adverse reactions among pro-U.S. Arab regimes. The collaboration of Israel would be essential to any direct use of the Rapid Deployment Forces, the new combat teams, established to specialize in the protection of U.S. corporate access to oil. South Africa's and Israel's military power and the willingness to use it thus fits in nicely with the Reagan Third World policy, at a time when other Third World and Western European allies have proven refractory to the Reagan view of East–West confrontation.

The capacity for U.S. intervention is thus twofold: In the first instance, direct support and supply of the established military-dictatorial regimes and in the final instance the effort to construct a regional based police force that can provide for the collective security of any particular regime threatened by upheaval. The impact and consequences for the Third World of U.S. policy are profound: the decline of diplomacy and political negotiations as instruments of policy in the face of the ascendancy of the arms build-up. This does not mean that all negotiations will be eschewed, especially in light of the constant pressures by Western allies. What it does mean, however, is that negotiations and summit meetings with socialist and revolutionary regimes will be ritualistic affairs in which Washington will hope to "demonstrate" their ineffectiveness— they will become themselves propaganda forums to reinforce the commitment to policies of confrontation. International meetings with adversaries will be arenas to "warn" or "threaten" or "pressure" them to accommodate U.S. interests or face retaliation. Negotiations and meetings thus become an extension of the confrontational relationship— a process that will affect every area of international exchange. The Reagan administration's decision to proceed with confrontational policies was taken unilaterally—the allies are presented accomplished facts and the alternatives of accepting them or being subject to U.S. pressure. The strategy of the Reagan administration is to "create facts" which polarize East/West, forcing the rest of the capitalist world to follow suit.

The main criteria today in shaping Reaganite policy are how a regime lines up on the issue of East–West polarization and whether it is willing to subordinate itself to U.S. leadership in pursuit of the politics of confrontation. The revival of the doctrine of a bipolar world, and the attempt to submerge all conflicts into this pattern, will be resisted by many allies of the U.S.: West Germany, with its trade ties with the Eastern bloc; Saudi Arabia, with its fears of Israeli expansionism; Indonesia and Malaysia with their fears of Chinese "hegemonism"; Mexico, with its fears of U.S. domination, and so on. The ideology of bipolar global confrontation and the polarizing effects that it evokes will not only have an adverse effect on "nonaligned" forces, but will undercut the position of middle class liberal-democratic and nationalistic movements within Third World countries. The right-wing and repressive political terrain will favor clandestine groups over legalists; the supply and training of military forces will encourage violent, as opposed to electoral, activity; the attacks on the center will force centrists out of politics or over to the left. Global confrontation which polarizes international politics will have a tendency to do likewise internally. The end of policy is to reconstruct the structure of power that existed in the 1950s and to recuperate the economic position that accompanied uncontested military supremacy.

The commitment of the Reagan administration to the reconstruction of the world in the image of the 1950s requires a number of fundamental changes, most of which are beyond the realm of possibility (including "military supremacy over the USSR," dominating European economic and foreign policy). What appears to be the first strategic task is to prevent any further changes in power—"containing revolutions" in the Third World. This involves a major effort to make El Salvador an example of the "testing of the wills," the willingness of the United States to maximize the use of force to sustain a repressive regime, even at the cost of massive loss of civilian lives, even in the absence of allied support. Beyond the revival of preventive interventionism is the serious planning of policies to reverse established revolutionary regimes. The attempt to retrieve the past involves efforts to destroy the present: the danger is that it can lead to global nuclear war. Washington, under Reagan, is not reconciled with the established revolutionary governments in Angola, Nicaragua, Grenada, or Cuba. Policymakers have developed a strategy of confrontation to create the basis for "regionally based" military intervention. The image of revolutionary societies that Reagan projects is revealing: according to him, they are crisis-wracked systems devoid of popular support and dependent on outside power to sustain them; the strategy adopted by the Reaganite is to neutralize Soviet assistance (through a military buildup) and then, through combined United States and regional allies, engage in a military assault for power.

These extremist positions—even by U.S. standards—reflect the new personnel in Washington whose ideological propensities and styles are divorced from the practical exigencies of day-to-day business operation: The extreme voluntarism manifested in U.S. foreign policy—the will to power—substitutes individual desires and powers for the objective circumstances that allow for the realization of policy goals.

The adventurism in this approach is obvious. The same subjectivity is evidenced in the Reagan approach to the market; the problem is the "psychology" of Wall Street for not investing in industry and stock, not the high interest rates or the availability of other areas which provide higher profit rates. There is an emerging conflict between the militarist-voluntarist policy geared to reversing global trends over the past twenty years and the more sober-minded calculations of pragmatic Western businessmen who recognize the realities of post-revolutionary society—and try to maximize opportunities. The divorce between political power and economic power, however, has yet to manifest itself in any clear-cut alternative program. It finds expression only in opposition to particular policy measures.

The first manifestations of the new Reagan offensive strategy have already appeared: the deepening ties with Israel have found expression in the invasion of Beirut and the bombing of Iraq. Despite Washington's disclaimers, the action was followed by a Washington initiative to formalize a relationship of "strategic collaboration." The rapprochement with South Africa is evidenced in Washington's veto of a Security Council resolution condemning its invasion of Angola. The South Africa invasion established terrain for the operation of the United States–promoted UNITA terrorists in Angola and attempts to create a zone between Angola and Namibia to isolate SWAPO from its Namibian supporters.

Massive bombings, full-scale invasions, massive internal political crackdowns, are the first fruits of the new era of the Cold War. While the strategic collaborators thus follow the policy of open warfare, the Reagan administration pursues a policy of unremitting pressure on Europeans and moderate nationalist governments in the Third World. Following the French-Mexican declaration of support for the Salvadoran Democratic Revolutionary Front, twelve Latin American countries were mobilized to denounce the declaration. Vernon Walters, Reagan's roving ambassador, is the liaison with the most extremist forces in the Latin American military, and the key figure organizing support for U.S. positions. The process of integrating and subordinating Latin countries within the United States orbit has been operating primarily at the military-strategic levels, as the growing pattern of economic diversification make more difficult a greater control by the United States (e.g., Argentina's heavy dependence on grain sales to the Soviet bloc).

The revival and extension of Central Intelligence Agency activity as a factor in destabilizing nationalist regimes in the Third World is once again evident in the recent reports of attempts on the life of the Libyan head of state. The activation of terrorist activity against the Angolan government and the harrassment of the Cuban government are also likely indications of stepped-up CIA activity, following patterns established earlier.

The mounting pressures on Japan and Europe to rearm for confrontation is promoted by a demagogic campaign centering on the efforts in Poland to extricate itself from Soviet and local Stalinist domination. The Soviet-Polish confrontation has been manipulated by the Reagan administration as a means of mobilizing and militarizing Western Europe under U.S. hegemony. By focusing on Soviet-Polish relations, Washington hopes to extend its own brand of interventionism; brandishing the threat of Soviet intervention in Eastern Europe, it hopes to subordinate Western Europe to its efforts to polarize the world.

The goals of the Reagan administration include:

(1) Reestablishment of U.S. military-economic hegemony over the Third World, through the development of a network of stable strategic collaborators capable of jointly participating in armed occupation of target areas: (2) Displacement of European and Japanese hegemony in areas which it has undercut U.S. positions, deflecting competition, and striking a more favorable "balance" between the partners regarding their economic gains and their military expenditures, and (3) Creating new opportunities for U.S. capital expansion and new markets for U.S. goods by universalizing the free market economic strategy. Rejection of large-scale public funding and the proposals for a New International Economic Order are centerpieces of the new strategy.

Central to the Reagan strategy of "making the United States number one again" is the restructuring of U.S. society and economy: The federal budget is oriented toward cutting taxes and social services to free capital to accumulate, compete, and increase its share of markets worldwide; the increase in the military budget is to provide the imperial state with the armaments to defend and create the opportunities for expansion. Thus the Reagan approach is a new historical project based on a sharp reconcentration of capital for export which leaves out the labor movement; it represents a shift from "social" or "welfare imperialism," in which domestic reform accompanies outward expansion to an approach in which internal exploitation becomes a necessary condition for imperialism. The basic difference is the enormous growth of competition between advanced countries and the new challenges from the Third World which have vastly increased the costs of participation in the world economy. The cost of external expansion, however, point to one of many contradictions between the goals of the new historical project of the Reagan administration and the historical realities of the world economy.

## The United States and the Horn of Africa

The Horn of Africa is of particular importance to Washington because of the adjoining regions of which it forms an integral part, namely, the countries facing the Red Sea and with access to the Indian Ocean. Thus while the Horn in itself does not have great economic interest, it does have "strategic significance," namely, that influence in the region provides major powers leverage in shaping policies in countries where economic interests are paramount—in particular, the oil-rich Middle Eastern countries.

Thus the formulation of U.S. policy toward the regimes in the Horn is shaped by how these interact with U.S. policy toward larger regional issues. One of Washington's prime concerns in the Middle East has been to refashion a collaborative framework involving Egypt-Israel-Saudi Arabia, thus excluding the Soviet Union. The Camp David Agreement achieved part of this goal. (Saudi Arabia and most other Arab states rejected it.) The basic concern of U.S. policymakers was to mobilize support behind the Egyptian position. Behind the support for Egypt and the overall Camp David framework, Washington envisioned the reinsertion of the United States in the Middle East—through its clients and allies—as the major power shaping development agendas and political direction. This core concern with projecting U.S. power in the Middle East radiated outward toward the adjoining region, including the Horn of Africa. For Washington, a crucial determining factor of U.S. policy toward the countries in the region was their relationship toward Egypt and its participation in the Camp David framework; the ties between Sudan and Somalia with Egypt are decisive elements in shaping Washington's favorable policy. There are other issues that define U.S. policy toward the countries of the Horn—namely their relationship with the USSR and their disposition to U.S. bases facing the Indian Ocean. Washington's commitment to Sudan, Somalia, and Kenya is dictated in part by their hostility to the Soviets and their willingness to provide bases for U.S. forces near the Indian Ocean.

United States–Ethiopian relations deteriorated subsequent to the overthrow of Selassie in 1974. According to policymakers in Washington, the points of conflict revolved around three issues: Ethiopia's close ties with the USSR; its failure to compensate expropriated U.S. corporations (roughly $28 million); criticism of U.S. policy in regard to South Africa, Puerto Rico, and the failure to criticize Soviet policy in Afghanistan. The same policymakers perceived little prospect for improvement in relations in the near future. As a result, U.S. aid is directed toward those regimes that serve its larger interests. Or, as one policymaker stated: "We will stand closest to our best friends in the area. . . . These are Kenya, Sudan, Egypt, and Saudi Arabia." The following U.S. aid figures for 1982 in millions of dollars confirm this statement:

| | |
|---|---|
| Sudan | 206.6 |
| Kenya | 116.2 |
| Somalia | 78.5 |
| Djibouti | 5.3 |
| Ethiopia | 3.4 |

Nevertheless, Washington is aware of the superficial nature of Ethiopian military Marxism, the willingness of the regime to maneuver and, most fundamentally, that the Ethiopian regime continues to be basically integrated into the capitalist world market. Soviet involvement has not changed this basic link since it has mainly provided military assistance and sales and Soviet links to the Ethiopian economy are much weaker. The economic basis exists, therefore, for the Ethiopian regime to make a shift in its international policy once it has exhausted its strategic needs from the USSR and once it decides to tap into Western financial resources and marketplaces. Washington policymakers are aware of these possibilities. As one U.S. official stated in 1981: "... We seek to continue a dialogue with the Ethiopian Government. We provide humanitarian assistance and we intend to continue to do so and *we are ready to take advantage of opportunities which may come up in the future to improve our relations with Ethiopia*"[1] [my emphasis]. In 1982 there were the first signs that in fact a rapprochement between Washington and the Menghistu regime were in the offing. One influential policymaker in Washington testified, "We have indications from the Ethiopians that they desire to improve relations between our two countries and they have taken some steps in this direction. For example, the government of Ethiopia has begun to settle various nationalization claims."[2] It would be no great surprise then, given the class nature of the Ethiopian state to see it switch sides in the Cold War, shifting its supplier from Moscow to Washington. The latter was virtually unaffected by the "nationalization" (most of those expropriated were local landlords); hence there are few "pressures" among U.S. businessmen for a hostile policy. The key is Washington's ability to replace Soviet influence and retake strategic military positions and what they can offer the Ethiopian regime in exchange.

## Conclusion

In the final analysis the Ethiopian experience demonstrates that no progressive social reform can be sustained internally while an imperial war is pursued abroad. This is true from a practical point of view (expenditures) and from an ideological perspective (military brutalization abroad reverberates at home and vice versa). The initial responsiveness of the military regime to mass demands was eroded by the constant pressure of war abroad. The stagnation of the economy is directly related to the growth of the military. Prior to 1974 there were 44,000 soldiers in the armed forces and expenditures of $40 million. By 1980 there were 230,000 soldiers and expenditures reached $385 million. Meanwhile, in the areas of education and health the central government's expenditures per capita were the same in 1978 as they were under the Selassie regime. With agricultural and industrial production virtually stagnant, it is obvious that the regime cannot sustain its commitments to development and military expansion in Eritrea.

The peasants, being the recipients of land reform, were pressed into the military as cannon fodder to sustain the imperial pretensions of the regime. The forced conscription of peasants by the regime, and their subsequent death marches, are in their own fashion as exploitative of the peasants as the rent-gouging carried out under Selassie feudal monarchy. The location of peasant sacrifice is different, the rhetoric is certainly novel, but the result is the same: peasant life and labor is sacrificed for alien ends. The overall balance sheet of military-agrarianism or, better still, reformism harnessed to military conquest, clearly demonstrates that from the perspective of the peasant, life has not impoved: landlord-induced insecurities are replaced by new state-inflicted concerns.

While some writers on the left have emphasized the international realignments and internal changes carried out by the regime, they have with grand simplicity overlooked the state and class context within which those changes have taken place. The harnessing of the peasants and workers to an expansive chauvinist state, the alignment with the USSR precisely in order to secure arms to maintain a colonial relationship do not speak to a revolutionary regime but describe a colonial version of state capitalism—one in profound crisis and without the internal flexibility to rectify its course.

## Notes

1. Foreign Assistance Legislation for Fiscal Year 1981 (Part 7), Sub-Committee on Africa of the Committee on Foreign Affairs, U.S. House of Representatives.

2. Foreign Assistance Legislation for Fiscal Year 1982 (Part 8), Sub-Committee on Africa, Committee on Foreign Affairs, U.S. House of Representatives.

# 12

## Reflections on the Iranian Revolution

JAMES PETRAS

### Introduction

The Iranian revolution raises at least four important issues that are of great interest to socialists throughout the world:

1. The nature of imperialism and its impact on Third World social formations, and the resultant nature and orientation of the various strands of "anti-imperialist" movements; the complexity of anti-imperialist forces and the profound historical differences that divide them raise the issue of the proper relation (if any) that should exist between them.

2. The changing structure of power and relations within the world capitalist economy, and the importance of recognizing the consequences of the decline of U.S. domination and the incapacity of Europe or Japan to replace it.

3. The importance of recognizing the capacity of precapitalist classes to utilize their political power to compensate for their lack of economic power in modern economies. This requires an analysis of their capacity to adapt to the demands of capitalism and to co-opt "modern classes"; moreover, in some cases precapitalists can be at least partially "converted" by fusing cultural elements derived from precapitalist social formations with the imperatives of capitalist production. Deductive definitions of class behavior (product of a rigid structuralist view of class) fails to recognize the salience of class *context* (relations and struggle) in redefining the behavior of classes.

4. The combined and uneven development of capitalists, creating antagonistic "ethnic classes"; in particular, in countries which have experienced rapid capitalist growth under autocratic rulership there are marked spatial disparities in the implantation and location of productive forces. Captial located in the "center" regions appropriates the surplus value of labor from the outlying regions which serve as "labor reserves."

These regional patterns of exploitation, when juxtaposed upon diverse ethnic populations, find expression in class-regional-ethnic conflicts in which the dominant ethnic capitalist of the center cities exploit the subordinate ethnic peasant proletarians of the hinterland.

## The Two Faces of Imperialism

In the recent period there has emerged a wide-ranging debate on the nature and impact of imperialism on the Third World. Warren and his followers have disputed the effects of imperialist penetration, arguing that it has contributed to the development of productive forces and paved a way for national capitalist development. In opposition, the traditional neo-Marxist schools maintain that imperialism led to stagnation and underdevelopment through the appropriation of surplus. Both the Warren school and the neo-Marxists cite Marx's writings: The former dicuss Marx's early positive discussion of English imperialism's role in India; the latter cite his later writings on the consequences of British penetration of Ireland.

A great deal of confusion has been engendered by this discussion because it is largely divorced from the state and class relations that shape the impact of imperialism in each historical context. Equally misleading is the tendency to construe the development of imperialism in a linear rather than a dialectical fashion. The contradictory nature of the implantation of imperially induced capitalist development is flattened out—it is either "development" or "underdevelopment." Imperialist expansion has had a differential impact on Third World societies, depending on the level and development of the internal class forces and their capacity to influence its trajectory. In colonial regimes, local influence was minimal, and there was little capacity to direct imperialist penetration, hence surplus extraction and underdevelopment was characteristic of this type of regime. In the post-colonial period this uniform pattern alters, depending upon the nature and structure of the post-colonial states. Leaving aside the revolutionary societies, which completely rupture their relations with imperialism, there are, among the capitalist Third World countries, a variety of relations and development outcomes resulting from their links to imperialism. In part, these differences are a reflection of the different state structures and class configurations and, in part, a reflection of imperialist needs (i.e., access to markets or strategic raw materials). Essentially we can identify three class-state patterns: (1) the classical *neo-colonial* regime, which contains a large expatriot elite in key decision-making positions and which continues to participate in the traditional division of labor with little external or internal diversification of the economy from the colonial period; (2) the *developing collaborator capitalist* regime, which is closely linked with imperial capital and state but which increasingly appropriates and channels part of the surplus into internal productive activities, leading to fundamental changes in the internal structures of production (shifts from agriculture and mining to industry and urban construction); and (3) *state capitalist* regimes, which redefine their relation with imperialism by limiting its participation to specific economic sectors and attempt through the nationalization of the commanding heights of the economy a pattern of national capitalist accumulation.

Iran under the Shah appears to fit the second type. Under his regime, there was both large-scale imperial expansion and extensive local, including state, investment in the economy, resulting in an explosive growth of urban areas, industry, construction, commerce, and real estate. This *growth* of productive forces, directed by the *autocratic* regime in collaboration with local and imperial capital, systematically *displaced* the previous influential precapitalist classes (cleric merchants, landlords) while *exploiting* the new working and salaried middle classes. As the process of expansion accelerated, so did the displacement and exploitation of new layers of the labor force increase: More and more strata from precapitalist society were converted into wage laborers or displaced from petty-commodity production. The *dynamic* of the developing collaborator capitalist regime induced the very class *antagonisms* that would, in the first instance, *paralyze* the growth of productive forces, and secondly, *overthrow* the regime. Thus imperialism that was induced through autocratic-elite domination polarized society; this polarization, in turn, acted to brake the further development of the productive forces; the "stagnation of the economy" in turn acted back upon the population, accelerating political and social mobilization and fragmenting the institutions upon which the regime relied for control. In this context of institutional disintegration, class polarization, and economic paralysis, the regime was overthrown.

In summary, unlike the mechanical views of Warren and his adversaries, imperialism engendered *growth and stagnation*, the development of productive forces and class antagonisms. The process was not linear, *nor* was the role of imperialism *at any point politically or socially* progressive: The productive forces expanded under the aegis of a regime imposed by the CIA, guarded by the SAVAK, and secured by the systematic murder and torture of thousands of militants. At all times during the transformation process, there existed alternative forces—within the working class and professional petit-bourgeoisie—capable of accomplishing the same historic task, developing the productive forces, within the framework of a democratic-socialist framework. It is the existence of this alternative democratic-modernizing force within the Iranian capitalist economy that marks out the historically reactionary nature of the Shah's development of the productive forces. Warren's extrapolation and revindication of the development of the productive forces out of the historical, political, and class context is what marks his work as a veritable apologia for imperialist exploitation.

On the other hand, the neo-Marxists who failed to recognize the expansive and developmental nature of the Shah's dictatorship, and who simply defined it by its reactionary political and social character, were unable to come to grips with the dual character of the opposition. Imperial-collaborator-induced capitalist expansion uprooted and displaced precapitalist classes opposed to and blocking the development of the modern forces of production as well as exploiting workers and salaried employers. The neo-Marxists operating with a market definition of capitalism (so-called "circulationists" who defined capitalism in terms of profitable exchanges of commodities in the market) viewed the Iranian social formation as homogeneously "capitalist." Failing to recognize the heterogeneity of the social formation, they did not give sufficient attention to the fact that opposition to the anti-imperialist Shah was developing from two diametrically opposing positions: one a democratic-progessive configuration of modern classes rooted in capitalist production and struggling to *transform* it, in some cases to socialism; the other a reactionary coalition of precapitalist classes seeking to restore the privileges, power, and prerogatives of merchant-clerical society. By reducing Iranian society to imperial-capitalist domination, it was easy (and false) to conclude that all anti-imperialist forces were "progressive." The enormous weight of the precapitalist classes manifested itself in the post-Shah period, when the clerical-reactionary forces completely overwhelmed the secular-democratic coalition.

While the Warren school would have failed to recognize the *sociopolitically reactionary* content of the Shah-developed productive forces, the neo-Marxists failed to grasp the *contradictory* nature of the transformation of the productive forces. By simply defining the totality of productive and social relations as *reactionary*, the neo-Marxists fell victim to the ideology of the anti-industrial, antimodern anti-imperialism of the clerical forces.

Clearly the *centerpiece* for any progessive transformation of a dynamic imperial-collaborator regime was the modern working class and petit-bourgeoisie. Alliances that subordinated these classes to the leadership of a precapitalist coalition was *not* an *advance* over imperialism but a *return* to clerical-merchant domination. Historically secular democratic anti-imperialist classes have forged alliances with precapitalist anti-imperialists, but these alliances have paved the way for progressive changes only when the modern classes exercised clear hegemony in the alliance. In Vietnam the Marxists allied with the Buddhists, in Cuba the Fidelistas allied with the small merchant and petty commodity producers, as did the Sandanistas in Nicaragua, but in all cases the worker-peasant forces were the *dominant* group in the alliance, and clearly recognized the divergent interests among the anti-imperialists in the post-revolutionary period. In Iran, as in the case of Cambodia, the petty-commodity collectivists, with their despotic methods, seized control of the anti-imperialist movement and attempted to reconstruct centralized despotism based on the ideal of small-scale producers; in Iran through private, in Cambodia through collectivist property forms. In both cases, the revolutionary democratic forces who participated in the revolution were not its beneficiaries.

## Rethinking the World Economy

The second issue that is raised by the Iranian experience is the changing nature of the capitalist world economy. Between 1945 and 1970, U.S. dominance was the primordial fact in defining the structure of the world economy. It became fashionable to conceptualize world capitalism in terms of a center/periphery, and within certain limits this was a useful, if overly simplistic, conception. Over the last decade and a half, it has become abundantly clear that U.S. dominance of economic and political relations within the capitalist world has been in decline. However, no other capitalist country has been able to replace it as the dominant center of the system. In this context, we are witnessing the proliferation of "regional centers" of power, of newly industrializing countries laying claims to regional domination, and the elaboration of regional networks of economic relations. The fragmentation of power and the growth of conflicts to establish regional hegemony is directly related to a major issue in contemporary Iranian foreign and domestic policy: In the face of the decline of U.S. imperialism, the Iranian regime has attempted to assert regional hegemony in the Gulf region. Those who operate with the center/periphery world-system perspective have failed to grasp the significance of the changes in this conjuncture in world capitalist development and the new dynamic within the region; the Khomeini regime has pursued the same regional hegemonic aspiration as its predecessor, the Shah. The political-cultural ideological basis of expansion in the present period prepares the ground for the commerical-economic domination in a subsequent period. The Iraqi regime is the mirror counterpart; a state-capitalist regime attempting to carve out a mini-empire of regional satellites. While one should not discount the internal uses of external wars—especially in times of crisis—there is a whole history of late-capitalist developers who seek to appropriate land, labor, and resources in order to fuel the engines of capitalist expansion. Beginning with Japan and Germany at the turn of the century, this tendency manifests itself today among several regional powers, especially in light of the loss of a single dominant capitalist center.

## Two Faces of Clerical Reaction

The Khomeini regime, dominated by the clerical caste linked to pre-capitalist classes, initially defined a sharp break with the course of capitalist development. As in the case with many precapitalist social formations, the economic base was subordinated to the politicoreligious and military bureaucracy. The first efforts to attempt to create a new Islamic economy, regulated and controlled by the religious leader, led to economic disintegration, the flight of skilled technicians, and the disaggregation of the working class. Production declined in all areas of the economy, including most notably petroleum production. The stratification of the economy, the expropriation of bourgeois property, did not result in raising production but in closing down productive units or running down available stock. The decline in production led to the socialization of poverty: Instead of raising the lowest wage and salary sectors to the highest, all were pulled down to the lowest levels. This equality of poverty was sanctified by the religious leaders as a virtue; a sign that the capitalist devils were being defeated. At the same time, the purge of class-conscious militants ensured that the "communist devils" would not be in a position to define a new course for socialized production. The demise of major industrial and construction industries led to the deproletarianization of the urban population: a large reserve army of former peasant and former wage workers began to depend on subsistence handouts from the mullahs. Nonetheless, while the religious leadership may have been realizing their vision of a return to precapitalist society, factors outside their control quickly shattered their dreams. The war with Iraq, the rising internal opposition from the Left, the ethnic rebellions, and the increasing pressures from the East and the West made it clear that without a modern economy Iran would cease to exist—it would become a fragmented and subordinate satellite of regional forces, and subject to all the machinations of the superpowers. Against their whole philosophy and social roots, the clerical caste was forced by historical imperatives to turn to the only class that could operate a modern economy: the technical and professional petit-bourgeoisie. In the subsequent period, the clergy ruling class has had to share power with this managerial-technical elite. A *de facto* division of labor has emerged in which the managerial-technocrats run the economy and the religious mullahs control the cultural-educational and political sphere. Clearly the impossibility of building Islam in one country, and the need to participate in the world market, encouraged the emergence of more cosmopolitan, pragmatic forces into positions of economic responsibility and led to the eclipse of the mullahs in certain strategic economic sectors. The result of this shift and sharing in political power was a partial recovery of the economy, especially evidenced in the steady increase in oil production. The religious caste, thrown back to the more limited spheres of political-culture-education control, have attempted to compensate by laying down ever more rigid codes of conduct and indoctrination. While the clerical caste continues to voice uncompromising principles, to issue pronouncements about the building of an Islamic economy, they have been forced to adapt to the demands and direction of the new technobureaucracy. The Islamic clergy's contrasting behavior—rigid appearance and flexible adaptation—and the emergence of dual spheres of action generates unavoidable tensions. The economic and technical imperatives of modern production and distribution come into conflict with the narrow organizational and educational demands of the clergy. The increasing expansion of the economy, its reinsertion in the work market, the reconstruction of the working class and salaried groups will increase pressure on the reluctant clergy to return to a narrower role in society or, as appears to be the case, precipitate divisions between "modernist" and "traditionalist" clergy. Cleavages among the clergy will be defined as those who will increasingly adapt or "convert" to the demands of the managerial/ technocrats and those who will feel that the initial concessions need to be reversed to return to the original spiritual (precapitalist) goals of the "revolution." The push-pull between these factions within the regime will resonate among the oppositon, as the alliance of technomangerialists and modernist clergy offer opportunities for "struggle from within." The critics of this position, however, might point to the enormous programmatic sacrifices involved in such as "insiders" strategy—the exchange of democratic, secular and socialist goals in order to increase production, within a clerical-statist regime.

In summary, the dominant clerical traditionalist class has developed a two-faced policy, one of intransigent commitment to cultural-political control and the other of flexibility in adapting to the imperatives of participating in the capitalist world marketplace.

## Uneven Development and Class/Ethnic Confrontation

One of the striking elements during the rule of the imperial collaborator capitalist regime (the Shah) was the tremendous uneven development of the productive forces; the great concentration of wealth, capital and power in particular regions and classes and the relative impoverishment of other regions. These differences in wealth, translated into Marxist categories, reveal that the regional centers became the owners of the means of production and the outlying regions the centers for the recruitment of proletarians. The appropriation and transfer of surplus value from labor generated in the exploited regions to the centers (Teheran) created the economic basis for the ethnic-regional struggles against centralized autocratic rule. When this pattern of spatial con-centration and exploitation was overlaid on a pattern of different ethnic populations, conditions were created for the emergence of ethnic class conflict: Kurdish petty-commodity producers and proletarians against Farsi speaking capitalists. No doubt this account oversimplifies the social structures within each region, but it also points to the importance of avoiding class reductionism in heterogeneous social formations in which ethnicity is an important factor determining one's position in relation to the means of production and the structure of state power. The historical legacy of regional concentration of power and control over the means of production has been taken over by the Khomeini regime. Because of the disintegration of the economy, the regime has attempted to impose political-religious homogeneity as a means of control and domination over the exploited and oppressed minorities. However, while the profound economic-political inequalities exist, the internal bonds among the ethnic minorities are stronger than any appeals or exhortations from the alien clergy. Thus the continual resistance by the ethnic minorities, thus the increased use of force by the centralized clerical state. The ultimate failure of the central regime to come to terms with the historical issues of uneven development raised by the ethnic minorities will escalate their demands for separation and could lead to the disintegration of the Iranian state into a series of ministates. Thus while the pattern of uneven development led to the concentration of capital and the expansion of productive forces, the political and social forces antagonistic to this process have set in motion a process which can explode the political framework that engendered that growth. The dialectics of uneven spatial development have created a situation in which the greater growth of capital has created the deepening of ethnic particularism. Instead of capital "uniting the people" in a common national market within the nation-state, it has established conditions to disintegrate both. The attempts by the religious zealots to reimpose the oppressive framework (with a heavy varnish of religious rhetoric) can only deepen the alienation of the oppressed people. Neither secular managerial-technocrats working toward a state capitalist regime nor self-styled holy men can exercise the spectre of fragmentation. Only a genuine democratic-socialist movement that recognizes and moves to restructure the state and economy and place it in the hands of the councils of the direct producers can come to grips with the regional issues.

# 13

## The Crises in Market Collectivist, and Mixed Economies: Puerto Rico, Cuba, and Jamaica

JAMES PETRAS
MIGUEL E. CORREA
ROBERTO P. KORZENIEWICZ

*I*

All of the social systems in the Caribbean are in crisis. Up to now, proponents of one ideological model or another have been acute critics of their adversaries, while blandly unobservant of the deficiencies of their favored approach. By crisis, we mean deep-seated structural-organizational features of the economy and society that adversely affect periodically the capacity to transcend fundamental social and economic development problems. Regime crisis in the region can be ascribed in part to (1) the historical legacy of colonial domination and neocolonial exploitation; (2) contemporary external conditions reflecting inequality in competitive opportunities, concentration in the distribution of capital and technical resources, and limited influence on markets, flows of capital and the terms of exchange and finance; and (3) the general crises in social systems to which the regimes are entwined: the inflationary-recessionary cycle that afflicts the capitalist world, the technological and bureaucratic-centralist constraints that manifest themselves in the collectivist countries.While past and external factors play an influential role in circumscribing the universe in which the contemporary crises unfold, that is not the final and determining factor. Shaping the regime crises are a set of policies and strategies rooted in distinct class structures organized in specific state formations in the present. While all regimes

Paper presented at the Caribbean Studies Association Meeting, May 25–30, St. Thomas, Virgin Islands.

have experienced crisis, each crisis reflects a particular configuration of forces and embraces a distinct set of problems. Moreover, the challenges that emerge are of a distinctly different order within each regime. For example, to anticipate our discussion, the visible and pervasive problem of mass unemployment that profoundly affects Puerto Rico and Jamaica is clearly absent in Cuba, which has successfully resolved that issue, even as it grapples with its intractable problems arising from low productivity in some sectors, limited diversification, and so on. While all regimes are in "crisis," the nature of the crisis—its impact on the populace—varies considerably between the socialist and capitalist countries. This caveat should not distract from the structural character of the crisis as it affects all regimes in the area. What is at issue, however, are the sources and consequences of the crisis which vary with the kind of regime and development strategy that has been pursued. In this regard, by emphasizing economic, political, and social structure in shaping policy, we are deliberately downplaying "geographic" factors (e.g., the small size of the countries, the fact that these regimes are located on islands in close proximity to the United States, the limited resource base), even though these are not altogether insignificant factors. The focus is rather on the historical crises which have emerged from particular regime-models embodied in particular country experiences, namely, (1) *Puerto Rico*, with its external growth model, open door to foreign capital and total dependence on foreign capital; (2) *Cuba*, with its revolutionary redistributive approach based on centralized collectivized ownership of the productive forces; and (3) *Jamaica* (under Manley) with its reformist attempt to combine dependency and nationalization in pursuit of a welfare state.

Before we proceed further in our analysis, it is worthwhile to summarize both the similarities and the differences in economic structure which characterize these regimes.

## Similarities and Differences in Economic Structure

Independently, whether the regimes are socialist, populist, or market, a fundamental feature of these regimes is the fact that they are all "externally oriented." There are numerous indicators of this aspect: foreign trade accounts for a high percentage of their gross national product[1]; major productive activities are oriented toward the external market (see Table 13.1): All regimes import a substantial proportion of their capital and consumer goods; a high percentage of the technology that is applied is generated elsewhere; all regimes are heavily indebted, and depend on external finance to sustain their development effort (see Table 13.2).

These common features reflect the inexorable realities inherited from *past* integration and subordination in the world capitalist system, the long and difficult task of breaking with the past, and continued need to relate to one or another world economic system to obtain necessary

The Crises in Market, Collectivist, and Mixed Economies

Table 13.1   GNP and Exports in Cuba, Jamaica, and Puerto Rico

Cuba

| Year | GNP[a] | Exports as % of GNP | Exports: Sugar and derivatives as % of GNP |
|---|---|---|---|
| 1958 | 3,322.2 | 22.1 | 17.6 |
| 1966 | 4,417.9 | 13.4 | 11.4 |
| 1974 | 7,895.8 | 28.1 | 24.3 |
| 1978 | 10,356.0 | 33.0 | N.A. |

Jamaica

| Year | GNP[b] | Exports as % of GNP | Exports: Crude materials, inedible, except fuel as % of GNP |
|---|---|---|---|
| 1971 | 1,202.6 | 36.1 | 23.6 |
| 1973 | 1,708.6 | 31.8 | 21.0 |
| 1975 | 2,574.4 | 38.3 | 25.0 |
| 1977 | 2,846.5 | 32.9 | 23.4 |

Puerto Rico

| Year | GNP[a] | Exports as % of GNP | Food and animals as % of GNP | Chemicals as % of GNP |
|---|---|---|---|---|
| 1947 | 705.3 | 43.0 | | |
| 1962 | 1,683.9 | 56.6 | | |
| 1968 | 2,455.3 | 60.1 | 9.0 | 6.0 |
| 1977 | 3,594.4 | 63.1 | 7.5 | 21.6 |

[a]= In millions of 1965 constant pesos.
[b]= In purchasers' values at current prices ('000s Jamaican dollars.

*Source:* Elaborated on the basis of U.S. Department of Commerce, *Economic Study of Puerto Rico,* Washington: 1979; U.N., *Economic Survey of Latin America,* 1978; CIDE, "Cuba: Politica Economica bajo la revolucion", *CIDE,* September 1978; MacEwan, Arthur, *Revolution and Economic Development in Cuba,* 1980; Department of Statistics, *Statistical Abstract,* Jamaica: 1972–1978.

goods absent or too costly to produce from within (and to avoid the pitfalls and draconian measures associated with autarchic self-reliance, if that is even feasible).

Having noted similarities in economic structure, it would be deceptive to submerge the countries in the region under some common rubric such as "periphery" or "underdeveloped countries." For the impact that these structures have on society, and the context in which they function, is profoundly dissimilar. More important, the historical direction and the possibilities and potentialities for redefining the relations and structures that currently define the region vary greatly with the particular regime, for example, while Cuba is technically dependent, it has through a vast training and education program created an impressive

Table 13.2    Imports in Cuba, Jamaica, and Puerto Rico

Cuba

| Year | Import as % of GNP | Machinery, equipment and manufacture as % of imports | Idem as % of GNP |
|------|------|------|------|
| 1958 | 23.4 | 37.9 | 8.9 |
| 1966 | 20.9 | 30.0 | 6.3 |
| 1974 | 28.2 | 33.1 | 9.3 |
| 1978 | 34.4 | N.A. | N.A. |
| Jamaica | | | |
| 1971 | 43.7 | 52.6 | 23.0 |
| 1973 | 41.4 | 46.1 | 19.1 |
| 1975 | 46.1 | 41.8 | 19.3 |
| 1977 | 34.1 | 31.3 | 10.7 |
| Puerto Rico | | | |
| 1947 | 61.6 | N.A. | N.A. |
| 1965 | 88.7 | 45.2 | 40.1 |
| 1971 | 101.2 | | |
| 1977 | 102.7 | 39.9 | 41.4 |

Source: Ibid.

cadre of technicians who have already begun to adapt technology to Cuban realities and even to design an autonomously anchored technology.[3] Given the dominance of U.S. multinationals in Puerto Rico and the close control exercised over technology, this is not even a prospect in Puerto Rico, unless, of course, there is a change in regime.

Thus, while it is important to note the common economic structural features among the regimes, it is equally vital to observe their dissimilarities:

1. *Ownership in the means of production.* In Puerto Rico, apart from utilities and some declining enterprises, private capital, and especially U.S. capital, controls all of the major productive and some service activity. For example, in 1974, as a percentage of total gross capital stock (at current cost valuation) the private sector represented 69.4% and the public sector 30.6%, while in 1970 the figures were 73.1% for the private sector and 26.9% for the public sector. In 1977 the distribution was 72% for the private sector and 28% for the public sector. On the other hand external capital inflow represented 44.2% of total investment during the period 1947–63, going to 61.3% during 1963–73, and jumping to 81.6% in the 1973–77 period. In Cuba, the state owns all the principal means of production, though a residual small farmer class remains;[5] Jamaica possessed both private and state enterprises, as well as mixed ownership in key industries.[6]

Table 13.3   Puerto Rico: Capital Intensive Industries, Unemployment and Food Stamps

| | | Industrial Output | | | |
|---|---|---|---|---|---|
| Year | GDP[a] | Labor-intensive industries | Capital-intensive industries | Unemployment | Food stamp program cost[b] |
| 1947 | 664.0 | 70.9 | 23.4 | N.A. | — |
| 1950 | 844.1 | N.A. | N.A. | 14.7 | — |
| 1955 | 1,058.3 | N.A. | N.A. | 14.3 | — |
| 1960 | 1,431.9 | N.A. | N.A. | 12.1 | — |
| 1967 | 2,475.4 | 61.6 | 35.4 | 11.6 | — |
| 1970 | 3,067.8 | 60.7 | 38.0 | 10.8 | 40.66 |
| 1974 | 3,787.2 | 47.6 | 51.9 | 13.3 | 88.10 |
| 1977 | 4,048.1 | 32.1 | 66.6 | 19.9 | 629.44[c] |

[a]In constant 1954 millions of dollars.
[b]In millions of dollars.
[c]1976.

Source: Elaborated on the basis of data from U.S. Department of Commerce, op. cit.

2. *Role of the state.* The state in Puerto Rico is largely the classical policeman of liberal economies; economic plans are generally reflections of private initiatives and usually involve the design of incentives to attract capital; the colonial nature of the state further limits its attributes, leaving it with essentially the role of cushioning the negative consequences of market operations, of food stamp distribution (see Table 13.3). In Cuba the state controls, manages, and directs all major economic activity; the central plan allocates investments, resources, financing and manpower. Under centralized collective ownership, the economic and political systems are unified. In Jamaica, the state plays a more active role in directing investment and the plan attempts, through fiscal as well as investment policy, to shape the economy,[7] but its role is curcumscribed by the preexisting and continuing activities in the still substantial private sector and the operations of the local and international

Table 13.4   Puerto Rico: Relation of Profits and Labor Income to Net Domestic Income (in percentages)

| Puerto Rico | 1950 | 1955 | 1960 | 1970 | 1974 | 1977 |
|---|---|---|---|---|---|---|
| Profits | 30.6 | 36.4 | 37.5 | 38.4 | 50.5 | 59.3 |
| Labor income | 69.4 | 63.6 | 62.5 | 62.6 | 49.5 | 40.7 |

Source: U.S. Department of Commerce, op. cit.

market. The state intervenes in, but it does not control, the consequences and reactions of the other (private) economic actors.

3. *Income distribution.* In Puerto Rico, the income curve is heavily skewed toward property owners with returns to capital appropriating a substantial share of total income (see Table 13.4). In Cuba, income distribution tends toward equalization, with small variations approximating 3.5 to 1; in Jamaica, income distribution is skewed (perhaps not as acutely as in Puerto Rico), though the redistributive efforts initially attempted by Manley were undermined by the deterioration of the economy and the loss of purchasing power.[8]

4. *Relative importance of local and foreign private and state capital.* In Puerto Rico, foreign capital predominates over local, and state capital is subordinate to both; in Cuba, state capital is controlling, private capital subsists in the interstices, and foreign capital is nonexistent (except in the form of state to state loans). In Jamaica, while the state sector grew during the Manley years, it was unable to gain control over the commanding heights of the economy, which remained in the hands of private capital.

5. *Labor market.* Both Puerto Rico and Jamaica have a massive surplus labor force, with unemployment ranging from 30 to 40 percent of the working-age population. Cuba has full employment, in some areas labor shortages, though there is some evidence of overstaffing (a disguised form of unemployment).[9]

The meaning of these differences in economic structure is found in the way in which property ownership, class and income structure, and labor market mediate the relations to the world market and to external dependency. External exchanges that generate economic surpluses can be distributed in a variety of ways depending on the class structure, the social and political orientation of the state, the principal holders of property. Thus, for example, income generated by a multinational firm selling industrial goods to the United States can siphon off its earning to the U.S., pay a high salary to upper-class Puerto Rican executives, and provide a minimum amount of tax revenue to the state (and nothing for local technological development). On the other hand, the income generated by the sale of Cuban sugar to the Soviet Union or Japan can provide the state with income for increasing social services, funds for new investments in technology and/or reinvestment in the expansion of productive capacity. The point is that the social and political meaning of "external-oriented" Caribbean economies varies with the type and structure of social order and state. The imperatives flowing from depending on the world market are filtered through the political program and organizational capacities of the local class structure. The manner in which a society articulates its economy within the world market is fundamentally shaped by the nature of the predominating productive system. Simply to note that all Caribbean societies must relate to the world market is to repeat an obvious commonplace practice.

To derive from that fact a notion of market determination of the ordering of Caribbean society is to overlook the profound differences in income, employment, labor market, that define each society. The class differences among Caribbean societies are more consequential than their common classification in the "periphery." For the changes in the world order, if they are to be, are attached to the particular "national" systemic transformations that create the organizational, technological, and institutional capacities to redefine global relations. Our analysis of the contemporary crises of the Caribbean regimes will focus on the interface between internal class contradictions and global economic forces. Our discussion will begin by outlining the common historical problems that faced all three regime models, and will conclude with a discussion of the emerging crises. Essentially we will focus on how one set of solutions to an earlier crisis embedded in a matrix of policies and circumstances contributed to the contemporary crisis. This underlines the fact that dynamic changes have taken place and that new social forces and programs are emerging. It rejects the view that we are dealing with some sort of circular process within a static and stagnant ambience in which one crisis resembles another—the kind of sterile tunnel vision that characterizes the primitive literary exercises of a V.S. Naipaul.

## II: Historical Problems: The Point of Departure

The regime models confronted a common set of economic, social, and political problems forming the basic challenges to which their development strategies were directed. In order to evaluate the successes and failures of each model, it is appropriate to outline the salient issues before proceeding to discuss the strategies and outcomes.

The economic problems were fundamentally fourfold: (1) underdevelopment of the productive forces—absence of technology, skilled labor, and machinery leading to stagnant economies and low levels of productivity; (2) monoculture economies—the specialization in one or a few export products, subject to the fluctuations of the world market; (3) dependence on external sources for capital, technology, finance, and the absence of a developed "home market"; and (4) a local bourgeoisie lacking capacity to organize sustained and rapid growth. While the social issues are numerous, at least four key problems can be identified: (1) substantial class inequalities, especially between large property-owning classes and wage earners; (2) massive long-term, large-scale unemployment and the proliferation of low paying "service jobs"—a permanent class of subproletariats; (3) uneven regional development, clearly expressed in the distribution of social services, income, and government expenditures between country and town; and (4) absence or inadequate supply of social services, resulting in high infant mortality rates, malnutrition, and the like. In the political realm, several features constrained effective popular participation in the making of national decisions: (1) political independence was limited by economic dependence and external penetration both of which preempted vital areas of decision-making; (2) clientelistic styles of political organization in which vertical ties between propertied and propertyless groups prevented the articulation of social issues and the organization of political organizations with coherent socioeconomic programs; and (3) authoritarian structures expressed by the permeation of the state by elite dominated representatives (e.g., police, bureaucracy, development agencies), and in some cases (Batista's Cuba) the use of physical constraints on political mobilization.

Faced with these enduring problems, products of centuries of colonial and neocolonial domination, three sets of responses were pursued, reflecting different strategies and divergent political and social coalitions.

## III: The Divergent Responses to Underdevelopment: Populism, Colonial Capitalism, and Revolutionary Socialism

We will focus on three distinct types of regimes and development strategies which confronted the problems of underdevelopment.

### Class Coalitions and Development Strategies

Each development strategy evolved from a particular configuration of class forces that exercised decisive control over the state apparatus and consequently over the agencies and mechanisms of economic development. In the case of Puerto Rico, an alliance of petty bourgeois politicians (some of whom descended from downwardly mobile hacienda-owner families), technocrats, and U.S. corporate capital dominated the political structure for over forty years, fashioning a model of capitalist development "from above and the outside." The enlargement of the private and public sectors on behalf of corporate expansion, and particularly the inclusion of Puerto Ricans as executive and administrative officers, created a substantial satellite "middle class" linked to U.S. corporate politics and identified with their interests. The growth of U.S. corporate enterprise became identified by this satellite middle class with its own advancement and mobility. The pursuit of development policies promoting U.S. corporate growth was taken over and identified by Puerto Rican auxiliaries as their "own" political-economic project. Ultimately, the logic of this position led to the growth of substantial imperial assimilation sentiment expressed in the pro-statehood movement. The deepening integration of Puerto Rican classes within the U.S. political economy, and the emerging crises of colonial industrialization, deepened the attachments of the dependent classes to the U.S. corporate economy.

In the case of Cuba, the revolutionary government is essentially an alliance of workers, peasants, and professionals rooted in the anti-

Batista, anti-imperialist and anticapitalist struggles covering the ten-year period 1953–63. Sectors of the petty and national bourgeoisie failed to capture the anti-Batista struggle and turn state policy toward a variant of capitalist development. As a result, the political class that emerged was based on and represented the mass of urban and rural propertyless groups and small farmers, even as it developed an autonomous frame-work for formulating policy. The government in Cuba thus *represents* the peasantry and the working class without being *democratically controlled* by its social base. The collectivization of production, the egalitarian norms evidenced in the pattern of redistribution, and the full employment policy are all evidence of the determining indirect influence of the worker-peasant forces in the regime, while the centralized decision-making process is cause and consequence of the growth of a political bureaucratic stratum in the state apparatus. Cuba's development strategy is thus shaped by worker-peasant demands from below and bureaucratic imperatives from above, the outcome reflecting the relative weight of the different forces in each conjuncture.

In Jamaica, the Manley government attempted to lead a coalition of contradictory classes, national capitalists and workers, peasants and bankers, state collectivists and multinational executives, toward a mixed economy described as democratic socialism. This multiclass coalition provided a broad basis of support for two electoral victories, but proved to be an untenable basis to sustain a coherent development policy. The regime's plural character prevented any decisive breaks either toward a straighforward path of capitalist or collectivist development strategy.

*Capitalist Development from Above and the Outside.* The Puerto Rican model is rooted essentially in a strategy of adaptation and collaboration with multinational corporations and subordination to the U.S. imperial state. The regime evolved from a welfare-reform movement in the 1930s to embrace an unadulterated version of free-market economies, sacrificing indigenous ownership and public controls in order to provide the maximum opportunities for foreign, mainly U.S., capital. Essentially, the agency for development was U.S. industrial enterprises, with the state development corporation designing the wage and fiscal policies that facilitated capital accumulation. The appeals to foreign capital were rooted in the opportunity to exploit lower labor costs in Puerto Rico, and at the same time take advantage of the free entry into U.S. markets. The prolonged tax holidays, low tax bases, and the freedom to remit profits that the regime provided further enhanced the "exploitation opportunities." The notion behind this strategy was that "late industrializing" countries needed to provide differential (greater) benefits to advanced corporate enterprises to attract them from the advanced countries in order to begin the process of capital accumulation. Industrial growth through multinational capital would allow the back-ward economy to "skip stages" and move rapidly into the stage of "advanced development" combining high growth and high technology. The strategy was based on an extreme form of "big push – unbalanced growth"—a massive concentration of resources toward the industrial sector at the expense of agriculture. State resources, credits, financing, and subsequently manpower were focused on industry, leading to the virtual demise of agriculture.[10] The notion was that industry could absorb the surplus population through rapid expansion; the rest of the labor force would migrate to the United States. The social problems would be solved through stages. First, industrial development would take place, then social welfare would trickle down to the masses. Once the industrial foundations were established, the "big pie" created, there would then be space to discuss redistributive measures. Premature redistribution and public control would inhibit capital flows, hinder the growth of industry and jobs, and prevent the pie from growing. Capitalist development from above and the outside was cast then in the form of a "stage theory," in which foreign domination and economic growth would create the basis for a modern national economy and the spreading of social benefits.

The Puerto Rican model was based on the premise of deepening its ties to the world market, extending its dependence in the hope of harnessing its external growth toward an internal transformation. To the critics who attributed the island's backwardness to past capitalist exploitation, the Puerto Rican proponents of the model would argue that it was the insufficient level of capitalist penetration that was perpetuating underdevelopment.

*The Revolutionary Socialist Model.* The Cuban revolution ushered in a new approach to the perrenial problems of Caribbean underdevelopment. The revolutionary regime grew out of an armed political struggle against the Batista regime and eventually succeeded in destroying the old state apparatus and establishing a new society based on the collectivization of the means of production. The revolution developed out of the social polarities emerging from an economy heavily controlled by U.S. business and tightly integrated into that country's market. The effort by the Batista regime to unleash state and labor constraints on private capital accumulation and to contain welfare demands probably detonated some of the wage-earner discontent that ultimately provided the social revolutionary forces with their durable base of support. Unlike that of Puerto Rico, the Cuban model ruptured the vast network of imperial tutelage that presided over its economic affairs, and established a new configuration of social classes to sustain the regime and pursue its economic development strategy. While the Puerto Rican model rested principally on an alliance between state technocrats, clientele politicians, and foreign industrialists, the Cuban model was based on a coalition of mass organizations that were predomiantly of a wage-worker and peasant composition. Thus the origins, institutional matrix, and the ascendent social forces in each model were essentially different; this had far-reaching consequences for the type of development strategy that each regime pursued.

The Cuban model was based on the notion of the primacy of economic development through social equality, mass participation, and collective ownership of the means of production. The first preoccupation of the Cuban revolution was to redistribute wealth, land, and social services, to overcome regional disparities, to raise the standard of living of the poorest sectors, and to eliminate unemployment, illiteracy, and malnutrition.[11] Economic growth was perceived as taking an impetus from the social transformation; the social transformation was envisioned as providing the social and political discipline and commitment to sustain rapid and equitable economic growth. The agency of development was the public sector, which took control of the means of production.[12]

The notion was that through state ownership, the economic surplus siphoned off to the exterior would be channeled into the economy. Likewise, the "potential surplus" embodied in fallow fields, unused industrial capacity, and the vast umemployed sector could be harnessed toward rapid growth, overcoming the economic constraints imposed by the adversary relations incurred in the rupture with U.S. tutelage. The sectoral strategy zig-zagged. Initially, an effort was made to shift from agro-export production toward an industrialization strategy. Subsequently, the regime returned to an agro-export approach as a means of eventually financing industrial expansion.[13] This policy, however, in its implementation was transformed into an "unbalanced, big-push" agricultural development strategy in which urban-industrial growth and social consumption were sacrificed in favor of high rates of investment in agriculture, mainly geared toward the export sector. The Cubans were following their own version of a stage theory: First, all-out investment to promote agricultural exports; this was to be followed by a second stage in which industrial growth would be financed and linked with the dominant agricultural sector, and the eventual diversification of the economy and external partners. As the big push in agriculture proceeded, the emphasis on egalitarian and moral incentives remained, but increasingly social relations of production were controlled by the state and the planning-public allocation of resources was centralized, concentrated in the bureaucracy. The post-1970 model represents a modification with increasing emphasis on decentralized decision making, utilization of price mechanism, material incentives, and limited inequalities. Industrialization has regained primacy though closely linked to agricultural growth; investment rates have been lowered and consumption increased. The importance of foreign trade as the engine of growth remains, however, as does dependence on Soviet financing.[14]

Thus, if the Puerto Rican development model was one of adaptation and collaboration with the dominant capitalist forces in the region, the Cuban model stressed innovation and confrontation. While both continued to depend on the world market and tended to become integrated into larger social systems, the manner in which the internal forces articulated with the larger system and the consequences were profoundly different.

*Welfare-Populism.* An attempt to combine aspects of the market integration with social redistributive methods of the Puerto Rican and Cuban models was tried in Jamaica under the Manley regime. Measures were taken to increase public ownership and control over the commanding heights of the economy; financing, however, continued to be linked to the creditor institutions of the capitalist world. Social services and income redistribution were objects of policy, but private capital and the traditional bureaucracy controlled the means of production and the state apparatus, the sources from which income was to be derived. The notion essentially was to combine public and private ownership, national and foreign capital, social welfare and capital incentives, into a development package within a parliamentary electoral institutional framework. Through the growth of a public sector in mining and agriculture, the national share of income would increase and be channeled into social measures (employment for the redundant) and economic incentives for the local bourgeoisie. A multiclass coalition, including big and small propertied groups, affluent middle-class professionals, wage laborers, and small rural producers formed the social base of the Manley regime, and would be sustained through this reform strategy. The parliamentary framework would ensure government responsiveness to the demands of its constituents and foreclose foreign opposition on the assumption that Western, and particularly U.S., hostility was directed mainly at communist-initiated redistributive measures. The "democratic socialist" ideology and the affiliation with the Socialist International would facilitate financial assistance from European counterparts, thus avoiding dependence on either of the "superpowers." An active role in the nonaligned movement would provide a ready forum to address the deep-seated structural issues arising from the international economic order. Thus, international affiliations congruent with the internal policies converged and were thought to provide sufficient leverage to stimulate development and avoid the dislocations of revolution and the subordination associated with adaptation.

The regime looked toward the technocrats in the Planning Agency, executives in the multinationals and local capital and the functionaries in the public enterprises and co-ops to provide the financial resources to stimulate investment and growth, while it increased tax revenues and redistributed income toward the poor. The changes and development policies were to be pursued through the existing state apparatus (e.g., civil service, police force) on the assumption that they were politically neutral and professional institutions loyal to the constitution. The ideological identification, "democratic socialism" referred not only to the "method" of change (parliamentary and electoral strategy) but also connoted that a multiplicity of classes (propertied and nonpropertied) would jointly share in making decisions affecting the distribution and production of goods and services. Hence, a more accurate ideological term describing the Manley regime would be "national-populist" regime, a genre familiar to students of Latin American politics. Insofar as there was common purpose within the heterogenous groups composing the regime, it would be found in their common claim to be increasing the capacity of the national economy to control its productive forces, and secondly their common concern to increase the level of consumption of the masses. Competing factions within the regime differed over precisely the scope and nature of these measures, but none seriously broached any manner of effort to redefine the terms of the struggle.

## THE BUREAUCRACY VERSUS THE MARKET

The development models discussed above provide evidence that illustrates the importance of the debate over the role of the state and market. The Puerto Rican and Cuban models polarize the debate between a laissez-faire state in which market relations permeate all levels and sectors of the economy, and a collectivist state in which market relations are constrained by the central plan, largely confined to external exchanges and to less substantial activities among the shrinking private farmer sector. In both the Puerto Rican and Jamaican models—despite the latter's efforts at state planning—the state was ultimately subordinated to the market. The success or failures resulted from the regime's efforts to insert itself into the universe of capitalist exchanges, finances, and production. The "market," including flows of capital, loans, as well as goods, shaped the economic and social relations between and within enterprises; the state's role was essentially to complement the role of the market through the providing of incentives to capital (Puerto Rico) or through regulations to redirect income (Jamaica). The demands of accumulation and reproduction of capital established the parameters for state activity, defining its strategic goals and possible instruments. Encroachment on the prerogatives of capital, such as too radical a tax bite or too deep-cutting income shifts, led to the withdrawal of capital on the economic front and social antagonism and political polarization, as was illustrated in the latter years of the Manley regime. The challenge to the marketplace had profound repercussions on the political sphere, leading eventually to the growth of a broadbased coalition of forces under the hegemony of pro-big business political representatives. Serious tampering with the dominance of the market by a regime that depends fundamentally on the market is a sure formula for crisis. Puerto Rican subservience to the market, and particularly the U.S. market, is evidenced by the limited autonomy of action of the state, the constraints on the trade union movement, the enormous growth of a high proportion of unproductive labor, ironically sustained by high levels of state financed transfer payments. The dictatorship of the market is expressed by its imperious demand for unmitigated power; whosoever conflicts with its prerogatives runs the risk of finding empty assembly shops, declining mining production, empty hotels, and the flight of "national" and "patriotic" professionals to Miami.

Counterposed to the dictorship of the market and those who slavishly follow its commands is the central plan administered by the state bureaucracy. The growth of central planning and the subordination of civil society to the state-party apparatus were two convergent processes accompanying the radical redistribution of wealth in Cuba. The plan abolished the market as the principal allocator of resources. In its place emerged a centralized administrative structure that permeated all decisions affecting production, distribution, and exchange. Corporate capital's dictatorship was replaced by the bureaucratic regime, conditioned by the burgeoning mass movements which laid consequential claims on the regime. Bureaucratic centralism with popular support established boundaries within which socioeconomic policies were pursued. Full employment and income equalization demanded by wage workers were combined with elite designation of investment targets, sectoral proportions, and other pivotal decisions.

While the market model clearly represents the interests of corporate capital, both systems avoid 'the third system of self-managed collective ownership. As in other parts of the world, the pendulum swings between bureaucracy and market, whereby the prerogatives of power and privilege become redistributed within elite groups. There is no mystical iron law of oligarchy here but the common interests of coherent groups—one rooted in property, the other in the state apparatus—whose prerogatives conflict with the socialization of the social relations of production. It is easier for a bureaucracy to shift from centralist control to the market, because it can retain its political power even if it must share its economic privileges. Likewise, property groups prefer statification, especially when it is well compensated, because it frequently offers opportunities to retain managerial prerogatives and privileges in the new regime.

## Social and Economic Impact of the Models on Development

Both the Cuban and Puerto Rican models, whatever their shortcomings, have had a profound impact on the structures of economy and society. The Jamaican experience appears to have made much less of an impact, in part because of the continuities with the past and in part because of the limited time frame in which it took place. The Puerto Rican model of capitalist development from "above and the outside" has transformed the country from a primarily agricultural to industrially based economy;[15] this has been accompanied by a massive demographic shift from the countryside to the city and abroad to the mainland cities.[16] Puerto Rico is overwhelmingly an urban industrial capitalist society with a large wage-labor force, a substantial salaried petty-bourgeoisie and dependent local capitalist class. The small agrarian producers, already substantially undermined by the corporate plantation system, were further decimated by the industrialization strategy. All sectors and strata of the Puerto Rican population are linked to market transactions and state activity. There are virtually no areas of precapitalist production or autonomous self-sufficient communities. Market integration, and class incorporation, have created the bases for a modern class-divided society. Income levels and the gross national product have increased significantly between the mid-1940s and the early 1970s, as the island was invaded by most of the major U.S. corporations seeking to take advantage of low labor costs and long tax holidays.

The very terms that successfully attract industry to the island, however, were the same factors that led to its decline; as labor was employed and then organized, labor costs increased. Given the sparse capital investments, it was easy for industry—especially the garment firms—to "island hop," or shift their operations to the Far East, where new sources of cheap labor could be employed.[17] Having displaced agriculture, the slowing down of industrialization led to a growing urban subproletariat, increasingly dependent on state subsidies.[18] Laissez-faire capitalism has become the catalyst for the expansion of state activity; food stamps subsidize the casualities of international capital mobility. The industrial solution to low incomes and unemployment in agriculture has led to a new set of problems—long-term massive urban under- and unemployment.[19] The stimulation of the inflow of foreign capital has led to the growth of income and the subsequent outflow of capital. The dependence on foreign capital as a means for stimulating growth has been the source for the financial dependence and growing debt to finance government activity in light of the decline of foreign capital. The growth of the economy based on exports to a single market constrains the regime's efforts to seek alternative markets. The unbalanced growth of industry has increased the need to import food precisely when industry's capacity to generate export earnings is declining and food costs are increasing. In a word, dependent colonial industrialization by solving some problems created new ones: The growth of productive forces raises the question of their control, their anchorage in the social system, their impact on the social system. The transformation of the agricultural population into wage workers raises the question of the capacity to redistribute income and effectively employ the labor force. The transition from agrarian to industrial capitalist society solved some problems but exacerbated others. Puerto Rico is no longer a "monoculture" but its many products are dependent on a single market, a single source of technology and finance, namely, U.S. banks and corporations.

The diversification of the class structure, the growth of income and wage levels, has been accompanied by a growing deracinated surplus labor force of under- and unemployed. Among classes, property groups appropriate a disproportionately large share of national income, sustaining and expanding social inequality. Regional differences have widened as rural areas and small towns are abandoned, and San Juan becomes a magnet attracting the poor and ambitious through the concentration of industrial capital and public expenditures.[20] The growth of welfare payments has been accompanied by the reinforcement of clientelistic political associations in which state payments are linked to political loyalities, encumbering most efforts at independent popular mobilization among the urban poor.

*Cuba.* The Cuban revolution succeeded in totally transforming the Cuban social structure, eliminating all large property holders, leveling incomes, and providing free social services for all. Moreover, it succeeded in eliminating all foreign ownership of productive and natural resources. The transformation of the economy and the society was accompanied by the destruction of the old clientelistic political relationships characteristic of both the Batista dictatorship and the previous parliamentary system. In its place a mass-based single-party system linked to mass organizations was established. While the Cuban revolution made a major impact in the realm of social problems and evening out disparities between country and town, its efforts to develop the productive forces were much less successful. Cuba still depends on sugar exports; the levels of growth are hardly impressive and per capita income has not grown greatly over the past two decades.[21] Moreover, while Cuba has broken its dependence on U.S. investment and markets, it now depends on the USSR for financing and trade. The transformation of Cuba was accomplished through the bureaucratization of the economy; in that context, the solution to ownership and exploitation has failed to solve the problem of confronting work organization or, more generally, social relations of production, manifested in low levels of productivity, absenteeism, mismanagement of resources, and an incapacity to convert high levels of investment into productive activity. The bureaucratic mechanisms for equalization of income have hindered the development of the productive forces, creating pressures to revert to market and price mechanisms, material incentives and differential payments. The reallocation of resources from the cities to the countryside reduced rural poverty and regional inequalities but was pursued with a singlemindedness that sacrificed opportunities for diversification and dynamic growth in industry. The attempt to pursue economic targets through moral exhortation without representative political institutions led to excessive reliance on voluntaristic concentrations of growth ("willpower" was exaggerated over material-technical conditions), which led to "societal mobilizations" that disrupted planning and rationality. Beginning in the early 1970s, efforts have been made to resolve these deepening contradictions; for example, planning has become less centralized, and some institutions of local control have been delegated authority. The central contradiction between social ownership and centralized control, however, continues to plague the economy and limit the potentialities inherent in a planned economy.

*Jamaica.* The Manley experiment with "democratic socialism" was short lived and only recently concluded; it therefore is difficult to evaluate and determine its impact on the problems of underdevelopment. In the economic sphere, the government increased Jamaican ownership in agro-export production and natural resources, including a partnership in the bauxite industry. Yet, financial dependence increased, as loans

Table 13.5   Jamaica: Rates of Growth of Selected Sectors of the Economy

| Year | GDP | Government services | Dis-trib-utive trade | Agri-cul-ture | Mining | Manufac-turing | Construc-tion |
|------|-----|---------------------|----------------------|---------------|--------|----------------|---------------|
| 1973 | −1.1 | 11.8 | − 2.9 | −0.3 | − 0.2 | −2.0 | − 2.8 |
| 1974 | −2.0 | 1.8 | −12.1 | −4.8 | 50.0 | 1.6 | −10.8 |
| 1975 | −0.4 | 7.0 | 8.2 | 5.4 | −22.3 | −3.4 | 0.7 |
| 1976 | −6.6 | 6.2 | −23.4 | 3.4 | −19.9 | 2.0 | −22.9 |
| 1977 | −4.1 | 0.4 | − 5.2 | −0.1 | 14.1 | −4.0 | −25.5 |

Source: Elaborated on the basis of data from U.N., *Economic Survey of Latin America,* 1976 and 1978; and Department of Statistics, *National Income and Product,* Jamaica, 1978.

and debts spiraled and international bankers demanded an increasing role in setting Jamaica's development agenda. Jamaican exports continued to depend upon primary products though industrial goods demonstrated some growth. In the years leading up to the 1980 elections, the rates of growth and productivity were negative and the overall development of the productive forces was quite insignificant (see Table 13.5).

In the realm of social changes, after initial efforts to increase mass consumption and the availability of the social services, the government's attempt to meet the austerity demands of the International Monetary Fund led to a precipitous decline in employment, income, and social services.[22] The local bourgeoisie and the affluent professionals took advantage of the lack of adequate state controls and sent substantial savings and capital abroad, not infrequently accompanying it. In the political realm, the regime was not able to break the pattern of vertical links between property owners and masses—clientelistic relations between local leaders, property groups and lumpen street gangs were found in both the JLP and PNP. While frequent "popular rallies" were held, the "plebescitarian style" of politics failed to provide a mechanism for institutionalizing new forms of direct representation for the producing classes. The Manley regime, bound by the constraints of parliament, the security forces, the civil service (and its ideology), did not envision the conversion of the mobilized masses into new governing councils. The electoral defeat of Manley's democratic socialist regime occurred in the midst of an increasingly demoralized mass. In the end, the regime was unable to guarantee the elementary condition of political order; it lacked the instruments and capacity to control the forces of extra-official violence. The multiclass coalition that brought the democratic socialist regime to power was the very condition that prevented the formulation of a coherent development program and a clear notion of class power.

The fragmentation of power was cause and consequence of the internal polarization within society and the party (PNP). Between the imperatives of capital accumulation (both local and international, financial, and industrial) and the mass demands for redistribution and consumption, the regime wavered and eventually collapsed, unable to satisfy either, lacking the political organization to discipline one or the other. The political breakthrough at the international level, the independent political line—the ability to carve out a nonaligned foreign policy, develop ties with Social Democracy, open relations with Cuba—came to nought because it was not anchored in an independent, coherent, disciplined class movement capable of sustaining production and making effective claims on its new allies abroad. In contrast to Puerto Rico or Cuba, Jamica has returned full cycle: Manley's defeat has brought forth a regime that promises to pursue "free market" policies—in a sense, a more radical version of the policies of the late 1960s, the socioeconomic consequences of which produced Manley's initial victory in 1972. Whether the Seaga regime can consistently apply these policies within a parlimentary system and facing a labor force clamoring to recuperate its living standards is open to question. The alternative practiced elsewhere is to bend the political system toward a form of authoritarian rulership and repress the discontent that grows out of the application of free market economics.

## Impending Crises

The Cuban and Puerto Rican models have radically transformed their societies. Both have demonstrated at the aggregate national level an enormous capacity to mobilize resources: Puerto Rico, by attracting foreign capital, Cuba by internal mobilization and external borrowing. Below the aggregate national level, however, profound disjunctures exist. In Puerto Rico, the growth of capital has been accompanied by the multiplication of unemployment; in Cuba, the high rates of investment have not led to the spectacular growth of the productive forces and individual levels of consumption. In the case of Puerto Rico, the process of economic growth has been dominated by an imperial capitalist class, appropriating wealth and exploiting labor power, which has led to a disjuncture between the production of surplus value and its reinvestment in activity generating employment in Puerto Rico; the mobility of international capital stands in contrast to the immobility of "Puerto Rican labor." Productive forces embedded in an international circuit of capital has led to the *growth* and *decline* of employment and income, the proletarianization of peasants, and the lumpenization of the proletarian. The cyclical nature is intimately related to the comparative costs and availability of labor within the international circuit of capital at different historical moments; the opening of new cheap labor markets in adjoining islands, in Central and South America and in the Far East, has led to the relative decline in the flow of capital to Puerto Rico.

The crises in contemporary Puerto Rico is *not* that of an underdeveloped country in transition from an agricultural to industrial society. Rather, it is the crises of a dependent (colonial) capitalist country that is deindustrializing. Industrial unemployment, bloated service sectors, expanding real estate and financial activities and stagflation, features found in the imperial capitalist centers, are present in Puerto Rico. On the island, the crisis runs deeper because the power of the state is derived (and its power to cushion the effects more limited) and the conditions for industrial growth much more contingent on a limited set of options. Out of this matrix of stagnation and deindustrialization has emerged a massive army of deracinated masses, susceptible to appeals from the extreme right (statehood) with its offers of food stamps and petty patronage; on the other hand, the rising welfare costs and the loss of economic vitality impinges on the U.S. at a time when big business is imposing austerity on its own Labor force: the possibility exists that if the U.S. government substantially reduces its welfare subsidies, this army of unemployed will become available for radical leftist movements. Up to now, the political contradictions of the deepening economic crises have been only marginally expressed.

In Jamaica, the collapse of "democratic socialism" reflected the incapaity of the regime to link welfare and redistributive measure to economic growth, a process which would not have been possible within the existing state and class structure. Efforts to control and direct capital provoked capital flight. Attempts to control wage claims led to electoral defections and political defeats. The problem was not "too much state control" as the conservatives would have it, but rather the lack of sufficient control, on one level, and more fundamentally the absence of control over the state by those forces directly linked to production—namely, the working class and their technical allies. Paradoxically, the conservative Seaga regime recognizes the need for direct control over the state by the agencies of development—in the case of his model, the capitalist class and its financial backers. The contradictions at the national level were replicated at the international level. While the government promoted anti-imperialist policies and nationalization of multinationals, it sought to finance them through the same imperial agencies. It is not surprising that a credit squeeze was put on. What is astonishing is that the Manley regime expressed surprise. The laws of action and reaction, popular measures and reactionary counter-measures, are played out in all arenas today, there is no "national economic strategy," least of all in the Caribbean. The Jamaican road to socialism came into conflict with the IMF prescriptions for a return to laissez faire capitalism. While it is important to recognize and take account of pecularities of national history, social structure, and so on, in the transition to socialism, it is essential to recognize the need for an international strategy which *assumes* political confrontation and develops alternatives.

The Cuban revolution is passing through a prolonged low-pressure crisis which manifests itself in a variety of "political" and "apolitical" ways—stagnant productivity despite substantial investments, absenteeism, low growth, failure to meet economic targets. The fundamental contradiction in Cuba is between *the high levels of national commitments* expressed in the aggregate investment and *the low level of direct control over the means of production by the direct producers*. The central problem facing the Cuban model is that it depends upon mass participation to sustain it, but decisions continue to be controlled by a restricted political elite. Unlike capitalist society, which depends upon fear and coercion of the market place, reinforced by state repression, the Cuban model is explicitly designed to produce through the active involvement of the producers: without worker control, job security leads to declining production and the proliferation of ineffectual bureaucratic controls and punitive edicts. The policy debates and oscillations between centralization or decentralization, region- or industry-based organization, remains an intrabureaucratic exercise that fails to confront the more fundamental issues rooted in the relations of production. External imposition of discipline will continue to be ineffective; material incentives may or may not increase production but, in any case, run the risk of provoking greater inequalities and sharpening social conflicts. The regime's recognition and criticism of the ultravoluntarism of the political leadership during the 1960s—when political "will" was sometimes assumed to conquer all material obstacles—is a step forward. But the decision to focus on the development of the productive forces can take place through a technocratic-managerial approach that will exacerbate social differences, or through a program of worker self-management within which the workers' productive practice will become the school of social discipline. Effective control by direct producers and respectable growth rates are two sides of the same coin. The alternative is the pattern of Eastern Europe: oscillation between collectivism and the inequities and inequalities of "market statism."

## Notes

1. However, in the case of Cuba, "(. .) over two thirds of its foreign commerce remains unaffected from fluctuations and unfavorable international prices, and from the contradictions which derive from world economic crises." Cepal, *op. cit.*, 146. Of course, Cuba's relation with the Soviet Union creates a particular set of contradictions which will be examined later in this paper.

2. In the case of Jamaica, the external Public Debt rose from $229.0 million in 1970 to $896.3 million in 1977 (World Bank, *World Development Report*, 1978, 1979). In the case of Puerto Rico, the Public Debt rose from 404.0 million 1954 constant dollars in 1960 to $2,767.7 million in 1977 (U.S. Department of Commerce, *op. cit.*). In the case of Cuba, although there is no available data on its debt, the latter often assumes the form of subsidies paid by the Soviet Union to balance Cuba's foreign dificit. In the 1970–74 period this deficit reached 1,400,000,000 Cuban pesos, and it is estimated at 4,000,000,000 for the whole revolutionary period. It should be noted that as internal consumption grows, so imports rise, as a result of existing obstacles to the rapid expansion of the productive sector.

In the case of Puerto Rico, the U.S. government notes: "Public debt issuance has been a major source of funding for the growing role of government in the Puerto Rican economy in this decade, funding public capital investment and to some degree operating expenditures." U.S. Department of Commerce, *op. cit.*

3. Higher education enrollment in Cuba has risen from 19,500 in 1960–61, to 35,110 in 1970–71, to 123,000 in 1977–78. (CMEA, *Statistical Yearbook*, Moscow, 1979).

4. U.S. Deparment of Commerce, *op. cit.*

5. After the Revolution, the agricultural sector remained the most privatized; in particular, this was the case of sugar cane production: in 1962 the private sector represented 59.8% of the total, but it fell to 18.0% by 1975. In the same period, the State sector grew from 40.2% to 82% (*Source*: Cide, *op. cit.*).

6. Foreign capital was substantial in bauxite, agriculture (bananas), commerce and tourism. Public ownership emerged in the bauxite and sugar industries, tourism and banking. Earlier the state controlled areas of communication and transport. The rest of the economy was in the hands of private Jamaican businessmen—a substantial part of which was in the hands of ethnic minorities.

7. In the case of Jamaica, state disbursements grew from 186,000,000 Jamaican dollars in 1969 to 1,074,200,000 in 1978. (Department of Statistics, *Statistical Abstract*, Jamaica, 1979).

8. Unemployment in Jamaica went from 18.5% in 1968 to 22.5% in 1972, reaching 26.0% in 1978. At the same time production of bauxite and alumina declined from an index of 100 in 1974 to 76 and 71 respectively for 1977.

9. "Although at present time the goal of full employment has been reached, there persists a serious qualitative disadjustment between the requirements of the productive structure and the available human resources. The educational system, with its new conception of "Study-Work," has gradually developed human resources that are highly qualified and that will fulfill the needs of the productive structure as the latter expands. Until this is achieved, the country will continue to maintain relatively low levels of production in some service sectors where the employed labor force exceeds the real needs. In other words, although 100% of the labor force is employed, it seems that part of it remains "underemployed", a term that may not be all that adequate, for in the Cuban case it refers to low productivity and not to low levels of income or the lack of access to the mass consumption market, nor to the inability of people to incorporate themselves in services such as health, education, culture, sports, etc." Cide, *op. cit.*, 145.

10. Agricultural production as % of GDP fell from 9.7 in 1960 to 3.5 in 1977. (Dept. of Commerce, *op. cit.*).

11. For example, life expectancy at birth rose in Cuba from 61.8 in 1960 to 69.8 in 1975. (*Caribbean Review*, vol. 8, no. 3, 1979). Also, "By the end of (1961), the adult literacy rate was listed as 96.1 percent—the highest in Latin America and among the highest in the world." (Dominguez, Jorge, *Cuba: Order and Revolution*, Harvard University Press, London, 1978).

12. See, on the initial years of the revolution, O'Connor, James, *The Origins of Socialism in Cuba*, Cornell Press, 1962.

13. For a synthesis of a CEPAL monograph on the different stages of Cuban economic planning, see Cide, *op. cit.* In Cuba according to CEPAL, three stages of economic planning can be distinguished from 1959 to the present time. The first stage, 1959–62, structural in character, accomplished an agrarian reform, tenency reform, urban reform, nationalization of foreign enterprises, banks, statization of foreign trade, and the nationalization of education. A second stage, 1963–70, characterized as the transition to Socialism, was initiated amidst an international blockade (led by the United States), which redefined the strategy for development. A heavy emphasis was placed on agricultural development, both in terms of technology and diversification. Although the main emphasis went towards the sugar industry, inroads were also made into developing livestock production and the myriad infrastructural works necessary to articulate a coherent agrarian strategy. Several problems arose with these first two stages of economic planning: First, a heavy reliance on sugar to generate foreign revenue subordinated other sectors of the economy to the fluctuations of agricultural production and international prices; second, the equalization,

increased income, and full employment of the population outdid the availability of internally produced goods and services, and thus led to an increase of imports. The shortage of consumer goods, in turn, led to the accumulation of large amounts of idle currency (generating inflationary pressures); in response to this problem, after 1970 the Cuban government adopted a discriminated policy of price increases so as to absorb this mass of money and further promote new areas of production. Thus, production of buses grew from 300 units in 1970 to 1,267 in 1976; gas stoves from 6,000 units in 1970 to 50,000 in 1976; refrigerators from 5,800 in 1970 to 43,700 in 1976; radios, from 19,100 in 1970 to 94,100 in 1976.

Thus, during the third stage of economic planning 1970–75, the Cuban model has sought to perfect work norms, increase efficiency, adopt a realistic wage policy. In this new stage, special importance has been given to medium-range planning; at the same time, there has been greater industrialization, as in the examples above, and the efficiency of the non-sugar sectors of agriculture has been increased. Sugar production, however, has not risen as expected, thus creating pressures on the balance of payments. In short, according to CEPAL, each stage attempts to articulate and resolve the problems of the previous ones.

14. See Cide, *op. cit.*

15. Manufacturing grew from 21.6% of GDP in 1960 to 33.5% in 1977 (Department of Commerce, *op. cit.*).

16. However, "As already noted, the migration trends, which from the 1940's to the late 1960's showed a sustained net flow out of Puerto Rico, have reversed dramatically over the past decade. During the last 6 years the net inflow of migrants has been estimated by the Planning Board of the Commonwealth to have averaged 34,400 per year. In fact, the inflow over the July 1976–June 1977 period has been estimated to have run even higher—about 47,000 persons.

The reasons for the reversal of the migration trends are obviously hard to determine, but several factors can be suggested: The 1967–68 riots in some large American cities, which made them less desirable places to live in; the deterioration of the employment situation in the United States both because of the 1970–71 recession and the much more severe 1974–75 recession; the substantial narrowing of the wage gap between Puerto Rico and the mainland; the extension of various income transfer programs, such as food stamps, to large sectors of the Puerto Rican population; and last but not least the unusually cold winters which have hit the mainland over the last couple years. It might be of some interest to note here that at the same time that many Puerto Ricans were returning to the island, reversing the traditional flow, many blacks were also leaving the large cities of the Northeast and returning to the South.

In any case, the net inflow of migrants to the Island must be considered as a disturbing development of Puerto Rico, which has long been suffering from high population pressure. The question is "to what extent are the immigrants hindering the economic progress of Puerto Rico by competing for jobs and other scarce resources with local residents." U.S. Department of Commerce, *op. cit.*

17. "Textile exports have fallen from a high of 170 million and 10% of the U.S. market in 1973 to only 48 million and a little over 1% of the import market in 1977. The factors causing this shift are the high energy cost and the recent rise in average hourly compensation stemming mostly from increases in the minimum wage. Wages in Puerto Rico's textile industries are well above those in countries which are Puerto Rico's main competitors." Note, however, that "high energy cost" affects all countries equally. The following list shows the *average hourly earning in textile industries, in 1976 $U.S.*

| | |
|---|---|
| Taiwan | .42 |
| Korea | .44 |
| Hong Kong | .78 |
| Mexico | 1.29 |
| Japan | 2.06 |
| Italy | 2.14 |
| Puerto Rico | 2.36 |

The same applies to the shoe and electrical equipment industries. On the other hand, the chemical industry is not affected, for "This industry is capital intensive—labor inputs are a small percentage of total cost; thus the recent rise in the minimum wage has not affected these industries seriously." U.S. Department of Commerce, *op. cit.*, 109.

18. See, for example, the growth of public services from 12.2% of total employment in 1964 to 19.3 in 1977 (ibid.).

19. Also, ". . . Statistics for Puerto Rico . . . show that a large proportion of the local labor force which has jobs is severly underemployed." U.S. Department of Commerce, *op. cit.*, p. 597.

20. Whereas in Puerto Rico as a whole the unemployment rate in 1978 was 20.0%, in San Juan it was only 15.7%, as compared to an average 23% in the rest of the country. U.S. Department of Commerce, *op. cit.*

21. "According to official figures, from 1958 to 1974, material production increased at an annual rate of 5.6%. Taking into account that the population increased from 6.8 to 9.2 million people in the same amount of time (yearly increased being 2%), material production per capita had increased during that time at a rate of 3.5% per annum." Cide, *op. cit.*

22. Consumer prices rose from (index=100.0) in 1970 to 326.7 in 1978. International Labor Organization, *Yearbook of Labour Statistics*, Geneva, 1978. Unemployment rose from 18.5% in 1968 to 26.0% in 1978 (Department of Statistics, *The Labour Force*, Jamaica 1972; World Bank, *World Development Report*, 1979).

# 14

# U.S. Policy Toward the Middle East

JAMES F. PETRAS
ROBERTO KORZENIEWICZ

## Introduction

A discussion of U.S. policy in the Middle East must begin by taking into account the long-term, large-scale economic interests that operate in the area. These economic interests embody social classes which inform the policy-making structure that allocates resources and define strategic goals. The heterogeneity of interests, as well as their vital stakes in the region, lead to a common purpose in pressuring for a strong U.S. presence without necessarily agreeing on the form in which it will be manifested. While economic interests are of paramount importance in understanding U.S. policy, the policy-making apparatus representing those interests defines and establishes the instruments and time schedules that structures policy. While the state represents corporate interests, it is not identical with it. Moreover, the political realm has a logic of its own—within the larger economic imperatives—and the various phases of policy-making must be analyzed in their own terms.

We proceed by outlining the overarching U.S. economic interests in the region and follow with an analysis of the perceptions and perspectives of U.S. policy discussed in responsible business journals. Recent U.S. policy is then analyzed in its various phases, with equal concern with the context and consequences of each policy and its larger implications.

## Economic Bases of U.S. Policy

The parameters of U.S. policy in the Middle East are set by a variety of economic interests whose cumulative effect is decisive in shaping the

Reprinted by permission from pages 69–96 in *U.S. Strategy in the Gulf: Intervention Against Liberation,* edited by Leila Meo (Belmont, MA: Association of Arab-American University Graduates, 1981).

substantive concerns of military and strategic thinking. Three levels of economic linkages exist between the U.S. and the Middle East: the first is structural and is found in the fact that U.S., European and Japanese economies depend on access to Middle East oil for survival. The collapse of one area would lead to a major crisis throughout the capitalist world. The second linkage is between particular capitalist segments who are directly involved in large-scale, long-term relations within the region and who are influential in having U.S. policy-makers define the defense of their corporate interests as matters of "national security." These three major segments include petroleum corporations, banking concerns and defense industries. All three segments have vast undertakings in the region and all have access to significant policy-making bodies in the government. The third linkage, the U.S. and Israel, is based on subsidies by the U.S., the result of a powerful domestic pressure group (the Israel Lobby). Moreover, Israel's relevance to military-strategic planners revolves around its role as a political contraceptive against revolutionary nationalist upheavals in the Middle East. Thus U.S. economic interests condition military and political decisions, as well as being shaped by them. There is a dialectic inter-play between the imperatives of economic expansion and the projection of military power in the region that undermines any effort to separate the two in any practical analysis of U.S. policy.

In examining the economic relations, it is important to focus on the multiple aspects of the relations and not to single any one area and examine it in isolation. Secondly, it is important to understand the dynamic aspects of the relation, to observe the direction it is moving. Thirdly, it is important to understand the qualitative aspects of the relationship, to recognize that particular products may have more importance than quantitative ratios may indicate. Finally, it is important to understand that it is social factors that define and influence "national policy"—particular class interests and corporate groups, not abstract notions such as investment earnings as a percentage of gross national products, oil income as a percentage of total trade, etc. The interests of corporate actors establish what is vital to a country.

In considering U.S. policy, it is important to consider both the specific interests of the U.S. and the interrelated interests of its foremost allies and trading partners, Japan and the European Economic Community (EEC). U.S., EEC and Japanese trade with the Mid-East has been growing steadily over the past 20 years. Middle Eastern trade has more than doubled its share of total U.S. trade since 1960, almost tripled its share of Japanese trade and increased by nearly 50 percent of EEC trade (see Table 14.1).

More significantly, the U.S. competitive position in the Mid-East, in relation to the EEC and Japan, has declined precipitously. In 1960, 11.7 percent of Mid-East trade was with the U.S., 27.5 percent with the EEC and 5.2 percent with Japan. By 1980, EEC had increased its share to 35.4 percent. Japan had jumped to 16.1 percent, while the U.S. share

Table 14.1    Composition by Middle Eastern Trade with U.S., EEC, Japan (in percentages)

|  | 1960 | 1970 | 1978 |
|---|---|---|---|
| U.S. exports to the Middle East (as % of total U.S. exports) | 3.3 | 3.1 | 7.6 |
| U.S. imports from Middle East (as % of total U.S. imports) | 2.6 | 1.0 | 5.7 |
| U.S. trade with the Middle East (as % of total U.S. foreign trade) | 2.9 | 2.1 | 6.6 |
| EEC exports to the Middle East (as % of total EEC exports) | 3.9 | 2.0 | 5.9 |
| EEC imports from the Middle East (as % of total EEC imports) | 5.1 | 3.6 | 7.8 |
| EEC trade with the Middle East (as % of total EEC foreign trade) | 4.5 | 2.8 | 6.9 |
| Japan's exports to the Middle East (as % of total Japanese exports) | 4.4 | 2.8 | 10.0 |
| Japan's imports from the Middle East (as % of total Japanese imports) | 8.5 | 12.6 | 27.4 |
| Japan's trade with the Middle East (as % of total Japanese foreign trade) | 6.4 | 7.1 | 17.3 |
| Middle eastern exports | | | |
| % to U.S. | 7.5 | 3.8 | 9.4 |
| % to EEC | 27.8 | 29.1 | 33.1 |
| % to Japan | 6.2 | 18.3 | 18.7 |
| Middle eastern imports | | | |
| % from U.S. | 16.0 | 18.0 | 15.0 |
| % from EEC | 27.3 | 24.7 | 37.8 |
| % from Japan | 4.2 | 7.3 | 13.6 |
| Middle eastern foreign trade | | | |
| % with U.S. | 11.7 | 10.9 | 12.2 |
| % with EEC | 27.5 | 26.9 | 35.4 |
| % with Japan | 5.2 | 12.8 | 16.1 |

Source: Elaborated on the basis of figures from United Nations, *Yearbook of International Trade Statistics,* years 1961, 1971, 1978.

still vegetated at about 12.2 percent. In overall trade terms, the U.S. is becoming more dependent on trade with "developing countries" which now account for 38 percent of U.S. exports and are the fastest growing export market for American exports. If the displacement occurring in the Middle East spreads, the U.S. economy will be in serious trouble, given its mounting trade deficits—largely from growing oil imports. Thus the massive markets of the Middle East are a growing and increasingly important area of U.S. interest and involvement, an area economically lucrative and militarily weak, a combination which easily invites power projections by U.S. policy makers.

Apart from trade, the Mid-Eastern countries are major suppliers of oil—providing almost 20 percent of U.S. supplies, almost 70 percent of EEC supplies and over three-quarters of Japan's. Without Mid-East

Table 14.2    Near and Middle Eastern Crude Oil Imports as Percentage of Total Supply
for U.S., EEC, and Japan

|  | 1977 |
|---|---|
| United States | 19.1 |
| EEC | 68.7 |
| Japan | 77.8 |

*Source:* Elaborated on the basis of figures from OCED, *Oil Statistics,* 1977.

oil, Japan and Europe's economies would collapse in a few months and
the U.S. would be in dire straits. (See Table 14.2.) Access to markets
and raw materials are areas of concern to overall U.S. policy. In addition,
however, three sets of socio-economic forces have particular interest:
namely, the defense industry, the petroleum companies and the big
banking houses.

Of particular importance for U.S. trade with the Middle East is the
sale of weapons: "In the first half of the 1970's, U.S. arms sales in the
Middle East averaged $3.2 billion *per year*—more than the total sales
($2.3 billion) over the previous 15 years. Arms sales almost tripled again
from 1975 to 1979, to an average $8.9 billion per year. As a percentage
of total U.S. arms sales, the region jumped from 19.7 percent in the
1955–69 period to nearly 52 percent in 1970–74 and 69.4 percent in
1975–79. The Middle East share of worldwide U.S. military grants and
credits in 1979 was 89.3 percent.[1]

Apart from the growing importance of the Mid-East arms market
for the defense industry, the oil industry is increasingly dependent on
the Mid-East for a growing share of its profits. In fact, Mid-East oil,
which accounts for only 1.8 percent of U.S. investments, accounts for
33.8 percent of total U.S. foreign earnings (see Table 14.3).[2]

Table 14.3    U.S. Investments in the Middle East (in percentages)

|  | 1973 | 1974 |
|---|---|---|
| U.S. direct investments in the Middle East (as % of total U.S. investments abroad) | 2.5 | 1.8 |
| U.S. adjusted earnings in the Middle East (as % of total U.S. foreign earnings) | 12.9 | 33.8 |
| Rate of return of adjusted earnings |  |  |
| of total U.S. investments abroad | 16.4 | 21.2 |
| of U.S. investments in Middle East | 84.5 | 399.5 |

*Source:* Elaborated on the basis of figures from Lupo, Leonard A., and Julius Freidlin,
"U.S. Direct Investment Abroad in 1974," in U.S. Department of Commerce, *Survey of
Current Business,* Oct. 1975, Vol. 55, No. 10.

Table 14.4    Deployment of Oil Exporters' Surpluses

|  | 1977 | 1978 | First 9 mos. 1979 |
|---|---|---|---|
| Total deployment (in billion US$) | 33.5 | 13.2 | 33.2 |
| % to U.K. | 12.2 | −2.0 | 39.8 |
| % to U.S. | 27.4 | −1.7 | 4.8 |
| % to other countries | 59.4 | 103.0 | 57.5 |
| % to international organizations | .8 | .7 | −.7 |
| Of total deployment |  |  |  |
| % in banks | 23.6 | 43.1 | 34.3 |
| % in property and equity in U.S. and U.K. | 17.0 | 24.2 | 2.7 |
| Of deployment within U.S. |  |  |  |
| % in treasury bonds, notes, and bills | 38.0 | −192.3 | −6.3 |
| % in bank deposits | 4.3 | 53.8 | 68.8 |
| % in property and equity | 57.6 | 238.5 | 37.5 |

*Source:* Elaborated on the basis of figures from *Middle East Economic Digest,* special report on banking, May 1980.

Finally, the newest and most active capitalist sector involved in the Mid-East are U.S. bankers. Western banks, particularly English and U.S., have been the major recipients of Mid-East oil surplus which they have recycled as loans to debt-ridden Third World countries at lucrative interest rates (see Table 14.4).

This power bloc of oil companies, private banks and defense industries projects its power into the U.S. executive branch. The major threat to their profits derives from revolutionary movements in the region which will nationalize oil profits, decrease military purchases and reinvest oil earnings in domestic productive activity. The obvious reason behind the massive U.S. military build-up is the vital interest that this power bloc has in the existing social order and relations of production. In addition to these large-scale profitable aspects of U.S. policy, the unprofitable areas of U.S. investment must also be considered, namely, the U.S. subsidy for the Israeli military machine. Israel accounted for almost 70 percent of all U.S. aid in the Middle East. This investment amounted to 3.4 billion dollars, largely because of Israel's military-strategic importance as a bulwark of anti-communist, anti-Arab nationalism. (See Table 14.5.) The economic investment has a politico-military pay-off. The basis of this high subsidy is largely the result of the very influential Israeli lobby, which has successfully sustained the U.S. commitment over and against whatever opposition has emerged from corporate interests linked to Arab wealth.

Since 1976, the U.S. has maintained its economic aid to Egypt, and increased it particularly since the Arab boycott of Egypt, which came as a result of the Camp David Agreements.

**Table 14.5   U.S. Aid to the Middle East**

|                                            | 1973 | 1976 |
|--------------------------------------------|------|------|
| Total U.S. aid to the Middle East (in billions) | 1.3  | 3.4  |
| % to Israel                                | 32.9 | 68.0 |
| % to Egypt                                 | .9   | 13.8 |
| % to Iran                                  | 21.3 | 1.2  |
| % to Jordan                                | 9.9  | 5.9  |
| % to Morocco                               | 3.2  | 3.8  |
| % to Turkey                                | 25.2 | 2.0  |
| % to rest of Middle East                   | 6.6  | 5.3  |

*Source:* Elaborated on the basis of figures from Congressional Quarterly, *The Middle East: U.S. Policy, Israel, Oil and the Arabs, 1977.*

These economic interests and the social and political forces that back them provide the basis for discussion of the growing U.S. military intervention in the Middle East and form the overarching reality behind the rhetoric of "national security."

## U.S. Business and Foreign Policy

At first impression, U.S. corporations seem to call upon a shift in domestic policy to solve a potential Middle East crisis. "Doing this means the U.S. must continue to push the U.S. inflation rate down rather than restimulating it; it means developing a rational energy policy, including accelerating oil decontrol; it means producing a coherent export policy and a consistent foreign policy. In short, it means rebuilding U.S. industrial strength."[3]

However, the strongest emphasis is placed upon a better coordination of U.S. foreign policy according to the needs of U.S. corporations abroad.

Until last year, business was reticent to exercise U.S. military power abroad: "Though most favor a reassertion of U.S. power and more awareness of the economic stakes abroad, few want any return to gunboat diplomacy or subversion of unfriendly regimes by the Central Intelligence Agency. 'If we tried to rule the world with an iron fist', says Edwin Van der Bark, senior vice-president for world exploration and production for Phillips Petrolleum Co., 'I think that would probably hurt business more than it would help.' "[4]

However, this latter position began to shift soon after the takeover of the U.S. embassy in Tehran. On November 7, 1979, soon after the event, the *Wall Street Journal* remarked in an editorial: "Given the importance and volatility of the Middle East, the need for some kind of military presence there has been apparent for a long while—certainly since the Shah failed. In the long run, this calls for a larger navy which the Administration has not requested. In the short term, it calls for redeployment of forces toward the major trouble area, which the Administration has not ordered."[5] And Irving Kristal, contributor to the *Wall Street Journal,* went further to state: ". . . as the post World War II international order falls apart—not only in the Middle East but probably in Latin America as well—. . . what will be relevant is an American foreign policy in which power, and the readiness to use it boldly, will play a far more central role than has ever before been the case in our history."[6]

U.S. businessmen at the moment are trying to find a balance between two extreme positions: they are no longer willing to rely merely on the natural laws of the market to maintain their economic interests abroad, but at the same time realize that military might alone will not secure their positions abroad. As Philip Moon, senior vice-president of the National Bank of Detroit stated last year: "Using military power abroad might make us feel more secure, but it won't make us more welcome."[7]

In this emerging balance, U.S. military presence in the Middle East is increasingly accepted as a necessity. And, as Sam Nakagama, vice president and chief economist for Kidder, Peabody and Co. recently remarked: "President Carter had previously declared that the United States would use military force if necessary to maintain the flow of oil from the Gulf, but the emerging commitment to Saudi Arabia is turning rhetoric into reality."[8] However, the author states, a contradiction arises from the root of the crisis and the way it is being resolved: "Any further rise in the trajectory of military spending will inevitably add to inflationary pressures in the United States."[9]

The answer to this problem, the author concludes, "must be found in a broader sharing of the burden of maintaining security in the Persian Gulf area [for] it is obvious that our allies in Europe and Japan have a far larger economic stake in the stability of the Persian Gulf than does the United States.

"Thus, it would not be too much to ask the Europeans and the Japanese to bear a larger part of the burden in preserving stability and keeping the oil flowing from the Persian Gulf."[10]

Thus, as conflicts in the Middle East intensify, internal economic stability within the United States comes to depend upon the degree to which other major industrial powers are willing to share the responsibility of enforcing stability through force in those areas which are vital to the Western world.

The position of U.S. business on the Middle East must be understood at the different levels in which it is expressed. The importance of the region to the U.S. economy is emphasized by U.S. corporations to underline the need for security in the area. Second, certain parameters are defined within which U.S. foreign policy can best accommodate the needs of U.S. business: security is sought, but at the same time it is emphasized that military adventures can be potentially harmful to the U.S. economy. This is the balance between two positions that was mentioned earlier. Third, these corporations do not formulate specific policies for the Middle East, but rather they seek to make clear within which parameters the U.S. government should weight its options in the area.

## U.S. and the Mid-East

In recent years U.S. policy toward the Middle East has passed through three phases: (1) the politics of regional influentials, (2) disintegration and crises in the alliance, and (3) direct U.S. presence. The politics of regional influentials during the period 1970–77 had its main emphasis on the promotion of a series of de-facto alliances with regimes which were either clients of the U.S. or whose ruling classes shared U.S. strategic perspectives. Each regime brought into the relationship specific sets of resources for sustaining U.S. economic and military interests. Those countries included Iran under the Shah, Israel, Saudi Arabia and Sadat's Egypt. The Shah proved extremely valuable not only as a stable source of oil, but also served as a gendarme in policing the Gulf states— sending troops to repress revolutionary nationalist forces in Oman. The Israelis served as a constant military-political pressure against any and all radical Arab nationalist movements—serving to buttress reactionary regimes and threatening others, thus indirectly and directly serving U.S. interests. As one commentator close to the Israelis has noted:

> Israelis argue . . . that their stability and military prowess has been an asset to moderate (sic) Arab states. They cite King Hussein's request, made via Washington in 1970 when Jordan was under attack by Syria, for Israeli air strikes against the Syrians. Israel instead concentrated forces on the Syrian border, and the Syrians withdrew. Some Israelis also contend that were it not for close Israeli-American ties, Washington's influence would not have revived in Egypt. After the 1973 war standoff, Egypt became convinced that only the United States could act as a broker for peace with Israel.[11]

Together Israeli and Iranian military forces were the glue that held the region within the U.S. sphere of influence. The later inclusion of Sadat's Egypt reinforced and extended the axis. Sadat's acceptance of the Camp David accords and the subsequent accommodation with Israel has been amplified and now includes joint military activities with U.S. armed forces from common bases within Egypt. The fourth element in the political alliances was Saudi Arabia, which maximized the availability of petroleum, subsidized reactionary regimes and financed right-wing, anti-communist movements. Together these forces, allied with the U.S., provided the political, economic and military miracle to promote U.S. hegemony without necessitating the overt presence of the U.S. This was especially important at the time because this was a period in which U.S. military forces were over-extended in Southeast Asia, domestic politics were strongly opposed to further direct U.S. state involvement and European allies and third world countries were hardly likely to support unilateral U.S. military initiatives. Up through the mid-1970's less than 15 percent of the U.S. public favored greater military spending, while over 40 percent favored further cut-backs.[12] The alliance of these collaborator regimes was based on the pivotal role of Iran in sustaining both the military and economic ties, linking the Arab and Israeli groups into one formidable bloc subordinated to U.S. interests.

The crisis and disintegration of the Shah's regime led to an irreparable breach in the alliance: the emergence of an anti-U.S., anti-Israeli Islamic regime broke the bond that held together Saudi Arabia and Israel in the same camp. Henceforth, the Saudis felt increasingly vulnerable to pressures from Iran and Muslim forces within their own society, as the same plunder and inequalities existing in Iran were present in their Arabia. Moreover, Iran's renunciation of its role as regional policeman—and the de-facto disintegration of its military machine—undermined one of the major props sustaining the reactionary rulers in the Gulf states. U.S. defense, corporate and political interests could no longer be defended by what Brzezinski referred to as "regional influentials"—sub-imperialist forces. While the Iranian revolution precipitated the rupture in the alliance and dissolved the basis of U.S. policy, there were several underlying long-term forces which were and are active and which threaten to deepen the crisis for U.S. policy makers in the region. The growing accumulation of oil wealth is accompanied by growing social inequalities between two sets of forces—the ruling classes and the old and new productive and commercial classes which are excluded from the political process. The alienation of traditional pre-capitalist as well as modern classes has set in motion the rise of reactionary clerical, as well as modern, nationalist forces. The limited capacity of the narrowly based political regimes of the region to contain social and political discontent has been recognized by the U.S. Since U.S. economic and political interests are intimately tied to these regimes and since there no longer exist local or regional forces capable of policing the area, the U.S. has been forced to build up its military presence as the sole guarantor of its interests, cloaked in the usual jargon of "defending the area from Soviet expansionism."

The disintegration of the alliance built to fortify and promote U.S. interests created a crisis; specifically, an enormous disjuncture between growing U.S. economic interests and a declining military-political apparatus with a capacity to defend and promote those interests. The centrality of U.S. economic interests was spelled out by then Secretary of State Vance in a speech before the Los Angeles World Affairs Council listing the basic interests that underlie U.S. foreign policy:

> We must maintain a defense establishment modern and strong enough to protect ourselves and our allies.

> We must protect American investment overseas and insure continuing access to vital raw materials.[13]

## Military Buildup to Protect U.S. "Vital Interests"

The response from Washington to the collapse of the regional alliances and the role of "regional influentials" was the relatively rapid insertion of direct U.S. military presence in the Middle East. Though most of the press handouts continued to emphasize the defensive reactive nature of the military build-up, Presidential advisor Brzezinski clearly spelled out the use of power as a form of intimidation—to bludgeon and undermine efforts by countries who attempt to carry through changes that adversely affect U.S. interests. Explaining the concerted military build-up, he stated:

> We have to be able to project our power credibily, and to make it clear to all concerned that American power exists and that it could be used and that our decision makers will not shrink from using American power when either our vital interests or the vital interests of our friends are jeopardized. . . . In recent years, the Middle East . . . emerged as a central strategic zone of vital importance to us and to Western Europe and to the Far East . . . we are now engaged in trying to fortify the stability and security of that part of the world.[14]

U.S. military presence in the Middle East was built in stages. Almost always, Washington justified each increase in military forces by referring to whatever conflict emerged at the moment.

The first major build-up occurred precisely in the aftermath of the Iranian revolution, which overthrew the Shah. As early as mid-1977, Brzezinski had advocated the creation of a rapid deployment force for use in creating a "security umbrella over the Persian Gulf."[15] But with the Shah still operating as an effective policeman, and the Pentagon and State Department in opposition, brzezinski's proposal did not take hold until the Shah's overthrow early in 1979. The first moves were to increase the U.S. naval presence and the sale of arms to allied regimes. The establishment of rapid deployment forces began to become a political reality. The second phase of the U.S. military build-up coincided with Carter's attempt to inflate the significance of Soviet training groups in Cuba. The factual basis of this early effort to invent a "Soviet threat" to promote a U.S. military build-up was deflated rapidly, even by the mass media—which pointed out that they had been there for over 15 years. Nevertheless, the consequences of this political promotion were to accelerate the operational effectiveness of the interventionary forces (the Rapid Deployment Forces). Carter directed Secretary of Defense Harold Brown "to further enhance the capacity of our rapid deployment forces to protect our own interest and to act in response to requests for help from our allies and friends. We must be able to move our ground, sea and air units to distant areas—rapidly and with adequate supplies."[16] A month earlier, before Carter had invented the Soviet threat in Cuba, Secretary Brown told the Senate Foreign Relations

Committee that "rapid response is likely to be crucial in a limited contingency" in the Persian Gulf and other regions. He went on to point out that the Pentagon's budget gave a "high priority to improving American military force."[17] Clearly, Carter's demagogic response to the non-existent Soviet threat in the Caribbean was a useful device in building up U.S. interventionary forces in the Gulf.

The third and most dramatic build-up of U.S. military build-up coincided with the Iranian hostage issue and the Soviet involvement in Afghanistan. Apart from the ill-fated U.S. military excursion into Iran, ostensibly to rescue the hostages, there has been a multi-pronged and sustained increase of all three branches of the U.S. armed forces in the region. Military bases have been established in Somalia, Kenya and Oman—convenient jumping off spots for combined land, sea and air operations. There has been a veritable armada of U.S. destroyers and air-carriers dispatched in the area—a throw back to the gun boat diplomacy so prominent in U.S. policy toward the Caribbean. The U.S. has 31 ships in the Arabian Sea and Persian Gulf, including two aircraft carriers.

Large-scale arms sales and working agreements for joint military efforts have been worked out with Egypt; the Begin regime has volunteered to offer its forces to assist the U.S. militarily if needed. While Saudi Arabia has formally declined U.S. offers of troops and bases, U.S. forces in fact control and operate a substantial part of the Saudi Airforce, air defense, training and arming of its ground forces, etc. Despite Jordan's rhetoric, about half of its budget is covered by U.S. aid in exchange for which Jordanian officers serve to buttress the regimes in Oman, Bahrain and the United Arab Emirates. Along with the transformation of the island of Diego Garcia into a major U.S. naval and air support facility, the U.S. has established a full-scale presence in the area.

The fourth phase in the U.S. military build-up coincided with the Iraq-Iran war. First, the U.S. used the conflict to begin an intense propaganda campaign to pressure Europe to become directly involved—joining the fleet. France and England agreed. Next, the U.S. sent and manned four radar war planes to the Saudis, in addition to two tanker planes and a guided missile cruiser. With Saudi Arabia leaning toward Iraq, the possiblity of U.S. military involvement in regional warfare increases. More important, the placement of U.S. forces in Saudi Arabia gives Washington greater leverage in totally integrating and subordinating Saudi foreign policy to the U.S. needs and in reshaping a new regional alliance. One Pentagon official, commenting on the radar plane transfer, noted:

[The quick response] opens the door to much more extensive military collaboration with the Saudis.[18]

A White House official was somewhat more specific:

[Washington was now] in a much better position to move ahead on building a security framework for Southwest Asia.[19]

Clearly, the overall goal of the new military build-up is bearing fruit: breaking down regional solidarity, subordinating and tying Arab wealth and resources to a U.S. led alliance. By focusing on Soviet, Islamic and internal discontent, Washington has built up leverage where it had been losing. U.S. military power in the region allows Washington to take advantage of the vulnerability of politically isolated rulers in the Gulf and, under the guise of "protecting" them, to shape their economic policies (increase oil production, holding down prices) and political alignments—tie them closer to the U.S.-European-Israeli axis. As Fred Halliday has noted: ". . . the rhetoric about "outside" (i.e. Soviet) influence was designed to divert attention from the *reality* of U.S. military deployment and from the fact that the main threats were internal, from the population of these countries . . ."[20] The justification for this U.S. military encirclement of the Middle East was laid out in Carter's June 23, 1980, State of the Union speech, in which he clearly enunciated a doctrine embracing unilateral military intervention:

> Let our position be absolutely clear: an attempt by any outside force to gain control of the Persian Gulf region will be regarded as an assault on the vital interests of the United States of America, and such an assault will be repelled by use of any means necessary, including military force.[21]

The speech then proceeded to outline a complete militarized foreign policy, including a massive increase in military spending, registration for subsequent conscription, modernized nuclear forces, increasing naval forces in the Indian Ocean, navy and air bases in northeast Africa and the Persian Gulf, removal of restraints on the CIA and arms arrangements with Pakistan. Only the latter fell through. Carter's speech brought together various strands of his interventionist policy which had been building over the past two years. The sudden convergence of these policies into a single foreign policy address made abundantly clear to all willing to see the new reality that the United States was preparing for war with the Third World in general and revolutionary challenges in the Mid-East in particular.

### *"Soviet Threat" Invoked*

The whole justification for this explicitly interventionary policy was the supposed growing menace of Soviet expansionism, highlighted by its Afghan policy. As Carter phrased it, "the greatest threat to world peace since World War Two." The most thorough refutation of Washington's justification for its own military expansionism was presented by the January issue of *The Defense Monitor.* After a comprehensive study of trends in Soviet influence in 155 countries since World War Two, it concluded: "Outside Eastern Europe, Soviet influence has lacked staying power. Inability to accumulate influence in foreign countries over long periods is a dominant feature of Soviet world involvement. Starting from a very low base of political, economic, and military involvement, the Soviets have increased their influence in the world. Starting with influence in nine percent of the world's nations in 1945, they peaked at 14 percent in the late 1950's and today have influence in 12 percent of the world's nations. Of the 155 countries in the world today, the Soviets have significant influence in 19 . . . Soviet setbacks in China, Indonesia, Egypt, India and Iraq dwarf marginal Soviet advances in lesser countries. Temporary Soviet successes in backward countries (sic) have proved costly to the Soviet Union. They provide no justification for American alarmism or military intervention . . ."[22] Washington's hyperbolic rhetoric concerning the Soviet intervention in Afghanistan and its massive publicity campaign has been an ideological diversion to screen the massive U.S. military build-up in preparation for direct intervention and possible occupation of oil rich Middle East countries. This fact is understood by the business community: the day after Carter's bellicose speech, the financial pages of *The New York Times* announced "Stocks Rise Sharply in All Areas, Defense Issues Lead."[23] The militarization of U.S. political life is evidenced in the outlook projected by respectable mainstream business journals. *Business Week* noted:

> Again and again, as OPEC pushes the West toward the edge of economic survival, the option of a military response becomes more and more reasonable. As one monetary official put it recently: "OPEC price actions are really getting out of hand. If they don't call for a military response, I wonder what would. I don't know what would happen if we intervened militarily. I hope some intelligent people are discussing this seriously, so that if we have to act we won't go off half-cocked. I don't see much danger of crippling damage to the oil fields. Even if there were sabotage, it would have very temporary effects in the Arabian peninsula, where you can strike oil with a hatpin. I don't think many other OPEC countries would dare to shut down for very long, if at all, in the face of a determined, united NATO military action."[24]

Clearly, the Carter Administration in 1980 had moved fast and far from the rhetoric of 1977, during which time it had proposed demilitarizing the Indian Ocean, and cutting back U.S. military spending and sales to third world countries. Under the pressure of corporate and banking interests, whose increasingly vulnerable position was made manifest in the aftermath of the Iranian revolution and the collapse of U.S. regional alliances, Carter had no choice but to respond to the crises through a comprehensive remilitarization of U.S. foreign policy, disguising corporate pressure as Soviet expansionism. In retrospect, it is clear that Carter's human rights doctrine was a transitional policy reflecting a particular conjuncture within which Washington was dependent on regional alliances, lacking domestic and European support

**Figure 14.1**
Rising Concern About Defense Spending

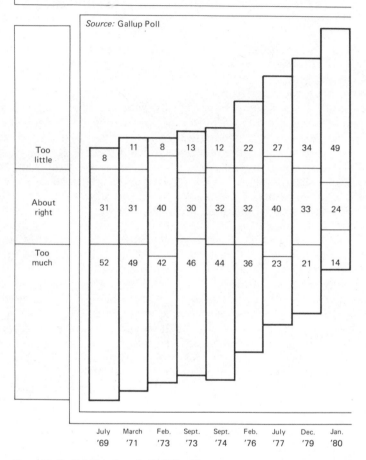

"There is much discussion as to the amount of money the Government in Washington should spend for national defense and military purposes. How do you feel about this? Do you think we are spending too little, too much or about the right amount?"

*Source:* Gallup Poll

|  | July '69 | March '71 | Feb. '73 | Sept. '73 | Sept. '74 | Feb. '76 | July '77 | Dec. '79 | Jan. '80 |
|---|---|---|---|---|---|---|---|---|---|
| Too little | 8 | 11 | 8 | 13 | 12 | 22 | 27 | 34 | 49 |
| About right | 31 | 31 | 40 | 30 | 32 | 32 | 40 | 33 | 24 |
| Too much | 52 | 49 | 42 | 46 | 44 | 36 | 23 | 21 | 14 |

*Source: The New York Times.* September 21, 1980. p. 58.

for a militant policy. Carter's opportune grabbing of a series of external issues to rearm and remilitarize public opinion over such issues as the Iranian hostages (rather than the corporations who were excluded and nationalized) is indicative of a concern not with "outside" threats but of internal revolutions. The capacity of the U.S. to remilitarize the Middle East was hindered by the "Vietnam syndrome", the widespread anti-military sentiment among many Americans. Carter's shrewd manipulation of the hostage and Afghan issues, aided by the mass media and the corporate world, led to a drastic shift in public opinion (see Figure 14.1).[25]

The second obstacle to the new U.S. military policy in the Middle East was the policy and involvement of European and Japanese powers. U.S. policymakers asked whether they would provide support and cooperate in joint ventures in policing the area? From the Pentagon's view, the "allies" have not assumed the political-military costs commensurate with the economic benefits that they have obtained in the Middle East. Robert Komer, the Under-secretary for Policy in the Defense Department, has voiced Washington's demand for joint military roles in the Persian Gulf:

> For a long time Europe has not borne the proportion of the common defense burden which would seem warranted by its political stake and economic growth. Japan has done even less.

> This was understandable when Europe and Japan were recovering from the ravages of World War II. Does it any longer adequately reflect the balance of mutual interests or that of our comparative strength? Indeed, we Americans are increasingly asking whether Europe is interested in its own defense as is the United States.[26]

Komer and the Carter policy were based on a reassertion of a dominant military role for the United States, supported and aided by Europe and Japan, based on the latter's growing economic exploitation of the region. Directing his remarks specifically about the Persian Gulf, Komer bluntly called on European governments to collaborate in the U.S. military build-up.

> But what will be Europe's role in this endeavor, since Europe is even more dependent on Middle East oil than the United States? We Americans feel entitled to ask our allies to share the burden of this joint responsibility, in terms of aid to threatened regimes, joint politico-economic measures and such military assistance in crises as is feasible.

> If the United States rearms, but much of Europe does not, I foresee sharp divisions between Europe and America which could undermine the security partnership which gives NATO its deterrent power.[27]

More recently, during the early phase of the Iraq-Iran conflict, the United States put heavy pressure on West Germany to send warships to the Persian Gulf and Indian Ocean. When Schmidt resisted, one U.S. official was quoted as saying German references to the Constitution as a reason for keeping the navy from the area of the Gulf "is beginning to irritate people. . . . It is legalistic, bureaucratic and open to question."[28] Washington's willingness to flaunt law and strong public pressures against intervention is matched by the willingness of the U.S. Executive branch to bypass Congress in the commitment of military personnel in war zones, contrary to Congressional legislation (War Powers Act, 1974) by sending pilots and personnel to Saudi Arabia.

European and Japanese reticence in committing themselves to the U.S. position is based in part on their growing competitive gains through an increasingly independent position in which a plurality of regimes reflecting different international alignments has emerged. The reconsolidation of political regimes under exclusive U.S. hegemony and linked to the U.S. politico-military apparatus could weaken the European and Japanese position in the area. Europe and Japan seem to best prosper with the relative weakening of neo-colonial regimes linked to the U.S.— just as the U.S. benefited from the demise of colonial linkages that tied the regimes of the region exclusively to Europe.

While Europe and Japan have not been enthusiastic supporters of the revival of militarism and intervention in the Middle East, one country in the area has been offering itself as a strategic staging area— namely Israel. For some time, Israel has been the prime exponent for direct action, frequently offering itself as helpmate to U.S. military intervention. In the post-Vietnam period, Israel was hostile and dismayed by U.S. public opinion's aversion to military intervention. Given Israel's unwillingness to renounce its settler policies, it has become a pariah state in the universe of modern nation-states, depending primarily on military power and U.S. subsidies and arms to sustain itself. Lacking any political options, unwilling to take any diplomatic initiatives that conflict with its internal colonialist constituency, it has been working to convince Washington of the necessity of projecting its military power in the Middle East. The convergence between the Israeli brand of direct interventionism in the Third World and the drift of U.S. policy toward the right is evidenced in the common contempt with which both the U.S. right and the Israelis view antimilitarist programs and democratic controls in U.S. secret police operations abroad. As one reporter describes it: "Like American conservatives, prominent Israelis have deplored the 'emasculation' of American intelligence services and Pentagon failure to keep pace with Soviet military growth."[29] In the current drive to build up U.S. military forces in the Middle East, the Israelis can be counted upon to provide logistical support and military forces if necessary.

### Basis of Policy of Direct U.S. Involvement

Two factors shape current U.S. policy in the Mid-East: (1) a power bloc containing powerful corporate interests, military strategists and policy makers who have major interests in the region and (2) the inability of U.S. policy makers to fashion local forces capable of sustaining those interests by themselves. The presence of U.S. military forces serves as a pole of attraction for all the politically isolated and vacillating regimes in the Gulf: it serves to discourage new regional alignments that might increase the energy costs to Western economies. The general structural weakness of U.S. allies—namely Saudi Arabia and the Gulf states—has spurred Washington to accelerate its own build-up and to extend its state apparatus as a bulwark to the regimes. Moreover, the policy is not only to support the regime but to increasingly shape all aspects of their policy—to protect by limiting their area of international policy, namely their role in OPEC. Secondly, by projecting its power in the region, Washington prevents its allies (Israel and Egypt) and local state-capitalist regimes from establishing regional hegemonic positions. Washington's policy is to harness these regions to its needs and wants; to avoid local wars in which local interests take precedence over global U.S. concerns. Thirdly, U.S. military power offsets the economic advantages that have given Europe and Japan a competitive edge. Henceforth, the new military definitions created by the U.S. presence can be expected to include greater economic leverage for the U.S. and fewer political initiatives from the Europeans, especially those which conflict with U.S. policy. Specifically, while Washington has its armada in the Gulf "protecting" the flow of oil to Europe and Japan, it is unlikely that the latter will pursue any new policies on the Palestinian issue. Washington's "military protection" can be an element of pressure forcing the Europeans into the background. The unilateral build-up thus serves Washington's desire to promote its own set of military-corporate interests, even at the expense of its competitor allies. Fourthly, the present involvement of Washington in the Middle East has as its goal the policial isolation of the Soviet Union: freezing it out of regional affairs that front on its border. Washington's policy rhetoric of noninterference applies only to the U.S.S.R. and not to the U.S.A. Washington is betting on translating Iraq's closer economic ties with the West toward an eventual political rapprochement. Likewise, there is hope in Washington that the war will lead to greater centralization of power in the hands of the standing army, leading to an eventual reopening of relations. These are middle range prospects that Washington is pursuing; in the short-run, its principal concern is to avoid having the current fragmentation and rivalry among Arab regimes spill over and adversely affect its corporate-military interests in the region. Rather, the hope is that fragmentation and rivalry can eventually be turned to advantage, as each regime exhausts its political and economic resources, and the people tire of empty religious, ethnic and bourgeois nationalist slogans.

Fifthly, Washington has a major liability in pursuing policies in the Middle East—the colonial-settlers of Israel inhibit overt military collaboration between the two countries. Hence, while Israel is useful as a pressure on Syria, the Palestinians, Lebanon, etc. and can be unleashed in a crisis (as a military staging area), its presence has to be kept in the background, guarding the West flank of the Mid-East, while U.S. forces occupy the eastern, Gulf zone. The unacceptability of colonial Israel as a policy force for collaborator regimes in the Gulf area thus forces the U.S. to rely on its own forces, more tuned into supporting rather than replacing local rulers.

Finally, the demise of colonialism, the growing market power of Europe and Japan, the anti-imperialist and anti-military sentiment within the mass social democratic and communist trade unions and parties have limited Europe's effectiveness as a military partner to the U.S. in the Middle East. Europe and Japan have concentrated their statecraft on promoting economic relations and building commercial bases, counting on the strength of these relations and the economic dependence of the regimes to avoid consequential losses. Washington and its corporate supporters therefore cannot count on its allies for support and must depend on its own military forces if it is going to pursue policies linked to "projecting power" in the region. In response to Washington's perception of European and Japanese weakness, it has assumed the major role in elaborating a new military policy to sustain its economic interests. Europe and Japan hope to piggy-back along as free-riders, ready to jump off if confronted by major policy blunders.

## Consequence of U.S. Policy

The immediate impact of the new U.S. policy of direct military involvement will be to strengthen Washington's political and economic position at the expense of Europe. Moreover, the "threat of intervention" will increase U.S. political leverage with bourgeois-nationalist and other regimes in the area. The weakness of the policy is that it commits the United States to regimes which have little historical viability—thus increasing the likelihood of the deployment of troops. In turn, the forcible intrusion of U.S. troops will be viewed throughout the region as an alien occupation army, with potential colonization projections. Thus an eventual U.S. direct invervention will serve to illegitimize regimes linked to it and unify otherwise fragmented and opposing religious groups, classes and ethnic collectivities. Short-term gains could lead to prolonged armed and political confrontations: short-term stability could be gained by large-scale upheaval.

Within the short-term perspective, the growing opening of Saudi Arabia to U.S. military forces and its increasing dependence on the extension of the U.S. military apparatus is leading to the growing subordination of Saudi policy to U.S. needs. If the current level penetration deepens, it could simply obliterate any notion of national sovereignty—Saudi Arabia might become the fifty-first state of the union, and the first Arabic speaking one. The integration of Saudi Arabia in a U.S. projected security alliance will certainly impose serious political constraints and onerous obligations which U.S. advisors will only be too willing to organize on behalf of their allies.

Imperialism lacks an original ideology which can appeal to the masses: it can only govern through force or by harnessing preexisting cultural formations which lend themselves to the defense of property and opposition to socialism. There is a great likelihood that Washington will pursue a policy of rapprochement with the Islamic Right—gaining military influence and economic opportunity in exchange for cultural domination. The revival of Islam, insofar as it develops in opposition to class politics, contains the seeds of this strategic alliance, especially as it lowers its goals to the cultural realm and renounces its "two devils" theory (opposition to industrial capitalism and socialism). Only by accepting the subordination of petty commerce and production to the imperatives of large-scale capital growth can the Islamic Right hope to consummate an alliance with capital, local and foreign, powers to preserve spheres of control. The present conception in Washington is based precisely on this division of power and is behind Carter's statement that the U.S. welcomes the Islamic revival. The failure to break the current conflict will lead to a further exacerbation of the triangular struggle between pro-U.S. regimes/ the Islamic Right/the Marxist Left. In the long run, the Islamic Right is not a viable political formula: it cannot retain or sustain production based on petty commodity production, it cannot defend the nation with religious texts and small-scale productive units. Planes and tanks are made in modern factories by engineers and workers with technical and scientific skills. The demise of the pre-capitalist Right as a national, hegemonic force then could set the stage for a renewed confrontation between Marxist nationalist forces and pro-western forces. The presence of U.S. armed forces while strengthening the military capability of regimes will weaken their political appeal. The likelihood then is that a new regional security alliance orchestrated by Washington and including Saudi Arabia and Israel and bringing in its wake a host of lesser Gulf states might generate short-term stability at the cost of eventual regional upheavals.

## Conclusion

U.S. hegemony in the Middle East has been eroded by the emergence of three forces: (1) the growing competition of western and Japanese capital; (2) internal revolutionary forces of a pre-capitalist and socialist nature; and (3) the growth of regional forces attempting to carve out their own spheres of influence. These developments have evoked an essentially military response from U.S. policy-makers. This effort has been aided and abetted by the increasing vulnerability of the Saudi regime and, until the assassination of President Sadat on October 6, by his effort to benefit from being the chosen client of the United States. The result has been the unmaking of the pan-Arab, nationalist alliances in favor of a return to the 1950's and earlier patterns of Western dominated regional alliances.

The intensification of competition among the advanced capitalist countries is a product of the uneven and dynamic growth which has occurred over the past 30 years. Europe and Japan have narrowed the economic gap between themselves and the U.S. and in the course of global expansion have increasingly found the international politico-military framework which the United States devised for "defense" a major constraint in developing their economic relations. It has become clear to the Europeans that the politico-military links that the United States had developed outside of Europe were also extremely useful in securing and favoring U.S. economic expansion. In this fashion, the alliances and East-West summit agreements for the United States were the functional equivalents of the colonial arrangement for the Europeans. For the Europeans to penetrate U.S. economic markets and investment territory, they have in some cases to undermine political and military alliances. This link between U.S. economic advantages and political alliances was pointed out recently:

> Politics, the Europeans believe, has worked for Americans in the past. Before Carter, Brezhnev's summit in Vienna, Creusot-Loire [French corporation] thought it was ahead in the running, an official at the French Foreign Ministry in Paris said. Then came Vienna, and Armco from the United States got the contract. I think that may have been a political decision.[30]

As a result, Europe has in part rejected the renewal of the Cold War and its concomitant boycott of the Soviet Union, picking up important trade contracts which were previously agreed to with U.S. companies, totalling in the hundreds of millions of dollars. While the U.S. embargo halved American trade with the USSR (from $1.7 billion to $857 million), France's trade rose from $3.8 billion to $4.7. West German exports to Eastern Europe totalled $8.7 billion, nearly three-fourths of the value of the goods Germany sent to the U.S., its major trading partner.[31] The same pattern occurred in other areas, including the Mid-East. In mid-October (1980), France signed a $1.4 billion contract to modernize and train the Saudi Arabian navy—after the Saudis had already signed for navy purchases from the United States.[32] The refusal of European capitalist countries to subordinate themselves to U.S. political-military strategy is a result of their recognition that in doing so they will be outmuscled economically. The growing political independence of Europe is in part an outgrowth of its efforts to seize new markets and its competition with U.S. corporations. The breakdown of the post-war neo-colonial system in the Mid-East constructed by the United States was both an opportunity and a threat to European and Japanese capital. Political change provided an opportunity to develop ties with newly independent rulers and displace U.S. corporations. On the other hand, lacking the military machinery of the United States, the Europeans did not have the capacity to ensure that the breakdown of the neo-colonial system did not spill over and endanger all capitalist relations. Europe was not inhibited from developing political ties with so-called "radical nationalist regimes" (anti-U.S. imperialist) to promote trade, just as the United States had earlier cultivated anti-communist nationalists who declared their independence from European colonialism. The relative loss of U.S. economic domination to Europe and Japan on a global level and in the Middle East in particular has forced it to shift back to projecting its *military power* as a way of reasserting its economic influence. For in that area, Europe and Japan are at a distinct disadvantage. The build-up of the military presence is a compensation for the lack of economic competitiveness. The military presence brings in its wake political linkages which turn on the economic spigot. The long term economic crisis in the West, the high levels of inflation and unemployment and the continuing economic recession intensify the need for economic markets in the one area which is still booming—the Mid-East oil countries. The economic crisis heightens the need for each competitor to seek new outlets; in this regard the United States has chosen to pursue its economic advantage through military means.

The revolutionary upheavals in the region, principally in Iran, have eroded the energy "cushion" which has underwritten U.S. and European capitalist expansion. As one oil research and investment house has noted:

> There is no margin of safety in the world crude supply system to offset any one of a number of possible adverse developments.[33]

The analyst went on to point out that the changing structure of the industry—the growth of state owned producing companies had increased "risks." Citing the impact of the Iranian revolution, he concluded, "Any new development—political, mechnical, labor or military—could lead to a crisis of the first order."[34]

The U.S. projection of military power is aimed at preserving the status quo and preventing future losses that cannot be absorbed by Western capitalism without severely affecting major economic interests, profit margins and perhaps the stability of the existing political order. New revolutions in the Mid-East are thus closely linked with the continuation of Western capitalism. Facing the economic abyss, the U.S. projects military power as the final and only solution.

The growth of regional forces—such as Iraq attempting to establish hegemony in the region—is a threat to U.S. efforts to reassert its dominance. Ironically, however, the course of the ensuing Gulf War has as its major consequence the strengthening of the U.S. position on several counts: Saudi Arabia and the Sheikhdoms of the Gulf have initiated a major opening to the U.S. Saudi Arabia's growing military ties with the United States and its agreement to increase oil production gave away a great deal of leverage for very little. The growing direct involvement of the U.S. in the Saudi military-state apparatus is, in effect, a loss of sovereignty in exchange for which the Saudi elite secures its voracious appetite for accumulating wealth. In exchange for securing the family wealth, regional Arab interests were squandered.

Under the facade of making the Saudis the new "Guardians of the Gulf," Western countries (the U.S. and French naval forces) are mounting a new colonial presence. As one Palestinian observed, "We are . . .

back to square one, just where we were before Abdel Nasser came to power and started chasing foreign powers out of this area."[35] The major loser in the Gulf War is the PLO: under the pretext of the war, the United States has accelerated its military buildup in the area, strengthening its ties with Israel and Egypt and weakening pro-PLO initiatives from Western Europe; the war is weakening both supporters of the PLO and dividing Mid-East efforts away from putting pressure on Israel. Finally, the Iraqi occupation of Iranian territory provides a rationale for Israeli occupation of Arab territory.

In response to the threats posed by capitalist competitors, regional powers and internal revolutionaries, the United States has pursued a policy of consolidating and integrating Egypt and Saudi Arabia in a U.S. dominated alliance, which includes bases, troop training facilities and joint maneuvers—reminiscent of the heyday of CENTO, SEATO, NATO alliances. For the first time in decades, 1,400 U.S. ground forces are being deployed in desert training exercises with Egyptian troops.[36] With Egypt guarding the Western flank and U.S.-Saudi forces in the eastern flank, a new military axis has been established, one which, however, requires the direct involvement of the United States. The significance of this axis is that it unmakes the politics of regional nationalism that has been dominant since the 1950's. Together with the growing inter-penetration of economic ties, the closer integration of Saudis into the American military orbit, reinforced by the Egyptian connection, sets the framework for a new round of regional and global conflicts and interventions.

## Notes

1. Joe Stork, "The Carter Doctrine and U.S. Bases," *MERIP Reports,* Sept. 1980. p. 4.

2. Over 99 percent of U.S. adjusted earnings in the Middle East came from oil production. It is clear from Table 14.3 that in the Middle East a seemingly small investment leads to very high profits. Also, it should be remembered that these are conservative estimates of U.S. foreign earnings, for, as a *New York Times* article recently noted, "Western industrialized countries have consistently underreported their true income from foreign trade". (*New York Times,* September 29, 1980).

3. *Business Week,* Editorial, July 28, 1980.

4. *Business Week,* March 12, 1979.

5. *Wall Street Journal,* November 7, 1979.

6. *Wall Street Journal,* November 26, 1979.

7. *Business Week,* March 12, 1979.

8. *The New York Times,* November 2, 1980.

9. Ibid.

10. Ibid.

11. *New York Times,* February 3, 1980, p. E3.

12. *New York Times,* September 21, 1980, p. 58.

13. "Foreign Policy Decisions for 1978," *The Secretary of State,* Bureau of Public Affairs, Office of Media Services, Department of State, January 13, 1978.

14. *New York Times,* March 30, 1980, p. E4.

15. *New York Times,* January 25, 1980, p. A6.

16. *New York Times,* October 2, 1979.

17. Ibid.

18. *New York Times,* October 12, 1980, p. 22.

19. Ibid.

20. Fred Halliday. "The Gulf Between Two Revolutions, 1958–1979," *MERIP Reports,* No. 85, February 1980, p. 10.

21. *New York Times,* January 24, 1980, p. A12.

22. *The Defense Monitor Report,* Vol. IX, No. 1, January 1980, p. 1.

23. *New York Times,* January 24, 1980, p. D1.

24. *Business Week,* November 19, 1979, p. 190.

25. This is clearly shown in an article in the *New York Times* entitled "Iran is helping U.S. to shed fear of intervening abroad": "Administration officials, members of Congress, specialists on foreign policy and others, liberals as well as conservatives, speak of a political and psychological watershed far more important than the immediate concern over the American hostages in Teheran. They view the situation as a pivotal event making the close of the post-Vietnam era.

" 'In terms of domestic politics, this has put an end to the Vietnam syndrome,' said a senior official who has served several administrations.(. . .)

"Now, officials explain, the public can see that defense spending relates to protecting oil supplies, and that gives it more of a bread-and-butter impact with more natural public support." (*The New York Times,* December 2, 1979.) This shift in public opinion is evident from Figure 14.1.

26. *New York Times,* February 10, 1980, p. 10.

27. Ibid.

28. *New York Times,* October 13, 1980, p. 16.

29. *New York Times,* February 3, 1980, p. E3.

30. *New York Times,* October 5, 1980, p. 6

31. Ibid.

32. *New York Times,* October 19, 1980, p. E5.

33. *New York Times,* October 27, 1980.

34. Ibid.

35. *New York Times,* October 19, 1980, p. E5.

36. *Philadelphia Inquirer,* October 17, 1980, p. 24D.

# Index

Abrams, Elliot, 14
Account deficits, 90, 91
Afghanistan: Soviet intervention in, 28
Africa: Cuban military aid to, 153; industrialization of, 76, 81, 82, 83; market development in, 73
Agrarian reform: in Algeria, 180–81, 183, 184; in Central America, 229–30; in China, 141–42, 144; in Venezuela, 251, 253, 254
Agricultural production: in Central America, 222–23; labor force in, 85
Agriculture: collectivization of, 141–42
Algeria: agrarian reform in, 180–81, 183, 184; Banque Centrae d'Algerie (BCA), 182; Coopratifis de la Reforme Algaire (CCRA), 182; FLN, 179, 180, 182, 183; nationalization in, 179–80; Office National de la Reforme Algaire (RA), 182; UCTA, 179, 180, 181, 182, 183; workers' self-management in, 179–80
Allende, Salvador, 185, 188
Althusser, Louis, 96, 97, 101, 112
American Institute for Free Labor development, 54, 55, 56
Andean Pact, 262, 263
Angola: South African invasion of, 27, 281, 283; U.S. policy toward, 26; workers' self-management in, 178
Argentina: class struggle in, 164; El Salvador, relations with, 23; industrial financing in, 84; manufacturing industry in, 81, 82; U.S. policy toward, 14–15, 19
Asia: industrialization of, 76; in international division of labor, 130; market development in, 73
Autonomy, 107, 108

Baker, Howard, 58
Baran, Paul, 71
Batista, Fulgencio, 305
Ben Bella, Ahmed, 179, 182, 183

Bolivia: El Salvador, relations with, 23; nationalization in, 189–90; workers' self-management in, 189–92
Bonapartism, 106–7, 110
Boumedienne, Houari, 183
Bowdler, William, 48
Brazil: agricultural labor force in, 85; class struggle in, 164; industrial financing in, 84; in international division of labor, 130; manufacturing industry in, 81, 82
Brown, Harold, 12
Brzezinski, Zbigniew, 155, 327, 328
Buckley, James L., 21
Bureaucracy, market vs., 308-9
Burnham, Linden Forbes, 145
Bushnell, John A., 19, 242

Camp David Agreement, 285, 323, 326
Capital: expansion of, 9; fictitious, 74–76, 94; finance, 74, 75, 90–94; foreign basis of, 9; industrial communities and, 198; production and, 73–76; reinvestment of, 187, 208; rentier, 74, 94
Capital accumulation: in China, 169; class struggle and, 164–65; colonialism and, 73, 171–72; normal, 73–74, 75; primitive, 72, 75; raw materials and, 75; regional, 171; in Russia, 169; in Third World development, 72–76; in Western countries, 72–76
Capitalism: alternative conceptions of, 171–75; in Central America, 220–23; colonialism and, 171–72; economic specialization and, 171–74; network system of, 173–75; productive force destruction by, 161–63; regional centers of, 292; social relations of production under, 167–70; in socialist transition, 160–64; Third World, effect on, 71–72; in Venezuelan development, 249–70; in world economy, 292
Capitalist countries: economic change in, 123; labor productivity in, 76; revolu-